McGRAW-HILL SERIES IN
SOCIOLOGY AND ANTHROPOLOGY
RICHARD T. LaPIERE, *Consulting Editor*
SANFORD DORNBUSCH, *Associate Consulting Editor.*

McGRAW-HILL SERIES IN
Sociology and Anthropology

RICHARD T. LaPIERE
Consulting Editor

Methods in Social Research

Methods in Social Research

WILLIAM J. GOODE

Associate Professor, Department of Sociology
Columbia University

PAUL K. HATT

Northwestern University

INTERNATIONAL STUDENT EDITION

McGRAW-HILL KOGAKUSHA, LTD.

Tokyo Auckland Beirut Bogota Düsseldorf Johannesburg
Lisbon London Madrid Mexico New Delhi Panama
Paris San Juan São Paulo Singapore Sydney

METHODS IN SOCIAL RESEARCH

INTERNATIONAL STUDENT EDITION

XXI

When ordering this title use ISBN 0-07-085260-X

TOSHO PRINTING CO., LTD., TOKYO, JAPAN

PREFACE

This volume was written out of our teaching experience with the students of Princeton University, Wayne University, Ohio State University, Northwestern University, and Pennsylvania State College and is an attempt to meet some of the problems which were part of that experience. Its primary debt must therefore be to those students who have suffered with us in seminars, classes, and projects over the past ten years. The book attempts to steer a course between a simple anecdotal account of research studies with their technical details, and a set of broad generalizations about research methodology. Its aim is to make both the elements of basic logic and the research procedures of modern sociology understandable at the undergraduate level, where the student should first be introduced to them. It has been a working assumption in our classes that such an understanding of research techniques is indispensable to the student, whether or not he wishes to become an active researcher. In the changing field of sociology, the person who is unwilling to learn *how* conclusions are reached cannot judge properly whether or not the conclusions he reads are correct.

It has also been a working assumption of our teaching that no amount of lecture material, summarizing in general propositions what has been learned about research techniques, can communicate to the student the meaning of research or excite in him any of the fascination which the social process possesses. We have, then, attempted to present, where possible, accounts of specific research experiences, taken in many cases from recent unpublished work.

In addition, as teachers, we have tried to see that all the students in such classes obtain actual field experience. This serves two important objectives: (1) it gives some concrete meaning to the general rules and allows the student some basis for learning when these rules do not apply; (2) equally important, it teaches the student who is easily able to criticize published work that it is much easier to criticize on a lofty level than it is to conduct good research. The objection has been made to putting students at work in research that such research is not "good," and that the student therefore has an idea that it is easy. It has been our experience that no student comes out of such a field experience with a smug feeling that now he is a "trained researcher." Although field expérience requires that the teacher devote considerable energy to his course, the difficulties of supervision are reduced somewhat if the outside work is made into a genuine group project.

Perhaps a third advantage to early field experience can be added to the two previously mentioned. This advantage applies more specifically to students who go on to do research at the graduate level. It is preferable for the student to make his blunders at a phase in his development when it costs him much less, than later to make the same blunders in his own research, often after a great investment in time and energy.

Because the complaints, comments, and difficulties of our students have contributed so much to this book, we wish to record here our gratitude to these students for their patience and their enthusiasm. In addition, of course, we wish to thank our many colleagues at other universities who have read and criticized this manuscript, in whole or in part. Many conferences with Melvin Tumin of Princeton University have added greatly to a clearer understanding of the problems which students face on first coming into contact with the difficulties of research. Read Bain of Miami University has helped us by pungent reminders that this idea or that procedure was not clearly expressed. Edward A. Suchman of Cornell University contributed by his detailed criticism of a substantial portion of this manuscript and gave special attention to the chapters on scaling. Several of our graduate students have worked on specific sections of the manuscript in seminars, adding to its usefulness. Among these may be mentioned Nicholas Babchuk, Arnold S. Feldman, Leonard Moss, Irving Rosow, and John Tarini.

As the teacher will recognize, this volume owes much to the thinking of Robert K. Merton and Paul F. Lazarsfeld, and to the Bureau of Applied Social Research, Columbia University, with which they have done so much creative work. Peter H. Rossi and Alice S. Rossi, formerly of the Bureau and now of Harvard University, contributed several useful suggestions which were drawn from their own research.

William J. Goode
Paul K. Hatt

NEW YORK, N.Y.
EVANSTON, ILL.

July, 1952

CONTENTS

CONTENTS

CHAPTER 1

The New Sociology

Within the past 15 or 20 years, courses in methods of social research have come to occupy an increasingly important role in sociological curricula. It is likely that at the present writing every major university offers such courses. In part, the increase is a reflection of the growing job opportunities in the field and the consequently greater number of students who plan to make their careers in sociology.

In addition, however, an interest in research methods is growing among those whose job interests are not specifically sociological. Anyone who has a serious interest in understanding society must give some thought to the ways in which social facts can be and are gathered. Thus we find a range of needs which the study of research techniques may help to satisfy. The student with a career interest in sociology must acquire the research tools which he will later need in holding his job, and he must embark upon an intensive training program for that purpose. The student who hopes, instead, to obtain an administrative position in government or business must also acquire some of this knowledge. As he moves upward through the various jobs, he will often be faced with the problem of evaluating reports. These are likely to be technical summaries of studies and research carried out by others, and he must be able to decide when they are reliable enough to be used as the basis of his decisions. The market analyst, the public-opinion expert, the investigator of communication and propaganda—all are gathering facts for governmental and business needs. A knowledge of social research is useful for interpreting and weighing such reports.

The lay citizen faces a similar responsibility. Wise decisions about current events are difficult to make unless he can judge the truth of published and spoken reports. Newspaper accounts, radio broadcasts, summary statements by governmental agencies must all be evaluated. This is a civilization in which decisions are increasingly based upon scientific fact, and those who cannot understand how the facts are reached will be unable to separate fact from speculation and wish. Furthermore, the prestige of the "scientific study" is great enough that many reports are given this label without justification. The consequence is that a growing number of nonscientists wish to know about the methods of social science.

At a deeper level, however, it is clear that more courses in research methods are being offered than before as a result of the growth in the field of sociology itself. The growth of every science has been accompanied by the development of research techniques in that field. This fact is not surprising, since the substantive growth, the gathering and ordering of facts, is based upon these new techniques. Techniques alone do not guarantee such a substantive expansion, but they are absolutely indispensable.

The increasing emphasis upon research method is, then, a sign of healthy development within the young science of sociology.

THE CONFLICT OVER SCIENCE

The preceding sentence will seem startling to few readers, and this is also a measure of the acceptance by sociologists of the scientific approach. Only a few years ago such a statement would have been the signal for a fierce debate. Those who wanted to model sociology after the image of the established sciences and those who objected to this view were in opposition, and there were many accusations and counteraccusations in this polemic. This conflict has now almost vanished, but we should attempt to understand its basis.

The main points at issue can be stated in four dogmatic propositions:

1. Human behavior changes too much from one period to the next to permit scientific, exact predictions.

2. Human behavior is too elusive, subtle, and complex to yield to the rigid categorizations and artificial instruments of science.

3. Human behavior can be studied only by other human observers, and these always distort fundamentally the facts being observed, so that there can be no objective procedures for achieving the truth.

4. Human beings are the subject of such predictions and have the ability deliberately to upset any predictions we make.

These are actually very complex propositions, and many corollaries can be elaborated from them. However, in one form or another they represent the center of the strife, and it is clear that if they are true, then sociology has a weak scientific foundation. It would then become the study of infinitely variable, unique, and nonmeasurable situations, rather than the investigation of repetitive, simplifiable, and observable behavior.

It is at least clear on the common-sense level, as noted in elementary sociology texts, that we are *all* engaged constantly in predicting social behavior. Indeed, if we could not do so, the society could not exist at all. We *abstract* various factors from the behavior of other people, and thus find their behavior understandable. In the same way, physicists abstract from the complex behavior of matter. It is true that we cannot predict the unique, but that is true for all sciences. All sciences simplify their subject matter, and the physicist would give scant comfort to the sociologist who complains that his own field, human behavior, is "more complex" or "more mysterious" than that of nuclear forces. In short, both common sense and scientific experience suggest that it is possible to develop methods of controlling observations, abstracting adequately, and reducing variability and complexity, so that sociology can become more scientific.

In many ways, the champions of this latter point of view and their opponents were never so far apart as it seemed. There was much overstatement and even more misunderstanding concerning the application of scientific methods to social data, so that great heat but only slowly increasing light was contributed to the controversy. Opponents of the "radical scientific" position stated that the nature of social data was such that the physical sciences could not serve as models for the social sciences. Today only a few sociologists would deny this charge, but at the same time almost all would accept what Julian Huxley has described as the fruitfulness of analogy from other sciences as one origin of hypotheses. They would maintain in addition that it is not the models of physics but the underlying thought-ways of science that are significant in modern social science.

At the present writing the conflict has died down, and the contributions of both schools of thought are appreciated by all sociologists. One has only to name men such as Znaniecki, Waller, and MacIver, on the one hand, and Chapin, Ogburn, and Odum, on the other, to realize that both approaches (sometimes given the unfortunate labels "intuitionist" and "neopositivist," respectively) have contributed greatly to the present level of sociological achievement.

The most valuable outcome of the conflict period was not in the "victory" of either side, but in the fact that all concerned were forced to reexamine their concepts, premises, and procedures. As a consequence, the benefit accruing to both from the development of quantitative techniques and social theory was very great. We no longer oppose theory and empirical research as opposite and conflicting elements in sociology. It is simply accepted that refined techniques applied to theoretically sterile questions produce barren results, and similarly that theory which cannot be put to the test is equally unprofitable. Attempts by sociologists to obtain precise measurements of important social forces have led to increasing theoretical and conceptual clarity. The insistence on attacking important (but difficult) problems has led to greater precision of measurement.

The outcome of the conflict has, therefore, been beneficial in producing a higher level of methodological sophistication and consequently greater precision in sociological research than were ever known before.

THE SIGNIFICANCE OF THE SCIENTIFIC APPROACH FOR THE STUDENT

This increase in technical precision and methodological sophistication has changed the situation for the sociology student in at least two ways. One of these is a consequence of the changed *position* of sociology itself; the other is a consequence of the greater *demands* made by sociology upon the student.

By the first we simply mean that in practical terms sociology is a success. The evidences for this are many and varied. In colleges and universities, sociology courses have multiplied, and their enrollments have steadily increased. Few institutions of higher learning fail to offer a wide range of courses in the field, and this in spite of the fact that only a few years ago sociology was viewed with mistrust in many places, often being taught by philosophers or economists.

The changing position of the discipline has not, however, been restricted to academic centers, for today the techniques of social research are employed in the forefront of programs aimed at slum clearance, the improvement of institutional management, the decrease of racial tensions, and the planning of long-range civic improvement and also in industrial relations.

In these and other areas, government, business, research foundations, and labor unions have become employers of the sociologist. What is more, this employment is often *as sociologist*. It is now no longer necessary for him always to masquerade as a statistician, an economist, a public-opinion analyst, or a social worker.

If the growth of sociology as a science has had the effect of increasing the range of activity for sociologists, it has also had the effect of demanding more from those who wish either to work in sociology or to understand and appreciate its products. One of these demands is the need for a basic understanding of the methods employed in the discipline.

When sociological principles are stated in "common-sense" terms, no technical knowledge is required for their understanding. When, however, as increasingly happens, they are stated in operational terms, that is, in such a way as to describe *the conditions and procedures for which they hold,* then a failure to understand these conditions leads to a misunderstanding of the principle. Such an error is perhaps best illustrated by the "failure" of the election polls in 1948. Actually the polls were no further off than in many earlier predictions. The error lay not in the scientific knowledge about polling methods but in its inadequate application, along with a failure to state all the conditions under which the predictions might hold. In addition, of course, the public did not understand the nature of polling and its limits of error.

Similarly, the significance of the findings of Faris and Dunham with reference to the distribution of mental disorder in urban areas cannot be appraised without knowing the methods applied. Nor can Shaw's law of recidivism, the principle of "relative deprivation" discussed in *The American Soldier,* the indexes of segregation developed by Schmid and others, and the whole series of prediction studies ranging from success in marriage to success on parole be meaningful to those who fail to understand the operations performed in each case.

The purpose of this book, then, is to acquaint the student with the modes of thought and the techniques that characterize modern sociological research.

TECHNIQUES AND METHODS

The growing methodological sophistication and technical skill of sociologists are a direct outcome of the fact that at last they see their field as having the same *foundations* as any other science. The first task of this volume, therefore, is to deal with the application of the fundamentals of science to the field of sociology. This is essentially what we mean by *method. Techniques* are thought of as comprising the specific procedures by which the sociologist gathers and orders his data prior to their logical or statistical manipulation. These are discussed in the remainder of the book.

The technical sophistication of research in sociology has grown from scientific techniques that have been useful in a variety of fields. Sociology may not, of course, blindly apply the operations or formulas of any other science without careful consideration. Nevertheless, within the field a process of the continuous *adaptation* of such methods has resulted in the growth of sociological techniques. The past half century has witnessed this type of cross-fertilization among all the sciences.

The process of the development of techniques, rather than the specific tools themselves, is the most significant indication of the increasing maturity of sociology. Many types of scales for the measurement of diverse types of phenomena have been devised and subsequently discarded. The *technique of constructing scales,* however, has gone forward. Similarly, we may observe that the application of rudimentary principles in such areas as statistical manipulations and the interview situation has resulted in the increasingly fruitful use of statistical processes and in the continuous improvement of the procedures for securing valid and reliable interviews.

This growth of technical knowledge and standardization does not by any means imply that sociology provides a series of automatic recipes for "making research." On the contrary, the possibilities for the improvement of techniques and the effective application of techniques in new areas challenges the young sociologist more than ever to apply insight, imagination, and creativity.

The purpose of this volume, then, is (1) to show how the principles of scientific method apply to the field of sociology; and (2) to give the beginning student an elementary command over the techniques being used in modern research. With this in mind, the next seven chapters will deal with the more general and basic problems of the relation between the foundations of science and social data. The remaining chapters will cover a variety of the empirical tools commonly employed in sociological research.

SUGGESTED READINGS

Barnes, Harry Elmer, and Howard Becker, *Social Thought from Lore to Science* (Boston: Heath, 1938). 2 vols.

Cobb, John Chandler, *The Application of Scientific Methods to Sociology* (Boston: Chapman & Grimes, Inc., 1934), pp. 21–64.

Cohen, Morris R., and Ernest Nagel, *An Introduction to Logic and Scientific Method* (New York: Harcourt, Brace, 1934).

Dewey, John, *Logic: The Theory of Inquiry* (New York: Holt, 1938).

Einstein, Albert, *Relativity: The Special and General Theory* (New York: Holt, 1920).

Fisher, R. A., *The Design of Experiments* (Edinburgh: Oliver & Boyd, 1937).

Lundberg, G. A., *Social Research* (New York: Longmans, 1942), Chap. 1.

——, "Alleged Obstacles to Social Science," *Scientific Monthly,* Vol. LXX, No. 5 (May, 1950), pp. 299–305.

Merton, Robert K., *Social Theory and Social Structure* (Glencoe, Ill.: Free Press, 1949), pp. 3–18.

Parsons, Talcott, *The Structure of Social Action* (New York: McGraw-Hill, 1937).

Planck, Max, *The Philosophy of Modern Physics,* trans. W. H. Johnston (New York: Norton, 1936).

Sorokin, P. A., *Society, Culture, and Personality* (New York: Harper, 1947), pp. 6–18.

Weber, Max, "Science as Vocation," *From Max Weber,* H. H. Gerth and C. W. Mills, eds. (New York: Oxford, 1946).

CHAPTER 2

Science: Theory and Fact

Science is popularly defined as an accumulation of systematic knowledge. Such a definition is adequate only to the extent that the words "systematic" and "knowledge" are themselves properly defined. Logical argument or systematic theology might otherwise be equated with natural science.

It is therefore necessary to elaborate upon the hidden content of these terms before the phrase can stand as a definition of science.

In the first place the fundamental character of science is ignored in this definition. Science is a *method of approach* to the entire empirical world, *i.e.,* to the world which is susceptible of experience by man. It is furthermore an approach which does not aim at persuasion, at the finding of "ultimate truth," or at conversion. It is merely a mode of analysis that permits the scientist to state propositions in the form of "if—, then—." Thus, no matter how systematic any body of knowledge may be, it is not science if it merely begins with axioms, or "self-evident" propositions, and ends with deductions from those axioms.

Put succinctly, the sole purpose of science is to understand the world in which man lives. What is meant by understanding the empirical world is, however, very complex and will require considerable explanation.

THEORY AND FACT

Basic to modern science is an intricate relation between theory and fact. The popular understanding of this relationship obscures more than it illuminates. Popular opinion generally conceives of these as direct opposites: Theory is confused with speculation, and thus a theory remains speculation until it is proved. When this proof is made, theory becomes fact. Facts are thought to be definite, certain, without question, and their meaning to be self-evident.

Furthermore, in this popular misconception science is thought to be concerned with facts alone. Theory ("speculation") is supposed to be the realm of philosophers. Scientific theory, therefore, is thought to be merely the summation of facts which have been accumulated upon a given sub-

7

ject. Even this function, however, is a restricted one, since facts are thought to speak for themselves.

If, however, we look at what scientists actually do when engaged in research, it becomes clear (1) that theory and fact are not diametrically opposed, but inextricably intertwined; (2) that theory is not speculation; and (3) that scientists are very much concerned with both theory and fact.

The way the scientist views theory and fact is indeed quite different from the popular conception of them. A fact is regarded as an *empirically verifiable observation*. The careful reader will see that this statement is very complex and one which would require an extensive philosophic treatment to explain fully. The implications of the statement will, however, become clearer later. To the scientist, *theory refers to the relationships between facts,* or to the ordering of them in some meaningful way.

Facts, or empirically verifiable observations, could never have produced modern science if they had been gathered at random. One scientist might count the grains of sand in a sand pile; another might survey the range of size and shape of leaves on a maple tree; still another might record the variations in color of rainbow trout taken from a particular river eddy. The infinity of possible procedures, objects for observation, and of ways to make those observations would effectively prohibit any substantial progress from one generation to the next. Without some system, some ordering principles, in short, *without theory,* science could yield no predictions. Without prediction there would be no control over the material world.

It can therefore be said that the facts of science are the product of observations that are not random but meaningful, *i.e.,* theoretically relevant. Thus we cannot think of facts and theory as being opposed. Rather, they are interrelated in many complex ways. The development of science can be considered as a constant interplay between theory and fact.

Theory is a tool of science in these ways: (1) it defines the major orientation of a science, by defining the kinds of data which are to be abstracted; (2) it offers a conceptual scheme by which the relevant phenomena are systematized, classified, and interrelated; (3) it summarizes facts into (a) empirical generalizations and (b) systems of generalizations; (4) it predicts facts; and (5) it points to gaps in our knowledge.

On the other hand, facts are also productive of theory, in these ways: (1) facts help to initiate theories; (2) they lead to the reformulation of existing theory; (3) they cause the rejection of theories which do not fit the facts; (4) they change the focus and orientation of theory; and (5) they clarify and redefine theory.

THE ROLE OF THEORY

Theory as orientation. A major function of a theoretical system is that it narrows the range of facts to be studied. Any phenomenon or object may be studied in many different ways. A football, for example, can be investigated within an economic framework, as we ascertain the patterns of demand and supply relating to this play object. It may also be the object of chemical research, for it is made up of organic chemicals. It has mass and may be studied as a physical object undergoing different stresses and attaining certain velocities under various conditions. It may also be seen as the center of many sociologically interesting activities—play, communication, group organization, etc.

Each science and each specialization within a broader field abstracts from reality, keeping its attention upon a few aspects of given phenomena rather than upon all aspects. Only thus can the work of science be reduced to manageability. The broad orientation of each field, then, focuses upon a limited range of things while ignoring or making assumptions about others. It is in the light of these considerations that much of nineteenth-century sociology may be understood, for a major task of such masters of theory as Comte, Spencer, Tönnies, or Simmel was to define the task and object of study for the future science. Theory, then, helps to define which kinds of facts are relevant.

Theory as conceptualization and classification. As is discussed more fully in Chapter 5, every science is also organized by a structure of concepts, which refer to the major processes and objects to be studied. It is the relationships between these concepts which are stated in "the facts of science." Such terms make up the specialized vocabulary that the scientist uses. They change as the science develops, for different phenomena come to be of major importance. However, it is clear that if knowledge is to be organized, there must be some system imposed upon the facts which are observable. As a consequence, a major task in any science is the development of systems of classification, a structure of concepts, and an increasingly precise set of definitions for these terms. As the student has probably learned from the history of sociology, much of sociology has been the development of elaborate conceptual schemata. These pointed to certain phenomena as the most important to be studied and thus helped to organize the facts of social relations. Some of the concepts now used may be mentioned to remind the student that he is already familiar with this function of theory: invasion and succession, marginal man, status and role, class system, socialization, social mobility, and social distance.

Another task of theory: summarizing. A further task which theory performs is to summarize concisely what is already known about the object of study. These summaries may be divided into two simple categories:

(1) empirical generalizations, and (2) systems of relationships between propositions.

Although the scientist may think of his field as a complex structure of relationships, most of his daily work is concerned with a prior task: the simple addition of data, expressed in empirical generalizations. Entomologists may be studying the habits of social insects in order to summarize these observations in a set of descriptions. The sociologist or social psychologist may gather data on the differences in the child-rearing practices of various classes. The demographer may tabulate births and deaths during a given period in order to ascertain the crude rate of reproduction. These facts are useful and are summarized in simple or complex theoretical relationships.

Summarizing at this level is often not even considered theory, and certainly it was going on long before there were scientists. Man's continuing existence depends upon such empirical observations: "objects fall," "wood floats," "strangers are dangerous," etc., are propositions of this kind, embodied in tribal wisdom.

It is clear, on the other hand, that such statements go beyond a single observation or a single group of observations. They may become very complex, and contain some expression of the conditions under which they are accurate. Furthermore, as a body of such summarizing statements develops, it is possible to see *relationships between the statements*. Hazing of freshmen, ordination of a minister, ritual circumcision, graduation ceremonies, and baptism are phenomena about which a number of summarizing propositions can be made, but they can also be seen as related to one another: ways by which a group gives a different status to an individual, patterns of asserting group control, ceremonial expressions of group unity, etc.

Theorizing on a still larger scale, some may attempt to integrate the major empirical generalizations of an era. From time to time in any science, there will be changes in this structure of relationships between propositions. Newton's *Principia* was such an example, as was Einstein's work on the special theory of relativity. Talcott Parsons has shown in his *Structure of Social Action* that major shifts of this kind may be traced in the work of Weber, Durkheim, and Pareto as each of them moved from older systems of theory toward a more acceptable system.

It is through systems of propositions that many of our common statements must be interpreted. Facts are seen within a framework rather than in an isolated fashion. Let us look at a few examples: "A social group is not just the sum of its members." "This is a patrilineal society." "The delinquency rate is higher in slum areas than in middle-class areas." If we study such apparently simple statements more closely, it is clear that behind each of them is a complex series of observations, a set of assumptions about the effect of social factors upon behavior, and a system of propositions about the way in which groups act. There is an implicit or explicit fact-chain or theory which gives such "simple" statements their full meaning.

Usually, of course, the existence of such theoretical systems is taken for granted, and we do not give them much thought. However, when we wish to communicate with great accuracy or to explain complex ideas, the systems are made explicit. For the scientist, then, it is important that such structures of facts be stated openly. Theoretical clarity demands that the scientist must be more conscious of the thought system being employed than is the average man.

Theory predicts facts. If theory summarizes facts and states a general uniformity beyond the immediate observations, it also becomes a prediction of facts. This prediction has several facets. The most obvious is the extrapolation from the known to the unknown. For example, we may observe that in every known case the introduction of Western technology has led to a sharp drop in the death rate and a relatively minor drop in the birth rate of a given nation, at least during the initial phases. Thus we predict that if Western technology is introduced into a native culture, we shall find this process again taking place. Correspondingly, we predict that in a region where Western technology has already been introduced, we shall find that this process has occurred.

Similarly, we should be surprised to find that delinquency rates in an American slum are lower than in the rest of the city, or that the remarriage rates of divorcees aged 25 to 34 are lower than the marriage rates of single persons at those ages. We have recorded many observations which have led to these generalizations. We expect to find the same patterns in areas for which we now have no data, and we expect to find these patterns in the future.

We expect the same patterns, however, simply because (1) we believe we know *which factors* cause these patterns; and (2) we believe that *these factors* will be found in the new situation. This is a common-sense way of saying that behind our empirical generalizations is a body of theory. The theories state that under conditions X, Y will be observable. A given theory may be incorrect, but it does make predictions about observations of phenomena. It is a set of directions, stating how certain operations, observations, and calculations are to be made, with a prediction about the outcome. Because sociology as a science is in its infancy, the predictions that can be made are relatively crude. Often we have not identified the causal factors and may make an erroneous prediction. For example, the factors that lead to a high remarriage rate for divorcees in this country may not be found in other countries, and a mechanical prediction from the United States pattern might be incorrect.

Nevertheless, it is clear that theory performs the task of stating what facts are to be expected. This becomes a set of directions to the researcher, telling him what data he should be able to observe.

Theory points to gaps in our knowledge. Since theory summarizes the known facts and predicts facts which have not yet been observed, it must also point to areas which have not yet been explored. As noted above, the simple fact of prediction suggests where to test our knowledge. If a theory states a general relationship, such as an inverse correlation between income and fertility, we can see immediately where further facts might be sought. We can break our income classes into smaller groups to see whether fertility might be higher (instead of lower) at the extreme upper income groups; we can ascertain whether this pattern is to be found in rural as in urban areas, or in other countries; or we can study the historical relationship between income and fertility. These are only examples, and the student can work out others suggested by the general proposition.

However, theory also points to gaps of a more basic kind. While these gaps are being filled, changes in the conceptual scheme usually occur. It might be noted in addition that "seeing the gap" is very easy once it has been done. An example may be taken from criminology. Although a substantial body of knowledge had been built up concerning criminal behavior and its causes by the time Sutherland began his researches, most of it related to the more common crimes such as murder, arson, theft, burglary, and so on. It is now possible, with good hindsight, to see that the body of theory dealing with causation was oriented almost exclusively to the crimes committed (in the main) by the lower classes. Almost no attention was paid to the crimes committed by the middle classes or, more especially, to the crimes which may be labeled "white collar" and which grow out of the usual activities of businessmen. Sutherland saw this as a major gap in criminological theory, which pointed to a lack of knowledge about this kind of crime. Soon many other researchers began to investigate this area.

Such a gap would not be visible if our facts were not systematized and organized. As a consequence, we may say that theory does suggest where our knowledge is deficient. The beginning student must, then, acquaint himself with existing theory. It will then become clearer to him why one research problem seems productive, and another sterile. As we shall see later, the formulation of a good question in science is an important step in the development of knowledge. Alerting oneself to the gaps in theory and fact will increase the likelihood of formulating good questions.

THE ROLE OF FACT

Theory and fact are, then, in constant interaction. Developments in one may lead to developments in the other. Theory, implicit or explicit, is basic to knowledge and even perception. Theory is not merely a passive element. It plays an active role in the uncovering of facts. We should expect, however, that "fact" has an equally significant part to play in the development of theory. Science actually depends upon a continuous stimulation of fact by theory and of theory by fact.

Fact initiates theory. Many of the human-interest stories in the history of science describe how a striking fact, sometimes stumbled upon, led to important new theories. This is what the public thinks of as a "discovery." Examples may be taken from many sciences: the accidental finding that the penicillium fungus inhibits bacterial growth; that excision of the pancreas in the dog is followed by the symptoms of diabetes; that radium will expose film even through opaque objects; that many errors in reading, speaking, or seeing are not accidental but have deep and systematic causes; or that a pendulum of given length, in free motion, will swing back and forth in equal time. Many of these stories take on added drama in the retelling, but they express a fundamental fact in the growth of science, that an apparently simple observation may lead to significant theory.

Merton has called this kind of observation "the unanticipated, anomalous, and strategic datum" and cites an example from the Craftown research.[1] The datum was the frequent report from interviewees that community participation was easier because there were so many baby sitters available for any event. This fact was anomalous and unanticipated because the research team possessed the relevant population data: actually, these were mostly young couples with infants or young children, and the proportion of teen-age children was lower than in the general United States population. Attempting to account for the anomalous datum in this case led to an interesting development of theory: It was not the absolute number of adolescents that was the important fact, but the number that had a *social existence* for these couples seeking baby sitters. There were fewer teen-agers, but they were all part of the community which was real to these couples and were thus available. This development can, in turn, be related to the larger body of theory dealing with social perception.

It must be emphasized that such strategic facts do not "speak for themselves." Nor will every researcher be capable of responding to the challenge. Almost every "discoverer" was preceded by others who saw his discovery first and thought no further about it. "Everyone" knew that many slips of the tongue and errors were caused by other factors than accident, but it was Freud who used his own experience to begin an elaborate, useful theory of such common observations. The fact can

[1] Robert K. Merton, "The Bearing of Empirical Research on Sociological Theory," *Social Theory and Social Structure* (Glencoe, Ill.: Free Press, 1949), Chap. 3, esp. pp. 98*ff*.

initiate theory only if the student is alert to the possible interplay between the two.

Facts lead to the rejection and reformulation of existing theory. Facts do not completely determine theory, since many possible theories can be developed to take account of a specific set of observations. Nevertheless, facts are the more stubborn of the two. Any theory must adjust to the facts and is rejected or reformulated if they cannot be fitted into its structure. Since research is a continuing activity, rejection and reformulation are likely to be going on simultaneously. Observations are gradually accumulated which seem to cast doubt upon existing theory. While new tests are being planned, new formulations of theory are developed which might fit these new facts. One result of this situation is that at any given time there may be several scientists who have come to doubt older theories, without having actually developed a satisfactory new body of theory.

Perhaps the classical case in sociology is Durkheim's work on the phenomenon of suicide. Suicide had occupied the attention of many analysts prior to Durkheim. Some had explained suicide by theories of psychopathology, while others had used climate, race and nationality, etc., in an effort to take account of all the facts.[2] However, as Durkheim showed, there were acceptable bodies of fact which did not fit any of these varied theories. In particular, when any one of these factors was held constant, the suicide rate was not constant. Durkheim then attempted to demonstrate that all these facts were in conformity with a classification of different *kinds* of suicide (*i.e.*, a new conceptualization) and a theory of social and personal disorganization. Later, of course, new facts led in turn to a reformulation of Durkheim's theoretical structure.

This relation between fact and theory may be expressed in syllogistic terms. A theory predicts that certain facts will be observable: "If X condition exists, then Y is observable; if Y is not observable, then X condition does not obtain." However, if X condition *does* exist, and Y is *not* observable, then the original proposition is denied. Unfortunately for the scientist's peace of mind, such a syllogistic pattern of logic does not guarantee that the original theory *is* correct when the facts *are* as predicted. Conformity merely guarantees that certain other theoretical propositions are *not* correct. Thus, the scientist is engaged in a process of narrowing possibilities, not of pinning down a certainty. His new facts can lead to the rejection of old theories and thus lead to new formulations, but these must in turn be tested by still further observation and experiment. The older notions of "bad blood" and race as factors in juvenile delinquency were based upon *some* facts (the high rates of delinquency in certain families and ethnic groups). These theories were, however, inconsistent

[2] See Émile Durkheim, *Suicide*, trans. J. A. Spaulding and G. Simpson (Glencoe, Ill.: Free Press, 1951).

with a growing body of fact about (1) how delinquency is recorded by the police in different areas, and (2) the social causation of crime as against biological theories of crime. Within each decade, however, new facts are recorded which demand that the most recent theory be changed in some particulars.

Note, however, that reformulation usually means a new *focus* for the scientist, for it is from the theoretical system that the major lines of research come. In turn, then, new facts will be recorded. Once we become sensitive to the fact that juvenile delinquency cannot be understood in biological terms but rather has social dimensions, we then become sensitive to *further* facts about the social determination of this phenomenon. We begin to explore these new data by further study. By leading to new theoretical formulations, facts may change the direction of scientific search. Thus, even negative facts may be useful.

Facts redefine and clarify theory. Usually the scientist has investigated his problem for a long time prior to actual field or laboratory test and is not surprised by his results. It is rare that he finds a fact that simply does not fit prior theory, or tests two alternative hypotheses for each of which there is an equal amount of evidence. In the main, his work consists in demonstrating what he has already come to believe is true.

However, new facts that fit the theory will always redefine the theory, for they state in detail what the theory states in very general terms. They clarify that theory, for they throw further light upon its concepts. Finally, they may actually present new theoretical problems, in that the redefinition may be far more specific than the theory. An example is the general hypothesis that when individuals from a rural population enter the urban environment we expect a considerable amount of personal disorganization. This process has been studied in most detail for immigrant groups and the children of such immigrants. We also expect that many changes in habit patterns will occur in this adjustment process. One of these is a decline in fertility. As a consequence of these notions, we would predict that when Negroes settle in large cities their birth rate will drop. Actually, the net reproduction rate of urban Negroes *is* much lower than that of rural Negroes, and we can say that the fact is in accord with the theoretical prediction.

The theory, however, is a general expectation, while the demographic facts are specific. The theory does not state how *much* the difference will be. In actuality the fertility of urban Negroes is even lower than that of urban whites. We are thus left with a redefinition of the theory toward greater specificity, and we also see that our older theory simply does not account for these new facts. The facts do not reject the older theory; they are simply more complex and definite than the predictions of the original theory, and they call for further research.

Indeed, it is one of the major experiences of researchers that actually testing any existing theory is likely to redefine it. The concepts that have been accepted as simple and obvious turn out to be elusive, vague, and ill defined when we fit them to the facts. It is not that the facts do not fit. It is rather that they are much richer, more precise and definite, than concept or theory. Furthermore, such redefinitions and clarifications may in turn lead to the discovery of new hypotheses. For so long as our theories use general terms and make rough predictions, it is difficult to disprove them. We may predict that in any social system there will be some integration between the political and the religious structures, for example. Investigation shows that such a proposition is true, but it is so general as not to predict all the varied ways and degrees of integration. How much integration of what? Priests and politicians? Magicians and chiefs? Ritual devotees and lay citizens? Taxes and devotional gifts? Temples and judicial chambers? When we look at the facts, we find that we have to sharpen our theories considerably to be able to disprove or prove them.

Facts, then, become a stimulus to the redefinition and clarification of theory even when they are in conformity with it. This process leads in turn to the reformulation of theory and the discovery of new facts.

SUMMARY

In this chapter, the discussion has centered on the interplay between theory and fact. Although popular opinion thinks of theory as being opposed to fact, since "theory is mere speculation," observation of what scientists actually do suggests that fact and theory stimulate each other. The growth of science is seen in new facts and new theory. Facts take their ultimate meaning from the theories which summarize them, classify them, predict them, point them out, and define them. However theory may direct the scientific process, facts in turn play a significant role in the development of theory. New and anomalous facts may initiate new theories. New observations lead to the rejection and reformulation of existing theory, or may demand that we redefine our theories. Concepts which had seemed definite in meaning are clarified by the specific facts relating to them.

The student of sociology must, therefore, succumb neither to the pose of the armchair theorist who deals with important principles while disdaining the fact grubbing of the field researcher, nor to the viewpoint of the fact collector who is certain of his facts while ignoring the question of their importance. The sociologist must accept the responsibilities of the scientist, who must see fact in theory and theory in fact. This is more difficult than philosophic speculation about reality or the collection of superficial certainties, but it leads more surely to the achievement of scientific truth about social behavior.

SUGGESTED READINGS

Cohen, Morris R., and Ernest Nagel, *An Introduction to Logic and Scientific Method* (New York: Harcourt, Brace, 1934), Chaps. 6 and 7.

Hull, Clark L., "The Hypothetico-deductive Method" in Melvin H. Marx, *Psychological Theory* (New York: Macmillan, 1951), pp. 218–232.

Lundberg, G. A., *Foundations of Sociology* (New York: Macmillan, 1939), Chap. 1.

Marx, Melvin H., "The General Nature of Theory Construction" in Melvin H. Marx, *Psychological Theory* (New York: Macmillan, 1951), Chap. 1.

Merton, Robert K., *Social Theory and Social Structure* (Glencoe, Ill.: Free Press, 1949), Chaps. 2 and 3.

Parsons, Talcott, *The Structure of Social Action* (Glencoe, Ill., Free Press, 1949), pp. 6–15.

CHAPTER 3

Values and Science

The preceding chapter has touched upon the subject of values in at least two places. No attempt was made to clarify the relationship between science and values at that time because of its complexity.

First of all it was stated that the work of science is not persuasion or conversion, but rather a demonstration that, given certain conditions, certain events inevitably follow. Persuasion or conversion may be systematic; they may even make use of scientific findings; but fundamentally they differ from simple demonstration. Their function is to convince that something is *right, good, proper,* or in some other way *desirable.*

Demonstration aims merely at stating that a given relationship *exists,* regardless of its goodness, rightness, or beauty. In effect this amounts to an assertion that science is devoid of value judgments. The careful student should not accept such an assertion, however, without a much more detailed consideration of the nature of science and the scientist.

Values were touched at another point in the preceding chapter in referring to the evaluation of a fact in terms of its theoretic relevance. It was suggested, indeed, that needed facts might be *evaluated* in advance by an adequate body of theory. This is the equivalent of an assertion that science discriminates between problems, judging one as more important than another and thus more desirable of solution.

It must also be seen that the question of the "importance" of a particular fact can be asked in two ways. It may be put as the question, "Of what scientific *significance* is this finding?" Or it may be put, "Of what practical *utility* is this finding?"

While it was suggested in the preceding chapter that scientific theory may help point to the answer of at least the first question, science must introduce values in order to answer the second. Furthermore, there is always the question as to whether the first can itself ever be scientifically answered. There are two reasons for this difficulty. The preference for one problem over another—when neither is dependent upon the answer to the other—must be made on the basis of a belief that one is more pressing than another. However, this belief is only a conviction, a faith, and it must be based upon values. Secondly, even as a *prediction* of what the answer to the problem will lead to in the future, such a decision has at best a flimsy basis in fact. Those who feel that such decisions are easily made will do well to ponder an answer reportedly given by Benjamin Franklin. To a critic who asked what importance could possibly be attached to his findings about the relationship between thunderclouds and electricity, he replied, "Of what use is a newborn child?"

These comments suggest that the sociologist needs a thorough understanding of the relationships between values and science. Before analyzing these relationships, however, several other connections between values and science may be noted, of which two have a particular significance for sociologists.

A broad value problem, of concern to all science, is posed by the spectacular destructiveness caused by some of the *applications* of modern science. The question is usually phrased in some such manner as, "What is the moral responsibility of the scientist in the world today?" Scientists of all branches have indicated their awareness of this problem, even going so far as to form special organizations for its consideration. It is true, of course, that such a problem refers to the *uses* of science rather than the *methods* of science. Nevertheless, it seems obvious that the answers given to this question will affect the course of science markedly.

Of a somewhat different order are the two areas of the *interaction* of values and science that are of particular interest to sociologists. One of these arises from the fact that much of the *subject matter* of sociology is values. The ways in which this fact may possibly interfere with the application of scientific method to sociology must be investigated.

The other arises from the fact that *moral involvement* with his subject matter may tempt the social scientist rather more than the physical scientist to bias his results in favor of his own values. For example, it has frequently been observed that in American communities certain families associate more with each other than with other families. Furthermore, club memberships, childhood friendships, and marriages follow these same clique lines. It may also be observed that this group of families possesses the most material advantages and receives deference in one way or another from the other families in the community. These statements, of course, simply represent observations of the social relations that actually exist.

To the scientist this is a description of the facts. In a society where social class has moral implications, however, such facts may produce emotional reactions. Some may feel resentful, on the grounds that such distinctions should not exist in a democratic society. Others may feel that these distinctions are perfectly justifiable and right. Whatever the scientist's feelings may be, it is certainly necessary for social science to distinguish between statements of what *is* and statements of what *should be*.

Several ways in which science and values do interact have been illustrated. There are, of course, others, but these should suffice to indicate the need for a systematic treatment of the relationships between values and both science and the scientist. In spite of its brevity, the following discussion presents an outline for such a treatment.

THE BASES OF SCIENCE

Science itself rests upon a series of postulates, or assumptions, which are themselves fundamentally unproved and unprovable. We can *assert* that these postulates are true; we can *believe* them; but we cannot prove them. They represent those problems in the area of the philosophy of science which is usually called epistemology. These postulates deal with the validity of human knowledge. Since this is not a book on epistemology but rather a work on scientific method, it is only necessary to make clear that these problems exist and then simply to assume their truth. This, of course, is what all scientists do, except when writing in a philosophical vein. Here are some of these "nonscientific bases of science."

The world exists. Those students who are acquainted with philosophical literature, particularly with the great names of Locke, Berkeley, Hume, and Kant, will recall that every attempt to prove the existence of the world has resulted in failure. Indeed, it is possible to deny philosophically its existence. Science, however, rests upon the *assertion* that this elementary statement is true, and further asserts that the world is a *physical* world.

We can know the world. This proposition is no more provable than is the assumption of the world's existence. It *must* be true because we *wish* it to be true, and because science depends upon the acceptance of the proposition.

We know the world through our senses. Science assumes that through our various sense organs, aided in most cases by extensions of those sense organs through such devices as rulers, scales, telescopes, etc., we can know the world. There is no other mode of knowing the world. Once more, this postulate cannot be proved, but if it were not true, then science could not exist. This is the case because science depends upon the agreement of sense impressions for verification of its observations. To arrive at an answer by "intuition" is not satisfactory as a scientific method.

Phenomena are related causally. There is some controversy as to whether science actually posits this or not. There is reason, however, to believe that this disagreement is largely verbal. What is assumed in science is that events may be related in such a way that under specified conditions, event *A* will be observed to follow from event *B*. It is further to be noted that the relationship is assumed to occur in time and space.

The foregoing statements are fundamental postulates of science. They are not provable, but they are "true" because we wish them to be true. In this sense, then, science itself is founded upon evaluative assertions.

ETHICS IN SCIENCE

An ethic is more than the presence of a basic value or values. It is also an injunction to action. In science the basic value is most simply stated as the faith that "it is better to know than not to know." The injunction to action contained in this simple proposition is that knowledge should be actively sought. This value, the seeking after knowledge, does not apply to the scientist alone, however, and carried with it, therefore, is the further injunction to disseminate knowledge. Since knowledge is believed to be better than ignorance for ordinary people as well as for scientists, the findings of science must be made public. They are not to be closely guarded secrets, but essentially unpatentable and unsalable, a part of the public domain, freely given.

The acceptance of the belief that knowledge is good is by itself sufficient to indicate the ethical quality of science. There are, however, some further corollaries of the proposition which make this even plainer. If knowledge is a value, then all factors which endanger its achievement are undesirable. One such clear danger is the personal involvement of the scientist in his results. Thus the scientist must always be willing to throw aside his ideas in the face of contrary evidence. The man who fails to do this suffers through loss of esteem and severe criticism, for this is an *ideal*, an emotionally toned value.

The training of the scientist, of course, prepares him to behave in this way, not only by moral injunction but also in a practical fashion. It is early learned that falsification or distortion of facts cannot succeed for long. Science is the most pitilessly public activity in which men can engage.

Reputations are frequently made by young men through finding holes in the work of older scientists. Every important bit of research is repeated many times—in Japan, in Russia, in England, or in a South African laboratory. As a practical matter it is impossible to falsify anything in which other scientists are interested. Absolute honesty, therefore, is required of the scientist, not only by morality but also by necessity. The full acceptance of this kind of honesty requires that the scientist admit his error when he is wrong, since truth is rated a higher value than sparing one's own feelings.

The biasing of data through the personal involvement of the scientist, however, is by no means the only source of interference with the goal of securing knowledge. Another of these is the presence in a society of any form of social organization which restricts the freedom of inquiry or the dissemination of knowledge.

This is a somewhat complicated proposition, since under even the most repressive kind of political, religious, or special-interest domination, some sorts of science may continue to grow. Social sciences, in particular, however, cannot make significant advances without a maximum freedom from external control. The reason for this necessity, of course, lies in the fact that the social sciences wish to study objectively the important values of the society, whereas a totalitarian regime demands that they remain unquestioned. This restriction is not confined to the social sciences, as is amply demonstrated by the examples of violence done to biological science by the racial dogmas of National Socialist Germany and the state genetics of the Soviet Union.

·It seems safe to assert, however, that a positive interest in academic freedom is another ethical principle characteristic of modern science, which together with absolute honesty, and the willingness to admit being wrong, can be derived from the basic value that knowledge is superior to ignorance.

THE APPRAISAL OF SCIENTIFIC WORK

Dr. Vannevar Bush, head of the Office of Scientific Research and Development during World War II, was quoted as stating that during that period science practically came to a standstill. Since such a remark is so much at variance with popular opinion, it will bear looking into. Dr. Bush could not have meant that scientific activity ceased, since it is well known that scientists were working hard during the war period. What he meant, of course, is that work of *importance to science* diminished sharply. To say this is to make a value judgment about the importance of particular research activities. Such value judgments are based not upon the *validity* of research but upon its utility. Perfectly sound and accurate scientific research may be, and frequently is, criticized on an entirely evaluative basis.

There are two quite separate bases for such evaluations of research. One of these lies in the general culture in which the scientist lives, the other in the value systems of fellow scientists.

Robert S. Lynd, in his book *Knowledge for What?*, has pointed out that certain types of problems have been studied more frequently and thoroughly than others. Research to add to "creature comforts" has been supported far more heavily than have researches that might lead to a lower rate of neurosis or a wider implementation of democratic ideals. Science, in other words, has been widely supported because it produces market values. It pays off in "practical" terms, and research can be evaluated on this basis.

Only a small part of the scientific resources of the society is directed toward producing more scientists or conducting basic research. Most of the resources are expended on producing engineers and other applied scientists whose concern is the solution of "practical" problems. This indicates that our culture tends to emphasize the immediately useful, and the material. Such a value situation cannot but influence the course of science in our society.

The other basis for the evaluation of scientific research is the opinion of the scientific world. As in other professions, the scientist's success is measured by the opinion of his colleagues. They must be the judges of his work. They read his published works and utilize, criticize, or ignore his findings. To become a scientist it is necessary not only to acquire a knowledge of theory, methods, and techniques but also to enter into social relationships with others in the field.

This process might be termed "scientific socialization." In the childhood period of socialization, values as well as skills are acquired. The process of becoming a scientist is similar. It is not sufficient to learn the skills of interviewing, schedule making, titration, or microchemistry. It is also necessary to learn the "proper" style for reporting research and to learn whom and what to respect among other scientists and their doctrines. It is necessary to learn the folkways of the field—perhaps to sneer coldly at the scientist who "popularizes" his work or to disparage the man who seeks promotion by some means other than research contributions.

In the course of acquiring these folkways it is, of course, essential to learn which problems are most important. Here importance depends not upon possible financial reward but upon the theoretic value of the problem. As was pointed out in the preceding chapter, this is determined by the extent to which the solution to the problem also answers further questions.

Theoretic importance alone, however, is by no means the only value that may direct the scientist's selection of problems. For example, some questions may lead rather quickly and easily to published results because the techniques are known and the approach is familiar. Such a basis for the selection of problems can be considered one aspect of *motivation*, which will be treated in the following section of this chapter. Whichever factor operates, however, every research problem will be judged by the scientist's colleagues not only on the basis of the validity of the research but also on the basis of how far-reaching the results may be.

The areas in which science advances are thus at least partially influenced by two value systems, the one emanating from the general culture, the other from the scientist's colleagues. Research is needed to appraise the *extent* of these influences, but their existence is certain. It should, furthermore, be pointed out that the influence of the value judgments of colleagues is likely to be greater than that of the general public. This is a consequence of the fact that the scientist's products are generally "consumed" by other scientists, and scientific fields are likely to be rather closely knit fraternities. The importance of this fact is illustrated by a statement from the director of the Institute for Advanced Study, who is quoted as having said that gossip is the lifeblood of physics. That evaluation by colleagues may be "informed" evaluation does not remove the fact that value judgments are inseparable from the selection of scientific problems.

MOTIVATIONS TO SCIENCE

The relation between science and values is seen much more concretely when we ask: "What motivates a man to become a scientist?" Whatever the answer to this question may be, clearly it must be put in terms of the value judgments made by the scientist. The bases of choice are values. Science and its values must be chosen as a way of life in competition with other values, other possible vocations.

The nature of science itself as a value should be seen as operating at several levels. It is not proposed to treat these exhaustively, for such an attempt would lie beyond the province of this book and in the field of the sociology of knowledge.

Modern Western society holds science in high regard. This is the only major civilization ever to give such wide and increasing approval and respect to science. In many other times and places, saints, philosophers, holy men, political leaders, businessmen, or skilled engineers have been honored and esteemed. Never before, however, has the scientific method been given such wide approval or have scientists been granted such high prestige.

One consequence of this cultural approval has been the ability of science to secure both political and financial support. Another is the fact that to become a scientist in our culture is to achieve a high status ranking. This fact, of course, suggests another level at which values and science are related through motivation.

Science may be a means to the achievement of other values in our society. This is a somewhat more individual level than the preceding factor of general cultural patterns. It refers to the fact that science may become a vocation through which individual goals may be obtained. Since people are socialized toward the acceptance of such values as prestige, honor, promotion, money, power, etc., science may be used to secure these values. To be a successful scientist, in other words, is to have a successful career. This is not to say that science is the surest or only way to such rewards, but it is at least one path to success.

The reasons lying behind the choice of this particular path lead to a third level at which motivations relate to science. Particular motives, other than the general prestige or rewards attaching to science, may lead a man to become a scientist. A full treatment of this subject might be considered the psychological or perhaps even the psychiatric approach to science. A few illustrations, however, will make clear how values can operate to affect science at this very individual level. It does not need to be emphasized that these examples do not describe most scientists but merely show how science can be affected by the most individual of motives.

It is possible to cloak inhibited sex desires by becoming a student of the phenomenon. An individual who rebels against social controls may enjoy the study of social disorganization, criminology, or juvenile delinquency. The unhappily married may compensate for their deprivation by the scientific study of marital adjustment. And no one knows how much chemistry, astrophysics, or meteorology owes to long hours spent in work as an escape from a shrewish wife.

Since science is the work of scientists, and since scientists share in the values of their culture, it is clear that science and values are related through the motivations of men.

VALUES AS DATA

This particular relationship between science and values is applicable to the social more than to the physical sciences. Value judgments constitute a large share of social-science data. These range from studies of the major value systems of whole cultures down to investigation of the values of the individual by means of the case history. The study of socialization, for example, is the study of the gradual acquisition of values by the child, and comparative historical surveys measure changes in values within a cultural system.

The central position of value judgments in the social sciences lies in the fact that value judgments are merely the formalized expressions of sentiments and emotions derived from the culture and impelling men to action. Values are thus major determinants of human behavior and hence major areas for study by social science.

Since the social scientist who studies the values of his own culture is also involved in those values, it goes without saying that it is difficult for him to keep those values from interfering with his scientific work. This may be especially true when the subject of investigation is not merely the description of value systems, but the analysis of conflicting values. In such a case the temptation to be biased by one of the conflicting systems is surely great.

This particular problem is a significant element in Gunnar Myrdal's analysis of the American race problem, *An American Dilemma*. Here he shows that the "American Creed," embracing such ideals as equality of opportunity, the freedom of the individual without respect to race, color, or creed, is in direct conflict with the actual treatment of the Negro. The *description* of this value conflict is a scientific operation. An *evaluation* of the situation is not. The *exposure of logical contradictions in value systems* is a legitimate scientific activity, even though special pleading for one system or the other is not.

There are other conflicts between the values of science and other values. Such a conflict may arise when the findings of science run counter to an existing prejudice or value. This is possible because many prejudices are expressed as empirical statements, such as "Negroes have too little intelligence to become anything but laborers." Science will continue to destroy such superstitious beliefs just as genetics, psychology, and sociology have destroyed earlier beliefs in prenatal influences and the inheritance of such things as criminality, pauperism, and depravity. The older beliefs in the existence of separate races, each with its own temperament and behavior patterns, have been attacked by the findings of biology, anthropology, psychology, and sociology.

Thus, science is inevitably brought into relation with values, since it may be used to study the relations and contradictions between different values, or to study areas that have previously been covered by a mixture of empirical guess and evaluational thinking. The importance of this is not that the validity of social science is weakened but that the scientist must cultivate an awareness of these value relationships and their impact upon the sciences themselves. He must thereby develop an alertness to the distinctions between an acceptance of such values and the scientific study of them.

SCIENCE AS A MEANS

Science is essentially a means to an end. There are some scientists who would paraphrase the old slogan of "art for art's sake" and maintain that science is its own justification. Nevertheless, the basis for the prestigeful position of science in our society is its ability to solve problems.

Science provides the answers as to *how* to perform certain operations in order to secure given ends. But such knowledge is a two-edged sword. The same processes that led to the manufacture of aniline dyes set in motion physiological processes that ended in death for many of those who helped manufacture the dyes. The development of superior methods of keeping records, basic to the growth of social science, may also be the means of strengthening the grip of a repressive political dictatorship. Today the use of radioactive-isotope therapy promises much for the reduction of disease, but these isotopes are products of the same scientific knowledge which produced the atomic bomb and which has made possible the even more destructive hydrogen bomb. Science as a method gives power, but this is a power which may be used for disapproved as well as approved ends.

Science, then, can (1) offer a method of solving problems, *i.e.*, of achieving values; (2) offer *alternative* methods, so that relative costs can be calculated; (3) provide a means for predicting what the other consequences of a given course of action may be. If, for example, it is desired to clear a slum, it is good to be able not only to predict the financial and emotional costs of the specific program but also to know what other effects the slum clearance will have upon the community. This is a task to which only the scientific method may be successfully applied.

Since science operates as a technique of problem solving, and since problems in this sense are formulated upon the basis of value judgments, then it is clear that science and values are interrelated. The central and most common question, however, still remains. We have seen the many relationships between science and values. Now we must ask, "If science can tell us *how* to do a thing, can it also tell us *what* to do?"

THE POSSIBILITY OF A SCIENTIFIC ETHIC

This question is often debated, even though the answer is clearly in the negative. There are those who, valuing science highly, seem to wish that science should support other values that are also important to them. The wish that this be so is therefore transformed into the statement that it *is* so. The position that values may be scientifically *proved* is usually put somewhat as follows: The consequences of various values can be demonstrated by the application of the scientific method. Thus we can see that certain values ought to be accepted and others rejected.

The obvious weakness in this argument is that, given a knowledge of the consequences, the choice of which consequence is desirable must *still* depend upon some criterion of value outside the realm of science. The ultimate value to which the proponents of a scientific ethic are driven is to some such statement as "It is better to be well than sick" or even "It is better to be alive than dead." Were this true, much experimental medicine would never have existed. It would be impossible to raise an army, and the martyrs to religious or political values would never have died. Other values may often be held superior to life itself, and there is no scientific method of testing the *validity* of those values—only the *consequences* may be scientifically known. Science, in other words, can only tell us *how* to achieve goals; it can never tell us *what* goals should be sought.

VALUE JUDGMENTS AND ERROR

It is hardly necessary to add at this point that the distinction between a value judgment and a scientific proposition is not one between *error* and *truth*. A scientific proposition may be either correct or incorrect. The point is that it can be demonstrated to be one or the other. The distinction between the correct and the erroneous, however, simply does not apply to value judgments. They are essentially expressions of wishes, desires, or goals, and their "truth" or falsity is of a different order from that of empirical statements.

SUMMARY

Because this chapter has presented a set of complex relationships, it seems worth while to retrace briefly the steps taken. Several areas in which science and values are related have been described in refutation of the common statement that science and values are in entirely different realms.

It has been stated that science is based upon assumptions that are unprovable and that are essentially value judgments. It has been shown further that science itself has developed an ethic based upon the assertion that knowledge is superior to ignorance.

These two points do not mean, however, that science must therefore relinquish its claim to being the only adequate method for achieving empirical truth. They in no way impair the objectivity of the scientific method but rather point out that science itself has its own metaphysics.

It has also been shown that the appraisal and selection of problems, as well as the motivations behind the selection of science as a career, are value-related aspects of science. It does not follow from this that the validity of science is determined by values. The purpose of this discussion is merely to point out that these are *possible* sources of bias, to be guarded against.

Similarly, the fact that science may deal with problems that have evaluative content, or even with the values themselves, and the fact that the scientist himself may share the values, does not necessarily interfere with the growth of sociology as science. Rather, these too are points at which care must be exercised to eliminate bias. The scientific method is itself a tool to this end. A clear understanding of the relationships between values and science allows us to improve our science, as it helps us to see other values more sharply.

SUGGESTED READINGS

Bowman, Claude C., "Must the Social Sciences Foster Moral Skepticism?" *American Sociological Review*, Vol. X (1945), pp. 709–715.

Lundberg, George A., *Can Science Save Us?* (New York: Longmans, 1947).

Lynd, Robert S., *Knowledge for What?* (Princeton, N.J.: Princeton University Press, 1939).

MacIver, Robert M., "Is Sociology a Natural Science?" *Proceedings of the American Sociological Society*, Vol. XXV (1930), pp. 25–35.

Myrdal, Gunnar, *An American Dilemma* (New York: Harper, 1944), Vol. 1, Appendix 2.

Sullivan, J. N. W., "The Values of Science," in *The Limitations of Science* (New York: Mentor Books, 1949), pp. 50–175.

Weber, Max, "The Objectivity of the Social Sciences," *On the Methodology of the Social Sciences*, trans. Edward A. Shils and Henry A. Finch (Glencoe, Ill.: Free Press, 1949).

CHAPTER 4

Science: Pure and Applied

The first chapter of this book noted that the scientific work of sociology has become increasingly valid in recent decades. In the following two chapters the role of theory and fact and the importance of values for science were discussed. These areas interrelate logically when the question is raised: "How practical is scientific sociology?"

This is a basic question for the student of sociology. The major portion of sociological effort is expended in the solution of practical problems for government and business. If this is true, then most students will have more concern with these practical problems than with the theoretic advancement of sociology. A course in the methods of sociological research, then, should have some value in training for the solution of practical problems. Whether or not to emphasize theory is not, however, a question that faces sociology alone. It is common to all science and is generally thought of as the consequence of a controversy between pure and applied science. This dichotomy, like that between "values and science," rests in part upon false bases.

THE PRESSURES TOWARD APPLIED SCIENCE

It is commonplace to hear science decried as being deaf to the values of the arts, as being morally obtuse, or as being narrow in its range of problems. All this may be true, but there is still the brute fact that science grows ever stronger. The reasons for this lie in its practical applications. It takes no great sophistication to appreciate these. Members of the most isolated and simple preliterate society can appreciate that an ax designed on good engineering principles will fell a tree faster than one of their own design. It requires no knowledge of mathematics, chemistry, and physics to grasp their consequences in the modern world. As a result of the applications of scientific study, Western civilization will leave the most impressive ruins yet found on this globe.

Science is known to the vast majority of the public almost solely by its engineering results. These practical applications therefore become the most frequently used criterion of the degree to which a discipline is scientific. If sociology is a science, then this fact must be demonstrated by the achievement of practical results. All other activity will tend to be put aside as "pure theory," that is, as mere speculation and as evidence that the field is not scientifically oriented.

Such pressures, plus the widespread faith that science can solve problems—"can save us," in the words of one writer—result in the suggestion that sociology tackle immediate and practical problems. This pressure does not come from laymen alone but is also exerted by those in social agencies and by university administrators and professors.

Sociologists have further contributed to this situation, particularly those who allow their vision of the bright future to color their appraisal of present actualities. Again, this is not characteristic of sociology alone but of science in general. Persuaded by their belief in the progress of knowledge, many scientists have predicted too early the appearance of many engineering devices. The motor car and airplane are cases in point, for like other applications of science they were predicted hundreds of years before their appearance. Every important engineering triumph comes only after repeated failures to solve the problem. Sociologists who claim applications of the field beyond the range of present possible achievement do no service to their own discipline. They contribute instead to the pressures which demand that sociology prove its scientific nature by producing applications of a practical nature far beyond the limits of its body of knowledge.

COUNTERPRESSURES

Resistance to the foregoing emphasis upon practical results is of two types. First, there is resistance based upon the belief that science has best been able to achieve practical results when no goals other than those of science are considered. Those who hold this position maintain that if scientists are allowed to pursue problems dictated purely by theoretical concerns, the growth of science and hence the growth of its potential applications will best be served.

If the dichotomy of pure as against applied science is accepted, the logical question would be "Which of these should be emphasized in contemporary sociology?" However, not all scientists accept the dichotomy to begin with, and this refusal is the basis of the second type of counterpressure to the insistence that sociology be addressed mainly to practical problems.

The reader will notice a certain parallel between this problem and the discussion of the relationship between theory and fact in Chapter 2. It is indeed a similar question, and one that requires an understanding of the nature of theory as a basis for analysis. Let us see how a redefinition of the problem affects the decision to confine oneself to "practical" sociology.

A theoretical system is a way of organizing problems. All facts collected, all the analysis of these facts, even the perception of the data themselves are ordered within some sort of theoretical framework. Such a simple statement as "Water is wet" is understandable only if it is made within the proper frame of reference. In nuclear physics, for example, water has no such characteristic. Wetness is not a property of electrons or their nucleus. Similarly, in a "common-sense" frame of reference, it may be asserted that a particular table is black. If, however, the table is examined within the theoretical system of chemistry, no such quality appears. It is, instead, a combination of complex organic compounds.

These simple examples serve to make two rather complex points. First, there is a difference between the common-sense frame of reference and a scientific theoretical system. The latter is much narrower and is defined more precisely. As a consequence of this narrowness and precision, it is also clear that frames of reference shift among the several sciences, so that properties in one science simply make no sense, or do not appear, in another science. The significance of this point will be discussed later when the problems of the hypothesis are taken up. For the moment it is the difference between the common-sense viewpoint and the outlook of science which is of greater importance.

The "importance" of a fact depends upon the frame of reference. Thus, a fact may be significant in the theory of a science without making any common sense at all. For example, the classic Michelson-Morley experiment, which showed light to have a speed independent of its point of origin or its direction, was of great importance to physics. Although this is a basic datum in the special theory of relativity, its immediate impact upon the man in the street has been negligible. If the findings had been contrary—that is, that light moving in the direction of the earth's spin traveled at the equator about 0.3 mile per second faster than its customary speed of 186,300 miles per second—who would notice, and who would care?

A fact is of significance only with reference to a particular theoretical schema. It may be of great scientific importance, but of no significance to the common-sense world and vice versa. It might be concluded, however, that if science depends for its growth upon the acquisition of scientifically important facts, the scientist should concentrate on "pure" research problems. While there is undoubted merit to this proposition, it cannot be accepted as a necessary conclusion unless the common-sense world and the scientific schema are mutually exclusive.

The same fact may have relevance for both scientific and practical problems. A problem that occurs in the everyday world is set in a loosely defined frame of reference, and its solution usually depends on several sciences simultaneously. Its characteristics therefore may be quite different from those of a scientific problem. There is nevertheless a relationship between the two.

To take a simple example, the cook, unaccustomed to the altitude, who boils his soaked beans in Mexico City for the usual 45 minutes to an hour will find them inedible. The problem he faces is that, in spite of the cooking, the beans have remained perversely hard. The solution is simple: cook them much longer until they are "done." This is a practical problem solved in a common-sense context.

It is clear that such a problem is not a scientific one, at least as it is stated here. In the first place, it is not stated what constitutes "hard" beans or what is meant when they are said to be "done." Secondly, the problem is not stated in sufficiently abstract terms to permit its solution to add anything to a scientific theory. Finally, once the solution to this problem has been reached, there is no compulsion to discover the reasons for this situation. In short, it is entirely devoid of scientific interest. *It need not be so,* however. Nothing prevents the problem of cooking beans at various altitudes from being looked at from the point of view of science.

For example, the activities of scientists in the seventeenth century, most of whom were mechanics and men of practical affairs rather than university men, were focused on problems understandable to most people. The new telescopes and microscopes were turned on any and every subject of interest that struck them. These men made better gunpowder and new cosmetics, improved firearms, and looked at ordinary ditchwater. At that time, the great flowering of modern physical science, there seemed to be little difference between practical and scientific frames of reference.

The study and solution of these everyday problems was, however, accompanied by an eager search for an understanding of the principles behind each problem. It was this fact that distinguished these solutions from merely practical adaptations and raised the activity to the level of science.

During this period the eagerness of the search for truth was so widespread that new experiments were repeated and discussed before ordinary citizens as well as scientists. When Von Guericke, Mayor of Magdeburg, invented the air pump, he found the Diet of Ratisbonne a most interested audience.

This air pump had several consequences. First, it astounded the Diet by showing that two hemispheres from which the air had been exhausted could not be pulled apart by 14 horses. In this sense the pump served as an intellectual toy. Beyond this amusement, however, observations of the air pump led to the discovery of important facts about the weight of air, and air pressure. These discoveries in turn have produced such important practical inventions as the barometer, the thermometer, and—to solve the problem of the beans—the pressure cooker.

It is clear that the subject matter of early science was not far removed from common experience. Brewers, dyers, mayors, soldiers, merchants, and men of many other backgrounds were able to make important contributions. There was, in other words, a considerable *overlapping* between the frameworks of science and of common sense. Theoretical science and practical problem solving were not widely separated.

Since, however, men had been solving practical problems for millenniums before this period without creating natural science, there must be a marked difference between empirical problem solving and the scientific method. It is also clear that this difference does not separate practical questions sharply from the sphere of scientific interest.

COMMON SENSE AND SCIENTIFIC FRAMEWORKS

Some of the relationships between these two ways of seeing problems have already been discussed. They may be summarized as showing four major differences, even when the focus of attention is an everyday practical problem.

The scientific method goes beyond the solution of the practical problem. There is a compulsion to find better instruments to help in the solution or to find alternative ways of solving it more satisfactorily. In other words, the practical problem may be solved in the area of common sense, but not in the scientific frame of reference, for here many problems remain even after "the beans are cooked."

The scientific method of solution involves controlled experimentation. This means that, even though a practical problem may be solved by the application of casual empirical observation—that is, simply by cooking the beans longer—a scientific solution has not necessarily been reached. For this, precise definition, measurement, and control of the variables must be employed in an experimental framework.

The scientific solution looks for broader generalizations. As the scientist works at problems, he is conscious that he is building a science. He searches for those facts (negative as well as positive), wherever they may be found, that constitute empirical uniformities. These in turn are studied in the attempt to locate underlying principles. Thus the practical solution is merely an intermediate step and not the end of the road for the scientist.

Scientific experimentation is set against an existing body of generalizations. This statement is an extension of the previous point. Not only does the scientist seek generalizations, but he also wishes to extend their utility by relating them to other generalizations; in short, he wishes to create a system of theory. Thus, in the early years of the scientific epoch, experiments with boiling water at low temperatures by varying pressure, and studies on the height of mercury columns as affected by the air pumps, not only were entertaining but led to some practical results. Entertainment and practical usefulness were not, however, the only consequences of these studies. They were tests that had a bearing upon a body of learning concerning vacuums and the weight of air. Each test was part of the cumulative process that is the growth of science. The constant change induced in a science by this cumulative process results in the clarification of its generalizations through greater *specification of the conditions* under which the generalizations hold. This development in turn increases the *predictive power* of the science and divides the field into an ever-growing number of *specialties,* each of which is more *abstract* and further removed than its parent from the frame of reference of common sense.

THE INTERPLAY BETWEEN APPLIED AND PURE SOCIOLOGY

On the other hand, sociology is still in an early phase of growth, and its frame of reference is not much more abstract than that of common sense. It should follow, then, that practical problems can contribute to theoretical sociology, and vice versa. At the present time, it is wasteful to lose the theoretical knowledge that could be gained from well-designed applied research. Yet it should be possible to utilize in a practical fashion the discoveries of theoretical sociology. Let us sketch some of the possible interplay between these two.

From the side of applied research. 1. APPLIED RESEARCH CAN CONTRIBUTE NEW FACTS. As we have noted previously, much of science consists in simply finding out what the facts are within a rather broad definition of relevance. Before we can organize a study that will neatly test a hypothesis, a considerable amount of information is necessary. If we had to develop all this information for each study, scientific work would be impossible. We may need United States census reports, tabulations from divorce courts, description of farming patterns, diagrams of the structure of a corporation, and so on. Such data are useful for subsequent analysis, for solving practical problems, or for setting up new tests.

In addition, we have already noted that new facts may lead to the initiation, rejection, and reformulation of theory, or to its clarification and redefinition. A practical school survey, designed to solve the problems of teaching in an area dominated by an ethnic group, may lead to interesting questions about socialization and group integration patterns among local families. A practical study designed to aid the reformation of paroled criminals may stimulate theoretical analysis of group pressures, stratification patterns, the psychodynamisms of frustration, etc. In short, if we design our applied research well enough that we can rely upon the facts uncovered, the new information may be theoretically useful and stimulating.

2. APPLIED RESEARCH CAN PUT THEORY TO THE TEST. The reader of research reports has become somewhat more sophisticated than he once was. He is no longer willing to accept the facile statement of a social

observer, "I saw it." He wishes to know instead when it was seen, under what conditions, for how many people of what kinds, and so on. Since practical social problems are almost invariably studied in an atmosphere of political conflict, the resulting report must be technically acceptable. The study must follow scientific procedures, for it may have to face the criticism of partisan groups. For this reason a relatively formalized research design must be worked out and applied. The researcher must be conscious of what he proposes to do and of why he uses certain techniques. Thus he is able to justify the cost of the research to the sponsoring agency or foundation and to defend his results later.

A practical research study thus provides an excellent opportunity to put theory to the test. It attempts the diagnosis of a situation (*i.e.*, what caused *X*, or how are the factors in *X* related?) and a solution (*i.e.*, if stimulus *Z* is introduced, how does *X* change?). Pure sociologists are wrestling with logically similar questions, often about the same subject matter (factory morale and production, invasion and succession of ethnic groups, divorce, etc.). From his knowledge of theory, the sociologist should be able to develop hypotheses which predict what he will find in the study. The demand for formalized procedures requires that he sharpen his concepts and follow good research design. If new stimuli are introduced, *i.e.*, if "something is done about the situation," a quasi experiment is created to test his hypotheses still further. Until the theoretical framework of sociology becomes very abstract, many of its basic problems and concepts will not be far removed from common sense, and applied research offers an opportunity to test the validity of existing theory.

3. APPLIED RESEARCH MAY AID IN CONCEPTUAL CLARIFICATION. As in any changing science, many sociological concepts are not precise. Such notions as "integration of the social structure," "function," "class," "adjustment," or "primary relationship" occasion considerable argument among sociologists, since the referents of these terms are not entirely clear. Lack of clarity becomes crucial when research is planned. If we wish to know the consequences of social integration in a neighborhood or group, we have to find techniques for observing or measuring that integration. In order to do this, however, we have to clarify our concept considerably. A concept exhibits its vagueness most sharply when we begin to define the procedures and operations for dealing with it in research.

Applied and theoretical research are not differentiated in this respect. Both contribute to the process of translating concepts into manageable operations. A further contribution of applied research, however, may be the development of concepts, especially when the central use of a concept has not received much attention in theoretical sociology. An example may be taken from housing research.[1] "Expected duration of membership in a

---

[1] See Hanan C. Selvin, "The Interplay of Social Research and Social Policy in Housing," *Journal of Social Issues*, Vol. VII (1951), p. 182.

group" is of importance in applied investigations in this field, and particularly so with reference to "housing projects." This variable is used by managers as a basis of choice in order to reduce turnover. The variable may determine community participation to some extent, or reaction to proposed changes in the neighborhood. Yet it has not received the systematic attention in theoretical sociology which it deserves. A concept may thus be developed in applied research and then be utilized further in theoretical research once its importance has been noted.

4. APPLIED RESEARCH MAY INTEGRATE PREVIOUSLY EXISTING THEORY. Problem solving typically draws upon many sciences, for the problem is concrete and cannot be solved by the application of abstract principles from a single science. Bridge construction, for example, may draw upon such disciplines as economics, hydrostatics, stress analysis, demography, chemistry, geology, etc. "Slum clearance" requires the data studied by the criminologist, the social worker, the sociologist, the economist, and others. Thus, the solution of a concrete problem may require some integration of the findings from many theoretical as well as applied investigations in several fields. The same principle must be applied, however, *within* sociology. Studies of socialization may be used in planning for the interaction of children from different ethnic groups or in developing a program for adult education, in designing the project that replaces the slum. Demographic data must be used to calculate the expected number of children in the schools and to plan community recreation. Studies of neighboring behavior, of the impact of physical location upon social interaction, of the bases for community participation may be used in laying out the building entrances or locating the community center.

These contributions may be seen as the application of theoretical knowledge to specific problems. It must be seen, however, that we have a pattern, a total plan, and it must then be seen how these various factors *interact* with one another. For example, previous studies have shown that physical proximity is important in the formation of clique patterns, as are factors of class, ethnic group, religion, and so on. How do these principles operate *together,* when the influence of each is in the same direction? In different directions? We may ask similar questions about the association of juvenile delinquency with such factors as income, education, association with fringe groups, or "broken" homes. This example is taken from housing research. An analogous integration could be attempted in applied industrial research and other areas. We would then be trying to discover the weights to be given such factors, so as to be able to predict their total effects more accurately. Applied social research, then, can be useful in the actual integration of existing theory.

From the side of "pure" research. 1. BY DEVELOPING GENERAL PRINCIPLES, THEORY OFFERS SOLUTIONS TO MANY PRACTICAL PROBLEMS. The abstractness which removes a scientific generalization from ordinary experience also gives it a broader application. When we have ascertained the differential effects of various kinds of social backgrounds upon intellectual achievement in IQ tests, we can apply these rough principles to the analysis of test grades made by Southern Negroes or by San Francisco Chinese-Americans. We can predict what will happen when these groups migrate to other areas, or when new opportunities are given them. We can interpret more easily the different achievements of class strata. Although these judgments are not so precise or so well established as, say, those relating to the interaction between air pressure, altitude, boiling points, etc., they are similar in that there are many practical applications. Indeed, it can be said that nothing is so practical for the goals of diagnosis or treatment as good theoretical research. Too often, in contrast, practical problem solving confines itself to the concrete immediacy, so that the result is not applicable elsewhere.

2. "PURE" RESEARCH HELPS TO FIND THE CENTRAL FACTORS IN A PRACTICAL PROBLEM. All too often, those who adopt a common-sense approach see the problem in traditional ways and fail to abstract the key factors. As a consequence, the solution is likely to be an inefficient one. For example, in an area torn by racial dissension, a playground director may "solve" the problem of gang fights between boys of different races by allotting different playground hours or days to the various gangs. This may "work," in the sense that the fights are avoided. However, since it fails to grapple with the causes of the tension and this outlet for it, the solution is inefficient and very likely helps to maintain the existing situation.

On the other hand, by the development and application of general principles of social interaction, group morale and cohesion, socialization, and deflection of tension, it is possible to work out a solution that both avoids gang fights and integrates these different groups. Theoretical knowledge, then, can go beyond mere common sense.

3. RESEARCH AS AN ANSWER TO PROBLEMS MAY BECOME A STANDARD PROCEDURE FOR THE ADMINISTRATOR. Pure research may have an effect upon the pattern of administrative procedure, as the practitioner learns of its utility. This development has not been a common one, but both governmental and business organizations have begun to utilize "research and planning units" to evaluate the techniques which have been applied in the past and to develop new solutions to old as well as new problems. Such a unit may be given considerable freedom in its investigations. Large industrial corporations have, of course, used such units particularly in the biological and physical sciences. However, the utility of social-research units is obvious for both nonindustrial and industrial organizations, since problems of social relations are common to both. What is central to this development is the belief that problems should be anticipated where possible, that traditional procedures may always be questioned, and that the development of fairly general principles can be a practical activity. Thus

the pattern of pure research has an effect upon the solution of practical problems in that its aims and procedures become the usual, long-term approach to the latter type of problem.

4. THEORETICAL RESEARCH DEVELOPS MANY ALTERNATIVE SOLUTIONS, WITH THE RESULT THAT ALTERNATIVE COSTS MAY BE WEIGHED AND ULTIMATELY REDUCED. The solutions that theoretical research first develops are likely to be very expensive. Most of the applications of science which have become common in our civilization—the radio, television, mechanical refrigeration, sun lamps—were originally laboratory appliances, unwieldy, costly, and inefficient. The first isolation of elements or isotopes has almost invariably required a relatively large expenditure of time and money. However, pure science characteristically continues the investigation beyond a "workable" solution to more precise generalizations, discovery of the essential factors, and ascertainment of the exact conditions under which the process operates. Consequently, after a time there are many solutions for a given type of problem, with different main and subsidiary consequences. We are thus permitted to choose the best solution for our practical problem.

Because scientific sociology has had such a short history, the only acceptable examples of such multiple solutions must be taken from social-research techniques. With each improvement in these techniques, we are able to solve practical social problems with considerably less waste. Developments in social theory have offered alternative solutions to such problems as juvenile delinquency, racial and ethnic assimilation, low production in office and factory, etc., but in general these are improvements over common sense, rather than over scientific generalizations that had previously been applied. However, as we learn to isolate important social factors and to clarify the lines of cause and effect, we may be able to develop out of theoretical sociology still more efficient answers to our practical problems.

SUMMARY

Thus we see that at this stage in the development of sociology we should not think of pure and applied research as being opposed. The two are not mutually exclusive. There is interplay between them, and there can be still more. Good theoretical research may be applicable to practical problems, and applied research can contribute to theoretical sociology. What is essential is that, even in applied research, a scientific frame of reference should be kept in mind. For, ultimately, the great power of science appears to lie in the development of general principles which are applicable to many concrete problems. If practical programs of research have contributed less to science than might be desired, this reflects the need for more adequate scientific training and a more self-conscious scientific approach on the part of those who carry out the research.

This last point needs special emphasis because an increasing number of social scientists are engaged in practical research. Consequently, there are increasing opportunities for the sociologist to apply his knowledge to the concrete problems of the major social institutions. There is an increasing amount of money for such research. Community councils, city governments, labor unions, business concerns, and various special interest groups will in the future underwrite still larger programs of sociological research. Their interest, however, is not in the growth of sociology but in the achievement of a practical solution. Research is expensive, and funds are limited. The development of science could be greatly accelerated by such projects. The importance of this opportunity is heightened by the fact that there is relatively little money available for "pure" research.

It should be repeated at this point, however, that in applied research the work tends to be limited, the problem defined, and the frame of reference of the researcher specified without regard to the goals of scientific theory. When this occurs, we have an example of the possibly dangerous interference of personal values with science which was elaborated in the preceding chapter.

It is of vital importance that this danger be consciously recognized by the sociologist engaged in practical work. It need not handicap him so long as he designs his work within the scientific frame of reference as well as within the social-problem framework. The practicality of the results will in no way damage the scientific validity of work which is properly conceived and carried out.

The task for the student of sociology, then, is to develop his understanding of research design and techniques as well as his knowledge of sociological fact and theory. Whether he attempts "pure" or "applied" research, this training is necessary. It is perhaps particularly crucial when he must thread his way through complex everyday problems in such a way that he will not only help to solve them but also contribute to scientific growth.

SUGGESTED READINGS

Burgess, Ernest W., and Leonard S. Cottrell, *The Prediction of Success or Failure in Marriage* (New York: Prentice-Hall, 1939).

Campbell, Norman, *What Is Science?* (London: Methuen, 1921), Chap. 8.

Cohen, Morris R., and Ernest Nagel, *An Introduction to Logic and Scientific Method* (New York: Harcourt, Brace, 1934), Chaps. 1 and 2.

Herzog, Elizabeth G., "What Social Casework Wants of Social Science Research," *American Sociological Review*, Vol. XVI (1951), pp. 68–73.

Lundberg, G. A., *Social Research* (New York: Longmans, 1942), 2d ed., pp. 1–16.

Pollak, Otto, "Social Science and Child Guidance Practice," *American Sociological Review*, Vol. XVI (1951), pp. 61–67.

Selvin, Hanan C., "The Interplay of Social Research and Social Policy in Housing," *Journal of Social Issues*, Vol. VII, Nos. 1 and 2 (1951), pp. 172–185.

Stouffer, Samuel A., "Social Science and the Soldier," *Sociological Analysis*, Logan Wilson and William L. Kolb, eds. (New York: Harcourt, Brace, 1949), pp. 44–50.

Veblen, Thorstein, *The Place of Science in Modern Civilization* (New York: Viking, 1932), pp. 1–55.

Woodward, James L., "Making Government Opinion Research Bear upon Operations," *American Sociological Review*, Vol. IX (1944), pp. 670–677.

CHAPTER 5

Basic Elements of the Scientific Method: Concepts

The *systematic* character of scientific knowledge has been noted at various points in the previous chapters. A fact is not merely a random observation, for example, but is an empirically verified statement about phenomena. It thus embodies both scientific observations and a known theoretical framework into which those observations are fitted. Furthermore, the observations themselves are systematically guided by the existing structure of knowledge. The universe presents an infinite variety of phenomena to be studied, but science limits itself to a few of these. As has been pointed out before, science abstracts from reality, dealing with certain aspects of phenomena (such as mass, speed, valence, intensity of attitude, etc.), not with the whole phenomena themselves. Indeed, to separate any phenomenon from all that is connected with it is an act of abstraction.

Since science attempts to investigate particular sections or aspects of reality, with an abstract system of thought to interpret those segments, it should not be surprising that each science develops its own terms, or *concepts,* for communicating its findings. So much is this the case that we may refer to the theoretical system of the science as a *conceptual system.* Now, we use these terms to stand for the phenomena, or aspects of phenomena, which we are investigating. Consequently, when we formulate a proposition, we use concepts as *symbols* of the phenomena we are studying, and it is really these underlying phenomena which we are relating to one another. Because we deal directly with only the concepts, however, it is obvious that we may at times confuse the *concept* with the *phenomenon* it is supposed to symbolize. This is a common error, to be discussed in a moment under the term "reification."

A further point must be made. Since all these concepts are abstractions and represent only certain aspects of reality, it becomes important to know (1) which aspects we should study, and (2) how to develop concepts for them. The first problem properly belongs in a discussion of theories and hypotheses. The second is the process of *conceptualization* and is treated in this chapter, under these headings: (*a*) the concept as abstrac-

41

tion, (b) concepts and communication, (c) problems of definition, (d) re-conceptualization, and (e) the operational definition.

THE CONCEPT AS ABSTRACTION

It is sometimes forgotten that concepts are logical constructs created from sense impressions, percepts, or even fairly complex experiences. The tendency to assume that concepts actually exist as phenomena leads to many errors. The concept is not the phenomenon itself; that is, such logical constructs do not exist outside the stated frame of reference. The failure to recognize this is termed the *fallacy of reification,* that is, *treating abstractions as if they were actual phenomena.* This is such a common error that most of us are occasionally guilty of it.

A classic example of this error is found in sociology in the treatment and criticism of W. I. Thomas's "Four Wishes." Thomas felt that he had abstracted from human behavior certain elements that could be thought of as oriented toward (1) experiencing new situations, (2) securing the recognition of others, (3) retaining feelings of security, and (4) eliciting response from others. From his observations of human behavior, these were merely four major elements, not the totality. They were given these labels for conceptual convenience. However, some readers then reified these statements into something akin to instincts, and they were treated as though they were "forces" in their own right. As a consequence, they were subject to severe criticism because the existence of such entities was thought to be unproved.

Regardless of whether or not Thomas's observations were valid, criticism of this kind was really directed against these later reifications rather than against his concepts. Thomas was presenting his observations in conceptual terms, while his opponents were criticizing these ideas as though they were basic drives.

Since both facts and concepts are abstractions, they have meaning only within some frame of reference, some theoretical system. The discussion of the relationship between fact and theory to be found in Chapter 2 applies also to the relationship between concept and theory. A concept, like a fact, is an abstraction, not a phenomenon. It takes its meaning from the thought framework within which it is placed.

The distinction between fact and concept is that concepts symbolize the empirical relationships and phenomena which are stated by the fact. Thus, as noted before, a fact is stated as a relationship between concepts, for each term stands for the phenomena described by the fact. In this sense, then, a fact is "a logical construct of concepts." A concept, in turn, is abstracted from many sense impressions, or percepts. The process of conceptualization is one of abstracting and generalizing sense impressions. In this way, it is possible to manipulate, study, organize, and isolate the properties of objects. It is only by thought that such properties can be isolated, and thinking can proceed only by giving names to such properties. Thus, conceptualization is essential to thought.

We have been discussing the form of abstract manipulation called science. Concepts, however, are obviously not basic to scientific method alone: *they are the foundation of all human communication and thought.* Since, however, science requires a greater precision in communication, the process of conceptualization must be much more consciously a part of science than is the case for most common-sense and everyday contexts. So long as the scientist is aware of these relationships and of the abstract character of conceptualization, he can avoid the error of reification.

CONCEPTS AND COMMUNICATION

Concepts in science must be communicable in a very special sense. They must not merely arouse a vague "feeling" but must be so constructed that all their components are known. Deriving and clarifying the elements of such a construct are the major processes of definition, basic to the general problem of conceptualization.

Because of the differences between the common-sense framework and the scientific way of looking at the world, careful definition has a paradoxical quality. It facilitates communication within the sciences, but it also raises barriers to the lay understanding of scientific concepts. This is voiced in the common complaint that science uses "big words." Some critics are even cynical enough to suggest that science is a way of stating clichés in such polysyllabic words that no one else can understand what is said.

This same complaint is often registered by scientists against each other. The several sciences, as was seen in the preceding chapter, develop specialties which depend upon facts so abstract and complicated that no one scientist can know them all. Because each specialty deals with different phenomena, a variety of scientific vocabularies has been developed to communicate these special facts. The gap between these several sciences varies, depending upon the closeness of relationship between the frames of references. Between sociology and the physical sciences the gap is a chasm. The average sociologist cannot read with any great understanding most of the chemistry and physics reports in *Science,* the journal of the American Association for the Advancement of Science. He simply does not know the terms, does not possess the necessary concepts.

This is true even for many of the articles by biologists. For example, an article chosen randomly from this journal contains in its first paragraph the following terms: "specific adsorption," "antibody molecules," "angstrom units," "antigenic protein," "diluted antiserum," and "heterologous serum." Could this paragraph have been written so that even a "well-educated" but lay public could understand it? The answer is "yes," but it would no longer be a paragraph. It would be a series of volumes piling definition upon definition until much of the complex history of modern biochemistry was reconstructed. Each concept, in short, communicates to the specialist a vast amount of experience, abstracted and clarified for those who understand the term.

Consequently the basic equipment of any student is the possession of a scientific vocabulary adequate to understand the conceptual development of his field. These necessary terms are not merely big words chosen to impress the uninitiated, nor are they "just the difficult way of stating common sense." They are rather the "shorthand" of science, the precise terms which are basic to easy communication between scientists.

PROBLEMS IN DEFINITION AND COMMUNICATION

Not only is communication difficult between individuals who do not share the same conceptual systems, but similar problems often arise between those who do share a common frame of reference. In other words, definitions are not always clear; the concepts are not always adequately described. Several general reasons for the lack of clarity in some scientific communication are given below.

Concepts develop from a shared experience. The development of a conceptual system can, in fact, best be seen as the development of a new language. It is then easily seen why a group of scientists, in sharing experiences, is likely to develop a language not intelligible to others. This is a common problem of communication, not only in the scientific world but in translation from one language into another. Why is it so difficult to translate the German word *gemütlich* into English? Why do American sociologists continue to use the words *Gemeinschaft* and *Gesellschaft* in their original German form? Why has the word *Gymnasium* been taken from the German but given an entirely different referent in English?

The answer to these questions is that the two peoples either have experienced different things or have chosen to conceptualize different aspects of those things. Thus the word *gemütlich* refers to a series of qualities familiar to those who speak English—that is, a warm, pleasant, relaxed, "feeling-at-homeness"—but this conceptualization happens not to have occurred in English. *Gemeinschaft* and *Gesellschaft* exist in American sociology for the same reason. Each may require a paragraph of English to define. The terms "community" and "society," which are the English translations of these words, do not convey the particular *sociological* meanings of these two German words. The *Gymnasium* in Germany is a kind of high school and junior college combined, but only its physical-education aspects survive in our use of the term.

The fact that language represents a shared experience has important consequences for the student of a science. If verbal definitions of everyday German experience are so difficult to communicate to Americans, how much greater is the problem of communicating scientific meanings to a layman! Dictionary definitions of scientific terms are seldom satisfactory, either to the advanced practitioner or to the beginning student. What a chemist means by "titration," a histologist by "washing tissue," or a demographer by the "net reproductive rate" would require very elaborate verbal definitions. They are best learned by participating in the *operations* to which these terms refer and thus sharing the world of experience represented by them.

Terms used to denote scientific concepts may also have meanings in other frames of reference. Many scientific words are "contrived" by scientists in such a way that they will have no referent outside the specific scientific frame of reference. This is done in several ways. Frequently the terms are constructed from Greek or Latin roots, or they may be given the name of the man who first elaborated the concept, or perhaps geographic names are used. These concepts are relatively easy to keep clear linguistically, since the terms are not used in lay vocabularies, but many of the other words of science are also used in other contexts. The beginning student of physics, for example, must learn that a "mass" is not a "big pile of something" but is a quality of matter which can be measured by certain operations. Even the word "pile" has taken on a specific meaning in nuclear physics and does not refer merely to a heap of matter. Similarly the student of anthropology and sociology must learn that "culture" does not refer to an acquaintanceship with opera, painting, literature, or "good" manners, but rather to the totality of the social heritage of any society. On the other hand, the word has an entirely different meaning in bacteriology. In any similar case the simultaneous existence of more than one meaning constitutes a trap for the unwary student.

While the examples given above may seem very simple and easy to bear in mind, the compounding of such concepts and the complexity of some of them make trouble for even skillful scientists. Sociologists, for example, have studied "bureaucracy." It is not easy to read into this term *only* the precise meaning agreed upon by sociologists, because there always exists the temptation to give the term an altogether different referent. Instead of meaning only a particular type of social structure, the term "bureaucracy" may also evoke such value-laden images as "red tape," administrative waste, and official disregard for the public interest. Both the sociologist and the layman are likely to fall into this error.

If at such simple levels the student may be misled by multiple meanings, it is no wonder that at more complex levels the possibility of confusion is still greater. To deal with this problem its dangers must be borne in mind, and clear definition must always be a fundamental principle of scientific research and discussion. Let us look at further difficulties.

A term may refer to different phenomena. To illustrate this common experience in science, Robert K. Merton cites the complex usage of the term "function." [1] Leaving aside its many meanings in common-sense vocabularies, or even in the various sciences, we may note that even within the field of sociology it has diverse meanings. Especially in socioeconomic analysis it may refer to occupational phenomena. Sometimes, on the other hand, it is used in a mathematical sense: phenomenon X (divorce rates, fertility, social acceptability) is a function of phenomenon Y (economic position). Again, and more commonly in social anthropology, its meaning has been taken from biology to denote the contribution which a given practice or belief makes toward the continued existence of the society. It is not surprising, then, that both the beginning student and the advanced scientist will at times be puzzled by discussions of this concept.

Different terms may refer to the same phenomenon. We can understand both this and the previous type of problem if we remember that the linguistic usage develops in response to the different experience, and the selection of experience, of different scientists. Since the researcher may use any terms he chooses, he may select his concepts for literary or historical reasons. Or he may believe that he is writing about different things, while his readers can see that he has simply introduced different terms. For example, the four conceptual sets "structure-function," "ideal-real," "formal-informal," and "primary-secondary" overlap in meaning to such an extent that these very different terms are sometimes used to refer to the same phenomena. [2] The student must, then, be alert to these conceptual difficulties when reading or writing research reports. Both this and the preceding errors are not difficult to understand; they are, however, difficult to avoid, since the confusion exists in our own minds. If we can clarify our own thinking, the problem of the concept becomes merely linguistic. Later in this chapter, and at various points throughout this volume, some suggestions are made toward this process of clarification. Let us now, however, note further problems in the development and use of concepts.

A term may have no immediate empirical referent at all. There are two senses in which this may be true. Both may result in making concepts less well understood, but the first of them is nevertheless necessary and useful.

First, scientific theory often deals with things that have not been directly observed. Concepts of this kind have as referents the *logical relationships between other concepts.* Consider, as an example, the problem in isolating what is meant by the common sociological term "social structure." The structure of a group cannot be weighed and will respond to none of the

---

[1] Robert K. Merton, *Social Theory and Social Structure* (Glencoe, Ill.: Free Press, 1949), pp. 22*ff.*

[2] William J. Goode, "Structure and Function: Four Overlapping Conceptual Sets," *Sociological Review* (England), Vol. XLII (1950), pp. 171–178.

common physical measurements. The only data are the observations of the activities of people. Note that these data are not "acts," for so to conceive the problem would violate the original concept. Continuous *patterned* activity is the central characteristic of the social structure. Such a concept, then, has a very complex series of referents, through other concepts, before the empirical reference is clear. There is ultimately an empirical referent, but the basic concept properly refers to logical relationships between other concepts.

However, it is of the greatest importance for conceptual clarity that the *ultimate* empirical referents of a concept be determinable, even though they may be several logical operations removed.

Not acceptable to science, however, is the use of such concepts when those who use them are *unaware* of the fact that they have no empirical referent. A historian faced with not only a difficult problem of analysis but also a shortage of patience and paper might write that "the sweep of history forced the rulers to acquiesce." This use of "the sweep of history" would accord with the older use in sociology of such terms as "the social milieu," or (more simply) "environment," but it would be difficult to find the referent for these concepts. It may also be recalled that not long ago respectable sociologists and psychologists misused the term "instinct." Even today competent psychoanalysts write essays upon the "death wish" or "racial memory."

It is easy for man to become enchanted at times by the image-evoking power of his own eloquence. Nor is it necessary to turn to social science for examples. Until fairly recently it was possible to find elementary physics texts which referred to the concept "ether." Ether was assumed to be an invisible matter, without weight, and susceptible to neither taste nor smell. It was, however, the "medium" through which light was thought to travel, like the water through which ripples travel. It may actually have had some of these qualities, of course, for subsequent investigation revealed its sole existence to be in the word itself. Recently, however, the term has been reintroduced for purposes of mathematical description, and without these objectionable "qualities."

The meaning of concepts may change. Every science sees its terms continuously being modified as its knowledge accumulates. The more is known about the referent of a concept, the more specifically that concept can be defined. However, a somewhat different definition results, and the consequent shifts in meaning may confuse the student.

Another source of such changes in meaning is the changing *focus* of a science as it grows. Attention may be centered upon different *aspects* of the same concept in such a way as to change its meaning, although the same term is kept. Thus, a concept "grows" with the increasing experience of scientists with the phenomena to which it refers. As these experiences multiply, it is seen that the original concept "covers too much," and several concepts are used to refer to the different kinds of experience discovered by research. Thus, instead of "status" alone, we may come to use 'status," "rank," "role," "position," "situs," and so on.

The term "intelligence" has gone through such an evolution. It was not long ago that intelligence was conceived by psychology as being an inherited, fairly stable intellectual potential. Later, because so many conflicting data were discovered, it had to be redefined, and one way of describing it became merely the score made on certain types of test. With such changes occurring, it is easy to see that overlapping of meanings may occur and may well lead to confusion. It is precisely this type of misunderstanding which makes it difficult for a contemporary chemist to read treatises written two centuries ago in his field. Similarly, the sociologist of today finds the writings of even 50 years ago very confusing. Not only are some of the terms different, but those which are the same have different meanings in the two periods.

RECONCEPTUALIZATION

The situation, then, is not one of chaos. All these problems do arise, but as the science develops we see one conceptual difficulty after another disappear. Others, of course, take their place, but that is characteristic of communication when the things talked about are changing. These types of confusion are faced by the community of scientists in a given field and are gradually solved by joint research and discussion. Furthermore, these added considerations should be kept in mind:

1. In the main, the terms are clear and cause little difficulty.

2. Since scientists are working on much the same group of problems with similar techniques and vocabulary, an occasional confused or obscure conceptual usage may cause little difficulty. The *context* of the exposition, as is true for language generally, points to the intended meaning of the concept.

3. From time to time, conceptual analyses are made which point to confused or overlapping usage and suggest a solution. Thus, difficulties in communication do not proceed far without correction.

4. As the science develops, many conceptual problems are by-passed when the concepts themselves become irrelevant to the newer theoretical tasks.

We may say, then, that the student must learn the conceptual tools of his field. When concepts are ambiguous, he must become aware of the ambiguity. Since the only ultimate assurance of conceptual clarity in sociology is precise thinking about its phenomena and their interrelationships, he must not become lost in the mere manipulation of concepts.

It is worth while, however, to suggest some procedures for clarifying his thinking about the concepts used in his research problem. This process of clarification may be called "reconceptualization," or "respecification of a concept," following Robert K. Merton and Paul F. Lazarsfeld. This description of what the scientist does implicitly or explicitly is only a tentative statement. However, the careful student will compare some of these hints with the later discussions of the hypothesis, the logic of proof, the formulation of questions, and the analysis of data, for in each of these cases the main focus of discussion is the problem of clearly defining the research project.

1. After writing out the preliminary statement of the project, the student should carefully select from the statement a list of all the major concepts: "marital adjustment," "family ritual," "adolescent," "segregation," "social class," etc.

2. Next, an analysis of the apparent *meaning elements* of the concepts should be made. This is a first step in finding out how we are actually using the concept. For example, we may find that in our concept of marital adjustment there are elements such as these: (*a*) personal happiness; (*b*) conformity with the rules of the society; (*c*) acceptance of fate; (*d*) being in love with one's spouse; (*e*) liking the marital state; (*f*) acceptance of monogamy; (*g*) a clear realization of the problems of marriage; and so on. In this case, we would have to decide how many of these meaning elements we would be able to accept as part of our concept. We might, in some cases, find contradictions between these elements. Already, then, we would have located and specified part of our conceptual problem.

3. It would then be useful to return to the published literature in which the concept has been used, in order to discover the various usages of the term. Very frequently we find that the concept has not been clearly defined at any time, but we can see how it was applied in any study. In a few cases, we may find specific aids to clear thinking. Sometimes these further definitions will change our approach to the problem. "Juvenile delinquency," for example, may be defined in terms of commitment to a reform school, in one investigation. In another, it may be defined by conviction alone. In still another, it may be defined by reference to the court calendar, the police blotter, or even to records of police calls. Each of these definitions changes the research project considerably, since the phenomenon being studied is different in each case. Such differences in usage, however, may also turn our thoughts to the notion of *types* of delinquency, so that we must develop still further definitions. We may then reanalyze the usual practice of equating adult crime with juvenile crime. We may decide that we cannot accept certain types of police offenses as "juvenile delinquency." We come to select from the complex mass of behavior called "delinquent" only certain kinds of behavior, and we thereby redefine the concept with which we began. However, since each of these steps requires an explanation and constant reference to our subject matter, we will understand our

concept much more clearly. Its precision and its usefulness will both be greater.

4. A further step should also be taken—that of relating the phenomenon to similar phenomena which have been described by *other terms,* and often in other fields. This step should be taken separately from the previous one of bringing together the various phenomena or types of behavior that have been described by the *same* term. Although the student may at first be impatient with such steps, he will find that these operations are not mere exercises in ingenuity. The concept that seemed so clear and sharp will be shown to have many complex and often contradictory facets, and the final result will be a concept of much greater fruitfulness and definiteness.

Furthermore, respecification of the concept always leads to more fruitful *hypotheses,* as will be discussed later in this text. Of course, most sociological studies do not report these processes. When we read Max Weber's analysis of capitalism, we are not immediately aware of the complex ways in which the concept of capitalism was redefined in order to be more effective. There are two excellent analyses, however, that make explicit these procedures. They are even more useful to the student, since their major goal is not a discussion of these operations but the application of these techniques to modern sociological research. These are Robert K. Merton's codification of functional analysis, and Robert K. Merton and Alice Kitt's development of reference-group theory.[3] The student who believes that he needs only to "think a bit" about a given concept in order to develop it adequately will do well to study carefully both these essays for the useful conceptual techniques applied by Merton and Kitt.

The essay on reference-group behavior makes considerable use of this third step, relating the phenomenon to similar behavior described in other studies under different terms.[4] Beginning with the apparently concrete term "relative deprivation," used by Samuel A. Stouffer and his associates in *The American Soldier,* we are taken through many steps in the elucidation and development of this concept. Various elements in the term have been called, by one writer or another, "social frame of reference," "patterns of expectation," "definition of the situation," "in-group behavior," "generalized other," "emulation," "assimilation," etc.

Now, it must be kept in mind that the purpose of this operation is not to exhibit one's cleverness in conceptual manipulation, or even one's learning; the purpose is to isolate and recombine those elements which will be most fruitful in research. There are many examples of behavior

[3] Merton, "Manifest and Latent Functions," *op. cit.,* pp. 21–81; and Robert K. Merton and Alice S. Kitt, "Reference Group Behavior," *Continuities in Social Research,* Robert K. Merton and Paul F. Lazarsfeld, eds. (Glencoe, Ill.: Free Press, 1950), pp. 40–105.

[4] See Merton and Kitt, *op. cit.,* pp. 43*ff.,* esp. 48, 53, 100–05.

under each of these concepts which can be classed as identical, so that we are *codifying*, or collating, behavior from many fields. Many elements, however, are also dissimilar, and at these points we begin to see a more systematic framework emerge. We know that people in general see problems according to the notions of their own group. However, it is sometimes a *different* group that is taken as the basis of reference. Usually, it is the values and expectations of the group that must be the center of attention. We also note that the problem begins to divide: Which group or groups? Which individuals respond to which groups? Under what conditions? What are the relationships between the groups selected? What is the process by which the individual selects one group as a reference? Note that we are not only expanding our concept into many related but sharper concepts, but also developing specific hypotheses for immediate research.

It should be further noted that the usefulness of this operation is based in part upon the fact that it integrates various theoretical ideas which were the product of isolated studies. The use of different concepts for similar types of behavior may thus have obscured the common elements, while avoiding a clear definition of the differences between them. Moreover, we can also see that we are not analyzing concepts in pure abstraction but are redefining them in direct relationship to the social behavior being reported in these other studies. Thus they have a basis in fact, at the same time that they are being integrated with further theoretical development.

5. A final operation may be mentioned, of particular use for the theoretical fruitfulness of the concept: ascertaining the next higher (or lower) level of generalization of the concept. Here again, the goal is to clarify the concept, while increasing its usefulness for research. Although most research ideas with which students begin are likely to be rather highly general concepts, such as "function," "modern society," or "socialization," a few will begin at a concrete level with such concepts as "Hell Week at Ivy College," or "our corner drug store," or "my dislike of spanking." The first three will probably seem to the student to be more significant than the last three, but neither group possesses an unquestionable, intrinsic advantage over the other. The first group deals with broad forces, but when the student examines them through the procedures outlined here, they will turn out to contain many vague and complex elements. The latter group, although apparently less important, may be much easier to define clearly.

However, science must integrate both levels. Its specific research activities must always be concerned with the concrete, while its aim is to produce the general. Similarly, in sociology we may study the apparently trivial, but our work remains trivial unless we can generalize from it. Therefore, one aim in reconceptualization, as in the development of hypotheses, is to integrate carefully these different levels of observation and theory. At the same time, we learn much more definitely which elements we are really trying to abstract from the concrete behavior under study. The result is a greater clarity in the concepts we use.

This process may become fairly complex, but it is possible to indicate briefly its general form. For example, Hell Week at Ivy College has many aspects. We might count the numbers of individuals involved. We could map their physical location on campus. We could collect data on their health, weight, height, age, or shape of skull. We could, instead, study the flora and fauna at this particular time of the year. Most of these suggestions sound absurd, but the student must see that the *social* elements have not been picked from the concept: age-grade stratification patterns, rituals, customs, social isolation of the campus town, importance of sororities and fraternities.

Once we have done this, we begin to see Hell Week as, first of all, one example of common practices on college campuses—the initiation of freshmen. With this insight we have moved from a concrete case to a class of concrete cases. Although a survey might cover many cases on the one hand, on the other we are offered a hint of a still higher level of generalization when we study the elements in "initiation": physical and social punishment, out-group and in-group, and so on. Initiation, we know, is but one case of a still larger group of phenomena, which we may call "rituals of passage," *i.e.*, the rituals and customs which surround and give meaning to the *transition* from one status to another: confirmation, graduation, taking the oath of office, marriage, baptism, circumcision, etc. At each level, the concentration of interest may be in how these groups select, the aspirations and choices of those selected, the rituals themselves, the emotional responses of those selected, and other problems. What is noteworthy, however, is that at each step we are bringing our case under a still wider rubric. We must, then, see which of the relevant aspects of our case we are most interested in, so that our data will be relevant to the proper higher level category. In this case, we have moved toward the concept, "rituals of status transition," but we need not stop at this point. We could proceed to generalize this to "rituals of all kinds," or "all status changes." The still higher levels need not concern us, for we are only noting that our choice of focus at any level determines which direction our generalizing will take. To return to our poor freshmen, if we had decided to concentrate upon their emotional responses, we might have generalized toward "responses to situations of status ambiguity," or "responses to the temporary loss of status," or (at a higher level) "responses to strain."

Proceeding from the highly general concept to the more concrete simply challenges the student to translate his broad notions into concepts (such as Hell Week) that are concrete enough to be observable. From either direction, this operation forces the student to attempt an integration between theoretical levels, to locate concrete behavior for possible observation, to identify which conceptual elements are of primary concern, and thereby to have a much clearer notion of *how* general his concept is. The result is a more useful and more sharply defined concept.

THE OPERATIONAL DEFINITION

One facet of the polemic, mentioned in Chapter 1, between the "fact-oriented" and the "theory-oriented" sociologists has been a disagreement about the importance of the operational definition. The debate is a rather complex one, but its central point was whether a concept is most usefully and precisely defined by describing the operations which observe, measure, and record a given phenomenon. The "fact-minded" group has leaned toward the opinion that a concept like "mass" or "length" or "social cohesion" *means a set of operations.* Thus, the mass of an object is the number obtained when we go through the operation of weighing the object on a balance. We are not to confuse this meaning with the many other characteristics we think of when we have the notion of mass in mind.

Against this stand, the opposition group has contended that when we think of such a concept, we do not "mean" merely these operations. Rather, they are simply the techniques we have to use in order to get at, or measure, something *behind* those operations—the phenomenon itself. Such procedures, then, are useful because we cannot directly observe or measure, say, "social cohesion." However, it is "social cohesion" that we really wish to discuss, not these operations.

At the present stage of sociology, we may find a compromise between these positions, and indeed the debate is taken less seriously at the present time. Perhaps we may deal with the problem more easily by remembering that a concept *is* a set of directions, in one major sense: it directs the reader to a particular kind of experience, one which has to some extent been shared. If it does not do so, communication is difficult. Thus, whether the concept is defined in a literary fashion or by a set of laboratory directions, the definition turns attention to this experience.

Furthermore, it is clear that the physical sciences have laid great emphasis upon the operational type of definition. Relatively few concepts in these fields refer to direct experience, such as weight, length, or color, and even these are defined by a set of operations. Most concepts refer to phenomena that are not measurable or visible to the naked eye. By defining these phenomena through a set of directions, there is greater assurance that scientists from other nations, thinking in other languages, will "mean" the same thing. It seems likely that as sociology develops a more precise and more commonly shared set of research operations, there will be an increasing development of operational definitions.

We can easily see, however, where the possibility of confusion enters. Suppose, for example, the sociologist decides to define "status" by means of a set of directions which tell the researcher to mark on a standardized list of items whether the family possesses certain objects such as rugs, living-room lamps, or a radio or television set; whether its members belong to certain organizations such as Camp Fire Girls, Odd Fellows, or Kiwanis; to what extent its members have attended school; etc. The directions may further indicate what weight should be given to each item, so that a final "status score" can be calculated.

So far, there should be no confusion, and any experienced field worker should be able to follow such a set of directions and to obtain the same results for the same families. If we now attempt to analyze "status" on the basis of this research, however, we must not expect to find that our facts will be easily comparable to older analyses of status, for these used different definitions of status. Our operational definition has given the old concept a new meaning. In this case, there will be overlap in meaning, but status as traditionally defined does not refer to quite the same set of experiences. The confusion, then, arises because we are likely to use the same *term* to refer to different phenomena: (1) the data from our newly defined operations; and (2) the data traditionally associated with "status." This confusion has occurred widely in discussions of the intelligence quotient, or IQ test, since its results are often treated as relating to an innate complex of factors called "intelligence," whereas the IQ test is rather an operational definition of selected factors of intellectual achievement and potential. If we use "IQ" only in the second sense, there is no confusion; if we apply these results to the more common-sense meaning of "intelligence," many unnecessary problems arise.

An operational definition, therefore, may define a phenomenon with greater definiteness in that it outlines the directions for having the same experience as other researchers. On the other hand, the redefinition that is the result of such a definition may leave out important elements of an older concept. Furthermore, in order to develop an operational definition, considerable research must be done upon the phenomenon to be defined. Consequently, we should not attempt an operational definition merely to be in fashion. We must do so in full consciousness of its problems, knowing that the traditional term (such as "morale," "social cohesion," "social structure") is likely not to refer to exactly the same phenomena as defined by the operations we outline. And, in some cases, an operational definition may be more complex and unwieldy, while less fruitful in its results, than a traditional definition. With respect to some knotty problems in research, we may have to make a conscious decision as to which we need most—precision or significance. As our research project develops in precision and scope, however, we shall find ways, as the recent history of social research clearly shows, to obtain both.

SUGGESTED READINGS

Bergmann, Gustav, and Kenneth W. Spence, "Operationism and Theory Construction" in Melvin H. Marx, *Psychological Theory* (New York: Macmillan, 1951), pp. 54–66.

Cohen, Morris R., and Ernest Nagel, *An Introduction to Logic and Scientific Method* (New York: Harcourt, Brace, 1934), Chap. 12.

Eubank, Earle Edward, *The Concepts of Sociology* (Boston: Heath, 1932), Chaps. 3 and 4.

Goode, William J., "Conceptual Schemata in the Field of Social Disorganization," *Social Forces*, Vol. XXVI (1947), pp. 19–25.

———, "Structure and Function: Four Overlapping Conceptual Sets," *Sociological Review* (England), Vol. XLII (1950), pp. 171–178.

Langer, Suzanne K., *Philosophy in a New Key* (New York: Penguin, 1942), Chap. 3.

CHAPTER 6

Basic Elements of the Scientific Method: Hypotheses

THE FUNCTION OF THE HYPOTHESIS

Facts, as has been shown, are dependent upon a theoretical framework for their meaning. They are also statements of relationships between concepts. A basic requirement in the application of the scientific method, the clear definition of concepts, has just been discussed. The next step, how to ask the questions which lead to new scientific propositions, must now be considered.

Chapter 2 has shown how theory serves to order and give meaning to facts. It also pointed out that theory can give direction to the search for facts. A hypothesis states what we are looking for. When facts are assembled, ordered, and seen in a relationship, they constitute a theory. The theory is not speculation, but is built upon fact. Now, the various facts in a theory may be logically analyzed, and relationships other than those stated in the theory can be deduced. At this point there is no knowledge as to whether such deductions are correct. *The formulation of the deduction,* however, constitutes a hypothesis; if verified it becomes part of a future theoretical construction. It is thus clear that the relation between the hypothesis and theory is very close indeed. One scientist, in this connection, has stated: "In practice a theory is an elaborate hypothesis which deals with more types of facts than does the simple hypothesis. . . . The distinction . . . is not clearly defined." [1] While it is true that the two can never be satisfactorily separated, it is useful to think of them as two aspects of the way in which science adds to knowledge. Thus a theory states a logical relationship between facts. From this theory other propositions can be deduced that *should* be true, if the first relationship holds. These deduced propositions are hypotheses.

A hypothesis looks forward. It is a proposition which can be put to a test to determine its validity. It may seem contrary to, or in accord with, common sense. It may prove to be correct or incorrect. In any event, however, *it leads to an empirical test.* Whatever the outcome, the hypothesis is a question put in such a way that an answer of some kind can be

[1] William H. George, *The Scientist in Action* (London: Williams & Norgate, 1936), p. 220.

forthcoming. It is an example of the organized skepticism of science, the refusal to accept any statement without empirical verification.

Every worth-while theory, then, permits the formulation of additional hypotheses. These, when tested, are either proved or disproved and in turn constitute further tests of the original theory. In either case they may be of use to existing theory and may make possible the formulation of still other hypotheses. Such a simple outline, unfortunately, fails to indicate that the formulation of useful hypotheses is one of the most difficult steps in scientific method.

PROBLEMS IN FORMULATING THE HYPOTHESIS

As difficult as the process may be, it is necessary for the student to see the fundamental need of a hypothesis to guide sound research. Without it, research is unfocused, a random empirical wandering. The results cannot even be stated as facts with a clear meaning. The hypothesis is the necessary link between theory and the investigation which leads to the discovery of additions to knowledge.

The chief difficulties in the road to the formulation of useful hypotheses are three. First among these is the absence of (or the absence of knowledge of) a clear theoretical framework. Second is the lack of ability to utilize that theoretical framework logically. Third is the failure to be acquainted with available research techniques so as to be able to phrase the hypothesis properly. These obstacles will be treated later in the chapter, but at the moment it is possible to stop and consider the question, "Just how difficult is it to ask an important, testable question?"

Let the student answer this question himself. By the time he completes this course, he will have had several sociology courses. If he happens to be a superior student, he has also read several monographs in sociology. With this knowledge of sociological theory at hand, let him formulate one *good, definite, testable hypothesis*.

Many students will completely fail such a test. If so, they should not be discouraged, for this is not a simple task. In any case, one of the functions of this course is to improve the ability to formulate good hypotheses. If the student is able to formulate propositions at all, closer investigation will show many of them not to be hypotheses. Some students will have merely selected an *area* of study: the socialization of the child, juvenile delinquency, white-collar crime, or courtship behavior. Such formulations, of course, are not hypotheses; they do not formulate precise and testable questions.

Somewhat closer to the mark will be some who might suggest the *replication* of previous studies. That is, some may think it useful to repeat a previous piece of scientific work, duplicating the conditions exactly. This is useful work and does in one sense state a hypothesis, *i.e.*, that the results will be the same. But the utility of this procedure does not go beyond checking findings and it is likely to make no contribution to new knowledge.

Still closer to the formulation of a hypothesis would be those few who might suggest the study of *empirical regularities*. This type of research would be represented by the study of such things as the ecological distribution of mental disorders, the acceptance of contraceptive practices in Latin America, or the marital adjustment of rural Southerners. Such questions do suggest the *type of data* to be gathered, but they are hypotheses of a low level of abstraction; they merely predict that *some* type of patterning will appear without predicting *what* that pattern will be.

On the other hand, if we actually begin with a broad theory, and by deduction predict a social regularity as a relationship between two or more factors, we may develop a hypothesis. We might then obtain such formulations as the following, although space does not allow a statement of the entire chain of theoretical reasoning upon which they are based, or the detailed definitions necessary:

(1) *Principle:* A socially recognized relationship in which there are strains built into the situation will also be surrounded by institutionalized controls, to ensure conformity of the participants with implicit or explicit norms.

Deduction: We therefore predict that in those professions (such as psychiatry and psychotherapy generally, medicine, and law to a lesser degree) which deal with the more intimate aspects of clients' lives there are (*a*) more emotional strains in the client-practitioner relationship, and (*b*) more internalized and external controls upon both participants than is the case in other professions (such as engineering, architecture, dentistry). Of course, such a hypothesis can and must be broken down into subhypotheses. These would take these forms: (*a*) specification of the *degree* of difference; (*b*) specification of profession and problem, to separate criminal law from corporation law, types of contacts between profession and client, and types of strain-producing problems; and (*c*) specification of kinds of controls.

(2) *Principle:* Rather extensive, but relatively unsystematized, data show that members of the upper occupational-class strata experience less unhappiness and worry and are subject to more formal controls than members of lower strata.

Deduction: Our hypothesis would then predict that this comparison also applies to the marital relationships of members of these strata and would predict that such differential pressures could be observed through divorce rates. There should be an inverse correlation between class position and divorce rates. Again, we would have to define our terms carefully and show the systematic connection between our original premises and our deduction, but the result can be tested by the degree of our correlation.

The above examples indicate not only the difficulty of formulating a hypothesis, but also the need to do so. Early in any investigation a definite hypothesis should be formed. At first this may not be very specific. In such an instance it is referred to as a "working hypothesis," which will be subject to modification as the investigation proceeds. The utilization of a hypothesis, however, is necessary for any useful research results.

TYPES OF HYPOTHESES

What are the *kinds* of hypotheses with which the sociologist deals? There are many ways of classifying hypotheses. For the purpose of this book, however, it seems adequate to separate them on the basis of the level of abstraction. Three broad levels may be distinguished. These will be discussed in the order of increasing abstractness.

Some hypotheses state the existence of empirical uniformities. These hypotheses frequently, though not always, represent the scientific examination of common-sense propositions. Thus, we might make a survey of some area that seems to represent a "problem" in common-sense terms. It usually represents, also, a problem about which some "common-sense" observations already exist. There are many types of such empirical uniformities which are common in sociological research. These studies may show regularities in the distribution of business establishments in a city, the ethnic backgrounds of workers in an industry, the size of families on relief, or the distribution of Negroes in the nation.

Or, they may describe the behavior patterns of specific groups—for example, the students at a particular college in their freshman year. Here we might tabulate conformity and nonconformity to customary usage; the wearing of the "dink," the submission to "initiation" rites, or the pledging to a fraternity. From research of this type the tabulations will yield expressions of the *degree of uniformity* in social behavior. They may be symbolized by graphs, figures, or maps. In any event, their end product is a simple description of group activities.

It may be protested, of course, that these investigations do not involve the *testing* of a hypothesis at all, but are merely adding up the facts. Such a charge may have merit in a particular case, but the line is difficult to draw. Certainly, many such studies have actually sought to test common-sense statements about these phenomena, using such statements as hypotheses.

It may be further objected that these are not useful hypotheses, on the grounds that they merely represent what everyone already knows. There are two answers to this objection. First, "what everyone knows" is not put in precise terms nor is it integrated into the framework of science. The importance of these deficiencies has been discussed in Chapters 4 and 5. Second, "what everyone knows" may well be incorrect. To put common-sense ideas into precisely defined concepts and subject the proposition to test is an important task of science.

These statements are particularly true for sociology at its present, early stage of development. Folk knowledge of social relations is abundant, but it is often a confused mixture of clichés and moral judgments. Sociology thus has a large-scale job in transforming and testing these so that they can become useful knowledge. This requires that three tasks be performed: first, the removal of value judgments; second, the clarification of terms; and third, the application of validity tests.

For example, such statements as "Bad children are born that way" or its reverse, "Bad parents produce bad children," or "Wealthy people have a high divorce rate because they lead such self-indulgent lives" are the kinds of generalizations which, though commonplace, cannot be tested. As they stand, they merely express sentiment rather than describe fact, and the concepts are unclear. They could be made into adequate hypotheses, however, if cleared of moral overtones and put into carefully defined terms.

Not only sociology, as noted previously, but all science has found such common-sense knowledge fruitful for study—even when it has been wrong. "Everybody knew" that the sun revolved around the earth, that horsehairs in a watering trough would turn to worms, that a bag of asafetida hung around the neck would prevent colds (this last, at least, may have been true, since the smell kept others at a distance!). All those beliefs have been exploded by patient, plodding empirical checking of the facts, so that we now know that horsehairs do not turn into worms and asafetida has no effect on colds.

In social relations, too, there are many clichés which are not correct. The objection that it "elaborates the obvious" has been made by a good number of critics against the monumental work *The American Soldier* (Princeton, N.J.: Princeton University Press, 1949–1950; 4 vols.). It would seem, for example, that there was no need for the social researchers to prove the following hypotheses, since they were known already:

1. Soldiers from white-collar jobs were somewhat less adjusted in the Army, since they had sacrificed more than lower class men by going into the service.

2. Negro soldiers, knowing that the barriers against promotion were rigid, did not work for promotion so hard as did white soldiers.

3. Soldiers in units with high promotion rates had a more optimistic view of promotion chances and were more satisfied about promotion policies than were soldiers in units with low promotion rates.

Nevertheless, these were among the hypotheses tested—with the result that all three were proved to be *incorrect*. Often, we believe that "everybody knows that," but we make the statement *after* the investigation. We could not have predicted the result. We believe that the result is only common sense, since *some* of our experience fits the result. However, if the result had turned out differently, we would have found still other experiences, of a contrary order, to fit the different results. As a consequence,

many supposedly obvious facts must actually be tested.[2] It hardly needs
to be added, moreover, that even when we know in general that a given
relationship exists, we do not know to what degree or in what proportions
it exists. Science demands a higher precision than "in general."

In any case it is certain that "what everybody knows" is not known
until it has been tested. The simple level of hypothesis that seeks empirical
generalization plays an important role in the growth of science.

Some hypotheses are concerned with complex ideal types. These hypotheses aim at testing the existence of logically derived relationships
between empirical uniformities. If this test sounds difficult to understand,
an example may help to make it clearer. Human ecology early described
a large number of empirical uniformities. Land values, industrial concen-
trations, types of businesses, ethnic groups, mental disorders, and many
other phenomena appeared to show unquestionable uniformities in distribution. Further study and logical analysis of these and other related
findings led to the formulation of various hypotheses concerning the way
in which these were related. One such hypothesis was Ernest W. Burgess's
statement of the concentric growth circles that characterize the city.

This hypothesis was then tested against a variety of variables in a
number of cities. That this ideal type does represent the actual pattern
of city growth is not accepted by all ecologists, however, and so this
formulation remains a hypothesis until a more crucial test of it is made.

Another hypothesis concerning an ideal type resulted from these same
ecological empirical uniformities. This was the notion that areas tend to
represent certain characteristics in a series of predictable patterns. This
was called the hypothesis of "the natural area." Much research has been
done on this hypothesis, and the results, although they have modified the
original statement somewhat, have generally supported it. With the
growth of supporting evidence, notions about natural areas have become
a part of sociological theory rather than remaining hypotheses.

A similar type of hypothesis in another area resulted from the analysis
of minority groups. Many studies revealed empirical uniformities in the
behavior of members of a wide variety of minorities. Logical analysis then
led to the hypothesis that these uniformities produced an ideal type. This
was at first called by H. A. Miller the "oppression psychosis," but it was
subsequently modified to the "marginal man" by E. W. Stonequist and
others. Empirical evidence supported the hypothesis, and thus the "marginal man" is today also a part of sociological theory.

It is important to see here that this level of hypothesizing moves beyond
the expectations of simple empirical uniformity, by *creating* a complex
referent in society. Not *all* areas must be natural areas, not *all* members
of minority groups must be marginal men, not *all* cities must show per-

2 Paul F. Lazarsfeld, *"The American Soldier*—an Expository Review," *Public Opinion
Quarterly*, Vol. XIII (1949), pp. 377–404.

fect concentric circles, for these hypotheses to be useful. They must, of course, be verified in that under *certain conditions* of maximum opportunity such instances will occur, but in reality such hypotheses are purposeful distortions of empiric exactness. Because of their removal from empirical reality these constructs are termed "ideal types." The function of such hypotheses is to create tools and problems for further research in otherwise very complex areas of investigation.

Some hypotheses are concerned with the relation of analytic variables. These hypotheses occur at a level of abstraction beyond that of ideal types. Whereas the hypotheses of empirical uniformities lead to the observation of simple differences, and those dealing with ideal types lead to specific coincidences of observations, the study of *analytic variables* requires the formulation of a relationship between changes in one property and changes in another.

To take an example from sociology, the study of human fertility might show empirical regularities by wealth, region, size of community, and religion. If this were then raised to the level of ideal type formulation, one result might be the hypothesis that there are two high-fertility population segments in the United States. One would be the low-income, Southern, rural Protestant, and the other the low-income, Northern, urban Catholic. At a still higher level of abstraction the *qualities* of region, size of community, and religion might be abstracted and controlled; that is, their effects on fertility held constant. This would allow a better measurement of the relation between the *variables* of wealth and fertility. Similarly, the problem could be stated in such a way that any three could be controlled so as to allow the fourth to vary and hence to measure its relation to fertility. It is clear that this is a very abstract way to handle the problem because *there are no people* whose fertility is not affected by *all* the variables. Of course, not all the characteristics mentioned are as yet expressed as variables.

This level of hypothesizing is not only more abstract than the others; it is also the most sophisticated and the most flexible mode of formulation. At this level, the number of variables which can be abstracted and studied is limited only by theory; and since theory grows by the process itself, opportunities for new research are constantly being created.

In the event that it should appear that any of these types of hypotheses is "better" than another, a word of explanation may be needed. The function of the ideal-type method, it will be recalled, is to provide constructs for use in further hypothesizing. This is also one function of studies of empirical uniformities. Without the painstaking, grubbing labor which characterizes this type of investigation, none of the "brilliant" theories of a more abstract nature could have ever appeared. Particularly in sociology is it necessary for the student to learn that at whatever the level of abstraction the hypothesis lies, the need for careful work does not vary, nor is the significance of the findings automatically apparent.

Thus far in the chapter, three major points have been made: (1) that a hypothesis is a necessary condition for successful research; (2) that formulation of the hypothesis must be given considerable attention, to clarify its relation to theory, remove vague or value-judgmental terms, and specify the test to be applied; and (3) that hypotheses may be formulated on different levels of abstraction. At various points in the discussion, more or less casual references have been made to the question of the *origins* of hypotheses. At this point it seems useful, then, to look at this matter in greater detail and somewhat more systematically. It seems possible to distinguish four such sources more or less clearly.

The general culture in which a science develops furnishes many of its basic hypotheses. This point has been mentioned several times before in the discussions of science and values, pure and applied science, and the simplest hypotheses which state empirical regularities. It has been pointed out that science has developed in Western society and that this is no mere accident but is a function of the culture itself.

The fact that sociology is so new and that its growth has taken place very largely in the United States, England, Germany, and France means that the hypotheses which have been put forth and tested have been related to a particular cultural complex. To oversimplify the situation, let us assume that the American variant of Western European culture emphasizes individual happiness, mobility, and competition. This is in contrast, let us say, to the Zuñi type of Pueblo culture in which there is more emphasis upon the group, an avoidance of personal competition and achievement, and less concern about individual happiness. Flowing from this, certain hypotheses could be expected to occupy the attention of American sociologists. To say that these hypotheses are the product of the cultural values does not make them scientifically less important than others, but it does at least indicate that attention has been called to them by the culture itself.

For example, the American emphasis upon personal happiness has had considerable effect upon social science in this country. Not only is there an excellent market for books explaining "how to be happy," but the phenomenon itself has been studied in great detail. Much of textbook economics is based upon a theory of human action which is predicated upon personal happiness as the central motivation. There have been many studies of the factors which make for marital happiness. Even the term "adjustment" used by sociologists and psychologists customarily means happiness and is the focus of innumerable studies. Happiness in one way or another has been correlated with income, education, occupation, ethnic origin, social class, and parental happiness. The factors contributing to adjustment in sexual relations, marital relations, on the job, and in other social groups have been analyzed in detail. From all this it is at least clear that the cultural emphasis upon happiness has been productive of an almost limitless range of hypotheses for American social science.

Not only do the major cultural values serve to direct research interests, but folk wisdom serves as another source of hypotheses. In Western society, in varying degrees, race is thought to be an important determinant of human behavior. This is perhaps most widely and extremely held in the United States and in South Africa. The sociologist in this cultural setting cannot accept such a folk belief as fact but must test it scientifically. It would be very simple to think of an almost limitless number of similar common-sense propositions which have served or could serve as a source of hypotheses.

This raises still another point. It is not merely that the existence of such propositions is productive of hypotheses but also that social change increases the value of the culture as a source of scientific questions. Common-sense propositions are usually unquestioned. Ideas and behavior often seem so obvious as to call for no serious study. It is, in these cases, a real test of the investigator's ingenuity to see a question in such truisms. Social change, however, may call these into question, thus providing a hypothesis for study. Thus, doctrines of both "liberalism" and "progressivism" have played important roles in social science. The latter, by embracing change, challenges the old assumptions; and the former, by emphasizing the importance of the individual, insists that he not be prejudged. In either case there is present the kind of skepticism which is productive of hypotheses.

For example, the folk notions about race were called into question on *moral* grounds. The progressive and liberal ideology held the old notion of the racial determination of behavior to be false. Careful analysis of the Army Alpha tests of World War I, studies of the IQs of Negroes and whites, anthropological evidence about the learning ability of "primitives," and many other studies piled up scientific evidence opposed to the older folk beliefs. Similar results occurred in other areas, such as the inherent lack of capabilities in the lower classes. Alcoholism is no longer considered to be the result of weak moral fiber but is regarded as a disease. These examples could be multiplied almost indefinitely, but enough have already been given to indicate the role of "equalitarian" thought patterns and of social change, in the generation of hypotheses.

Hypotheses originate in the science itself. Mention has already been made of the fact that this operates in two ways. First, in the discussion on theory and fact it was pointed out that theory gives direction to research by stating what is known. Logical deduction from this leads to new problems. Second, in the treatment of values and science it was pointed out that science is a social relation and that the scientist must acquire the folkways of his discipline.

As an example of the way the first effect comes about, a development in communications research may be cited. It was first established in theory and fact that there existed people who could be considered as "opinion leaders." It was further seen that these were prestigeful people, that is, that they possessed high status in the community. Since it was also known that high status is a function of a number of variables, it was logical to hypothesize the existence of an ideal type, "the influential person." However, in an actual study, the influential persons did not seem to have many characteristics in common. This led to still further questioning and the development of two major categories, which Merton termed "cosmopolitan" and "local" influentials, each with its own set of characteristics. Thus, what was known led to the asking of still another question or, in other words, to the formulation of a new hypothesis.[3] Indeed, the student will find a number of suggested readings at the end of this chapter, which deal with hypotheses whose origins lay in the *deviant* cases.

The "socialization" process in learning a science also affects the hypotheses which will be developed by the scientist. First of all the student learns from his teachers which are the promising areas, which methods are adequate, which scholars are superior, and, of course, which are "inferior." Thus, the range of hypotheses open to him is limited by the direction of his learning experience. Later in his life, the scientist is affected by a similar process—the approval of his colleagues. Formally and informally, scientists continually discuss current research, both orally and in print. In this way consensus is reached as to which areas and problems are thought to be important. Through this constant interaction in the area, "fashionable" modes of thought, terminology, concepts, and problems develop. These, in turn, of course, operate to suggest further hypotheses.

Analogies are often a source of useful hypotheses. Julian Huxley has pointed out that casual observations in nature or in the framework of another science may be a fertile source of hypotheses. The hypotheses that resulted in the development of human ecology, for example, were an application of established theory in the fields of plant and animal ecology. Thus, the hypothesis that similar human types or activities may be found occupying the same territory came from plant ecology, where the phenomenon is known as segregation. When the hypothesis was borne out by social observation, the same term was taken into sociology where it has become an important idea in sociological theory.

Similarly, the observation that the behavior of human groups seems to exhibit some of the same patterns as found in gravitational and electric fields led to the basic hypothesis of what is called social physics. This hypothesis is that if people are related in some way similar to the struc-

[3] Robert K. Merton, "Patterns of Influence: A Study of Interpersonal Influence and of Communications Behavior in a Local Community," *Communications Research, 1948–1949*, Paul F. Lazarsfeld and Frank Stanton, eds. (New York: Harper, 1949), pp. 180–219.

ture of such a physical field then human behavior should show reliable correlation with the values secured by such a field analysis. John Q. Stewart has now published much evidence to indicate that the application of this analogy might be interesting.

The use of analogy as a source of hypotheses is not without its dangers, of course. There is reason to suspect any analogy from another science, since the models to be applied are clearly understood in their own theoretical framework but are not related to the new frame of reference. Thus, it is dangerous to assume that natural areas in human society are a product of symbiosis as is true in biology. We have no empirical method of applying the concept to human beings. Similarly, it is dangerous to assume, as in social physics, that "demographic potential" is the same phenomenon as "gravitational potential" in physics. In short, analogy may be very suggestive, but care must be taken not to accept models for sociology from other disciplines without careful examination of the concepts which make up the models.

Hypotheses are also the consequence of personal, idiosyncratic experience. Not only do culture, science, and analogy affect the formulation of hypotheses. The way in which an *individual* reacts to each of these is also a factor in the statement of hypotheses. Therefore, the individual experience of the scientist contributes to the type and the form of the questions he asks.

In just the same way that perception has been shown to be structured by experience, producing odd and interesting illusions, some persons will perceive an interesting pattern from what may merely seem a jumble of facts to another. The history of science is full of instances of discoveries made because the "right" individual happened to make the "right" observation because of his particular life history.

Thomas Henry Huxley is reported to have exclaimed, on reading Darwin's *Origin of Species,* "Oh, what an ass I was not to have thought of that!" Even if the story is apocryphal, it is pertinent, for Darwin had assembled many facts which had been known for at least two generations. In addition he had added many observations on his famous 4-year voyage on H.M.S. *Beagle.* Nevertheless, this enormous body of data did not take on any systematic order until a fortuitous event occurred. Darwin was pondering the problem of understanding what caused species to change, when he happened to read Thomas Malthus's notion that a population tended, in the absence of certain other checks, to overwhelm the resources for the sustenance of that population. In other words, the physical environment itself was always snapping at the heels of any species. If individuals change in certain directions they will be at an advantage; if they change in other directions, at a disadvantage. This, then, combined with Darwin's other information, resulted in the notion of the struggle for survival of the species. After its public expression and in spite of the fierce theological controversy it aroused, this explanation was quickly accepted by scientists. Huxley was simply exclaiming, because "anyone could have seen it." This was indeed the "right" man at the "right" time.

This should not be construed that certain ideas will be observable only by one particular man. In fact, Wallace independently worked out the same idea as Darwin but decided the latter's greater body of data justified publication by him. All discoveries are made not once but many times. It is merely that personal life histories are a factor in determining the kinds of perception and conception. These factors may, in turn, direct one person to certain hypotheses more quickly. Often, of course, these persons were not seeking the particular observation or hypothesis. They were simply trained to understand and use the strategic fact when it appeared. The story of Newton and the falling apple, however untrue, illustrates this individual, accidental process. Similar occurrences are by no means unknown in the scientific laboratory.

An illustration of individual perspective in the social sciences may be seen in the work of Thorstein Veblen. The product of an isolated Norwegian community in Minnesota, Veblen lived at a time when the capitalistic system was not usually called into question except by "radicals." His own community background, however, was replete with negative experiences concerning the working of the economic system, and he was himself a kind of outsider or "marginal man," able to look at the capitalist system objectively. He was thus in an excellent position to attack the fundamental concepts and postulates of classical economics. In a very real sense he was an alien who could bring a different experience to bear upon the economic world. As a result he made penetrating analyses of our society which have profoundly influenced social science since his time.

All these sources of hypotheses—value orientations of the culture, folk wisdom and cliché, rebellion against common-sense ideas, observation of deviant cases (the cases which "don't fit the rule"), social experience within the science, the application of analogies, and personal experience—provide a wealth of hypotheses. In fact it is an almost embarrassing profusion. The problem which this raises is how to select those ideas which may actually prove useful.

THE CHARACTERISTICS OF USABLE HYPOTHESES

In the privacy of the scientist's mind, alone or in social gatherings, in odd moments or in the press of business, many hypotheses are entertained. Most of them, having appeared, are fortunately left to die alone. A few survive, however, to be exhibited in "bull sessions" or to be tried out on sleepy undergraduates at eight o'clock on a wintry morning. Most are not destined to play any significant role in the growth of science. Some of these would seem to be the product of the fact, as the philosopher Suzanne Langer has argued, that man's mind, like his body, is often active without any immediate goal. It is only by the imposition of firm standards that it is possible to winnow out the good ideas from the bad.

Let us now look at some criteria for judging hypotheses.

The hypotheses must be conceptually clear. Enough emphasis upon this requirement was made in the preceding chapter to require little further elaboration. It should be repeated, however, that this involves two things. The concepts should be clearly defined, operationally if possible. Moreover, they should be definitions which are commonly accepted and communicable rather than the products of a "private world."

What to do: One simple device for clarifying concepts is to write out a list of the concepts used in the research outline. Then try to define them (*a*) in words, (*b*) in terms of particular operations (index calculations, types of observations, etc.), and (*c*) with reference to other concepts to be found in previous research. Talk over each concept with fellow students and other researchers in the field. It will often be found that supposedly simple concepts contain many meanings. Then it is possible to decide which is the desired referent. For systematic conceptual clarification, perform all the operations suggested in Chapter 5.

Hypotheses should have empirical referents. It has also been previously pointed out that scientific concepts must have an ultimate empirical referent. No usable hypotheses can embody moral judgments. Such statements as "criminals are no worse than businessmen," "women should pursue a career," or "capitalists exploit their workers," are no more usable hypotheses than is the familiar proposition that "pigs are well named because they are so dirty" or the classical question, "How many yards of buttermilk are required to make a pair of breeches for a black bull?" In other words, while a hypothesis may study value judgments, such a goal must be separated from a moral preachment or a plea for acceptance of one's values.

What to do: First, analyze the concepts which express attitudes rather than describing or referring to empirical phenomena. Watch for key words such as "ought," "should," "bad," etc. Then transform the notions into more useful concepts. "Bad parents" is a value term, but the researcher may have a definite description in mind: parents who follow such practices as whimsical and arbitrary authoritarianism, inducing psychic insecurity in the child, failure to give love, etc. "Should" is also a value term, but the student may simply mean, "If women do not pursue a career, we can predict emotional difficulties when the children leave home, or we can predict that the society will not be able to produce as much goods," etc. When, instead, we find that our referent is simply a vague feeling and we cannot define the operations needed to observe it, we should study the problem further and discover what it is that we really wish to investigate.

The hypotheses must be specific. That is, all the operations and pre-dictions indicated by it should be spelled out. The possibility of actually testing the hypothesis can thus be appraised. Often hypotheses are ex-pressed in such general terms, and with so grandiose a scope, that they are simply not testable. Because of their magnitude, such grand ideas are tempting because they seem impressive and important. It is better for the student to avoid such problems and instead develop his skills upon more tangible notions.

By making all the concepts and operations explicit is meant not only conceptual clarity but a description of any *indexes* to be used. Thus, to hypothesize that the degree of vertical social mobility is decreasing in the United States requires the use of indexes. At present there is no satisfactory operational definition of the status levels which define mobility. There-fore, the hypothesis must include a statement of the indexes which are to be used; that is, political office, occupation, effective income, education, etc.

Such specific formulations have the advantage of assuring that research is practicable and significant, in advance of the expenditure of effort. It furthermore increases the validity of the results, since the broader the terms the easier it is to fall into the trap of using *selective evidence*. The fame of most prophets and fortunetellers lies in their ability to state pre-dictions so that almost any occurrence can be interpreted as a fulfillment. We can express this in almost statistical terms: the more specific the pre-diction, the smaller the chance that the prediction will actually be borne out as a result of mere accident. Scientific predictions or hypotheses must, then, avoid the trap of selective evidence by being as definite and specific as possible.

What to do: Never be satisfied with a general prediction, if it can be broken into more precise subhypotheses. The general prediction of war is not enough, for example: we must specify time, place, and participants. Predicting the gen-eral decline of a civilization is not a hypothesis for testing a theory. Again, we must be able to specify and measure the forces, specify the meaning and time of decline, the population segments involved, etc. Often this can be done by con-ceptual analysis and the formation of related hypotheses; *e.g.,* we may predict that urbanization is accompanied by a decline in fertility. However, we gain in precision if we attempt to define our indexes of urbanization; specify which seg-ments will be affected, and how much (since in the United States the various eth-nic and religious segments are affected differently); specify the amount of fertil-ity decline, and the type (percentage childless, net reproduction rate, etc.). Form-ing sub-hypotheses (1) clarifies the relationship between the data sought and the conclusions; and (2) makes the specific research task more manageable.

Hypotheses should be related to available techniques. In earlier chap-ters the point was repeatedly made that theory and method are not opposites. The theorist who does not know what techniques are available to test his hypotheses is in a poor way to formulate usable questions.

This is not to be taken as an absolute injunction against the formulation of hypotheses which at present are too complex to be handled by contemporary technique. It is merely a sensible requirement to apply to any problem in its early stages in order to judge its researchability.

There are some aspects of the impossible hypothesis which may make its formulation worth while. If the problem is significant enough as a possible frame of reference it may be useful whether or not it can be tested at the time. The socioeconomic hypotheses of Marx, for example, were not proved by his data. The necessary techniques were not available either then or now. Nevertheless, Marxian frameworks are an important source of more precise, smaller, verifiable propositions. This is true for much of Émile Durkheim's work on suicide. His related formulations concerning social cohesion have also been useful. The work of both men has been of paramount importance to sociology, even though at the time their larger ideas were not capable of being handled by available techniques.

Furthermore, posing the impossible question may *stimulate* the growth of technique. Certainly some of the impetus toward modern developments in technique has come from criticisms against significant studies which were considered inadequate because of technical limitations. In any serious sociological discussion, research frontiers are continuously challenged by the assertion that various problems "ought" to be investigated even though the investigations are presently impossible.

What to do: Look for research articles on the subject being investigated. Make a list of the various techniques which have been used to measure the factors of importance in the study. If you are unable to locate any discussions of technique, you may find it wiser to do a research *on the necessary research techniques.* You may, instead, decide that this lack of techniques means your problem is too large and general for your present resources.

Some items, such as stratification or race attitudes, have been studied by many techniques. Try to discover why one technique is used in one case and not in another. Note how refinements in technique have been made, and see whether one of these may be more useful for your purposes. Look for criticisms of previous research, so as to understand the weaknesses in the procedures followed.

Again, other problems may have been studied with few attempts at precise measurement. Study the literature to see why this is the case. Ascertain whether some subareas (for example, of religious behavior) may be attacked with techniques used in other areas (for example, attitude measurement, stratification measures, research on choice making, etc.).

The hypothesis should be related to a body of theory. This criterion is one which is often overlooked by the beginning student. He is more likely to select subject matter which is "interesting," without finding out whether the research will really help to refute, qualify, or support any existing theories of social relations. A science, however, can be cumulative only by building on an existing body of fact and theory. It cannot develop if each study is an isolated survey.

Although it is true that the clearest examples of crescive theoretical development are to be found in the physical and biological sciences, the process can also be seen in the social sciences. One such case is the development of a set of generalizations concerning the social character of intelligence. The anthropological investigations at the end of the nineteenth century uncovered the amazing variety of social customs in various societies, while demonstrating conclusively that there were a number of common elements in social life: family systems, religious patterns, an organization of the socialization process, etc.

The French school of sociology, including Lucien Lévy-Bruhl, Émile Durkheim, Marcel Mauss, Henri Hubert, and others, formulated a series of propositions, at the turn of the century, which suggested that the intellectual structure of the human mind is determined by the structure of the society. That is, perception and thought are determined by society, not alone by the anatomical structure of our eyes, ears, and other senses. Modes of thought vary from society to society. Some of these formulations were phrased in an extreme form which need not concern us now, and they were often vague. Nevertheless, the idea was growing that the intelligence of a Polynesian native could not be judged by European standards; his thinking was qualitatively, not merely quantitatively, different.

At the same time, however, better techniques were being evolved for measuring "intelligence," which came to be standardized in the form of scores on various IQ tests. When these were applied to different groups it became clear that the variation in IQ was great; children of Italian immigrants made lower grades on such tests, as did Negroes. Northern Negroes made higher grades than whites from many Southern states. American children of Chinese and Japanese parents made rather high scores. Since it was generally assumed that these tests measured "innate intelligence," these data were sometimes generalized to suggest that certain "racial" groups were by nature inferior and others superior.

However, such conclusions were opposed on rational grounds, and liberal sentiments suggested that they be put to the test. There were, then, two major sets of conclusions, one suggesting that intelligence is in the main determined by social experience, the other suggesting that the IQ is innately determined. To test such opposing generalizations, a research design was needed for testing logical expectations in more specific situations. If, for example, it is true that the intelligence of individuals who are members of "inferior" groups is really determined biologically, then changes in their environments should not change their IQ. If, on the other hand, the social experience is crucial, we should expect that such changes in social experience would result in definite patterns of IQ change.

Further deductions are possible. If identical twins are separated and are placed in radically different social experiences at an early age, we might expect significant differences in IQ. Or, if a group of rural Negro children moves from the poor school and social experience of the South, to the somewhat more stimulating environment of the North, the group averages would be expected to change somewhat. Otto Klineberg, in a classic study, carried out the latter research. He traced Negro children of various ages after they had moved to the North and found that, in general, the earlier the move to the North occurred, the greater the average rise in the IQ. The later the move, the smaller the increase. Even if one assumes that the "better," more able, and more daring adult Negroes made this move, this does not explain the differences by time of movement. Besides, of course, the subjects were children at the time of the migration.[4]

In this research design a particular result was predicted by a series of deductions from a larger set of generalizations. Further, the prediction was actually validated. In justice to the great number of scholars who have been engaged in refining and developing IQ tests, it should be mentioned that other tests and investigations of a similar order have been carried out by many anthropologists, sociologists, and social psychologists. They do not invalidate the notion that IQ is based in part on "innate" abilities, but they do indicate that to a great extent these abilities must be stimulated by certain types of experience in order to achieve high scores on such tests.

From even so sketchy an outline of a theoretical development as the foregoing is, it can be seen that when research is systematically based upon a body of existing theory, a genuine contribution in knowledge is more likely to result. In other words, to be worth doing, a hypothesis must not only be carefully stated, but it should possess theoretical relevance.

What to do: First, of course, cover the literature relating to your subject. If it is impossible to do so, then your hypothesis probably covers too much ground. Second, try to abstract from the literature the way in which various propositions and sets of propositions relate to one another (for example, the literature relating to Sutherland's theory of differential association in criminology, the conditions for maximum morale in factories, or the studies of prediction of marital adjustment). Third, ascertain whether you can deduce any of the propositions, including your own hypothesis, from one another or from a small set of major statements. Fourth, test it by some theoretical model, such as Merton's "Paradigm for Functional Analysis in Sociology" (*Social Theory and Social Structure*, pp. 50–54), to see whether you have left out major propositions and determinants. Fifth, especially compare your own set of related propositions with those of some classic author, such as Weber on bureaucracy or Durkheim on suicide. If you find this task of abstraction difficult, compare instead with the propositions of these men

[4] Otto Klineberg, *Negro Intelligence and Selective Migration* (New York: Columbia University Press, 1935).

as explained by a systematic interpreter such as Talcott Parsons in his *Structure of Social Action*. What is important is that, whatever the *source* of your hypothesis, it must be *logically* derivable from and based upon a set of related sociological propositions.

SUMMARY

The formulation of the hypothesis is a central step in good research, and it is important to give it a great deal of thought. Because of this significance, we have looked at the hypothesis from several points of view.

1. We have shown why it is so crucial a step to take, and how it functions in a research. It is the question which we put to the empirical world, in such a form that an answer can be obtained.

2. We have also looked at some of the problems which occur when we attempt to formulate hypotheses. It is clear that the formulation of hypotheses does not occur automatically but is usually preceded by many false starts, evaluational propositions, vague statements, etc.

3. As an aid in understanding hypotheses, we noted that they may be developed at different levels of concreteness, from fairly common-sense statements to the relationships between complex, abstract variables.

4. Making hypotheses is a creative act, but we can study such acts. We saw that hypotheses come from many sources, from the general emphases of our culture to the most individual of experiences.

5. Finally, we sketched a few criteria for *selecting* the more useful hypotheses and offered a few suggestions for improving those hypotheses which seem to be weak.

Such an outline at least offers the student a set of preliminary but useful notions for thinking fruitfully about research problems. Many studies fail at precisely this point, the development of a good hypothesis. On the other hand, the history of science gives innumerable examples to prove that great strides were made when someone asked the right question.

SUGGESTED READINGS

Campbell, Norman, *What Is Science?* (London: Methuen, 1921), Chaps. 3, 4, and 5.

Cohen, Morris R., and Ernest Nagel, *An Introduction to Logic and Scientific Method* (New York: Harcourt, Brace, 1934), Chap. 11.

Marx, Melvin H., "Hypothesis and Construct" in Melvin H. Marx, *Psychological Theory* (New York: Macmillan, 1951), pp. 112–128.

Waller, Willard, "Insight and Scientific Method," *American Journal of Sociology*, Vol. XL (1934), pp. 285–297.

CHAPTER 7

Design of Proof: Testing the Hypothesis

THE ROLE OF LOGIC

The function of the hypothesis is to state a specific relationship between phenomena in such a way that this relationship can be empirically tested. That is, the hypothesis must be empirically demonstrated as either probable or not probable. The basic method of this demonstration is to design the research so that logic will require the acceptance or rejection of the hypothesis, on the basis of the resulting data. This requires control of the observations in order to eliminate other possible relationships. A basic aspect of research design, therefore, is setting up the research so as to allow logical conclusions to be drawn.

The basic designs of logical proof were formulated by John Stuart Mill and still remain the foundation of experimental procedure, although many refinements have been made. His analysis provides two methods with which this section of the chapter will be concerned.

The first of these is called the *method of agreement*. When stated positively this holds that, when two or more cases of a given phenomenon have one and only one condition in common, then that condition may be regarded as the cause (or effect) of the phenomenon. More simply, if we can make observation Z in every case that we find condition C, we can conclude that they are causally related. Thus, in Figure 1, if it is known that all the conditions in the two situations, X and Y, are described and designated by A, B, C, D, and E, and further if it is known that both sets of conditions result in observation Z, then it must be concluded that C and Z are related as cause and effect. Two common propositions which are examples of this kind of reasoning may be drawn from psychodynamics and sociology:

Early and repeated emotional rejection in all primary relationships will be followed by adult neurosis.

Whenever a small, socially integrated, and culturally distinct group is in close and constant contact with a larger, more powerful group, both will exhibit patterns of ethnic prejudice.

At this point the accuracy of these two propositions is not the chief concern. Rather, we are interested in the pattern of logic they represent. In both cases, observation Z has been made whenever condition C has been found. Although this type of proof has weaknesses, it can be shown that this canon has some usefulness and expresses one pattern of common-sense reasoning very well. First of all, it helps to rule out various factors as irrelevant, although error at this point is possible. Our research problem is thereby simplified. Second, it indicates that certain factors do seem to occur together. Third, it allows us to observe in the concrete situation that

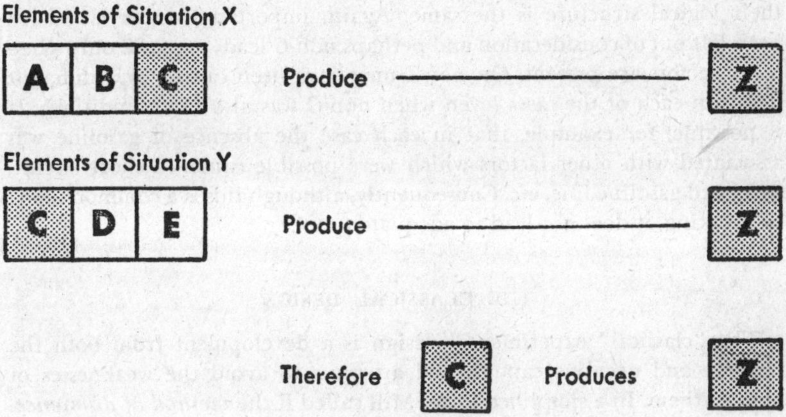

Elements of Situation X

Elements of Situation Y

FIGURE 1

factor C always occurs prior to Z. Now, if factor C is always found whenever Z is observed, it *could* be the cause of Z. Further, if among the other factors no one that is common to all our cases can be found, then these other factors could *not* be the cause. Thus, it has eliminated extraneous factors, and leaves the one, C, which could be the cause.

The weaknesses are equally manifest, however. As noted previously, some factors may not even be considered, when they are actually of great importance. Further, it is possible that C will operate only when certain other conditions are present. Finally, Z may have had a different cause in each of the cases. As a consequence, we are likely not to be satisfied with any research which stops at this point. Indeed, the observation of such an association will ordinarily be the starting point of a more carefully designed proof.

The *negative canon of agreement* simply states that when condition non-C is found to be associated with observation non-Z, we may assert a causal relationship between C and Z. An example would be:

Lack of social experience with ethnic stereotypes in childhood is followed by lack of ethnic prejudice in adulthood.

In general, this proposition, whether accurate or not, states that whenever, throughout all variations of other factors, an absence of factor C is associated with an absence of Z, it is possible to accept a causal relationship between C and Z. Assuming we have properly controlled all other factors, this canon has some claim to validity, and like the positive canon it is used in common-sense situations. We find, for example, that lack of gasoline is associated with a dead motor, so that when we find the former condition we expect to be able to make the latter observation soon afterward.

However, the same weaknesses are to be found in both canons, since their logical structure is the same. Again, important factors may have been left out of consideration and perhaps non-C leads to non-Z only when other factors are present. Or, non-Z may have been caused by a different factor in each of the cases (even when non-C was also a precondition). It is possible, for example, that in each case the absence of gasoline was associated with other factors which were possible causes—a short circuit, a clogged gasoline line, etc. Consequently, although this is a common mode of thinking, it does not lead to adequate proof.

THE CLASSICAL DESIGN

The "classical" experimental design is a development from both the positive and negative canons, and attempts to avoid the weaknesses of both of them. In a simplified form, Mill called it the *method of difference*. In its simple statement, it can be formulated in this fashion: If there are two or more cases, and in one of them observation Z can be made, while in the other it cannot; and if factor C occurs when observation Z is made, and does not occur when observation Z is not made; then it can be asserted that there is a causal relationship between C and Z. Figure 2 shows this relationship diagrammatically. In more common-sense terms, it can be stated that the first observation indicates that C *could* cause Z, while the second shows that the other possible factors could *not* cause Z.

It will be noted that there is one weakness which this design does not answer: the possibility of other factors being more significant than the ones included. However, any method of proof must operate within the limits of the variables designated in the hypothesis. If the hypothesis does not take account of current theory bearing on the problem, and if it works with irrelevant factors, no research design can cure the weakness. Indeed, it is a mark of the creative scientist that he is able to locate those factors which are central and to ignore the irrelevant. No set of recipes can supply this creativity.

To develop the classical design of proof by the method of difference, it is necessary only to make *two series* of observations and situations. As is the case for all patterns of proof, this has its counterpart in our thinking about practical problems. For example, the student may have had the experience of receiving unsatisfactory grades in some courses and satisfactory grades in others. If, by any chance, he also noted that the grade was adequate in those courses where he read the assigned materials, but unsatisfactory in those where he did not do the reading, then he is forced to the conclusion that grades and completing the reading assignments are related. This perhaps is not a perfect example since it assumes that in all courses the other factors related to grades are the same. Nevertheless, it illustrates the practical, everyday use of the classical design.

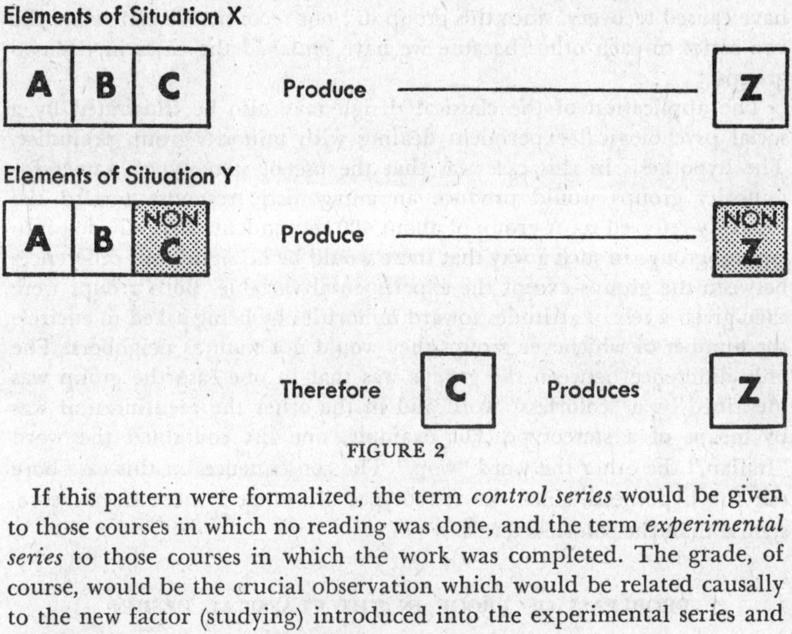

Elements of Situation X

A	B	C

Produce ————————————————— Z

Elements of Situation Y

A	B	NON C

Produce ————————————————— NON Z

Therefore C Produces Z

FIGURE 2

If this pattern were formalized, the term *control series* would be given to those courses in which no reading was done, and the term *experimental series* to those courses in which the work was completed. The grade, of course, would be the crucial observation which would be related causally to the new factor (studying) introduced into the experimental series and not present in the control series.

This type of research design is perhaps most familiar to the student from newspaper accounts of biological or medical experiments. If a new drug, atabrine, is to be tested as a treatment of malaria, for example, the classical demonstration might be applied. Two series, or groups of persons, suffering from malaria would then be selected. These groups must be matched in all relevant questions of health so that the method of differences may be applied. Atabrine is administered to one group, the experimental series, and withheld from the other, the control series.

The results as measured by subsequent symptoms of malaria are then observed. Should the experimental group recover and the control group not, the conclusion is warranted that atabrine and the remission of malarial symptoms are related. Should all recover, or none recover, in

both groups, or if no pattern is at all observable, then it can be concluded that atabrine does not affect malaria. The reasoning followed indicates, as noted before, that the classical design is made up of two *series*
of cases, each series corresponding to one of the two opposed cases in the
method of differences. Further, when each such case is made into a series,
each series corresponds to one of the canons of agreement. The experimental series (*C* causes *Z*) follows the logic of the *positive* canon. That
is, if the experimental group recovers, we see that atabrine might have
caused recovery. The control series (non-*C* leads to non-*Z*) follows the
logic of the *negative* canon. That is, none of the other factors could
have caused recovery, since this group did not recover. We can relate the
two series to each other because we have *matched* the cases in the two
groups.

The application of the classical design may also be illustrated by a
social psychological experiment dealing with minority-group prejudice.
The hypothesis in this case was that the use of stereotyped names for
minority groups would produce an antagonistic response toward the
minority referred to. A group of about 400 respondents were divided into
two subgroups in such a way that there would be no significant differences
between the groups except the experimental variable. Both groups were
then given a test of attitudes toward minorities by being asked to encircle
the number of whichever groups they would not want as neighbors. The
only difference between the groups was that in one case the group was
identified by a "colorless" word and in the other the identification was
by means of a stereotype. For example, one list contained the word
"Italian," the other the word "wop." The consequences in this case bore
out the hypothesis, since the stereotypes did elicit a more negative response than the colorless terms.[1]

PROBLEMS OF PROOF IN THE CLASSICAL DESIGN

The weaknesses of the methods of agreement and difference are, of
course, present in the experimental designs illustrated above. The problems of minimizing these are of the greatest importance to well-planned
research.

*The first problem is recognizing and controlling the variables which are
of importance in the research.* It is at this point that knowledge of theory,
of previous experimental work, and of fruitful concepts will help to
achieve good results. An immense amount of work may be wasted in
research, if the investigator fails to locate the important elements. In the
case of the atabrine experiment, for example, we might wish to know
whether there were different types of malaria, or stages of the disease,

---

[1] Research carried out by Paul K. Hatt.

and which physiological and health factors might affect the results. If these factors are recognized to be important, they must also be controlled.

"Control" may mean actual manipulation, *i.e.*, changing the values of the variables. Usually, however, manipulation is confined to the experimental variable. "Control," then, means that the values of the variables are known, or that their effects are deliberately minimized by equating them in the experimental and control series. This can be achieved by various statistical techniques, such as factor analysis, partial correlation, or analysis of covariance. More usually, the two groups are equated by (1) precision matching, (2) matching by frequency distributions, or (3) randomization. In precision matching, for any individual in the control series there will be one in the experimental series, with exactly (or almost exactly) the same characteristics. Thus, to ascertain whether changing the living pattern in a home for elderly people from a central building with all facilities in it to a cottage system, would increase the integration of the group, we might wish to control such factors as these when comparing a control with an experimental series of šuch homes: age and sex structures of the populations; number of visits from relatives; economic independence of individuals; health; church membership; previous occupation; work and recreation in the home; etc.

Ideally, for each individual with certain characteristics (age group, health, etc.) in one series we would find a comparable individual in the other. Actually, this is difficult. The loss of individuals is very great, and precise matching may cause as much as 90 per cent of the original cases to be without its twin. Consequently, one solution is to match *frequencies* instead. Thus, in the case used for illustration (which is complicated by the fact that we have to match *homes* with homes and *individuals* with individuals), if the experimental group averages 71 years of age, we would try to design our control group so that its average age would be about the same. If one series is 65 per cent female, we would draw our other sample series so that its sex composition would be similar. Frequency matching is thus much easier, though somewhat less precise, than pair matching. All that we seek is to have equal representation of the relevant factors.

An apparently less precise but actually more trustworthy technique is *randomization*, which may be used as the sole matching procedure or in combination with a frequency-matching plan. Pair or frequency matching may be more efficient when the number of cases is very small, but in sociological research we frequently have rather large populations. Now, precision and frequency matching have the weakness that there may be important factors other than those we have chosen for control. In randomization, we avoid this problem by using a random sampling design for *choosing which* individual shall be in the experimental and which shall be in the control group. We can thus assume that half those possessing any important characteristic will fall into each group, even though we may discover only later that a certain variable is significant.

The problem of interfering variables in the logic of proof is partially dealt with, then, by an experimental technique which avoids the introduction of a bias into either the experimental or the control group.

The second problem is that the causal relationship may not be clear. In the illustrations in Figures 1 and 2, it was stated that C was the cause (or effect) of Z. The direction of this relationship is not made clear by the experimental design. In fact, the possible relationship between C and Z, so far as the methods of proof are concerned, could be any one of many. Consider the following possibilities:

1. C is the cause of Z.
2. Z is the cause of C.
3. C and Z are both caused by another and unknown variable.
4. A, or B, may also be a cause of Z, but this is obscured by other unknown factors.
5. C may cause Z but only in the presence of other and unknown factors.
6. C does not cause Z because this is simply an accidental or fortuitous occurrence.

It is not to be wondered, then, that many scientists prefer to avoid the term *cause* altogether. However, there should be no difficulty if we simply mean that one event, C, is always followed (in time) by event Z under specified conditions. If this be the case a choice between possibilities 1 and 2 above can be settled on the basis of priority in time. Possibilities 3, 4, and 5 can never be removed with absolute certainty but can be lessened by adequate theory and proper sampling. Possibility 5, in fact, is characteristic of all empirical propositions since the negative assertion that no other factor exists can never be proved. Possibility 6 can be dealt with by statistical methods and will be discussed at a later point. The fact that the concept of causation always involves time brings up another problem in the logic of proof.

The third problem is that the element of time may confuse experimental results in social science. Any social variable requires time to affect social behavior. In those cases where the time span is long, cases may be lost through moving. Even if they are not lost, they may have gone through experiences which have modified the results of the original experimental stimulus. If, on the other hand, they are tested immediately after the stimulus, it may not have had enough time to effect any significant changes.

The more highly developed sciences, aside from biology, are not time-bound in the same way as sociology. The propositions of these sciences are therefore more likely to be stated in terms of constant relationships (*e.g.*, the pressure, volume, and temperature of gases). The stimulus or change can be measured with less likelihood that factors occurring between stimulus and measurement of effect have been of great importance. However, it seems clear that this reflects the stage of development of physical science, rather than the intrinsic qualities of its subject matter. Actually some physical scientists do study long-term causal relationships (*e.g.*, cosmogony, comet formation, vulcanology, etc.) and cannot at present achieve the elegance of other areas of these sciences. We cannot develop such mathematically pleasing equations until our data are much more precise, our conceptual framework more clearly defined, and our experimental techniques more highly developed. However, present research does move in such directions, and we can take the problem of time into account in our studies (1) by first learning how *powerful* or *continuing* stimuli affect social behavior over longer periods, instead of attempting to trace very intermittent or minor stimuli; (2) by studying the interrelationships of both minor and major stimuli within manageable time limits; and (3) by attempting to locate and measure subsystems (such as decision making, adjustment to crisis, etc.) of related variables, at definite moments in time.

A fourth problem in proof is that the classical design is stated in simplistic terms. For the purposes of simplification the classical design was presented in an all-or-nothing form. It states that, "given event *C*, event *Z* follows." It is thus stated in *qualitative* form. Event *Z*, however, may be a *quantity*. For example, not all the malaria cases treated with atabrine may recover. Further, some of those not treated may recover anyway.

Through the use of probability theory, however, statistical techniques allow the possibility of determining whether event *Z* expressed as a quantity is likely to be a consequence of event *C*. Thus, it is possible to compute the *increase in the proportion* disliking "wops" as neighbors, *over the proportion* disliking "Italians" as neighbors, which would be required to prove that the difference in the labels actually had an effect. More will be said on this matter in statistical terms later in the book. The fact of *quantitative* variation raises another of Mill's methods of proof, that of concomitant variation, which is increasingly being used in sociology as we learn to develop better techniques for measurement. However, let us first look at various study designs which are often used at present but which do not satisfy the classical design of experiment.

DEVIATIONS FROM THE CLASSICAL EXPERIMENTAL DESIGN

We have seen that the classical design of proof uses two series of matched groups, only one of which is exposed to the experimental stimulus. This "controlled experiment" can be diagrammed as follows: [2]

[2] Although the discussion in this section is based upon well-known principles, its immediate stimulus is the article by Samuel A. Stouffer, "Some Observations on Study Design," *American Journal of Sociology*, Vol. LV (1950), pp. 355–361, and its organization is derived from that paper.

	Before	After	Comparison: Before vs. After
Experimental Group	x	x_1	Difference $= x_1 - x$
Control Group	x'	x'_1	Difference $= x'_1 - x'$

As Stouffer dryly remarks concerning the impact of a film on soldier attitudes, "One of the troubles with using this careful design was that the effectiveness of a single film when thus measured turned out to be so slight." Much more "satisfactory" results were obtained when the "after" groups were selected by finding soldiers who admitted having seen the film. That is, those who remembered the film were also those who were most affected by it, so that the difference between "before" and "after" was great.

Practically, we may be unable to obtain such control over the situation as to be able to use this full design. Consequently, a frequent pattern uses only the experimental group:

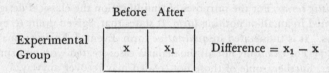

	Before	After	
Experimental Group	x	x_1	Difference $= x_1 - x$

In this case, the technique would be to have a preliminary observational period so as to measure "usual" (*i.e.*, control) behavior and thereupon introduce the stimulus. It may be called a "before and after," or "successional" experiment. Often used in laboratory research, it may take this form:

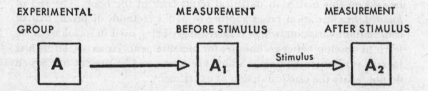

As noted, we thus lose the chance of comparing the reaction of a control group with the reaction of this group. Perhaps the best known example is the series of relay-assembly experiments in the Hawthorne study which was carried out by Mayo, Roethlisberger, Dickson, and others.[3] The attempt was made to measure the effect of several factors upon rates of production. The first period was one of intensive observation, in which

[3] F. J. Roethlisberger and W. J. Dickson, *Management and the Worker* (Cambridge, Mass.: Harvard University Press, 1939).

production and behavioral norms were ascertained (day-to-day variation in output, predictable interruptions, percentage of telephone relay assemblies rejected because of low quality, communication patterns, cooperation, etc.). This phase required several weeks of observation. Subsequently, at intervals, the variables to be measured were introduced.

The weakness of this design is simply that we have no control group for comparison. In the Hawthorne study, as in the illumination studies which preceded it, the fact of making these workers the center of attention thwarted the intent of the researchers to "control" the important variables. This change in the situational importance of the workers had greater impact than the other variables. In the illumination studies, an increase in light did increase production, but so did a decrease in brightness, to the ultimate point of the illumination on a bright moonlight night. As the student can readily see, it may be possible to assume that before the stimulus is introduced, the experimental group is the same as the control—but we have no notion what might have happened to the control group with *no* introduction of stimulus. In the illumination phase of the Hawthorne study, the investigators replaced bulbs with bulbs of the same or lesser power, but the subjects mentioned how much better they could see. Elton Mayo, who played a major role in this study, had a similar experience prior to Hawthorne. Attempting to improve conditions in one section of the mule spinning unit in a textile plant, he found that other sections responded in the same way, by both increased production and higher morale.[4] Although we may not always be able to "measure the effect of the nonstimulus" on the control group, when we are unable to contrive such a group, we must at least be aware of the dangers inherent in this gap.

On the other hand, our problem may simply be the measurement of changes, with no attempt to determine causes, and in such a case this "before and after" comparison is adequate. One example is the panel study. A similar time comparison is used in this design:

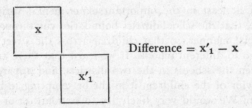

That is, the "after" group is an entirely different sample. Presumably, the latter was subject to the same stimuli as was the former. We must also assume that both were identical during the "before" phase. We have no

[4] Elton Mayo, *The Human Problems of an Industrial Civilization* (New York: Macmillan, 1933), pp. 43*ff*.

proof of either statement, and thus a comparison between x'_1 and x may not be legitimate. Further, since these are different individuals, we cannot trace the process of change. Since we do not have the other "cells," we cannot specify causes. If we recognize these limitations, on the other hand, this pattern may be of some use. It was applied as a practical device by Stouffer and his colleagues, since it was not always possible to find the *same* men for the "after" phase, once they had moved from the army center at which the "before" measurements were made. Consequently, a matched sample of men was drawn from those who had been comparable in most respects to the original group. Similarly, a study might be made which compared refugees now entering this country with a sample of those who have been in the country for several years.

A very common pattern in social research is to compare two "after" groups, in this fashion:

	Before	After
Experimental Group	x	x_1
Control Group	x'	x'_1

In this case, we really know little about the "before" phase, and simply try to reconstruct it historically. However, our basic comparison is a statistical one, in that we use various cross-tabulational and correlational techniques to eliminate one factor or another as a cause. For example, if the two groups differ in their education or age, we may wish to hold these factors constant in order to see whether some of the differences between the two groups decrease or increase.

This design is frequently used because we are faced with a situation which already exists, *i.e.*, an "after" situation for two or more groups which differ at least in the important experimental variable. Suppose, for example, that the school-district boundaries cut through a slum area in an artificial manner, so that children across the street from one another may go to different schools. If we learn that there are great differences between the schools in the two districts, and apparent differences in the behavior of the children, it might be tempting to make a formal investigation. We would very likely try to standardize or hold constant certain prior factors such as occupation of father, family pattern, etc., in order to see whether the differences between the schools seem to account for the differences in the children. Indeed, this is how many studies begin, *i.e.*, when we see differences between groups and believe that we can locate what caused the differences.

The problem of the missing "befores" is obviously that, if we do not have them, we cannot find out what difference the supposed experimental variable actually made in the situation. A common solution to this problem was used by the Army Research Branch during World War II. The question was asked, "How do the white soldiers feel about Negroes fighting beside them, in those units which have had a Negro platoon for several months of combat and other service?" The answer was that 7 per cent objected, as against 62 per cent in all-white units. The student can easily see the importance of the two missing cells: How did these units feel *before* the introduction of the Negro platoons? Although statistical standardization would help to check obvious differences, such as percentage of Southerners, education, etc., these are only one type of check. When the researchers asked the men about their attitudes prior to the change, it was learned that 67 per cent claimed to have been opposed, prior to the actual introduction of Negroes. Such a reconstruction is not a complete answer to the problem posed by the missing cells even in this case, but it does reduce uncertainty in some types of problem.

Perhaps an equally common "design" is the single cell:

After

Experimental
Group   x

This is actually a report on what exists at the time of the study. As such, it can be very useful. Presumably, we have gathered adequate data about the people in the group studied, so that we can relate various characteris-tics: *e.g.*, the young are more literate than the old; the very old speak only a foreign language while the very young speak only English, and the segments between these two are bilingual; four-fifths of the high school graduates whose fathers are in business desire to attend college, as against one-third of those whose fathers are manual laborers; etc.

However, the more we study such a single cell, the more certain we become that we really do know the "causes" of various patterns and characteristics. Our "theories" make good common sense, and perhaps we can even trace historically some of these supposed causes. Nevertheless, the student must recognize that a feeling of certainty is not demonstra-tion. By seeing any attempt at demonstration as one variation on the classical pattern, it is possible to see at once whether a given research has actually used both control and experimental series, matched for the "before" phase, and also studied at the "after" stage to see (1) how the previously identified experimental stimulus has affected the experimental group; and (2) how the lack of the stimulus has "affected" the control group. Variations on this basic design are many, and in one type, called the *"ex post facto* experiment," the situation was not contrived in advance by the researcher. However, such a study must also meet all the standards for good basic design. No amount of insight will substitute for the failure to include all the required cells. When we deviate from this minimum, we must do so in full awareness of the consequences, and only after making certain that the demands of even this minimum are greater than the practical situation will permit.

METHOD OF CONCOMITANT VARIATION

Because of the difficulties mentioned above in setting up a perfect qualitative experiment in the classical design, another mode of ap-

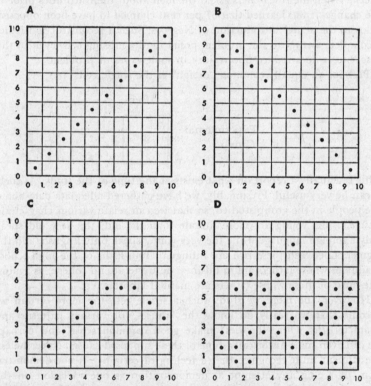

FIGURE 3. Scattergram representations of various types of correlation: (*A*) perfect positive correlation; (*B*) perfect negative correlation; (*C*) perfect curvilinear correlation; (*D*) very low correlation.

proach is often required. This was called the method of concomitant variation by Mill and is applied today as some form of correlation analysis. What this method holds is that if a change in the *amount* of one variable is accompanied by a comparable change in the *amount* of another variable in two or more cases, and the latter change does not occur in the absence of the first change, one change is the cause (or effect) of the other. Many types of this relationship are possible, the most common of which are shown in the diagrams of Figure 3. If such relationships are to be considered as causal connections between the variables X and Y, it is clear that the same problems of proof which faced the classical design also apply in this case. The direction of cause is not given. The presence of unknown factors and the statistical significance of the computations, however, are all problems to be met in the same ways as in the case of the classical design.

THE PROBLEM OF CERTAINTY

It is impossible not to come to the conclusion that certainty can never be reached by any design of proof. This is no cause for despair, however, for uncertainty can be diminished, and the *probable* accuracy of observation increased, with every addition to knowledge. Correlation techniques for controlling other variables through part and partial correlation have been developed, and wise sampling makes it easier to construct adequate designs.

The difficulty of proof has caused some sociologists to throw up their hands with the complaint that the social world is too complex to be studied scientifically. Nevertheless, research is already going forward. Similar problems are to be met in other disciplines. Certainly scientists in other fields would not agree that they face less complex problems, and we must rather conclude that science does not achieve absolutes but reduces the amount of uncertainty.

One of the most serious handicaps to the application of any sound design—classical, correlative, or other—to sociological problems is the tendency to deal with problems in the large. There simply is no "cause of juvenile delinquency" any more than there is for marriage, divorce, reproduction, or any other complex phenomenon. When a sharp focus is absent, the techniques of controlling other variables by the application of concomitant variation, good sampling, etc., are of no use, for such large formulations can lead only to the conclusion that almost everything is a cause of almost everything else.

It is clear, then, that by whatever design the hypothesis is tested the results are never certain but *are approximations stated in terms of probability.* This indicates the necessity for well-designed research to anticipate work beyond the formal demonstration of the hypothesis. That is, good design prepares the way for still further hypotheses. Moreover, it is only in this fashion that the organized knowledge of science can grow.

First approximations establish the original hypothesis. From this are deduced other, subsidiary, hypotheses. If the original idea is correct and the logic impeccable, the subsidiary propositions should also be correct. If later experimentation shows that these deduced hypotheses are correct, they thus yield more data to confirm the original proposition. If the deduced hypotheses are not correct, it becomes necessary to revise the original idea. As a consequence of this interrelatedness, science actually cumulates. It does not become a series of isolated propositions. And, with each such series of experimentation, all the related propositions have a higher degree of probability.

THE IMPORTANCE OF THE DEVIANT CASE AND OF THE PROCESS

It has been pointed out that experiments rarely, if ever, give results so conclusive as to answer the problem completely. Particularly in social research, correlations are likely to be low, and differences between experimental and control groups something less than obvious. As a result there will be many cases which deviate from the hypothesis.

A study of deviant cases may reveal additional factors which should be taken into consideration in order to increase the predictive value of the hypothesis. Such a detailed examination may also change the interpretation of an experiment considerably. For example, consider the following situation.

Using a simple "before and after" testing method, the effectiveness of a particular piece of propaganda regarding the United Nations was appraised. The experimental and control groups were both given attitude tests before the propaganda was employed. The experimental group alone was exposed to the propaganda. Then both groups were tested subsequently. Neither group showed any change between the two tests in average scores for the group. Consequently, the hypothesis that the propaganda affected these attitudes seemed at first to be untenable.

The question was then asked, "If there is no change *in general,* what are the known facts about the *exceptions?*" This led to an analysis of the apparent exceptions, those who had changed. This revealed that many changes had occurred in the experimental group. These, however, had just happened to balance so that an equal number moved an equal distance in both directions. This new fact meant that the original hypothesis was not voided but required further study. In this particular case it was also observed that when the changes were divided into the two groups— those who became more favorable, and those who became less favorable— one group was predominantly male and the other predominantly female.

This finding, of course, threw new light on the hypothesis and required its reformulation and retesting in different terms.[5] In this case, additional factors were uncovered by the analysis of the deviant cases. In some cases, we may find that our conceptual or theoretical notions were too simple. For example, the study of Orson Welles's "Invasion from Mars" broadcast began with the idea that they would find that only the late tuners had been fooled. That is, those tuners would have missed the explanation at the beginning of the program.[6] However, they soon found that early tuners were fooled just as were late tuners, even with the advantage of the explanatory introduction. They deviated from expectation because they had grown accustomed to having radio programs interrupted by news bulletins and assumed that the "invasion" broadcast was such a series of bulletins, unconnected with the prior explanation.

Analysis of these deviant cases may actually add further data to the hypothesis, by showing that there is an underlying principle for both deviant and nondeviant. In Merton's study of the Kate Smith war-bond drive, for example, it seemed reasonable to believe that those who had relatives or loved ones in the armed services would be more affected by her appeal. There were, however, individuals who failed to respond even though they did fall within this category. Further analysis demonstrated the importance of having a personal stake in the war, because these deviants had relatives or loved ones who were at bases in the United States or at fairly safe stations outside the continent.[7]

We may also learn from this analysis that we need to refine our indexes, or statistical variables. Any index we use may be relatively crude, for it is difficult to develop precise indexes for measuring or locating social patterns. For example, we may predict that neighboring and other local patterns of group orientation will be stronger in cities with a high level of moral integration. However, since the development of a good index for this phenomenon is difficult, we may decide to use certain crime rates as a composite index. Then, when we compare low and high level cities, we will find deviant cases. The analysis of these deviant cases may show us that our index needs considerable refinement. Some of the cities may deviate because of local police conditions, others because of natural barriers within them. Our original hypothesis has not been challenged, but

[5] Cf. similar analysis of the exception in *Cincinnati Looks at the U.N.* and *Cincinnati Looks Again,* National Opinion Research Center publications No. 37 and 37A (mimeographed) (University of Chicago, 1947).

[6] Hadley Cantril, *Invasion from Mars* (Princeton, N.J.: Princeton University Press, 1940). See also the article by Patricia L. Kendall and Katherine M. Wolf, "The Analysis of Deviant Cases in Communications Research," *Communications Research 1948–1949,* Paul F. Lazarsfeld and Frank Stanton, eds. (New York: Harper, 1949), pp. 152–179.

[7] Robert K. Merton (with M. Fiske and A. Curtis), *Mass Persuasion* (New York: Harper, 1946).

we will attempt to find a more effective measure of moral integration, so that our deviant cases may be fewer, and our principle more sharply tested.

The deviant cases should not, then, be lumped together as awkward or useless, but should be utilized further for the next stage of the study. This matter is dealt with again in the later section on the analysis of data.

Taking account of the deviant case suggests that we should also attempt to consider the *process* by which the social variable affects the individual or group. For example, if it is predicted that a particular motion picture will be an effective means of changing racial attitudes, and tests of the hypothesis reveal it to be true, the study is not yet complete. The process by which attitudes were changed must be studied if the results are to be generalized beyond the particular film and the particular subjects involved in the experiment.

Such an analysis would assume that different parts of the film affected different people in diverse ways. Thus, a series of subhypotheses would be developed for the study of the process itself. To some, the main impact of the film would be its race propaganda, to others its delineation of character and conflict. Still others might see it as the solution of a personal emotional conflict. The manner in which the film's impact operates to change attitudes may also be assumed to vary. For some, the film may have been an "eye opener," a new and dramatic experience. For others it may have simply crystallized a long process of "soul searching" in regard to race problems. For still others it may merely have served as a topic of conversation, which, however, brought them into contact with individuals interested in the question. This, in turn, may have caused a change of attitudes.

Clearly, all three of these hypothetical cases are processually different, yet in the sample cross tabulation of the classical design they would all be classified as having their attitudes changed as a consequence of exposure to the film. But for purposes of generalization, their treatment as a group, just as the treatment of the film as a whole, leaves much to be desired. Good research design, therefore, requires that both exceptions and processes be studied in order to understand the meaning of the test for the hypothesis. If this is carefully done, many wrong interpretations of results will be prevented.

In the following chapter, several additional problems in research design are discussed.

SUGGESTED READINGS

Chapin, F. Stuart, *Experimental Designs in Sociological Research* (New York: Harper, 1947), Chaps. 1, 2, and 7.

Cohen, Morris R., and Ernest Nagel, *An Introduction to Logic and Scientific Method* (New York: Harcourt, Brace, 1934), Chap. 13.

Fisher, R. A., *The Design of Experiments* (Edinburgh: Oliver & Boyd, 1937).

Greenwood, Ernest, *Experimental Sociology* (New York: King's Crown Press, 1945), Chap. 2.

Mill, John Stuart, *A System of Logic* (New York: Longmans, 1930), 8th ed.

Pearson, Karl, *The Grammar of Science* (London: A & C Black, 1911), 3d ed.

CHAPTER 8

Further Problems in Research Design

The previous chapter has dealt with some of the elementary principles of research design. This analysis is carried forward in the present chapter by a discussion of these problems: (1) delimitation of the factors to be studied, and (2) further variations of research design.

THE DELIMITATION OF VARIABLES

This problem has been repeatedly discussed in preceding chapters. Its importance may be phrased by stating that it is easier to answer a good question than a poor one. The history of every science contains many instances of wrestling with questions which would now be considered pointless. Consequently, this volume has placed much emphasis on seeing the problem in theoretical and conceptual terms. Although many sociologists find their work handicapped by the difficulty of laboratory experimentation, this problem may not be the most significant aspect of delimiting variables. Certainly of equal importance is discovering which variables ought to be controlled.

Thus, previous suggestions to this end should be followed: (1) studying the research literature on the subject; (2) analyzing the problem with colleagues and teachers, particularly with those who have worked on the problem; (3) attempting to locate unpublished materials or projected research on the subject; (4) attempting to carry out formally the steps in conceptual respecification; (5) developing in sharp detail the hypothesis, including its connections with social theory; and (6) actual contact, where possible, with the phenomena being studied.

Although this last item is discussed further in the later chapter on observation, it frequently takes the form of a *pilot study*, whose aim is to ascertain which are the salient field problems and the important variables. Depth interviews may be used, as well as all types of observation, and even the application of various hypotheses to see whether they seem to fit the situation. Usually, a pilot study will be limited to a few cases which are chosen as strategically as possible, *e.g.*, extreme cases, sets of cases which seem contradictory, "ideal" cases, etc. Usually, this exploration gives the student a much clearer notion of which variables will be of greatest importance.

Preliminary empirical results may, then, limit the number of possible variables, as does the continuing work of reconceptualization. Since we can never be absolutely certain that a given variable is unimportant, there are several bases upon which we may *eliminate* one or another factor. In general, these are (1) social theory, especially the general orientation toward sociological phenomena; (2) preliminary empirical results; (3) conceptual analysis; and (4) expense in time, money, and energy. The first merely points to certain factors (status and role, socialization, social definition of the situation, etc.) as being more important than others for sociological problems. The last is a matter of mere practicability. We cannot investigate all the interesting aspects of a problem, and at some point we must arbitrarily limit its size. However, by being aware of this limitation, we at least leave open the possibility of later integrating our results with other research which does deal with the variables we have ignored.

It is particularly necessary that the student recognize the role of the *observer as an important variable*. This matter is treated in greater detail in Chapter 10, and only a few comments need be made here. First, we must keep in mind that even in the physical or biological sciences the observer is a problem. The instruments used to extend the range or character of the observations (electron microscopes, X rays, etc.) may themselves interfere with the characteristics of the subjects. Therefore, one of the variables to be delimited, controlled, or taken account of, is the observer himself. Second, each observer has his personal or cultural frame of perception which determines in part what he sees. To deal with this problem requires standardized techniques for both observing and recording the data we need. Third, the knowledge on the part of individuals or groups that they are being observed may change their behavior. Fourth, when the social researcher is using existing data, such as agency records, census figures, school files, etc., his own interference may be minimal, but he must be aware that *someone* made the observations originally, and that earlier effect must be weighed. Fifth, both the questionnaire and the interview are modes of interaction between observer and observed, and the role of the former is a part of the system of variables in the problem itself.

The research plan will not, then, aim at eliminating the "effect of the observer variable." What is attempted, however, is either (1) eliminating this effect as far as *important* variables are concerned, or (2) keeping the effect within measurable and reasonable limits. As far as possible, this variable should be anticipated in planning the research. An example may be taken from an interview study of Puerto Rican fertility. This research sought information concerning family life, the birth of children, and other items which might have created a delicate situation between interviewer and subject. Puerto Rican mores would not have permitted these questions to be asked by a man of a woman. Since the reverse was not true, it was necessary to employ only women as interviewers on this project. Sex, age, class, and race differences may frequently so affect the interview situation as to interfere with the validity of the results. Many other factors are also of significance in this connection, but they can wait upon the general discussion of interviewing problems.

We have placed some emphasis upon the essentially conceptual and theoretical aspects of delimiting variables. Actual manipulation of variables, aside from that of the observer, has been achieved in many experiments, and examples are used throughout this text. The laboratory form of the experiment possesses no logical superiority over any other form, however. Its potential superiority lies in its effort to limit or to hold constant the *concrete* effect of various factors. This may require greater precision of observation than can be achieved in all areas of social research, at present. Whether or not the work of sociology a decade hence will take the form of laboratory experimentation, it seems clear that few of our present techniques operate at their greatest effectiveness in that situation. Laboratory work has been most fruitful in dealing with social aspects of perception, learning, and memory; the social structure of groups set to work on laboratory problems; and many types of studies of children. Further, ethical considerations prevent the manipulation of people in all the ways which might be demanded by a purely laboratory form of research.

We must not, then, take the laboratory as our ideal in social research. Its advantages, where they exist, are of a technical and practical nature, just as is true of its disadvantages. In terms of the logic of proof, neither possesses an intrinsic superiority. We must choose the area and site for our experiment on the basis of their suitability for demonstrating the hypothesis, not on the basis of a preference for or dislike of the laboratory.

FURTHER SIMPLE VARIATIONS IN EXPERIMENTAL DESIGN

Whether correlational or not, the basic pattern of the classical design is one of comparing the result of the experimental variable upon an experimental series, with the result of *not* introducing that variable into a nearly identical series, under the same conditions. In sociological as in biological research, it is often the case that changes occur without the new variable. Another problem emerges, in that we are introducing only one variable, usually with one definite value, into the situation. Perhaps it is only at that value that the variable has any importance.

Consequently, we may wish to answer this problem by a somewhat more sophisticated design, which attempts to approach the still more adequate factorial design by utilizing one control group but comparing it with several experimental groups. We may thus test *different intensities* of the same stimulus, or even *different stimuli*. This type of comparison would be diagrammed as shown in Figure 1.

If a different stimulus were used for the groups B, C, and D, the design would be the same. In both cases, the comparisons would be B with B_1, C with C_1, and D with D_1, in order to see whether the stimulus seemed to have a specifiable effect. However, the really crucial comparison, *be-*

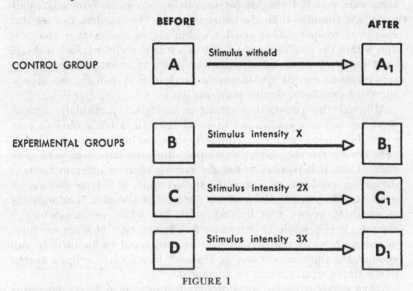

FIGURE 1

tween these differences on the one hand, and the difference between A and A_1, on the other, could be observed. For it cannot be assumed that A_1 will be the same as A, simply because it is believed that no stimulus was introduced into that control group. Laying aside the possibility of inadvertently or carelessly introducing a stimulus, there remains the fact that any group exhibits some variation from one period to another. Such a design takes this fact into account and allows the specification of the amount of effect from a given amount of stimulus. Such a pattern is very amenable to later correlational analysis.

An example of this type of experiment is the early study carried out by Gosnell on voting behavior.[1] In order to measure the effect of different stimuli upon the tendency to register as a voter and to vote, the residents of twelve selected districts (of which eight were voting precincts) were divided into experimental and control groups. The stimuli were directed

[1] Harold F. Gosnell, *Getting Out the Vote* (Chicago: University of Chicago Press. 1927).

toward the fall presidential election (1924) and the winter aldermanic election (February, 1925). The experimental group received a mail canvass stimulus to register, before the first registration day, and the same informative notice plus a cartoon before the final registration day. Of course, the control group did not receive these. Further, specimen ballots were sent to the experimental groups before the presidential election, and a cartoon notice urging voting, together with English instructions for voting, before the aldermanic election. The control and experimental areas were matched roughly for nationality, sex ratio, economic conditions, and stimulus from the political parties. The student can see that a series of comparisons is possible within such a design. It is also clear that within the conditions stated this is a true experiment. Such a design has also been used in order to compare different techniques for eliciting answers from mailed questionnaires (inclosure of money, use of self-addressed envelopes, double postcards, etc.).

Although this pattern is common in biological, particularly agricultural, research, its application to social research is fairly obvious even when difficult to carry out. However, since the measurement of social variables has not been highly developed, attributes have been used more often. Thus, it is possible to test the varying effect of different kinds of stimuli on productivity within the smaller units of a large factory, instead of different intensities of the same social stimulus. The difficulty of matching groups may be very great, but when we surmount this obstacle, it is possible to introduce a different type of wage incentive in one unit, while rest periods may be introduced in another. In still another, the illumination may be changed. In a fourth group, a change in the clique structure may be attempted.

When *different stimuli* are introduced, instead of different intensities of the same stimulus, the problem of interpretation is more difficult. In such a case, there are really *several simultaneous* comparisons, for which the single control group acts as a base. Although each such comparison may be valid, the relationship between the several stimuli remains unclear. For example, when the clique structure is changed production may fall, while it might rise with the introduction of a wage incentive plan. Yet there are many possible *kinds* of changes in the clique structure, and many *degrees* of change. Some of these might compare favorably in increased production with the effect of the change in wage incentives. Such possibilities remain unanswered until their solution is sought through further research. However, we may thus open several avenues of data, with limited numbers of cases.

The classical logical pattern is not confined to projective designs, *i.e.*, designs which look forward in time. It can also be applied in what Greenwood has called *"ex post facto* research." [2] This design differs from

2 Ernest Greenwood, *Experimental Sociology* (New York: King's Crown Press, 1945).

the projective design in two ways. First, it proceeds from the past to the present rather than being oriented toward the future. Second, the researcher can control the crucial variables only by selecting one which has already been *recorded*. In basic logic, however, projective and *ex post facto* experiments are the same. The aim of both is to compare two groups, similar on all relevant characteristics but one, in order to measure the effects of that characteristic.

In the case of the *ex post facto* design, however, we manipulate pieces of paper, that is, presently existing records which symbolize the behavior upon which the experiment is focused. Control is exercised by matching records in such a way that the similarity of the control and experimental groups in all but the crucial variable is assured. The records are then followed through by measuring the consequences as observed in present characteristics.

If, for example, it is hypothesized that two types of depression experience, the receipt of direct relief and the receipt of work relief such as WPA employment, have differential consequences in subsequent work adjustment, the *ex post facto* design could be employed. The procedure would involve securing lists of names of persons having each of these experiences, and no other relief history. These lists would then be matched on all relevant factors such as age, skills, race and nationality, education, health, etc. The next step is locating the people on the two lists, at some time subsequent to the relief history, and measuring work adjustment at that time. Any significant differences, if the matching was roundly done, could then be ascribed to the difference in relief history.[3]

It is clear that this design involves the same theoretical problems of adequate matching as in the projective design. *Ex post facto* research, however, adds two other problems:

1. It is necessary to find the cases or at least a record of those cases, after a lapse of some years. Because of death and mobility, this is often difficult. Thus, it is usually safer to locate both groups before matching, and then to match between those cases which are available for the second examination.

2. It restricts research to those problems and cases for which adequate records exist. If a crucial variable was not recorded, or an important population segment is absent, the gap cannot be filled when the study is undertaken some years after the event.

A variant of this design which minimizes the problem of locating cases is to state the problem in such a way that the total population can be located with certainty. This shifts the problem of location to that of finding earlier records. One such study, directed by Chapin, undertook to study the relation between scouting and delinquency.

[3] The student may profitably study this and other such researches in F. Stuart Chapin, *Experimental Design in Sociological Research* (New York: Harper, 1947).

In this case, older boys from a school system were classified as delinquent and nondelinquent. Matched samples on the bases of socioeconomic status, family structure, location, school grades, and other factors were taken from each group. Research upon these two samples was done to determine whether or not scouting characterized the nondelinquents and was absent in the experience of the delinquents.

In this case, there was no problem of locating the cases but, instead, a problem of securing access to their past histories. Sometimes one form,

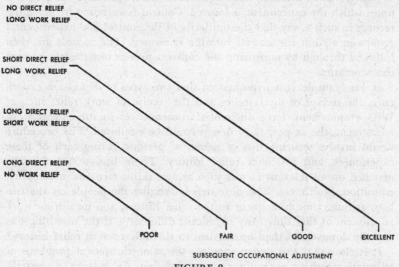

FIGURE 2

and sometimes another, of the *ex post facto* method may be employed. The decision must be based on the nature of the problem and the availability of the data.

Both *ex post facto* and projective designs, as has been noted, may utilize in their simplest form any of the patterns of empirical proof. In more complicated designs, however, the method of *concomitant variation* may also be applied. Thus, if the experimental variable and the measure of consequences can be expressed quantitatively, the demonstration procedure may involve correlation analysis.

In the foregoing illustration of the *ex post facto* version of the classical experimental design it was stated that the experimental and control groups consisted of matched series of persons, all possessing relief experience in the depression, but with the difference that one group had experienced *work* relief and the other *direct* relief. The test of the hypothesis was to lie in the relative proportions of the two groups present at a subsequent date in another category defined as "occupationally well adjusted." It seems clear that it would not always be a simple matter to secure a sample which was clearly differentiated at the earlier period. That is, many people would have had both experiences, and even those who had had only one of the types would have experienced the situation for varying lengths of time.

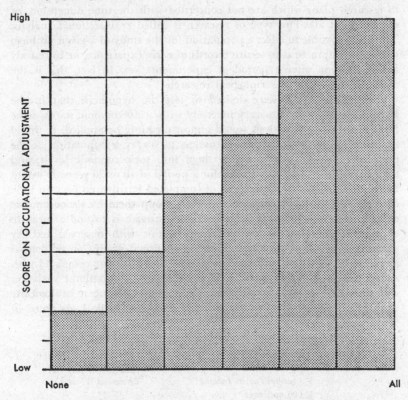

PROPORTION OF RELIEF EXPERIENCE AS WORK RELIEF

FIGURE 3. A vertical bar graph (histogram) showing hypothetical relationship between work relief and occupational adjustment.

One way to solve this problem is to frame the design so as to use correlation analysis. Then, the hypothesis would state that among those experiencing the same length of relief experience, the *longer* the experience of *work* relief and the *shorter* the experience of *direct* relief, the *higher* will be the score on some test of subsequent occupational adjustment. Figure 2 illustrates how correlation analysis thus incorporates a series of classical designs into one research plan.

There is no reason, of course, why the design reproduced in Figure 2 should not be applied directly as shown. The difficulty of securing "pure" types, however, will usually indicate the superior simplicity of the method of concomitant variation, with the consequent use of the technique of correlation. In this case the diagram of design would be that of Figure 3.

Concomitant variation, as a quantitative method of demonstration, is not only usable in projective and *ex post facto* designs. It is also applicable to research plans which are not concerned with the time dimension, or sequences, at all. This type of research is called *cross-sectional* analysis. Thus it is possible to select a population for the study of a given problem when it is impractical to secure records of early experience, or to restudy the population after a period of experimentation. In fact, this is the most common type of sociological research.

For example, if it were desired to test the hypothesis that in the United States birth rates vary inversely with socioeconomic status, some form of correlation analysis would almost certainly be applied. It would be quite impractical and indeed useless to survey a population at the beginning of adolescence, divide them into socioeconomic levels, and then await their fertility behavior for a period of 10 or 20 years. It would be equally difficult to secure cases of completed fertility, go back in time to their entry into adolescence and then group them by socioeconomic experience levels. What is normally done, instead, is to find a measure of socioeconomic status and to compare this with observed fertility patterns *at the time of study*. Thus occupational groups or residential areas can be scored on socioeconomic status and this score compared with an acceptable index of fertility. The method of concomitant variation will then demonstrate whether or not a relationship can be logically established between the two variables, as shown in Table 1. As noted in

TABLE 1

Fertility Rates Standardized for Age, by Family Income Groups *

Annual Family Income	Live Births per Thousand Wives
$3,000 and over	77
2,000–2,999	76
1,500–1,999	81
1,000–1,499	90
Under $1,000 and total relief	117
Total relief	147

* Taken from Clyde V. Kiser, *Group Differences in Urban Fertility* (Baltimore: Williams & Wilkins, 1942), Table 40, p. 169. Data from the National Health Survey, conducted in 83 United States cities, 1935–1936.

the previous chapter, the *relationship* can be demonstrated, but without a full cell design we do not know its direction or whether both factors are caused by a third.

The careful student will have noted that cross-sectional analysis does not do away with the problem of controlling other significant variables.

In the classical design these are controlled by sampling. That is, the experimental and control groups are so drawn, either by matching or randomization, that there is no reason to suspect that any bias has entered to disturb the experiment. The cross-sectional design meets the problem in logically the same fashion but with some technical differences. Control by *randomization* is sometimes used in this method. Thus, for example, if the relation of socioeconomic status to fertility were applied only to certain age groups, or certain types of communities, and not to others, the resulting relationship would be a distorted one. The nature of the population and the method of selecting cases from that population are quite as important matters in the use of correlation analysis as in the application of the classical design.

Sometimes, however, randomization is not an adequate control method either because it is impractical, or because it is prohibited by the problem, or because the distribution of the factor within the population is unknown. In such cases, cross-sectional design may fall back upon statistical methods of control. The most common of these is the use of the technique of *partial correlation*. This technique consists in holding constant the effect of other variables which might interfere with the desired observation. In the example used above it might be thought that age, education, and racial differences are confusing the relation between socioeconomic status and fertility. Partial correlation provides a means of asking, "How is socioeconomic status related to fertility, if all the people had the same education, were of the same age, and of the same race?" Such a statistical procedure operates in the same way as if several compound designs such as those shown in Figure 3 were actually applied. The student is directed to standard statistics textbooks for the procedures to be followed, although Table 2 shows a simple method of introducing such controls by

TABLE 2

Fertility Rates Standardized for Age, by Family Income and Occupation of Family Head *

Live Births per Thousand Wives

| | OCCUPATION | | | |
INCOME	Professional	Business	Skilled and Semi-skilled	Unskilled
$3,000 and over	80	74	71	59
2,000–2,999	79	76	73	78
1,500–1,999	102	75	84	78
1,000–1,499	99	89	90	94
Under $1,000 and total relief	102	105	119	130
Total relief	117	142	149	155

* Taken from Clyde V. Kiser, *Group Differences in Urban Fertility* (Baltimore: Williams & Wilkins, 1942), Table 38, p. 160.

simultaneous tabulation showing the effect of income, for several different occupational levels, on fertility rates.

COMPLEXITY OF RESEARCH DESIGN

This and the preceding chapter have tried to clarify several problems in the design of logical proof. First, there are many methods of logical demonstration which may be employed. Second, these methods may be used in three types of time designs: *ex post facto,* projective, and cross-sectional. Third, the selection of a method, or methods, of logic and the planning of the design in time do not guarantee sound results. These are only first steps. The effectively designed study must also calculate as closely as possible what are the logical variables to control and then devise methods to control them.

This last aspect of design is perhaps the most difficult to perform well, and the most affected by the theoretical knowledge or lack of knowledge on the part of the experimenter. Research design which clearly states the problem, controls the relevant variables, and selects an appropriate logic of demonstration is a goal difficult of achievement but worthy of great effort.

SUGGESTED READINGS

Chapin, F. Stuart, *Experimental Designs in Sociological Research* (New York: Harper, 1947), Chaps. 3, 4, 5, and 7.

Churchman, C. West, *The Theory of Experimental Inference* (New York: Macmillan, 1948).

Greenwood, Ernest, *Experimental Sociology* (New York: King's Crown Press, 1945), Chaps. 3, 4, 5, 6, and 7.

Jahoda, Marie, Morton Deutsch, and Stuart W. Cook, *Research Methods in Social Relations* (New York: Dryden, 1951), Part I, pp. 58–88.

Rice, Stuart A. (ed.), *Methods in Social Science* (Chicago: University of Chicago Press, 1931).

CHAPTER 9

Use of the Library

by Joseph S. Komidar

An important part of the preparation for research work consists in learning how to use the resources of libraries. It is important because all research inevitably involves the use of the book, pamphlet, periodical, and documentary materials in libraries. This applies to studies based upon original data gathered in a field study as well as to those based entirely upon documentary sources. In both types of studies there is the same need for using certain basic kinds of published materials. On the one hand, general source materials have to be consulted for the necessary background knowledge of the problem to be investigated. Obviously, no research project can be undertaken without this preliminary orientation. Nor should one be undertaken without knowledge of the research that has already been done in the field. It provides further orientation to the problem, and at the same time eliminates the possibility of unnecessary duplication of effort. In addition, valuable information on research techniques may be gained from reports of previous research.

In studies based upon original data gathered in the field, the use of library materials is seldom limited to this preliminary purpose. The specific needs that may have to be met by data already collected and available in a library collection are numerous and varied. They may be of importance—the information necessary to make a selection of a representative community for a sociological study; or the needs may be peripheral—the definition of a sociological term or the publication date of a book that is to be listed in a bibliography.

In selecting a topic for research, the student need not confine himself to considering only those problems which require field investigation. Not all research has to be of this kind in order to be significant; sound research studies can be developed from the materials available in library collections. An example is the historical study, which has to depend upon published and manuscript materials for its data. A biographical dictionary, such as the *Who's Who in America,* provides enough information for a meaningful study of the question of social mobility. There are many economic, political, and social statistics gathered by agencies, both governmental and private, which can serve as the raw data for analysis of a specific problem. A *demographic* study, for example, could be made on the basis of the different types of population statistics gathered and published by such agencies. A *synthesis* of the findings of research studies can be a useful kind of study, particularly when it draws upon the research of several disciplines and relates them to the same social phenomenon. *Content analysis* studies represent yet another type of research which can be based entirely upon materials available in a library collection. The analysis of the characteristics of the content of communication has been used for a variety of purposes, from that of exposing propaganda techniques to that of measuring the readability of materials.

Ability to do library research begins with an understanding of the ways in which libraries organize their collections and with a knowledge of basic bibliographic and reference materials. The general procedure followed in doing library research is the same in any library because all libraries organize their collections on the same general principles and provide similar resources for research. This means that they all have a system of subject classification, a card catalogue, and certain bibliographic and reference materials. There are local variations, of course, in the arrangement and location of certain types of materials, and in the extent and quality of the research materials that are provided. Therefore, orientation to the peculiarities of these kinds in the library being used is an essential preliminary to the efficient use of its resources. In spite of these variations, however, the same general procedure is followed and certain basic bibliographic and reference tools are commonly used in finding materials in libraries.

CARD CATALOGUE

In general, the first source to check for finding materials in a library is the library's card catalogue. It is an index which lists all the publications in the library collection, by author, by subject, and often by title. These three types of headings represent the ways in which one may need to look for publications: Does the library have any materials on this subject, or by this author? Does it have this book by this author? Does it have a book with this title?

The catalogue is arranged like a dictionary, with the cards filed alphabetically according to the first word on the card. The first word may be the name of the author, the subject heading, or the title of the publication. This kind of arrangement brings together in the catalogue the cards for all the books by a specific author, and the cards for all the publications in the library on a given subject. All the works of an author are filed alphabetically by title under his surname. When the title begins with an article, the *second* word is used for filing purposes. Under a given subject, publications are listed alphabetically according to author.

To find a publication by author in the card catalogue, it is advisable and often essential to know the given names as well as the surname of the author. There may be several authors with identical or similar names, and it sometimes happens that some of them have written books in the same subject field. The name Smith appears in the card catalogue as often as it does in the telephone directory of a large metropolitan area. Unless Smith can be identified more specifically, he will not be found easily. In addition, there should be enough information about the title of the publication to distinguish it from titles of other books in the library written by the same author. If the information on the author's name and title is incomplete, it may be easier to find the publication under its subject heading.

In looking up materials by subject, it is necessary to look under the heading which describes the subject most specifically. Public administration is a subject in the field of political science, but materials on it are listed under the heading "Public Administration," not under the heading "Political Science." A subject for which there are many books is subdivided to indicate its specific aspects. Thus, a book concerned only with the question of agriculture in a primitive society is listed under the heading "Agriculture, Primitive," not under "Agriculture"; and a book on the colonial period of American history is listed under "U.S. History, Colonial Period."

There are two types of cross-reference cards filed in the catalogue to assist the catalogue user in finding the heading under which materials on a subject are listed. One is a "see" card, which refers from a heading that is not used for a subject to one that is. A card reading

Primitive Society
see
Society, Primitive

indicates that the materials in the library on the subject are listed under the second heading indicated. A second type of cross-reference card is the "see also" reference. It is always filed *behind* all the other cards on a given subject to direct the user to headings under which the materials on related subjects are listed. After the last reference listed under the heading "Political Science," for example, there would be a card reading "Political Science, see also Elections, Political Conventions, Political Parties" (and other headings under which the library has listed materials that are related in subject content).

Examples of Cards

Subject entry

Author or "main" entry

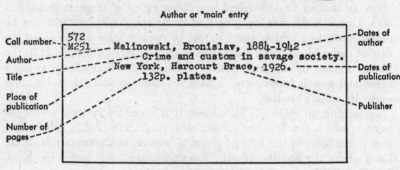

FIGURE 1

The information appearing on the face of the cards identifies specifically each publication in the library by author, title, place of publication, publisher, date of publication, number of pages, and other distinguishing characteristics. This information may be helpful in the selection of publications which may best meet a particular need. The *publication date* is a useful index to the *recency* of information contained in a book; the *number of pages* sometimes is an indication of the *comprehensiveness* of treatment; the *name* of the author or the name of the publisher may indicate the *authoritativeness* of the treatment of a subject or the special point of view which may be expressed in the publication. A book published by the National Association of Manufacturers, for example, would probably have a different approach to a subject than one published by the Congress of Industrial Organizations.

In addition to identifying a publication, the catalogue card supplies the information needed to locate it. It does this by giving the "call number" which appears in the upper left corner of the card. This number consists of (1) a classification symbol, which is the top line of the number and designates the subject of a publication (572 in the illustration); and (2) a "Cutter number" which is the second line and designates the author or title (M251 in the illustration).

The classification symbol is derived from the particular scheme of subject classification used by a library. It may consist of numbers, or letters, or a combination of the two, depending on the classification system used.

The Dewey decimal classification system, which is used by most libraries, has numbers only. The Library of Congress scheme, another system frequently used by libraries, has both letters and numbers to designate subject classes.[1] The purpose of using a classification system as the basis for arranging materials is to bring publications on one subject together in one location and near publications on related subjects. How this is achieved is illustrated in the following brief outline of classes in the Dewey system:

Main classes		Sociology		Political Science	
000	General works	300	Sociology	320	General
100	Philosophy	310	Statistics	321	Form of state
200	Religion	320	Political science	321.1	Family
300	Sociology	330	Economics	321.2	Tribes
400	Philology	340	Law	321.3	Feudalism
500	Pure science	350	Government	321.4	Democracy
600	Useful arts	360	Charities and	322	Church and state
700	Fine arts		corrections	323	Internal relations
800	Literature	370	Education		with groups and
900	History	380	Commerce		individuals
		390	Customs, folklore	324	Suffrage

The Cutter number consists of the first letter of the author's name, and a number which is a code for the combination of letters in the name. If there is no author, the Cutter number is derived from the title of the publication. This number serves to alphabetize publications within a subject classification and to bring together within each subject classification all the books of one author and all the volumes of a periodical. All the volumes of *Harper's* magazine, for example, would have the same Cutter number, H295, as well as an identical classification number.

The whole call number is the key to the location of a publication on the library shelves because no two publications can ever be assigned the same combination of symbols. Books within a subject classification are differentiated by the Cutter number, and books with identical classification and Cutter numbers are differentiated by additional symbols to indicate volume or edition.

INDEXES AND BIBLIOGRAPHIES

The main use of the classification number is to locate a given publication. For research purposes, it is at best only a rough guide to materials in the library on a particular subject. It is inadequate as a subject guide mainly because a publication can be assigned only one classification number while its contents may be pertinent to several different subjects.

[1] For a brief but informative description of these classification systems, see Margaret Hutchins *et al.*, *Guide to the Use of Libraries* (New York: H. W. Wilson, 1938), pp. 9–18.

The card catalogue also has its limitations as a guide to materials in the library. On the one hand, it is an index to the collection of only one library. In research, it is often necessary to use the resources of several libraries. At the same time, the catalogue does not index all the materials that are available in the library. Periodical articles, which form a large and important segment of published literature, are not indexed in the catalogue, nor, in general, are parts of books. There are some types of materials that libraries tend to organize in special collections which will not be listed in the card catalogue. Government documents, for example, are often organized separately, with special documents indexes used exclusively as guides to them. Most libraries maintain separate pamphlet collections, also, and do not attempt to prepare any detailed indexes to them.

To find all the materials which may be needed and which cannot be found through the card catalogue, it is necessary to use published indexes, bibliographies, and various types of reference books. Some of the more important of these are listed and described briefly in the following sections.[2]

Periodical indexes. To locate periodical articles on a specific subject it is necessary to consult one or more of a group of publications known as periodical indexes. One of the best known and most used of these is the *Reader's Guide to Periodical Literature,* which has been published since 1900. It indexes by author, subject, and title the articles appearing in about 100 periodicals of general interest, some of which are the *Annals of the American Academy of Political and Social Science, Fortune, Harper's, Life, Monthly Labor Review, School and Society,* and *Time. The International Index to Periodical Literature* (1907 to date) indexes more scholarly periodicals and includes many foreign publications. It is especially strong in science and in the humanities, but it also indexes periodicals in the social sciences. Important American and English periodicals of the nineteenth century are indexed in *Poole's Index to Periodical Literature,* which covers the period from 1802 through 1906.

In addition to these general indexes, there are indexes that are limited to special fields of interest or to special types of publications. A very useful index to materials in economics, political science, and sociology is the *Public Affairs Information Service* (1915 to date). It is a subject guide to books, pamphlets, and government documents as well as to periodical articles. Other special publications which index materials pertinent to the social sciences are the *Agriculture Index* (1906 to date), which is of

special value because it indexes many materials pertaining to rural sociology; the *Education Index* (1929 to date), which covers all aspects of
the subject of education and indexes books, pamphlets, government
documents, and periodical articles; the *Index to Legal Periodicals* (1908
to date); *Psychological Abstracts* (1927 to date), which abstracts as well as
indexes the book and periodical literature in the field of psychology; and
the *Writings in American History* (1906 to 1939–1940), a comprehensive
annual bibliography of books and periodical articles.

A useful index to current affairs is the *New York Times Index* (1913
to date), which is a detailed index to the contents of the *New York Times*
newspaper. Because the coverage of this newspaper is so complete, and
events tend to be reported at the same time in most newspapers, this
index is also a useful guide to materials appearing in other newspapers.
Facts on File (1940 to date), a weekly summary of current events, serves a
similar purpose.

National and trade bibliographies. National and trade bibliographies
are comprehensive lists of publications issued in a given country. They
are indispensable to anyone compiling a comprehensive bibliography on
a specific subject. They are useful, also, for verifying a reference to a
publication which has been listed incompletely or inaccurately in some
other source. Probably one of the most common problems in library
research is this need for verification of a reference. It often means the
difference between finding and not finding a publication that is needed.
The United States Catalog (1899 to 1934), which is kept up to date by
the *Cumulative Book Index,* is the bibliography for materials published
in the United States. It is an author, subject, and title index to publications issued in this country since 1898. Until 1928, this catalogue listed
only publications issued in the United States; since that date it has included publications issued in English in Canada and in other English-
speaking countries. Other countries have similar lists.

Subject bibliographies. The indexes and bibliographies described in
the preceding sections consist of many volumes and cover many subjects.
A considerable amount of searching through them is required to find
materials on a specific subject. It is often advisable, therefore, to determine whether a special bibliography on the subject has already been
prepared and published. If there is one, and if it has been carefully compiled, using it may save many steps in the process of bibliographical
searching. There are, for example, bibliographies such as the *Guide to
Historical Literature* (New York: Macmillan, 1936), an annotated bibliography of basic works and source materials in history; *Propaganda, Communication, and Public Opinion,* by Bruce L. Smith *et al.* (Princeton,
N.J.: Princeton University Press, 1946), a comprehensive reference guide
to materials on the subject of propaganda; and *A Bibliography of Negro
Migration,* by F. A. Ross and L. V. Kennedy (New York: Columbia Uni-

versity Press, 1934). These titles represent extensive bibliographies published in book form. But there are many good bibliographies that are published in pamphlet and mimeographed form, as parts of books, or in periodicals. *The Public Opinion Quarterly,* for example, includes a bibliography of materials on propaganda, communication, and public opinion; and organizations such as the Russell Sage Foundation and the Reference Division of the Library of Congress issue many useful bibliographies on subjects pertinent to the social sciences.[3] Bibliographies appearing in pamphlet or mimeographed form may not be listed in the card catalogue, but this does not necessarily mean that they are not in the library. They should be asked for because they may be filed in the pamphlet or the documents collections.

Library catalogues. Several major libraries of the world, including the Bibliothèque Nationale in Paris, the British Museum in London, and the U.S. Library of Congress, have published author catalogues of materials in their collections.[4] Because they represent some of the largest collections in the world, these catalogues are one of the best sources for verifying references. And because they are catalogues of existing libraries, they are useful for locating publications which it may be necessary to consult. If the person needing a publication in another library cannot go directly to that library, he can often get a copy of it through interlibrary loan if he is engaged in serious research. Should the publication be unavailable on interlibrary loan, a microfilm or photostatic copy can sometimes be obtained.

Union lists. Union lists are publications whose major purpose is to locate and list the actual holdings of specific publications in the libraries of a region. One of the most important of these is the *Union List of Serials in Libraries of the United States and Canada,* edited by Winifred Gregory (New York: H. W. Wilson, 2d ed., 1943; and supplement, 1941 to 1943), which lists all the periodicals to be found in a large number of libraries. A similar list for newspapers is *American Newspapers, A Union List of Files Available in the United States and Canada,* edited by Winifred Gregory (New York: H. W. Wilson, 1947).

---

[3] The following sources are useful for determining whether a bibliography on a particular subject has been published: Theodore Besterman, *World Bibliography of Bibliographies* (London: published by the author, 1947–1949); H. B. Van Hoesen and F. K. Walter, *Bibliography, Practical, Enumerative and Historical* (New York: Scribner, 1928); and the *Bibliographic Index* (1937 to date), a cumulative index to bibliographies, including those that have appeared as parts of books or in periodical articles.

[4] British Museum, Department of Printed Books, *General Catalogue of Printed Books* (London: Clowes, 1881–1900), 95 vols.; Supplement (1900–1905), 13 vols.; and the new edition which began publication in 1931 and now covers A through Cres. Bibliothèque Nationale, *Catalogue générale des livres imprimés: Auteurs* (Paris: Imprimerie Nationale, 1900–1947), 175 vols., which covers A through Soustov. U.S. Library of Congress, *Catalog of Books . . .* (Ann Arbor, Mich.: Edwards Bros., Inc., 1943–1946), 167 vols., which is brought up to date by supplementary volumes. Beginning in 1950, the Library of Congress began publication of a quarterly subject index to materials received.

REFERENCE BOOKS

General and special dictionaries, encyclopedias, yearbooks, directories, and biographical dictionaries are types of reference materials that are constantly useful in research. Because of their general character, these reference materials cannot be indexed in any specific way in the card catalogue or in indexes and bibliographies. The purposes they serve and the specific types of information they contain become apparent only with experience in using them; but the person doing research work should be familiar with at least the types of reference books and their potentialities as source materials. In using any of them, he must be alert to their individual peculiarities in scope, purpose, and arrangement. The need for a careful reading of *explanatory notes* in these publications cannot be overemphasized, since it is essential for correct interpretation of the data presented and for quick and efficient use of the publication. The following are representative titles among the types of reference books:

Dictionaries. In addition to the standard unabridged dictionaries of the English language, there are dictionaries that serve special purposes or interests. They include dictionaries of synonyms, which are useful writing aids, and dictionaries of terms and phrases in particular fields of knowledge. Some of those concerned with fields within the social sciences are the *Dictionary of Sociology,* edited by Henry P. Fairchild (New York: Philosophical Library, 1944); *Dictionary of Modern Economics,* by Byrne J. Horton (Washington, D.C.: Public Affairs Press, 1948); *New Dictionary of American Politics,* edited by E. C. Smith and A. J. Zurcher (New York: Barnes & Noble, Inc., 1949); *Dictionary of Education,* edited by Carter V. Good (New York: McGraw-Hill, 1945); and the *Dictionary of Psychology,* edited by Howard C. Warren (Boston: Houghton Mifflin, 1934). These dictionaries often include information about events and names important to the field, as well as definitions of terms and phrases.

Encyclopedias. An article in an encyclopedia can be useful for quick orientation to a subject and for specific items of information. If it includes a bibliography, as many encyclopedia articles do, it can be useful as a guide to general sources of information on a subject. There are several special encyclopedias of particular interest and value to the person working in the social sciences. One of the most important is the *Encyclopedia of the Social Sciences* (New York: Macmillan, 1930 to 1935, 15 vols.), which includes biographies of men whose work has been significant to the social sciences and articles on all the important topics in the field. Capitalism, Christian labor unions, coal industry, democracy, land tenure, law, League of Nations, legislative assemblies, libel and slander are typical of the subjects covered. The articles, which have been written by specialists, are long and include good bibliographies of source materials. Some of the more specialized encyclopedias pertinent to the social sciences are Walter S. Monroe, *Encyclopedia of Educational Research* (New York: Macmillan, 1950); A. C. McLaughlin and A. B. Hart, *Cyclopedia of American Government* (New York: Appleton-Century-Crofts, 1914, 3 vols.); and Glenn G. Munn, *Encyclopedia of Banking and Finance* (Cambridge, Mass.: Bankers, 1931).

Yearbooks. Many of the needs for specific and current information are met by yearbooks of various types. Since the information they contain is gathered from a wide variety of sources, yearbooks are useful indexes to the kinds of information that are available. Of special value are their references to the primary sources of the statistics included in them. The references are guides to source materials in which more detailed statistics can be found and which should be checked to assure getting accurate, authoritative information. One of the most useful and most comprehensive sources of miscellaneous information is the *World Almanac* (New York: New York World-Telegram, 1868 to date). *The American Yearbook,* issued since 1911 by various publishers, is an excellent review of events of the year, with statistics and bibliographies. The material is presented in articles grouped under broad subjects. The U.S. Bureau of the Census, *Statistical Abstract of the United States* (Washington, D.C.: Government Printing Office, 1879 to date) is representative of official yearbooks of national governments. It is an authoritative and useful summary of statistics gathered by government agencies and, in some cases, by private organizations. The original sources from which the statistics are obtained are always indicated. A supplement to the *Statistical Abstract,* which was published in 1949 under the title *Historical Statistics of the United States, 1789–1945,* is a brief summary of statistics which show the economic, political, and social development of the country. But this volume is more important for the information contained in its descriptive notes than for the statistics it includes. The notes indicate the extent to which historical statistics in each subject covered are available, and the source materials in which they can be found. For political, economic, and social data for the countries of the world, the *Statesman's Yearbook* (London: Macmillan and Co., Ltd., 1864 to date) is practically indispensable. In addition, its bibliographies are one of the most useful and complete guides to official and unofficial national yearbooks. Another source of detailed international statistics is the United Nations Statistical Office, *Statistical Yearbook* (Lake Success, N.Y.: 1949 to date), first issued for the year 1948.

Useful yearbooks more restricted in scope than those just described include the *Municipal Yearbook* (Chicago: International City Managers' Association, 1934 to date), a detailed review of economic, political, and social statistics relating to municipal governments. The bibliographies at the end of each section list sources of statistics, a selection of standard references, and new book and periodical materials. *The Book of the States* (Chicago: Council of State Governments, 1935 to date, biennial) is a summary of information on the organization and administration of state governments, with a selected bibliography of materials on problems of state government. Other examples of special yearbooks are the *Social Work Yearbook* (New York: Russell Sage, 1929 to date); the *Social Security Yearbook* (Washington, D.C.: Government Printing Office, 1939 to date), which is issued as a supplement to the *Social Security Bulletin;* and the United Nations Statistical Office, *Demographic Yearbook* (Lake Success, N.Y.: 1949 to date), first issued for the year 1948, and presenting in detail the demographic statistics presented in summary form in the *Statistical Yearbook* of the United Nations.

Directories. When information cannot be found in available published sources, it can sometimes be obtained from an organization. All organizations maintain files and records which relate to their particular interests and which may yield information invaluable to a research study. Directories which list organizations by their area of interest are, therefore, important types of reference books.

The classified telephone directory is always a helpful guide to organizations in a specific community. The most useful general directories are the U.S. Bureau of Foreign and Domestic Commerce, *National Associations of the United States* (Washington, D.C.: Government Printing Office, 1949), a classified directory of trade and professional associations in the country; *American Foundations and Their Fields, VI* (New York: Rich, 1948); and the *Handbook of Scientific and Technical Societies and Institutions of the United States and Canada* (Washington, D.C.: National Research Council, 5th ed., 1948). Examples of more specialized directories are *Public Administration Organizations* (Chicago: Public Administration Clearing House, 1948); M. M. Chambers, *Youth Serving Organizations* (Washington, D.C.: American Council on Education, (1948); the New York City Welfare Council, *Directory of Social Agencies in the City of New York, 1948–49* (New York: 1948); and the directory of national and state agencies in social welfare work and related fields which appears in the *Social Work Yearbook*. Some of these include brief notes on the history, purpose, organization, and publications of the organizations listed.

Biographical dictionaries. There are two general types of biographical dictionaries—historical and contemporary. In the first category, the authoritative reference work for persons notable in American history is the *Dictionary of American Biography* (New York: Scribner, 1928 to 1944, 22 vols.); for English historical biography, the important reference work is the *Dictionary of National Biography* (London: Smith, Elder, 1885 to 1901, 63 vols., and supplements). Both dictionaries are useful for their bibliographical as well as their biographical information.

Biographies of contemporaries are covered in international and regional "who's who's," and biographical dictionaries devoted to special subject fields. *World Biography* (New York: Institute for Research in Biography, 4th ed., 1948) is the most comprehensive of the international dictionaries. *Who's Who in America* (Chicago: Marquis, 1899 to date, biennial), the British *Who's Who* (London: A. & C. Black, 1849 to date, annual), and the *Who's Who in the Midwest* (Chicago: Marquis, 1949), are examples of national and regional biographical dictionaries of contemporaries. In the subject fields, there are publications such as *Leaders in Education,* edited by Jacques Cattell (Lancaster, Pa.: Science Press, 1948); the American Political Science Association *Directory* (Columbus, Ohio: 1948); and *American Men in Government* (Washington, D.C.: Public Affairs Press, 1949). The *Biography Index* (1946 to date) is a comprehensive guide to biographical information in other types of book materials and in periodicals.

SPECIAL MATERIALS

Periodicals. A group of publications with which the student should become familiar are the learned journals and periodicals which have materials related to his field of interest. They usually contain the most current information on a subject, and they are often the only sources for reports of research studies. In addition, their book-review sections provide a means of keeping up with the important book publication in a field. The following are a few of the important periodicals in the social science fields:

BUSINESS AND COMMERCE: *Commercial and Financial Chronicle, Federal Reserve Bulletin, Harvard Business Review, Nation's Business, Survey of Current Business, Revue des études cooperatives, Wirtschaft und Statistik.*

CULTURAL ANTHROPOLOGY: *American Anthropologist, Human Organization, Journal of American Folklore, Yale University Publications in Anthropology, L'Anthropologie, Zeitschrift für Ethnologie.*

ECONOMICS: *American Economic Review, Economic Journal, International Monetary Fund Staff Papers, Journal of Political Economy, Oxford Economic Papers, Quarterly Journal of Economics, Economica.*

EDUCATION: *Journal of Educational Research, Journal of Educational Sociology, School Review, Review of Educational Research.*

GEOGRAPHY: *Annals of the Association of American Geographers, Economic Geography, Geographical Review.*

HISTORY: *American Historical Review, Current History, Bulletin of the Institute of Historical Research, Mississippi Valley Historical Review, Revue historique.*

INTERNATIONAL RELATIONS: *American Journal of International Law, Foreign Affairs, Foreign Policy Reports, International Affairs, Revue d'histoire diplomatique.*

JURISPRUDENCE: *Journal of the American Bar Association, Lawyer's Guild Review, Law and Contemporary Problems, Journal du droit international, Journal of Comparative Legislation and International Law.*

LABOR: *International Labor Review, Monthly Labor Review, Personnel Journal.*

POLITICAL SCIENCE: *Annals of the American Academy of Political and Social Science, American Political Science Review, Journal of Politics, Journal of Public Administration, Political Science Quarterly, Revue politique et parlementaire.*

PSYCHOLOGY: *Journal of Abnormal and Social Psychology, Journal of General Psychology, Journal of Social Psychology, Psychological Monographs, Psychological Bulletin.*

SOCIAL WORK AND SOCIAL MEDICINE: *Social Service Review, Survey, British Journal of Social Medicine, Journal of Social Hygiene.*

SOCIOLOGY: *American Journal of Sociology, American Sociological Review, British Journal of Sociology, Sociology and Social Research, Rural Sociology, Register of Research in the Social Sciences, Social Forces, Jahrbuch der Sozialwissenschaft, Sociological Review* (England), *L'Année sociologique.*

STATISTICS: *Biometrics, Journal of the American Statistical Association, Econometrica.*

Among the many general periodicals which contain materials pertinent to the social sciences are *Atlantic Monthly, Commentary, Harper's Magazine, Nation, New Republic, Twentieth Century, Virginia Quarterly Review,* and *Yale Review.*[5]

United States government documents. Publications of the Federal government are particularly rich source materials for social research. For the political scientist, records of the proceedings of Congress and congressional committees, bills, laws, and reports of the many divisions of government are the raw materials for research in the field of government. For the person who has never had to refer to them, the term government document is frequently associated only with this group of publications. But there is a vast amount of government publication that bears little or no

[5] For a listing of important American and foreign periodicals in the various subject fields, see *Periodicals Directory, A Classified Guide to a Selected List of Current Periodicals, Foreign and Domestic,* Eileen C. Graves, ed. (New York: Bowker, 1951), 6th ed. One of the useful features of this directory is that it indicates in which publications each periodical is indexed.

relation to the problem of the machinery of government and whose value to social research generally is immeasurable. Government agencies gather and publish data reflecting political, economic, and social developments in the country on a scale that no individual or private organization could approach. Nor are the types of publications limited to compilations of statistics; they include dictionaries, handbooks, reproductions of historical documentary materials, bibliographies, periodicals, and other types of publications useful for reference and research. Among the numerous divisions that issue publications of value to social research are the Bureau of Agricultural Economics, Bureau of the Census, Congress, Federal Bureau of Investigation, Bureau of Foreign and Domestic Commerce, Bureau of Labor Statistics, Bureau of American Ethnology, Federal Reserve System Board of Governors, Public Health Service, Social Security Administration, Children's Bureau, and Office of Education.[6]

Some of the documents are indexed in the *Education Index, Agriculture Index,* and similar types of publications. The comprehensive index to United States documents is the *United States Government Publications Monthly Catalog* (Washington, D.C.: Government Printing Office, 1895 to date), which lists documents by name of issuing agency, and includes a detailed subject index in each monthly issue and for each year. In libraries which maintain separate documents collections, the *Monthly Catalog* and other documents indexes are often used exclusively as guides to them.

State and local documents. Some of the publications issued by state and local units of government are useful reference and research materials. At the state level, legislative journals, statutes, state yearbooks or legislative manuals, and the publications of departments of public welfare, of extension divisions, and of agricultural experiment stations are pertinent. The publications of the last two types are of special importance as source materials for questions relating to rural sociology. Many important state documents are indexed in publications such as the *Agriculture Index,* the *Education Index,* and the *Public Affairs Information Service.* The most comprehensive listing of them appears in the *Monthly Checklist of State Publications* (Washington, D.C.: Government Printing Office, 1910 to date), which is prepared and issued by the Library of Congress. There is no comparable list of publications issued by local units of government, but some of them can be found through the *Public Affairs Information Service,* the *Education Index,* and in the listings which appear in the *Municipal Yearbook.*

[6] The following books are useful guides to the publications of the Federal government: A. M. Boyd, *United States Government Publications* (New York: H. W. Wilson, 1949), 3d ed. revised by R. E. Rips; L. F. Schmeckbier, *Government Publications and Their Use* (Washington, D.C.: Brookings, 1939), 2d ed.: and H. H. Hirshberg and C. H. Melinat, *Subject Guide to United States Government Publications* (Chicago: American Library Association, 1947).

International organizations. Among the organizations which gather and publish international economic, political and social data are the American Society of International Law, the Inter American Statistical Institute, the Pan American Union, the Permanent Court of International Justice, the Carnegie Endowment for International Peace, and the United Nations and its allied specialized agencies—the Food and Agriculture Organization, the International Labour Office, the International Court of Justice, the International Monetary Fund, the World Health Organization, and others.[7] Publications of the United Nations and its specialized agencies form the most important single group of source materials for international statistics. They are comprehensive in scope and official in character, many of them continuing publications formerly issued by the League of Nations.[8]

EVALUATION OF SOURCES

The emphasis in this chapter has been upon the value of library resources to research, but it should not be inferred that all published materials are appropriate or reliable sources of information. Because of the errors they may contain as a result of the bias or incompetence of the compiler or the carelessness of the proofreader, secondary compilations should be used primarily as guides to original sources, and the original sources themselves checked whenever possible for the required data. Any secondary source that is used must be analyzed for any factors that might affect the accuracy or the validity of its information. Information about the compiler should be obtained to ascertain his competence, his interests, and his prejudices. The kinds of sources used and the purpose in gathering the material should also be determined if the data are to be evaluated properly. In using any published sources, whether primary or secondary in character, the data to be used must be analyzed within the limitations of the collection methods. Unless these are clearly understood, it is impossible to determine whether the data are applicable to the particular problem for which it is being considered. The student should, therefore, develop a critical attitude toward all published sources and analyze and evaluate carefully any source that is being consulted.

[7] For lists of organizations of this kind, the following directories are useful: Ruth Savord, comp., *American Agencies Interested in International Affairs* (New York: Council on Foreign Relations, 1948); Ruth D. Masters, *Handbook of International Organizations in the Americas* (Washington, D.C.: Carnegie Endowment, Division of International Law, 1945); and *Annuaire des organizations internationales, 1950* (Geneva: Union of International Associations, 1950).

[8] A good review of the indexing of League of Nations and United Nations publications appears in Everett S. Brown, *Manual of Government Publications, United States and Foreign* (New York: Appleton-Century-Crofts, 1950), pp. 100–110. The largest part of this book is devoted to a review of American and foreign government publications, with emphasis on materials of interest to the political scientist. The review is brief but very useful.

SUGGESTED READINGS

Downs, Robert B. (ed.), *Union Catalogs in the United States* (Chicago: American Library Association, 1942).

Fussler, Herman H., *Photographic Reproduction for Libraries; A Study of Administrative Problems* (Chicago: University of Chicago Press, 1942), pp. 1–47.

Hutchins, Margaret, *et al.*, *Guide to the Use of Libraries; A Manual for College and University Students* (New York: H. W. Wilson, 1938), 5th ed.

Russell, Harold G., *et al.*, *The Use of Books in Libraries* (Minneapolis: University of Minnesota Press, 1951), 7th ed.

Williams, Cecil B., and Allan H. Stevenson, *A Research Manual for College Studies and Papers* (New York: Harper, 1951), rev. ed.

CHAPTER 10

Observation

Science begins with observation and must ultimately return to observation for its final validation. The sociologist must, then, train himself to observe carefully. If he can become a good observer, he will start his investigation with more data at his disposal, be less likely to forget that his object of study is social behavior, and be able to maintain a continual check on his conclusions more easily.

Observation may take many forms and is at once the most primitive and the most modern of research techniques. It includes the most casual, uncontrolled experiences as well as the most exact film records of labora tory experimentation. There are many observational techniques, and each has its uses. Since the student should be able to choose which tools are most suitable for his research project, it is worth while to discuss these procedures, from the least to the most formal.

All of us notice some things and fail to see others. Our preferences and alertness, the range and depth of our knowledge, and the goals we seek all go to determine our pattern of selective observation. Few students take conscious note of social behavior. To illustrate this point, the student may use the following test either alone or as a member of a group. In the latter case, a study of the differences between individuals will be profitable. Take a field trip to a factory, a department store, a library, or even to a club meeting. During the period of observation take notes on what you see, writing a complete report on the trip. Now, analyze the report carefully to discover how much of it is concerned with *social* behavior. Many students will record the articulation of various processes in the assembly line, or the window display in the department store, and social behavior will receive scant attention. Others will respond emotionally to the gloominess of the factory, its noise, and the speed of the work pace; still others will comment on the vulgarity of the merchandise in the store, or the absurdity of proposals put forward by members of the club. Perhaps there will be some students who record the anomalous or striking social behavior, *i.e.*, the items of literary interest: the derelict who was sleeping in the library, the worker who seemed to be cursing the student group as it passed, the salesclerk who chewed her gum while explaining the ad vantages of the perfume being sold, or the near fight between two club members.

Relatively few, however, will record the items which are likely to be of even more sociological importance, such as the techniques of communication used by workers when they are spatially separated in a noisy factory; the deferential behavior of workmen toward the foreman; the swift change in role behavior when the salesclerk turns from her fellow clerk to the customer; the age and sex distributions of workers in different kinds of work units; the value assumptions implicit in the discussions at the club meetings; the varied social activities apparently being served by the library; or the informal hierarchical pattern of power which is evident among the club members. In short, we are not likely to be conscious of "obvious" social behavior, and few of us deliberately record the social interaction which goes on around us.

If the student finds, in the test just suggested, that he has mainly jotted down items which relate mostly to the physical situation, engineering relationships, or economic patterns, a first, obvious procedure for improving his power of observation is simply to develop an alertness to social phenomena. The student may smile at such advice, for it sounds like pulling oneself up by one's bootstraps. However, we do notice some social phenomena, since we are adjusting constantly to new social situations. We are aware of differences in status and changes in roles, for we act differently toward people of different social strata and occupations, or even toward different members of our own families (father, grandfather, brother, distant cousin, etc.). It may be true, on the other hand, that we have not consciously formulated these differences. We may "sense" antagonism between friends, or we may suspect the intentions of a stranger, without attempting to record the cues which led us to this feeling. Simply becoming aware of this failure may, therefore, cause us to see many items of social behavior to which we had given little previous thought.

SIMPLE OBSERVATION: UNCONTROLLED, PARTICIPANT AND NONPARTICIPANT

Most of the knowledge which people have about social relations is derived from uncontrolled observation, whether participant or nonparticipant. The controls in this case refer to the standardization of observational techniques or, in some cases, controls over the variables in an experimental situation. That is, we have learned about social behavior from the situations which we have witnessed or participated in, and our observations were not checked by other observers, by a set of specific items to be noted down, or by a detailed outline of experimental expectations. Scientific observation develops, however, from the most casual experience with a subject to the most formalized, abstract measurement of variables by the use of precision instruments. Even when a science has had a considerable growth, the simple forms of looking and listening are not superseded. Not only do they contribute to the basic, varied stock of knowledge about social relations with which we all begin our study, but they are the principal data-gathering techniques for many modern investigations.

Let us first discuss the uses and problems of uncontrolled, participant observation. This procedure is used when the investigator can so disguise himself as to be accepted as a member of the group. In his study of hobos, for instance, Nels Anderson often traveled and lived with these men without revealing that he was a social scientist. A recent study of professional dance musicians was carried out by a student who was accepted as a young piano player.[1] The English polling group Mass Observation has utilized various camouflage techniques. One observer may mingle as a laborer with other laborers or work as a porter in a barber shop.

The sociologist need not carry out exactly the same activities as others, in order to be a participant observer. He may, instead, attempt to find some other role which is acceptable to the group, while not divulging his real purpose. That is, he may find a role in the group which will not disturb the usual patterns of behavior. Thus, he may enter the community as a local historian or a botanist in order to record its informal social relations. The anthropologist also follows this pattern in part, since he usually participates in tribal activities if this is permitted. We see, then, that participant observation may vary from complete membership in the group to a part-time membership in the group.

It can be taken for granted that if the members are *unaware* of the scientist's purpose, their behavior is least likely to be affected. Thus, we may be able to record the "natural" behavior of the group. Furthermore, to the extent that the student actually participates, many of his emotional reactions will be similar to that of true members. Thus he has access to a body of information which could not easily be obtained by merely looking on in a disinterested fashion. He will feel the exhaustion and exhilaration of a tribal dance, the cold and hunger of the hobo, the bitterness of the steelworker who is bullied by the foreman. He thus obtains a greater depth of experience, while being able to record the actual behavior of other participants. Since his period of participation may continue for months, the range of materials collected will be much wider than that gained from a series of even lengthy interview schedules. He is able, further, to record the context which gives meaning to expressions of opinion, thus surpassing the richness of the usual questionnaire. He can also check the truth of statements made by members of the group.

[1] Nels Anderson, *The Hobo* (Chicago: University of Chicago Press, 1923); Dean Stiff (pseud.), *The Milk and Honey Route*, with unexpurgated glossary (New York: Vanguard, 1931); Howard S. Becker, "The Professional Dance Musician and His Audience," *American Journal of Sociology*, Vol. LVII (1951), pp. 136–144.

However, this tool has equally obvious disadvantages to be weighed before it is used in field research. Paradoxically, to the extent that the investigator actually becomes a participant, he narrows his range of experience. He takes on a particular position within the group, with a definite clique or friendship circle. He learns and follows a pattern of activity which is characteristic of its members, and thus is less able to find out what fringe individuals are doing. If there is a hierarchy of power, or a stratification of prestige, he comes to occupy one position within it, and thus many avenues of information are closed to him. Further, the role he comes to occupy may be important, so that he actually changes the group behavior.

Similarly, to the extent that he participates emotionally, he comes to lose the objectivity which is his single greatest asset. He reacts in anger instead of recording. He seeks prestige or ego satisfaction within the group, rather than observing this behavior in others. He sympathizes with tragedy and may not record its impact upon his fellow members. Moreover, as he learns the "correct" modes of behavior, he comes to take them so much for granted that they seem perfectly natural. As a consequence, he frequently will fail to note these details. They are so commonplace as not to seem worthy of any attention.

Finally, of course, it is clear that in both participant and nonparticipant observation the problem of observation control is not solved. To the degree that the investigator becomes a participant, his experience becomes unique, peculiarly his own, so that a second researcher would not be able to record the same facts. There is, then, less standardization of the data. Moreover, because the behavior of the group is not affected much by the investigator, the latter must passively wait for occurrences. He cannot set up a deliberate experiment, and he may not upset the social situation in order to change his position (to overhear an exchange of words, to see better, etc.) or leave it in order to observe a more important occurrence somewhere else. In short, his role of observer is handicapped somewhat by his being a participant.

Nonparticipant observation answers some of these objections. The anthropologist actually moves from one role to the other while in the field. He may, for example, go on a fishing trip as a participant, but during the preparations for an important religious ceremony he will interview formally the important participants, or record the ritual chants during the ceremony. This shift is made easier by the fact that the patterns of the society are not likely to be changed in important ways by the presence of an outsider, if the role of the latter is properly defined.

As the student can understand, purely nonparticipant observation is difficult. We have no standard set of relationships or role patterns for the nonmember who is always present but never participating. Both the group and the outsider are likely to feel uncomfortable. And, naturally, for many research situations it is almost impossible for the outsider to be a genuine participant in all ways. The sociologist cannot, for example, become a criminal in order to study a criminal gang, without running the risk of completing his report in prison. Neither can he be a true member of a juvenile gang, a spiritualist sect, a police squad, and so on.

On the other hand, it is not necessary that his role playing be complete. It is possible to take part in a great many activities of the group, so as to avoid the awkwardness of complete nonparticipation, while taking on the role of the observer and interviewer for other activities. This has been a classic pattern in social research. It was used by Le Play a century ago in his study of European working-class families, and by the Lynds in their modern studies of Middletown. In such surveys, the investigators have lived as members of the family, as participants in community activities, taking part in games and dances, or even in study groups. They nevertheless made clear that their purpose was to gather facts.

Nonparticipant observation is, then, usually "quasi-participant" observation. Carrying out both roles is simpler than attempting to disguise oneself completely. What is necessary, on the other hand, is a good plan for entering the group. In Merton's housing study, the research team developed a careful plan for dual entry into the community—privately at the higher administrative level of the housing project manager, and publicly at the level of community organizations.[2] Thus, they avoided the problem of being identified with the manager, while obtaining the official permission which was necessary for effective field work. Whyte, in his study of "corner boys" in an Italian slum, entered as a local historian under the auspices of Doc, a key member of a gang.[3] Similarly, a nonparticipant study of a self-determined selling group utilized the procedure of approaching a union representative first, but also obtaining permission from management before actual entrance.[4]

It is the experience of most field researchers that after the initial period of introductions and explanations, the members of the community or group accept the presence of the field workers as legitimate. If the first interview contacts are satisfactory, the succeeding contacts are facilitated. Although the role of social researcher is not a clear one in our society, it is sufficiently known to require no elaborate justification. And, as is discussed at length in the chapter on interviewing, the capable student explains his activities best by carrying them out with some competence.[5]

[2] Robert K. Merton, "Selected Problems of Field Work in the Planned Community," *American Sociological Review*, Vol. XII (1947), pp. 304–312.

[3] William F. Whyte, *Street Corner Society* (Chicago: University of Chicago Press, 1943).

[4] Nicholas Babchuk and William J. Goode, "Work Incentives in a Self-determined Group," *American Sociological Review*, Vol. XVI (1951), pp. 679–687.

[5] See Florence Kluckhohn, "The Participant Observer Technique in Small Communities," *American Journal of Sociology*, Vol. XLVI (1940), pp. 331–343.

The investigator then has several useful roles from which to select. He is a stranger, and thus less involved emotionally with the social situation. True members may thus feel relatively free to talk over tensions and delicate matters which they would not discuss with their own intimates. The researcher is also a listener. Further, he is a pupil, eager to learn, and by that eagerness indicating his belief that the community or group is a significant one. In addition, of course, for most interaction he may shift into his role of participant, so that he does not remain a mere alien.

AIDS IN SIMPLE OBSERVATION

Because there are relatively few controls on the observer in the use of this technique, he must self-consciously apply a range of tools for systematizing and recording the data which are part of his experience. Of course, the prime organizational factor for any research must be the research problem itself. From the hypothesis and the basic plan of the investigation will be drawn the categories of facts to be observed. Many facts must be ignored. Others will be ignored unless they are integrated into a system of recording phenomena which are significant for the project.

The basic document will be, of course, some type of field-experience log. This may take the form of a diary, or it may be a daily record of each item, written under appropriate subheadings. Thus, there might be a set of subheadings dealing with "socialization": crisis situations involving mother and child, scolding by mother, aggression by siblings of various ages, weaning, toilet training, etc. Since social action is swift and the day long, in many cases it will be profitable to keep running notes. These may be scribblings on small cards, key words written in a notebook, or typed notes written at odd moments during the day. It is not usual to be able to carry out the latter, except during periods of interviewing. In any event, the record must be relatively complete, and almost certainly will not be complete without the use of notes taken during the day, and a conscientious attempt to make a full log at the end of the day. It is a frequent failing to believe that a comment or occurrence is so striking that it will not be forgotten. The student will find, when he reads over his complete record several weeks later, that many items will seem novel and possessed of greater meaning than was obvious at the time of note taking. It is particularly important to write out details during the early phases of the field work, for later many of these details will have faded into the expected and taken for granted.

Whether or not the original notes are recorded under subheadings, they must later be reanalyzed and placed under the appropriate categories. The reasons are fairly obvious. If the study has been properly focused, certain types of data are more important than others. Analysis of the notes may show, however, that emphasis has been placed upon other types of data. Thus, the presumed purpose may be to study socialization, but the notes may be concentrated upon other "interesting" occurrences, such as conflicts and gossip, extramarital sexual behavior, or food habits. These may be relevant to socialization, but whether or not they have been chosen for that purpose, or for an extraneous purpose, can be seen when the notes are organized. Further, it is then possible to correct the error while field work is in progress. Otherwise, much time and money will be wasted. Moreover, by a continuing attempt to organize these observations, new categories will emerge, as well as related problems. It is likely that the student will not have time to carry out systematic coding and indexing operations, but even preliminary categorization is useful if it is done each day.

The investigator may find it profitable to record both observation and interpretation of the observation. In general, this cannot be done methodically, and too often the temptation exists to record the interpretation merely because it seems more meaningful. However, it is better research practice to separate the two, and to connect them by cross-indexing. If there is limited time, and this seems always to be the case, then a record of the item without the interpretation is more useful.

On the other hand, it is absolutely essential that continuing analyses or reports be made while the field work is under way. Ideally, these should be sent to colleagues who are not in the field, so that their added perspective may be used in the gathering of further data. Often, the researcher has failed to see or record items which the outsider believes are crucial. Such suggestions may, furthermore, lead to a restructuring of the research aims, or demand proof of tentative conclusions. If the field work is being done by a team, periodic analyses and reports will be discussed for the same purposes. However, for maximum fruitfulness, such reports should also be subjected to criticism from those not in the field.[6] When possible, the field worker may find it useful to leave the field from time to time, in order to think over the problems encountered and the data gathered, as well as to gain perspective on the research as a whole.

It is also the practice in such field work to supplement uncontrolled observation by schedules of information. These will have been drawn up in outline before beginning the work, and will be revised in the field. Often, these will contain such basic organizing data as age, sex, and numbers of individuals; occupational structure; religion; income; hierarchy of power; family pattern; etc. Even when these items are not the principal focus of the research, they will be essential for any description of the group, community, or organization. Sometimes a family schedule

---

[6] For a model pattern of utilizing both formal and informal techniques, and of utilizing the data at every stage to guide the research at the following stage, see the forthcoming *Patterns for Living: Explorations in the Sociology of Housing*, by Robert K. Merton, Patricia S. West, and Marie Jahoda (Harper).

will be used, with detailed questions about this institutional area, to be asked of all families or a sample of them. The point of such schedules is simply that recording only what is seen may dim the background against which those occurrences were seen. Everything seems so familiar to the investigator that he must be reminded to record the self-evident. For this reason, again, other aids may be used. For rural groups or for most communities, various maps may be used so as to report accurately the movements of people, their proximity to one another, or to set the detailed data in their physical context. Sociometric diagrams may be drawn, to develop with some precision the neighboring patterns, the likes and dislikes, or the structure of influence between individuals. Finally, of course, there are increasing attempts to use the modern tools of the film and the wire recorder.

Although uncontrolled participant and nonparticipant observation are often used as the exploratory phases of a research project, to ascertain whether a more sharply drawn hypothesis could be tested in the field, we must keep in mind that there is no opposition between these techniques and any tools of quantification that may be useful. Informal methods may be supplemented by highly structured observation, by detailed questionnaires, and by psychological or sociological tests. Furthermore, it is possible to quantify the protocols of case histories and field observation by the techniques of qualitative coding. Thus, what the sociologist or social anthropologist does in an unsystematic fashion, in order to arrive at any conclusions at all, can be carried out by more reliable procedures. For a discussion of qualitative coding, the student should read the chapter on qualitative analysis.

SYSTEMATIC OBSERVATION: CONTROLS OVER THE OBSERVER AND THE OBSERVED

It is clear, however, that as the precision of the hypothesis increases, so must the precision of the concepts and the data. Simple observation is most useful in exploratory studies, but the investigator gradually sees the need to supplement his notes with more carefully drawn schedules and questionnaires, with tests, and with better controls over the techniques of observation. It is the universal experience of every science that the perception of the individual observer must be corrected in various ways. Checks on his biases, his selective perception, and the vagueness of his senses must be built into the research. There must be objective standards against which to correct his measurements. Otherwise, it is difficult for other scientists to find the same facts. Vague impressions of body build are replaced by anthropometrical measurements. Guesses about distance can be corrected by exact maps. Casual hunches about friendship patterns can be checked by definite counts, cross tabulations, or sociometric diagrams. We can think of systematic observation, then, as being a later stage in the development of a project. As our ideas grow in depth and sharpness, we wish to rely much less upon uncontrolled observation. Since the sociologist is often in the position of the astronomer, the vulcanologist, or the comparative psychologist attempting to study the lives of animals in their natural habitat, in that it is rather difficult to control the *object* under investigation, he must at least put controls *on himself*. Thus he increases precision, and at the same time he protects his work from later attack. By reporting how he made his observations, under what conditions, when, and so on, he makes it possible for other scientists to know the limitations of his data, and to repeat the observations.

In these terms, the formal interview, the inventory or schedule, and maps are controls over the observer. They guide him to certain types of observations, and the instructions for using these tools are also instructions for other investigators. However, it is useful at this point to concentrate upon systematic controlled observation in the more usual sense, *i.e.*, the witnessing of social interaction.

Here, as in uncontrolled observation, the researcher is ordinarily not limiting the activities of the observed individuals to any great degree. Rather, he is trying to systematize the process of observation. However, as a consequence, in both these types he may be unprepared for new situations, and they may not be useful for his problem. Further, the role of the observer remains as a problem to be taken into account when the design of research is planned. The observer always affects the resulting observations in some fashion. What the scientist can do, however, is to reduce this effect, limit it to minor areas, or at least measure it.

Thus, we must consider (1) whether the situation is to be a "natural" one or a contrived one, and (2) whether those observed are to be aware or unaware of the observation. In most uncontrolled observation, the situation is natural, and those observed are aware that there is a witness. This may also be true for controlled observation, but variations are possible. A common tool for the observation of children in nursery situations, for example, is the one-way visual screen. Study of aggression, leadership, communication, patterns of play, etc., is thereby facilitated. Often this is carried out with a team of observers, each of whom is recording particular types of behavior. These may be synchronized through the use of time units, marked off on the recording paper. Either wire recordings or hand-written notes on language may be made. It is often the practice to integrate the observations further by having one student record the major patterns and movements, with which to compare the detailed notes. In this type of observation, of course, the children are in a natural situation, and they are unaware of the observation. As we shall note in the next section, the investigator may actually create new situations by introducing stimuli, again without the knowledge of the children.

Controlled observation may also be directed toward situations which are natural, but in which the subjects are aware that they are being observed. This has been done most successfully with "small-group research," a rather loose term used to refer to studies of the interaction between members of both formal and informal groups meeting face to face. When groups have been brought together for this purpose, the situation is contrived, but often the groups being studied are carrying out their usual activities. In either case, it is usually found that after an initial period of restraint due to the presence of observers, or awareness of their presence, the participants act naturally.[7] Thus it is possible to achieve some quantification of the data being gathered, even though the subjects have not changed their behavior in any fundamental way. It is almost unnecessary to comment that the use of precise observing observation techniques, including mechanical aids, films, etc., is fruitful only when the categories of data and the tentative hypotheses are clearly developed. Otherwise, the analysis of the resulting mass of material is likely to bog down in trivial tabulations, and the expense will not be justified by the result.

Systematic observation limits the bias of the individual observer partly by making the subjects feel the situation as natural, but far more through the applications of controls on the observer in the form of mechanical synchronizing devices, team observation, films and recordings, schedules and inventories, the development of elaborate categories for locating and coding observed behavior quickly. It is but a step from highly refined observational situations to the genuine laboratory situation, in which controls are applied to both observer and observed. That is, the situation is a contrived or manipulated one, in which definite stimuli are introduced, while the observations themselves are standardized as far as possible. As the student can note in the chapters on the design of proof, many of these studies are "quasi experiments" in that some element of the proof is missing, such as a control group. Thus, observation of nursery school children at play may be varied by introducing a single desirable toy in order to create rivalry situations, by changing the role of the nursery teacher, and so on.

However, the introduction of experimental variables into the situation creates no new observational problems. Whether the subjects are aware or unaware of the nature of the experiment, the role of the observer must be taken into account when planning the study. It is no great advantage to the result that the subjects are unaware, if the observational techniques

[7] Cf. R. Freed Bales, *Interaction Process Analysis* (Cambridge, Mass.: Addison-Wesley Press, 1950), and G. E. Swanson, "Some Problems of Laboratory Experiments with Small Populations," *American Sociological Review*, Vol. XVI (1951), pp 349–358.

are nevertheless loose, unstandardized, or with an unknown amount of distortion. The observer is a mediator between the actual situation and the data. Thus, he may affect the actual situation by interfering actively, or he may affect the data by either his skill at observation or his recording procedures. In any case, the final research is changed. Consequently, the researcher must keep in mind that "role of the observer" does not only mean the myriad ways in which the investigator may change the behavior of the group or persons being studied; it can also refer to all the ways by which the observer can affect the final results of the research. Within such a meaning must also fall the process of interviewing, which is discussed in later sections of this volume.

Social relations in factory situations have been the object of study in several studies which approximated experimental designs, as noted earlier. A good illustration of the complex ways by which the observer affects the data may be taken from the Hawthorne study.[8] Its earlier phases were occupied with the psychophysical problem of work output under varying conditions of illumination. The investigators carried out elaborate precautions to ensure standardization and precision of observation. However, the work led to apparently anomalous results, since the work output not only increased when illumination was increased, but also increased when it was decreased to almost the level of a bright moonlight night. However, analysis of this illumination research indicated that none of these controls, and perhaps none of the variables to be measured, was so crucial as the *fact* of being observed. The subjects responded to the changed social situation, in which they and their work were given attention, consideration, and prestige which had not previously been part of their factory experience.

On the other hand, various studies in the social structuring of perception have contrived quasi-experimental situations in which the subjects did know that they were to be observed, but did not know the *purpose* or meaning of the variables. Perhaps the classic case is Sherif's work on the autokinetic effect.[9] Subjects were placed in a room which was completely dark except for a pinpoint of light. They were told that the light would soon begin to move and were asked to estimate the amount of movement. Various social situations were then contrived so as to measure group influences upon individual measurement, differences between groups, etc. The subjects were misinformed, however, in that the light did not move, and of course they were told nothing about the interest in social influences. This design, then, maximized control over the observer

8 F. J. Roethlisberger and W. J. Dickson, *Management and the Worker* (Cambridge, Mass.: Harvard University Press, 1939).
9 Muzafer Sherif, *The Psychology of Social Norms* (New York: Harper, 1936).

and the observed even though the subjects were aware that they were under study.

SUMMARY

All scientific study depends ultimately upon the observer. As a science develops, its hypotheses require more precise data. In the physical sciences the observer's senses are extended and "standardized" by the use of mechanical devices. However, the observer is always a variable to be taken into account. In the case of sociology, much information must be gathered before a genuine experiment can be designed, and both participant and nonparticipant observation are used for this purpose. In either case, the groups being studied may be aware or unaware that the research is being done. However, the situation is not usually a contrived one. The social scientist may attempt to pass as a true group member, or as a member with some acceptable role other than his true one. On the other hand, after an initial period of establishing rapport, the nonparticipant may become a quasi participant who takes part in most social processes without denying his research activities.

Most studies are preceded by some uncontrolled observation of the relevant phenomena. This furnishes valuable preliminary data, while helping in the development of the more precise observations which should occupy a later phase of the investigation. Controls can be applied to the observer by controlling the situation itself, by restricting or defining carefully the participation of the observer, by the use of precise categories, and by utilizing schedules and other standardized tools for observation and the keeping of records. The laboratory experiment does not pose new problems beyond those faced in systematic, controlled observation, such as the study of small groups. In both cases, the need for precise data which are repeatable by other scientists must lead to the use of any tools which will be useful, and these often include mechanical aids such as films, recordings, the interaction recorder, timing devices, etc. However, it must be kept clearly in mind that we seek data which support or reject important hypotheses. Precision is necessary, but the achievement of precision in data which are of little significance is not an adequate justification for the use of such tools. We cannot eliminate the effect of the observer in science; we can, however, limit and measure this effect and thus gain some control over the variables in the research.

SUGGESTED READINGS

Anderson, Nels, *The Hobo* (Chicago: University of Chicago Press, 1923).
Kluckhohn, Florence, "The Participation Observer Technique in Small Communities," *American Journal of Sociology*, Vol. XLVI (1940), pp. 331–343.

Merton, Robert K., "Selected Problems of Field Work in the Planned Community," *American Sociological Review,* Vol. XII (1947), pp. 304–312.
Swanson, G. E., "Some Problems of Laboratory Experiments with Small Populations," *American Sociological Review,* Vol. XVI (1951), pp. 349–358.
Whyte, William F., *Street Corner Society* (Chicago: University of Chicago Press, 1943), Preface, Introduction, and Chap. 1.

CHAPTER 11

Constructing a Questionnaire

In the preceding chapters the specification of concepts, the formulation of hypotheses, and the development of research design have been discussed. More specific definitions of these must now be considered, as we discuss the construction of a questionnaire or interview schedule.

It is precisely at this point that the student will see concretely the difficulties confronting the execution of even the simplest research problem. It is frequently an easy matter to criticize a published report by pointing out ways in which its basic schedule could have been improved, or its design simplified or elaborated. The fact that such criticism is relatively easy reflects what can be called the "self-corrective" aspect of science. By this is meant the idea that one outcome of most good research is to point out how a similar problem may be better solved another time.

Criticism of research is all to the good and lays a significant foundation for future work. On the other hand, more than criticism is needed when the student begins his own first research project. He is likely to find that the standards for validity in field work are considerably more rigorous than is the case in most library research. When the student is faced with the concrete problem of proof by field demonstration, he usually discovers that many of the "important relationships" which he may have criticized other researchers for failing to demonstrate are very elusive and difficult indeed. He will find, if he submits a schedule or questionnaire to his classmates for their criticism, that their comments are similar to some he may have made in discussing previously published research.

One common experience is that the student is likely to begin with a problem of wide import but gradually be forced to narrow its focus upon discovering that his list of questions *will not answer the problem at all.* He may also learn that questions whose meaning seems perfectly obvious to him are not clearly understood by others. Or perhaps it will become clear that other questions which seemed entirely objective in content appear as highly biased to his listeners. The formulation of good questions is a much more subtle and frustrating task than is generally believed by those who have not actually attempted it.

Turning to the actual problem of constructing a questionnaire or similar research tool requires some brief comments and definitions. In general the word *questionnaire* refers to a device for securing answers to questions by using a form which the respondent fills in himself. Thus, anyone who has filled in a job application has had the experience of answering a questionnaire.

Schedule is the name usually applied to a set of questions which are asked and filled in by an interviewer in a face-to-face situation with another person. The two forms obviously have much in common, particularly the fact that in both cases the wording of the questions is the same for all respondents.

An *interview guide,* on the other hand, is a list of points or topics which an interviewer must cover during the interview. In this case considerable flexibility may be allowed as to the manner, order, and language in which the interviewer asks the questions.

Each of these three research tools contains a set of related *items,* that is, a set of questions all logically related to a central problem or problems. Not all items, obviously, have the same form, but in general they can be classed by the degree to which they are *structured.* By this is meant the fact that some ways of asking a question leave only a few alternative ways of answering it, while others allow a wide variety of responses. The questionnaire and schedule employ mainly *structured items,* while the interview guide uses a greater proportion of *unstructured,* or "open-ended," questions.

Some types of questions are automatically structured because of the precision of the only categories which can answer the questions. An example of such a structured question is "How old were you on your last birthday?" Another example, frequently asked, is that referring to marital status. This is best dealt with in a highly structured form. Thus the item might be formulated as follows: "Are you at present: Single____? Married____? Divorced____? Separated____? Widowed____?" To ask an open-ended question such as "What is your marital status?" might produce interesting but confusing answers, such as "Fine," "As good as could be expected," or "I'll have to ask my wife."

Many questions, however, cannot be structured so easily. This is particularly true when the responses to the item cannot be anticipated in detail. Thus, in National Opinion Research Center Survey No. 1044, respondents were asked to list what they thought were the main characteristics of a job which made it a position with high prestige. Another similar question in the same survey asked what factors about a job a young man should take into consideration before accepting it.

A more detailed consideration of the problems in the formulation of both structured and unstructured items will appear later in this chapter as well as in the subsequent chapters on scaling techniques, interviewing, and public-opinion research. At this point the task is to consider the basic difficulties which are common to questionnaires, schedules, or interview guides, regardless of whether they employ highly structured or open-ended questions.

RELATION OF ITEMS TO THE CENTRAL PROBLEM

Any questionnaire must be limited in its length and scope. In general, in the absence of special motivations for the respondent, an interview should not extend much beyond a half hour and even this length is difficult to sustain without fatiguing the informant. Self-administering questionnaires should not, usually, require more than 30 minutes to complete, and an even shorter period is desirable.

Such limitations result in an almost dismaying but necessary narrowness in the development of a questionnaire. When one considers the complexity of everyday life, the questions which can be asked are very few indeed. Consider, for example, all the questions which would be needed to explain to a person from another culture even the activities of yesterday, hour by hour. Every meal, with its cooking techniques, its raw materials, its timing, its rituals and manners, its taste ranges, its connections with friends, etc., would require a series of questions. Going to a movie could be the subject for hundreds of questions, ranging from the origin of the movie and its meaning, to the detailed reactions to various episodes as they were experienced. Spending an hour with one's family would require endless explanations of the American kinship system, the individual's relationships with each member, the specific meanings and emotional responses in each conversation of the day. How much more complicated, then, are most of the things sociologists wish to study.

It is clear, however, that when the questioner and the interviewee possess a more detailed experience with the subject of the inquiry, many questions become unnecessary. If they already know something of the kinship structure of the United States, the questions can be fewer in number and more focused in meaning. On a more personal level, a friend may ask, "Where are you going tonight?" and receive the answer, "I'm heading for Great Neck. Looks like a heavy freeze this weekend." This reply, although cryptic to an outsider, may convey a complete message to one familiar with the situation. It means that the respondent likes to hunt geese, and it is the season for hunting geese; he cannot afford to hunt often, and thus goes only when the weather is good; he has been waiting for a heavy freeze; etc. It is, in short, possible to fill in many gaps in information from your own knowledge.

The necessarily narrow picture which can be drawn from a schedule imposes upon the researcher the obligation *to learn as much as possible about his subject matter* before he begins to formulate the questions.[1] Ways of doing this have been mentioned earlier and will be discussed in several subsequent chapters.

The important thing for the student to bear in mind here is that *every item* in a questionnaire ideally constitutes a hypothesis, or part of a hypothesis, in itself. That is, the inclusion of every item should be defensible on the grounds that the researcher can logically expect the answer to be significant for his central problem. This obviously requires the fullest possible knowledge of the area in which he is working.

The process of actually collecting items for a schedule is a long and complex process requiring careful and patient effort, for the exclusion of crucial questions at this point may vitiate the entire research. It is worth repeating here that formulating a questionnaire is no different from the more general problem of determining, as was said earlier, *what are the important questions to be asked*. The fact that a questionnaire will *later* be put into the field does not differentiate the logical processes to be followed, from those of a scientific analysis of data already gathered.

In the ideal (and almost nonexistent) study, rival hypotheses to be tested are carefully worked out, and the logical relationships between those hypotheses and the type of data to be gathered are then analyzed. This process, then, points out those items which will be of value and those which will not be of value. Actually, however, a research originates more often in the existence of some unexplained fact. This then poses a problem for research. For example, one such case is analyzed by Merton, out of data from *The American Soldier:* the group which would seem to have "lost the most" by going into the Army, the better educated soldiers, were *less* indignant about having been inducted than those who would seem to have lost the least—those with less education and position.[2] This kind of observation is usually followed by discussion of the matter with colleagues, lectures on it in university classes, and a study of the apparently relevant literature, in a wide-ranging manner. These activities result in asking several specific questions which could be answered by data already gathered. It is precisely these processes which must be carried out in order to prepare a logically "tight" schedule.

Developing a questionnaire can be thought of as moving from the "inside" outward. What is meant by this is that the researcher should

[1] For an explicit development of this point as a technique, see Robert K. Merton and Patricia L. Kendall, "The Focussed Interview," *American Journal of Sociology,* Vol. LI (1946), pp. 541–557.

[2] For an extended analysis of various facets of this point, see Robert K. Merton and Alice S. Kitt, "Contributions to the Theory of Reference Group Behavior," *Continuities in Social Research,* Robert K. Merton and Paul F. Lazarsfeld, eds. (Glencoe, Ill.: Free Press, 1950), pp. 40–105; and Patricia L. Kendall and Paul F. Lazarsfeld, "Problems of Survey Analysis," *ibid.,* pp. 133*ff.*; as well as the corresponding sections in Samuel A. Stouffer *et al., The American Soldier: Combat and Its Aftermath* (Princeton, N.J.: Princeton University Press, 1949), Vols. 1 and 2.

first lay out tentatively the logical implications of his problem and then draw upon his own experience and the literature for questions which are relevant to those logical implications. At this point, the researcher should consult colleagues, friends, and acquaintances to get their thinking on his problem. Now, the researcher does not have even a rough draft of a schedule, but merely a list of areas to be covered and perhaps rough formulations of some of the questions. This total process is one of obtaining an even larger number of questions and of progressively uncovering omissions, biases, and ambiguities. Ultimately, a preliminary set of refined questions is arranged.

With the formulation of such a list of areas and questions the researcher is ready to move still farther "out" from himself and his friends. The next step should be to submit this list to experts both in the field of the problem and in related fields. With each consultation the same changes occur: (1) the list of possible questions grows; (2) the number of areas which are of interest increases; (3) the number of areas which the research *can* cover must be *decreased;* (4) ambiguities, biases, poor phrasing, etc., are corrected gradually; and (5) a closer logical relationship develops between the parts of the schedule.

Whether the final research plan will use a highly structured set of questions for a questionnaire, or a set of relatively open-ended questions for an interview guide, the researcher will find it necessary to carry out a number of unstructured exploratory interviews with the individuals who have most intimately experienced the social behavior being studied. These interviews are not to form part of the final tabulations. They are used as a guide to the formulation of the questions. No matter how carefully the student has studied the available materials, he must think of his schedule as a *draft* at this stage. He must use this draft in a very flexible manner, exploring with each experienced respondent the possible meanings of each question, probing beneath each answer given, and presenting alternative questions at many points. No matter how much the researcher believes he knows about the subject matter, he must go into the field in order to see how his best major draft seems to "fit the subject." This point, mentioned earlier, will also be discussed below as the pilot study.

THE SCHEDULE AS A UNIT

The foregoing, while emphasizing that each item must be logically related to the central problem, was focused upon the individual items. While each of the items must be judged carefully upon its own merits, another aspect of schedule construction which must be emphasized is fitting the items together in such a way as to make the entire schedule or questionnaire a unity. That is, there should be a logical progression such that the informant or respondent is (1) drawn into the interview by awakening his interest, (2) easily brought along from items which are simple to answer to those which are complex, (3) not affronted by an early and sudden request for personal information, (4) never asked to give an answer which could be embarrassing without being given an opportunity to explain, and (5) brought as smoothly as possible from one frame of reference to another rather than made to jump back and forth.

Turning to point 1 above, it may be noted that the introductory item should be as attention-catching as possible, without being controversial. In fact, schedules or questionnaires often begin with irrelevant or harmless questions. As a result, interview studies may avoid any bias from selective refusals. It seems to be more difficult for an informant to break off an interview or questionnaire than to refuse to begin it at all. Hence, if the first item is controversial, the proportion of people who are negatively oriented to *that particular issue* and who will refuse will be larger than would be the case if the item occurred further along in the interview. Thus if the schedule opens with a neutral item, the refusals will most generally be those from people who would refuse to answer *any* sort of schedule or questionnaire. It should be cautioned, however, that the opening item should either be completely neutral, that is, a type of information which is not part of some other current issue in the community, or it should be at least distantly related to the major issue under study. Above all, the beginning should have the power to evoke interest, to involve the respondent in the interview, without arousing a strong controversial response.

With regard to point 2, placing simpler items first and withholding the more complex ones, it is only necessary to point out that the more involved a respondent is the more difficult it is for him to break off the interview. Therefore, if any items require considerable thought they should not come too early in the schedule. Nor should they come too late, since *informant fatigue* usually sets in within a period of 15 to 25 minutes.

Point 3, the problem of dealing with "delicate" questions, is much the same as point 2, except that informant fatigue is not so important here and such items are generally well left to later sections of the questionnaire or schedule.

The question raised as point 4, that is, not leaving the informant in an embarrassing position without an opportunity to extricate himself, can be illustrated by a question often asked in sociological studies. To inquire of an informant, "Did you vote in the last election (national or local)?" can evoke feelings of guilt under certain circumstances. For example, the respondent may have happened to be a particularly responsible citizen, and may have answered "yes" to a preceding question inquiring whether he was a registered voter. If he had to say "no" to the question concerning voting, he might well feel guilty over this answer. It is useful, therefore, to include a further question as to why the informant did not vote. This provides him with an opportunity to explain his action and will thus serve to release any tension which may have been created. This should be done *whether or not the researcher is interested in the "why" question.* It is often a rather subtle task to anticipate whether or not a question may arouse tensions, though some instances are quite obvious. If a respondent is asked "Have you any children?" and replies in the affirmative, it is not good procedure to follow this with a question, "Are you married?" Nevertheless even such obvious slips have often been made, with damaging results to the study. The question concerning marriage should appear first, and the question concerning children second, and the latter should ordinarily not be asked of those respondents who state they are single, unless they are divorced or widowed. It is important that potential sources of unnecessary embarrassment, subtle or obvious, should be removed from the well-constructed questionnaire.

Point 5, that of moving smoothly from item to item, merely means that questions pertaining to the same general subject matter should be placed together so as to use whatever logical order or time sequence will aid the respondent in answering easily.

Though it seems too self-evident to require mentioning, no interview or questionnaire should be completed without an expression of appreciation for the efforts put forth by the respondent.

It may help to make these principles concrete if an actual schedule is analyzed with these points in mind. An interview schedule utilized in 1947 by the National Opinion Research Center is therefore reproduced below with annotations concerning the reasons for the inclusion of each item, as well as the positional aspects of the items.

The purpose of this interview was to ascertain the relative prestige standing of representative occupations in the United States, to discover whether these were constant among major population segments, and to see *why* high prestige was given to some occupations and low prestige to others. Thus the study was of the survey type rather than the closely knit experimental type. Nevertheless there had to be a rationale for the inclusion of each item. It should be kept in mind also, that while this is an interview schedule, with a few minor revisions it could have been a questionnaire, and the same logic would hold in its construction.

Question	*Comment*
1. Suppose some outstanding young man asked your advice on what would be one of the best occupations to aim toward. What *one* occupation do you think you would advise him to aim toward?	1. An opening question which invites the respondent's participation. He is asked to put himself in the position of giving *advice*—surely not a question calculated to arouse hostility. It is also well selected in that it provides a mental set toward the general subject of occupations.

Question

Comment

2. What do you think is the most important *single* thing for a young man to consider when he is choosing his life's work?

2. Similar to item 1 in function, thus involving the respondent more heavily in the interview. It follows item 1 because it is a logical extension of that question.

3. Last week, were you working, (keeping house), (going to school), or what?

Working for pay or profit or doing unpaid family work on farm or in business . . . . . . 1 *

Looking for work . . . . 2 *

Had job or business, but did not work because of illness, bad weather, labor dispute, or temporary lay-off with definite instructions to return to work within 30 days of lay-off . . . . . 3 *

Keeping house 4

Going to school . . . . . 5 †

Permanently unable or too old to work 6

Retired or voluntarily idle . . 7

Other main activity (specify) . 8

3. Note here that the major concern of the study is with items 3A and 3B rather than with the main body of that question. The reason for the earlier question (3 proper) is primarily to introduce the other questions without making any assumption that the respondent is employed. To have asked this question directly, that is "What kind of work do you do?" would have been a leading question which would bias the results.

Note also, that an explanation is provided, so that those who would have to respond "Not working" to a more direct question need not be embarrassed, but are given an opportunity to explain their position.

* A. What kind of work do you do?

Job _____

Industry _____

3A. This was related to the central problem through the hypothesis that persons of "low" and "high" occupational prestige would react differentially to the prestige pattern of occupations. One finding which bore this out was that people tend to rate their own type of employment higher than others do.

* B. Do you plan to change your general line of work within the next five years?

Yes . . . . 1 †

No 2

DK X

* If 1, 2, or 3, on Question 3, ask A and B.
† If "Plan to change work" or "Going to school last week," ask 3B1 and 3B2.

3B. This was placed after item 3A because having established the present pattern of employment it is easy to answer a question about the future. Its reason for inclusion was to attempt an estimate of whether the "mobile minded" rated occupations differently from those who were not, as well as to lead up to item 3B1.

Question

† (1). Exactly what occupation do you plan to go into?

† (2). How did you happen to decide on that occupation?

† See footnote, p. 139.

4. Now I am going to ask you how you would judge a number of occupations. For example, a *railroad brakeman*—which statement on this card (HAND RESPONDENT CARD) best gives *your own personal* opinion of the *general standing of a railroad brakeman?* (PAUSE.) What number of that card would you pick out for him? (RECORD ANSWER.)

1 2 3 4 5 X   Railroad Brakeman

Try not to judge a job according to your opinion of some one person you know who has such a job. . . . Now how would you judge a . . . ? (PROCEED THROUGH LIST OF OCCUPATIONS.)

4A.

1 2 3 4 5 X   Official of an international labor union
6 7 8 9 0 V   Farm hand

1 2 3 4 5 X   Owner of factory that employs about 100 people
6 7 8 9 0 V   Artist who paints pictures that are exhibited in galleries

1 2 3 4 5 X   Public-school teacher
6 7 8 9 0 V   Insurance agent

Comment

3B1. This follows logically from item 3B and its purpose was to discover what types of jobs represented the majority of "job intentions" among the American population.

3B2. This also flows logically from item 3B as well as from a "school" answer to item 3. Its purpose was to contribute to our understanding of why people elected to enter certain jobs rather than others.

4. By this time the respondent has been involved in the interview, first by giving advice and second by telling something concrete about himself. Now the more difficult part, that of making judgments, is introduced. Note that this is introduced fairly early, before the informant can be fatigued but only after he has already almost committed himself to an interview.

4A. This begins the listing of the occupations by the prestige ratings, which is the direct approach to the central problem under study—how occupations are rated in the United States today, according to prestige.

The occupations were selected from previous occupational studies and by the judgments of experts, in such a way as to provide as full and representative a listing as possible. Representativeness was considered from two points of view—the number of employed persons covered by the list, and the adequacy of the coverage of the potential range of prestige values.

	Question	*Comment*
1 2 3 4 5 X	Priest	
6 7 8 9 0 V	Policeman	

1 2 3 4 5 X	Janitor
6 7 8 9 0 V	Trained machinist

1 2 3 4 5 X	Traveling salesman for a wholesale concern
6 7 8 9 0 V	U.S. Supreme Court Justice

1 2 3 4 5 X	Musician in a symphony orchestra
6 7 8 9 0 V	Sociologist

1 2 3 4 5 X	Automobile repairman
6 7 8 9 0 V	Plumber

1 2 3 4 5 X	Playground director
6 7 8 9 0 V	Government scientist

1 2 3 4 5 X	Banker
6 7 8 9 0 V	Dentist

1 2 3 4 5 X	Radio announcer
6 7 8 9 0 V	State governor

4B.

1 2 3 4 5 X	Captain in the regular army
6 7 8 9 0 V	Restaurant waiter

1 2 3 4 5 X	United States Representative in Congress
6 7 8 9 0 V	Instructor in the public schools

1 2 3 4 5 X	Undertaker
6 7 8 9 0 V	Coal miner

1 2 3 4 5 X	Newspaper columnist
6 7 8 9 0 V	Barber

1 2 3 4 5 X	Owner-operator of a lunch stand
6 7 8 9 0 V	Civil engineer

1 2 3 4 5 X	Night watchman
6 7 8 9 0 V	Biologist

1 2 3 4 5 X	Garbage collector
6 7 8 9 0 V	Garage mechanic

4B. This is included to show how informant fatigue was dealt with in so long a schedule. The occupations were listed in *four blocks*. (C and D are not reproduced here.) The *order* of these blocks was rotated by the interviewer. The purpose was to avoid the possibility that bias due to informant fatigue would concentrate on a few occupations. Spreading it around this way helped to preclude any undue influence upon just a few occupations which were listed first.

Question	*Comment*
1 2 3 4 5 X Tenant farmer — one who owns livestock and machinery and manages the farm	
6 7 8 9 0 V Accountant for a large business	
1 2 3 4 5 X Architect	
6 7 8 9 0 V Railroad section hand	
1 2 3 4 5 X Psychologist	
6 7 8 9 0 V Airline pilot	
1 2 3 4 5 X Manager of a small store in a city	
6 7 8 9 0 V Bartender	

5. When you say that certain jobs have "Excellent standing," what do you think is the *one main* thing about such jobs that gives this standing?

5. This item is aimed at finding out what people think of as being the *basis* for prestige rankings. It is placed here because the respondent has already made a good many judgments as to the standing of occupations, so that the question is much more concrete than it would have been had it preceded the items on the specific occupations.

6. A good many people don't know exactly what a *nuclear physicist* does, but what is your *general* idea of what he does?

6. This item would not normally be included in a study of this kind since it does not really bear on the central problem. Its inclusion here was purely because of its topical interest.

7. About how much schooling do you think most young men need these days to get along well in the world? (PROBE FOR SPECIFIC ANSWERS.)

7. This item was included to secure a measure of the extent to which people feel that education is necessary to getting ahead vocationally.

8. May I ask your age? _____

Circle if estimated 1

8. This is the first question of the factual as opposed to the opinion items on the schedule. Note that the wording avoids the bluntness of simply asking "How old are you?" The purpose of this item is to test the hypothesis that people of different age groups rate jobs differently. It is also included, as are several of the items in the section, to provide a check on the representativeness of the sample, for we can

Question

Comment

compare the results with national census data.

9. (ASK EVERYBODY UNDER 45): Did you serve in any of the armed forces in World War II?

Yes . . . . 1 *
No 2

* (IF "YES," CIRCLE ONE):

Army . . . 1   Marines . . 3
Navy . . . 2   Coast Guard 4

9. This was included to see whether military experience seemed to provide any particular kinds of reactions to the prestige of occupations. This hypothesis was not borne out, and the preliminary findings showing that breakdowns by branch of service yielded such small numbers that these facts were not even tabulated. Except for the purposes of checking the sample this could be considered a wasted item. Almost every schedule or questionnaire will have at least one such result, since it is usually impossible to know enough in advance to include only items which will prove useful.

10. Who is the main earner in your family?

Respondent is main earner . . 1
Some other member of family
is main earner . . . . 2 *
(Relationship to respondent)

* 10A. (ASK IF RESPONDENT NOT MAIN EARNER): What kind of work does (he) (she) do?

Job _____
Industry _____

10. The purpose of this item is to learn whether the informant is the head of the household. It also seems to introduce the next question concerning the occupation of the head of the household.

10A. This information is for the purpose of securing an occupational identification of the head of the household, as providing further information on the hypothesis stated above under item 3A.

Note that, as in item 3A, the question does not ask for occupation but asks for a job description and the kind of industry in which the job is held. This allows for much greater accuracy in recording employment, since occupational designations can be sometimes misleading.

11. What is (was) your father's main occupation? _____

11. This item was included to gather data on a subarea of interest, that of intergenerational occupational mobility. Thus the answer to this item can be compared with the answer to item 3A. Because of the difficulty of recall

Question　　　　　　　　　　　　　　　*Comment*

it was necessary to ask only for *main occupation* rather than job and industry in this case.

12. What is (was) *his* father's main occupation? _____

12. The same as item 11.

13. (ASK EVERYONE BUT RURAL FARM QUOTA RESPONDENTS): Do you or your family rent or own the place where you live?

Rent . . . . 1 *
Own . . . . 2 †
Special conditions
　(specify) 3
Room and board 4
(ENCIRCLE IF RESPONDENT FILLS
　RURAL FARM QUOTA) . . . 5

13. This item was included as a measure of socioeconomic status and as a check on the representativeness of the sample, while also introducing items 13A and 13B.

* 13A. (IF "RENT"): May I ask about how much rent you pay each month? $_____

13A and 13B, These are included to test the hypothesis that different levels of socioeconomic status react differentially to the prestige pattern of occupations.

† 13B. (IF "OWN"): May I ask about how much you think your house would rent for, unfurnished and without utilities? $_____

14. Do you remember the name of the last school you went to? _____
_____

What was the last grade (or year) you completed in school?
Completed college 1
Some college 2
Completed high 3
Some high 4
Completed grammar . . . 5
Five to seven years grammar . 6
One to four years grammar . 7
No formal schooling . . . 8

14. This item was included to test the hypothesis that amount of education is an important determinant of occupational judgments. Note the way this question is phrased in asking for the name of the last school attended. This serves to introduce the question in a gentle fashion, at the same time so focusing the respondent's attention that an accurate instead of a "stock" answer will be forthcoming. The interviewer, of course, had no actual interest in the name of the school as such.

This item also serves as a check on the representativeness of the sample, since the tabulations can be compared with census figures.

Question	*Comment*

15. Did you favor Roosevelt or Dewey in the last Presidential election?

Roosevelt 1
Dewey 2
Neither 3
Don't remember X

15. This item was an attempt to link some measure of "liberalism" with patterns of occupational prestige. It did not prove very useful in the analysis.

16. Did you happen to vote, or were you unable to for some reason?

Did vote 1
Didn't vote 2
Too young to vote 3
Don't remember X

16. This item was aimed at associating political participation with occupational attitudes, but did not prove very useful. Note, however, the cautious method of phrasing so as to prevent possible embarrassment on the part of the informant.

17. SEX

Male 1
Female 2

18. RACE

White 1
Negro 2

19. ECONOMIC LEVEL
(Rate everybody)
A 1 B 2 C 3 D 4
ADDRESS Street_____
City_____ State_____
Interviewer's Signature_____

17, 18, 19 and 20. These items are not asked but are observed by interviewer, in accordance with instructions provided him. Note the completeness of identification which these provide. It is important to have this as complete as the situation will allow, to aid in controlling errors and rechecking where it becomes necessary.

20. Record date interview was made:
3/ /47.

PILOT STUDIES AND PRETESTS

It should be clear to the student that no smoothly organized schedule or questionnaire can be constructed purely on the basis of the procedures just discussed. That is, no amount of thinking, no matter how logical the mind or brilliant the insight, is likely to take the place of careful empirical checking. Two major questions still remain to be dealt with. One is "How does the researcher formulate items in areas where the literature is inadequate?" and the other is "How does he select items for the final schedule, whatever the source of those items?" The procedure called a *pilot study* furnishes an answer to the first, and the *pretest* to the second.

After the literature has been carefully studied and experts consulted, the researcher may still have only a rather vague idea of what are the crucial elements in his problem. A pilot study may then be launched as a step preliminary to the formulation of a schedule. At this stage, all that can be formulated is an *interview guide*. Thus the researcher interviews in the field in a very nondirective fashion. The questions are structured very little and controlled only by dealing with these general areas which he has reason to think are important. During this kind of flexible interviewing, he tries to follow up every promising lead which may appear, as to meaning of phrases, embarrassing areas of inquiry, differences of response to what seems to be the same question, new areas of subject matter, etc. The researcher, then, is not putting neat hypotheses to the test at this stage but is clarifying and formulating hypotheses for a subsequent study. Not only is he uncertain as to the materials he wants to inquire about, but he may even be uncertain as to whom he wishes to interview. This stage does not usually warrant a formal sampling design, but the student must be sure that he interviews a wide variety of the various types making up the final sample to be studied. Further, he must be alert to field-sampling problems which may warn him to take precautions at the stage of formal sampling design.

The results of these "intensive interviews" must then be written up and carefully analyzed, for they furnish the logical basis upon which the subsequent questionnaire will be based. If well done and thoroughly exploited, the pilot study will usually prove to be a substantial saver of time and effort by helping to avoid erroneous and insignificant hypotheses.

At this stage the researcher is ready to set up a *pretest* procedure. This is a much more formal step than the pilot study. It is, in fact, a "dress rehearsal" of the final study. Consequently every part of the procedure must be laid out exactly as the final study will be carried out. The *interviewing* instructions, whether for the individual or for a team, should be in final form, and followed precisely, so as to see whether they will be adequate. If the *questionnaire* is to be used, the cover letter or instructions should be put in final form, and the sample (though smaller) must have the same design as that to be used for the full-scale study.

It follows from this insistence on a "final form," that a good researcher will actually *tabulate* the data from this pretest, in order to see what weaknesses are present. This will include the proportion of "don't know" answers for difficult, ambiguous, or poorly worded questions; the proportion of respondents who refuse interviews or who refuse to return the questionnaire; as well as the marginal comments of interviewers or respondents concerning particular questions. This includes, in addition, some of the unexpected results of following the sampling design. For example, an overlooked area may be discovered, or a major change in ethnic or income distribution within an area, or a great difficulty in locating particular respondents. When the student attempts to cross-tabulate some of the answers to the questions, he is likely to find that certain bits of information are lacking and that the inclusion of one additional question will clarify a number of facts. Inconsistencies in answers may be discovered, and problems of space and typography may be seen. In short, an interplay is created between preliminary field data and later research operations. The best example of this process is to be found in the Merton-Jahoda-West housing study.[3]

In short, the pretest accepts the fact which has been documented thousands of times in scientific research—that no amount of intuition, native talent, or systematic thought will substitute for the careful recording, tabulating, and analysis of the research facts. These facts must be obtained before the final investment of much time, money, and energy in a full-scale project. It is quite likely that the undergraduate student, carrying out his first project, will be unable to divert so much energy to each phase of the study as is desirable. On the other hand, he must keep in mind that the project will, as a consequence, be deficient in many regards. Furthermore, if undergraduates form research teams for such projects, it is likely that each of these steps can be covered with a small sample.

MECHANICAL PROBLEMS

Good records are essential for good science, because no man's memory can ever adequately encompass the variety and quantity of data needed. It is necessary, then, to develop the mechanics of record keeping. This means more than a system for filing schedules and questionnaires, recording dates of receipts, checking forms and making certain that all questions are answered, while keeping sharp watch over the interviews yet to come in. It means more than working out a "flow chart," or "control sheet," for checking each questionnaire or schedule as it goes through the various steps of (1) issuance or transmission to the interviewer or respondent; (2) waiting for completion or return; (3) receipt after completion; (4) checking of the form; (5) filing of the form plus any additional records which may allow quick reference to it; (6) coding, which may be divided into several steps; (7) checking of the coding, whether done by spot checks of items or of whole interview forms; (8) tabulation, whether hand or machine tabulation, simple or complex; (9) tabular presentation; and (10) checking of the tabular calculations.

Before any of these steps in the mechanics of handling the schedule can be adequately performed, it is necessary to see that the form itself is properly designed. Some remarks on this subject are to be found in the chapter on the mailed questionnaire, but they bear repetition in this section, which applies to both the schedule and the questionnaire.

[3] See Hanan C. Selvin, "The Interplay of Social Research and Social Policy in Housing," *Journal of Social Issues,* Vol. VII (1951), pp. 180–181.

Thus, adequate *control* of the records can be obtained only if the form is suited to the needs of the research. For example, if the questions are open-ended in character, there must be a considerable amount of space available for each answer. There must, indeed, be *more* space than seems necessary, for the writing conditions in the respondent's home may be poor, forcing the interviewer to write in a large script for legibility. Again, liberal spacing is a stimulus for the questionnaire respondent to write more fully. Even when the form is to be mimeographed, the paper should be good enough to allow either ink or pencil, for either may have to be used in certain cases. The questions should be spaced, even in short-answer questions, so that the interviewer, concentrating on the interview situation, will not easily confuse the line from which he is reading.

Often a schedule or questionnaire must explore alternate lines of questioning. If the respondent answers "yes" to one question, then a series of questions is offered which is different from the series following a "no" answer. Such series must be set off spatially by indentation, asterisks, or some other technique, so that there is no confusion between the two series.

In a longer schedule, there are likely to be several sections, relating to different aspects of the problem. For example, in a study dealing with postdivorce adjustment, there were sections relating to finances, dating, marital conflict, religion, etc. As noted later, the shift from one section to another may be awkward, and often the designers of the schedule will find it useful to insert a transitional phrase, such as "We have been talking a lot about—; now, would you mind letting me ask you a few questions about—? First of all, —." Any such phrase should be set off spatially, or a different type face used, in order to call the attention of the interviewer to the item. Even if such a phrase is not written into the schedule, some arrangement should draw attention to the new subject matter. The respondent will feel the abrupt transition as a failure to explore adequately the previous subject matter unless it is appropriately shifted. Unless the shift is made obvious to an interviewer in the midst of the interview, the tendency is to rush into the new section without pause.

Very often the questionnaire or schedule is anonymous, in that the respondent's name is not written on the form. However, records are needed to keep track of the progress of the form through the various processes of the research. In addition, it is usually wise to relate the interview schedule to the interviewer who administered it. The date of receipt may also be of importance. At times, there are additional facts to be recorded after the interviewer leaves the respondent: race, type of dwelling or neighborhood, response of the interviewee, etc. For any of these items of information, there should be adequate preparation. A section of the form, often on the face sheet or end sheet, may be set aside for these items, to be recorded in a systematic, standard manner. Such a section will greatly facilitate the record keeping for the study.

Cross tabulations and mock tables. Since any study attempts to establish relationships between variables or attributes, many of the questions in the schedule are determined by this need. Other questions are rather in the nature of "survey" queries, establishing many of the facts needed to describe the social group or set of relationships being investigated. The student may have no particular hypothesis, for example, concerning the number of dates enjoyed by coeds, the amount of child support paid on the average in the state of Missouri, the percentage of Negroes who became noncommissioned officers in World War II, or the ethnic populations in a certain area, but each of these items may be of descriptive value in a study of such phenomena. When, however, certain cross tabulations are the focus of the study, the student will facilitate both his thinking and his formulation of specific questions by working out blank or mock tables; that is, tables with stubs and captions, but no data. Suppose, for example, a study is occupied with the relationship between birth rates and religious affiliation. The accompanying table is an example of a simple form that might be used.

Number of Live Births Per 1,000 Women, 15–45 Years of Age, by Religious Affiliation

Religious Affiliation	Number of Women, thousands	Live Births
Religion *A*		
Religion *B*		
Religion *C*		

Since, however, there is some evidence that one connecting variable between religious affiliation and birth rate is the use or nonuse of contraceptives, the data required (by interview, panel records, etc.) would call for further questions, exhibited in the second mock table here.

Number of Live Births Per 1,000 Women, 15–45 Years of Age, by Religious Affiliation and Contraceptive Experience

		NUMBER OF LIVE BIRTHS		
RELIGIOUS AFFILIATION	NUMBER OF WOMEN, THOUSANDS	Contraceptives Used Regularly	Contraceptives Used Irregularly	Contraceptives Never Used
Religion *A*				
Religion *B*				
Religion *C*				

The careful student will immediately see that the "use of contraceptives" must be broken down still further into *types* of contraceptives and into more definitely quantified *indexes* of use, such as "always," "half or more than half of the time," etc. Further, we know that birth rates do vary inversely, even though roughly (and except for upper levels), with educa-tion and income. Correspondingly, mock tables should be drawn up from the questions in the schedule, *in order to see just what kinds of data are likely to be available after the study is completed.*

This process performs several functions. Seeing concretely what kinds of information are being elicited by the questionnaire or schedule tells the student whether the data will actually prove anything at all. Such tables will help to point out important gaps in the questions and thereby to suggest other questions. Often, they will indicate that the researcher has used several questions to cover the same material, and this discovery helps to eliminate duplication and thus simplify the schedule or ques-tionnaire form. In addition, the tables will be close enough in form to tables already published on the same subject, allowing a decision as to whether the study will attempt to obtain data which can be compared with older studies. Often the student fails to do this, so that there is no cumulative body of fact—merely isolated studies.

Further, and perhaps more important, the student will sometimes find that when the tables are set up which (when the data are inserted) *ought* to prove or disprove a hypothesis, the cross tabulations do not correspond to the questions he has asked. For example, he may have formulated the hypothesis that for social-action purposes the white families living more than two blocks west of "The Wall" in Detroit are not likely to take part in any race friction. This notion is based on the underlying hy-pothesis that there is a decreasing *degree* of concern with racial matters as one moves westward from this traditional boundary. In other terms, the "reference groups" of those living farther away are different, and this is to be expressed by degree of involvement with other groups than those engaging in racial conflicts. However, the student is likely to find that he has many specific questions about racial matters, but none which could be substituted directly in a table whose stubs and captions would read: "Degree of Concern," and "Distance from 'The Wall.'" The latter cate-gory is spatial, and can be calculated easily. The former, however, must be an *index*, to be derived from several questions. At this point, then, the student is required to make certain just how he is going to measure "de-gree of concern." This may lead him to wonder whether "distance from 'The Wall'" can be measured only spatially. Perhaps certain routes are more traveled than others, so that a given distance along them yields different degrees of concern than along other routes. In short, these mock tables lead to a rethinking of the questions already in the schedule and to possible suggestions for other, sharper, questions. And, even when the decision is to make no such tables, it is absolutely essential to think through the cross tabulations to be made, if there is to be any adequate analysis later on.

Spontaneity and flow. Although the analysis of individual questions and groups of questions is necessary if the research is to obtain the required data, some analysis of the whole schedule is equally useful. The respondent must feel that the progression of questions is natural, that the transition from subject to subject is easy, that he is not merely being quizzed but is actually taking an active part in an interesting and useful process. This feeling aids the study, in that cooperation leads to more valid data. But the spontaneity and flow of a schedule also *aid the interviewer in doing a better job,* for he in turn finds the social situation a much easier one and is consequently more relaxed.

Although some researchers have begun their questions with the most central and pressing issues, the more usual and apparently more natural introduction is a section of emotionally neutral, objective questions which are rather basic for later cross tabulations. Some of these are age, sex, marital status, education, occupation, urban-rural origin, length of residence in the locality or neighborhood, and number and age of children. Not all these will be necessary each time, since cross tabulations with all of them may not be desired. On the other hand, many of these items have the double advantage of being basic to most sociological questions, and at the same time amenable to demographic checking by the use of census tract data. The latter data are available for many cities at the present time, and they offer a useful check on the resulting sample. If the demographic indexes in the resulting sample are very different from census or other reliable data, some doubt as to the representativeness of the sample is justified.

The questions should not, however, jump abruptly from such apparently innocent subjects to embarrassing ones. The respondent must be helped along the way by easy transitions. Since most extended interviews attempt to get at more than present attitudes and happenings, often a good transition to the central subject of the inquiry is a request for something about the *past.* Even when such a question is not to be tabulated, it may be useful as a "stage-setting question." That is, it starts the respondent on a train of thought centering on the major area of the study. Many respondents cannot begin to give detailed data until they have been helped to remember. A request for the recent history of the individual may be such a help. This is likely to be an open-ended question, allowing considerable latitude in the answers to be given. Nevertheless, if these data are important for the study, they can be coded and tabulated. The central function served, however, is to get the respondent to think seriously about the subject matter.

Other transitions may be more useful for a given study. In general, these are left to the discretion of the interviewer, but there seems good argument for inserting them into the document as standard forms. Such phrases as these have been used: "You've been telling me a little about yourself; now, I'd like to ask you a few questions about . . ." or "We've been talking about the background of . . . and have been leaving out some other important things like. . . . Let me ask you this . . ." or "You made a comment a moment ago about . . . ; now, there are a few questions I'd like to ask you about that."

Within the actual interviewing process, as discussed in the section on interviewing, various devices can be used to assure flow and spontaneity when the respondent seems unable to answer the question easily. What is important is that spontaneity is to be achieved so that the cooperation of the respondent will help obtain the facts.

These remarks are also relevant to the close of the interview or questionnaire form, where a final question may be used to make a socially appropriate ending to it. Again, it seems useful to include such questions and comments as parts of the document itself, not leaving them to be made up on the spur of the moment by the interviewer. Sometimes this final question may be a request for an *evaluation* of the questioning, which can be used for either the face-to-face interview or the self-administered questionnaire. A request for suggestions to improve it may be useful. A final note or comment of thanks for the cooperation should be included at the end of the form, in order that the interviewer will not forget.

Comparability and reliability. At some point in the development of a study, the student may question the necessity for such a formal document as a questionnaire or a schedule. It is clear that the competent journalist does not use this device, and some of the better social science has been carried out by anthropologists among nonliterate peoples, without using such a formalized set of questions for the primitives to answer. Most of us have a healthy respect for the person who has "lived through it" and a corresponding skepticism for the apparently less meaningful set of questions used in some sociological research. Although this kind of skepticism has been answered adequately in previous discussions, a few reminders are in order. The essence of an adequate scientific method is not merely accuracy in result but accuracy *that can be proved*. It is quite true that a good journalist may often capture more completely what is happening in a group than a poor sociologist. On the other hand, the journalist, like the person who has "actually seen it," is in the scientifically weak position of being unable to prove that what he says is accurate. Further, although in most anthropological monographs the investigative techniques are not presented, the trained anthropologist does have fairly standardized sets of questions to be answered within any primitive society. What is necessary is that the techniques be so formalized that the final results *can be checked.* A set of unique observations is of little scientific importance. Other scientists must be able to repeat them under similar circumstances and conditions. In spite of the many similarities between artistic and scientific creativity, one fundamental difference remains: in the latter activity, the scaffolding by which the edifice was built must be open to the public eye. In a basic sense, a research report is a *set of directions* to other scientists, informing them how they can observe certain data.

As the research becomes more focused, then, the nesessity of obtaining standard data, that is, *comparable information about each case in a given class,* increases substantially. If the information obtained about each case does not deal with somewhat the same items, no dependable statements about the cases can be made. If the age of some respondents is obtained but not that of others, income from some and not others, a life history from a few remaining ones, a job history from another group, courtship attitudes from others, and political participation from still others, a mass of data results, but none of them can be used for the analysis of the entire sample.

The simplest way to assure such comparability, given a definite hypothesis, is to formalize the questions. As noted previously, this requires clearer thinking concerning the kinds of data really needed. Further, the document becomes a protocol for future research as well as for the present study. When the query is made, "How did you come to such conclusions?" the answer lies partly in the questions themselves.

But this question, a basic one for all research, relates directly to that of *reliability,* that is, the extent to which repetition of the study would result in the same data and conclusions. For it is clear that standardizing the questions may yield a mere "paper stability"; the words may remain the same, but under different circumstances the meanings may shift. People forget, so that the answers may change over a period of weeks or months even when the objective facts *and* the questions remain the same. Perhaps a new set of interviewers will obtain different answers to the same questions, because their approach and interviewing technique are different. This is a fundamental set of considerations, and if sociology cannot give a satisfactory answer it must abdicate its claims to be considered seriously as a scientific discipline.

It must be kept clearly in mind that we are not now discussing whether the questions elicit "the truth" from the respondents, but the simple problem of *stability.* We shall deal with *validity,* or getting the truth, in a later section. Truth or untruth, can another sociologist repeat the results by repeating the study?

The immediately pragmatic answer to this problem is that sociologists actually can and do repeat each other's results. Mere repetition of a study is not common, but some studies repeat particular questions, allowing a check on reliability. This is predictable enough that those who are inter-ested in research can actually test *sampling designs,* using the same ques-tions, interviewing instructions, etc., but varying the design of sample. Research experience has shown that, within a known range of error, the answers are stable enough so that the differences can be ascribed to the differences in sample design.[4]

This pragmatic reliability of answers, it is assumed, is part of the under-lying order to be found in all natural phenomena whenever they are systematically studied. However, in the development of any science there are innumerable cases in which there is no apparent reliability. Jenner's attempts at vaccination were not always successful, nor were Pasteur's experiments with anthrax. Even in astronomy, the development of a "personal equation of error" was necessary to take account of the seeming instability of visual observations from one person to the next. However, in all these apparent cases of unreliability, once the underlying problem of technique was worked out, the results became considerably more pre-dictable. It is always discovered *that the previous "experiment" or tech-niques were not repeated exactly,* and new factors of importance for experimental control are then introduced.

In simpler words, another competent sociologist can obtain the same results by repeating the operations. However, he will come to the same conclusions *only by accident, unless he observes the same precautions.* He must keep such matters as these in mind:

1. The sample design must be repeated: If the "repetition" uses a random sample, and the first study used a quota sample, different results may be expected.

2. Interviewing instructions must be the same: If each interviewer has selected his own way of approaching the respondents and his own way of asking questions, or if the "repetition" has a different set of instructions, unreliable data result.

3. Actual changes in the factors being studied may occur: *e.g.,* one expects to obtain fluctuations in the "prowar sentiment" within a country from one month to the next; a group of respondents will very likely give a slightly older set of ages six months after the original study.

4. The meaning of the questions as understood by the respondent must be the same in both studies.

There is nothing mysterious about the last point. It is not true, as students are sometimes led to believe by the criticisms of their questions, that minor differences in meaning yield major differences in results.

---

[4] For example, see Norman C. Meier and Cletus J. Burke, "Laboratory Tests of Sampling Techniques," *Public Opinion Quarterly,* Vol. XI (1947), pp. 586–595; and Norman C. Meier, Cletus J. Burke, and Seymour Banks, "Laboratory Tests of Sampling Techniques: Comment and Rejoinder," *Public Opinion Quarterly,* Vol. XII (1948), pp. 316–324.

Rather, *minor* differences in *wording* sometimes create *major* differences in *meaning*, and the answers of respondents will reflect these differences, because of the simple fact that a different question has been asked. Much of the apparent unreliability between questions in different studies stems from the inability to see that two "similar" questions are very dissimilar. Consequently, we could not expect stable results. To take an extreme case, let us compare some positive and negative forms of a question:

1. Do you approve of spanking children?
2. You *do* approve of spanking children, don't you?
3. Don't you disapprove of spanking children?
4. You don't approve of spanking *children*, do you?

There are other possible variations, but the point is obvious. Forms 3 and 4 are highly suggestive. If accompanied by a sincere, earnest nod of the head, form 2 would cause many respondents to agree, and, correspondingly, if form 4 or 1 were accompanied by an unbelieving look, many individuals who do approve of spanking would deny it. Again, we are not discussing validity, but reliability: Do the same *percentages* of people, and the *same people,* give the same answers when apparently the same questions are asked? Let us note other cases in which what are apparently identical questions are actually quite different:

Now that the war is over, the workers in X industry are trying to get paid for 48 hours of work, while doing only 40. Do you approve or disapprove?

The workers in X industry are trying to get a raise of 20 cents an hour, and also want to cut down the number of hours they work each week. Do you approve or disapprove?

The essential facts are the same in the two questions, but it should surprise no one that researchers using the second form would not be able to repeat the results from the first.[5]

It is now possible to see that in this and the following examples the *unreliability* is basically caused by *validity* factors: the different questions get at different sentiments. Thus the results from one set of questions vary from those obtained from seemingly the same questions. There is, we may say, a fundamental difference of *themes* in the question forms. Roughly put, one form arouses the thematic response, "Nobody ought to get something for nothing." The second suggests a different theme, "Workers have a right to ask for raises." Both forms are open to the charge that they do not really tap public sentiment about the central issues of the labor dispute, but merely check on publicly expressed sentiments about these themes. A comparable set of differences, with different themes, would be the following:

[5] Cf. Arthur Kornhauser, "Are Public Opinion Polls Fair to Organized Labor?" *Public Opinion Quarterly*, Vol. X (1946), pp. 484–500.

A group of communist communities in Montana, the Hutterites, have refused to take part in many political affairs of the state, in the past. Now, however, they have had crop failures, and are demanding Federal aid. Do you approve or disapprove of our giving it to them?

A group of thrifty, independent religious communities in Montana, the Hutterites, have managed to run their affairs successfully as a group for a long time, sharing their land, labor, and crops. Now, however, they need help, and have asked Washington for aid. Do you approve or disapprove of our giving it to them?

Note the differences of themes here: "communist" as against "religious," "independent" as against "not taking part," "communist" against "sharing," "demand" as against "need," etc. Again, the facts are little different, but the emotional responses are greatly different. This underscores the point that the question is not one of bias, but one of obtaining low reliability because the two questions really deal with different things.

Unreliability from such a source takes various forms. Such thematic differences mean that the second researcher will not be able to repeat the data of the first. The differences also mean that different groups or classes of individuals will give different answers. Some of these themes may appear more important to one group than to another, so that even the *structure* of opinion or sentiment, *i.e.*, the amount of difference in attitude from one group to another, will seem different. Finally, since each group or individual may respond more to the themes than to other elements in the questions, the questions basically lack *validity*, that is, they *do not get at the kind of opinion or sentiment which was supposed to be explored.* We merely find out that some individuals accept certain themes which are contained in the questions.

Besides the unreliability due to differences in thematic references, another validity factor may be mentioned—the differences due to group references.[6] Here we see that questions which appear to be similar may yield variant results because not all respondents will use the same group standards when answering. Let us consider the following forms of a question used in World War II research: [7]

"Do you think you have been given enough training and experience so that you could do a good job of taking charge of a group of men on your own in combat?"

"If you were given a group of men and told to take charge of them all by yourself under enemy fire, how well do you think you would do?"

The key word "experience" elicited a consistent response difference, in that less "readiness to assume combat leadership" was tabulated for the first question. However, there was an equally consistent *pattern of response* between groups, which indicated that replacements, veterans, and green troops were using different standards for evaluation, in answer to either

6 See Merton and Kitt, *op. cit.*, pp. 40–105.
7 *Ibid.*, pp. 70*ff.;* and Stouffer *et al., op. cit.*, pp. 249–253.

form of the question. The combat veterans had had different experiences than the green troops. Further, the green troops in green units had only their *own* standards to go by; whereas green replacements in combat units measured themselves by the standards of the combat veterans, coming to very different conclusions. On a much more general level, many questions which ask for measurement, comparison, evaluations, or judgments will have to be shaped with this in mind. Most of the evaluational terms we use, such as "good," "enough," "wise," "often," "immoral," or "ethical" are ambiguous in any schedule, simply because different respondents will be referring to different group or individual standards when answering the questions. Again, this is not a mere matter of question ambiguity in itself, a simple problem of verbal confusion, but a pragmatic matter of not obtaining results that can be repeated by another researcher attempting to measure the same phenomena. With each variation in group reference, a *different question* is being asked in effect, and therefore the resulting data may vary. We must therefore understand this pattern in our respondents, if we wish to obtain stable answers or to interpret the differences.

A similar type of unreliability may result from difference in the *contextual references,* again a validity factor. That is, not only will the differences in group or individual *standards* result in differing data, even when the underlying phenomena are very similar. Equally important, the *context of fact* may be different, so that the question may reflect differences in knowledge, rather than differences in values, attitudes, or even behavior. As a consequence, many questions in public-opinion polls have resulted in data about nonexistent matters, when individuals were queried about a loan to Upper Querzog or the tax situation in Lower Amstk. Individuals will often answer questions concerning matters about which their ignorance is complete, and social scientists have sometimes wondered whether any results could be relied upon, so long as this is the case. This is a validity factor, because the failure of the question is that it does not get at the information sought by the researcher. However, what many such questions do get at is complex and difficult to interpret, and small differences in wording or interviewing may therefore elicit large differences in response, or low reliability.

RECOGNIZING POOR QUESTIONS THROUGH PRETEST RESULTS

Perhaps it is useful at this point to suggest a few signs which indicate that something is wrong in the early drafts of the questionnaire or interview. Specification of what is wrong, and elimination of the error, are the two succeeding steps, but the student must train himself to look for signs of trouble, so that he will know something must be done.

1. LACK OF ORDER IN THE ANSWERS. This is one of the most obvious signs. There is overwhelming evidence that social phenomena, like other phenomena, are ordered. That is, they fall into classes of similar items and into characteristic distributions. A purely scattered or random set of phenomena is unusual and calls for considerable scrutiny. Often the cause turns out to be a question or series of questions which do not tap the same experience in each respondent. This may be due to the use of difficult words, or questions which attempt to obtain too much data at one time, or other causes, but whatever the reason may be, totally unordered answers should always lead to a critical reexamination of the questions. This review of the question must be very thorough, for the lack of order may be caused not by the wording of the question but by a poor *conceptualization*. It may be found, for example, that a distribution of economic factors in a group shows little definite patterning, but that changing the question to deal with the *meaning* of these factors leads to a clearer ordering of data.[8]

Further, certain types of data have known distributions. We expect educational, occupational, fertility, salary, and other data to show characteristic patterns of distribution. If our data show a different pattern, we must at least restudy our questions.

2. "ALL-OR-NONE" RESPONSES. It is obvious that such responses should make us look at our questions again. Everyone is against sin, for patriotism and health, etc., and we can suspect that our question has elicited a mere stereotyped response or cliché, if all respondents answer the same way.

3. A HIGH PROPORTION OF "DON'T KNOW" OR "DON'T UNDERSTAND" ANSWERS. This is a good indication that the questions are improperly drawn, or that a bad sampling design has been used. Frequently, the "Don't understand" group gives the simpler, minimal answer "Don't know," so that these two can be treated together. Some proportion of such DK responses can be expected for almost any question, and of course the proportion to be expected will vary greatly for each stratum of respondent as well as for the kind of question. When the purpose of the question is to determine the proportion of respondents who do not know anything about the public issue, the organization in which they work, or the community in which they live, naturally this datum is valuable in itself. However, when the question is designed to measure public sentiment, or the past history of an emotional relationship, or the communication patterns of a worker with his superiors, a large percentage of DKs suggests (a) that the question

8 As an illustration, see the work of Mirra Komarovsky, *The Unemployed Man and His Family* (New York: Dryden, 1940); the analysis by Samuel A. Stouffer and Paul F. Lazarsfeld, *Research Memorandum on the Family in the Depression* (New York: Social Science Research Council, 1936); and William J. Goode, "Economic Factors and Marital Stability," *American Sociological Review*, Vol. XVI (1951), pp. 802–812.

is vague, or (b) that it is too complex, or (c) that it involves difficult answers on which the respondent needs expert interviewing help, or even (d) that the respondent simply is not in a position to answer the question. It is with reference to the latter point that the student may check the sample design. Perhaps too many respondents have been included whose experience does not relate to the questions. This kind of error may vary from a study of the importance of *Fortune* magazine among a sample which includes many slum dwellers, to an investigation of the beliefs among owners of Texas barbecue stands about the impact of Federal Reserve policies on their businesses. Sometimes the researcher learns thereby that the records or lists from which his sample was chosen are out of date, or improperly labeled. For example, he may ask questions about procedures at union meetings, using respondents selected from a list of supposed union members—only to find later that the list is 2 years old, or is actually a list of all the workers in the factory, not merely union members.

4. A GREAT NUMBER OF QUALIFICATIONS, OR IRRELEVANT COMMENTS. If many of these are offered by respondents when the question poses a choice between several supposedly clear and exhaustive alternatives, it is an indication of weakness. Often the researcher attempts a premature specification of the possible alternative answers. For example, a question relating to sources of news might be formulated as follows: "On the whole, from which of these sources did you prefer to get your news before the newspaper strike—from newspapers, or from the radio?" However, even if no other sources came to mind, a series of pilot interviews would record a number of comments or qualifications, or additional sources, to suggest that the list is inadequate. Some will prefer to get their news from magazines, while others will rely mainly on newsreels or even other people. All students have had the experience of having to answer examination questions whose alternative answer choices seem inadequate. The temptation is to record the qualifications to these choices, such as "*If X can be assumed . . .*" or "*If you mean. . . .*" Such additional comments suggest that the questions need revision and often indicate the precise revisions necessary.

5. A HIGH PROPORTION OF REFUSALS TO ANSWER. If a considerable percentage of respondents refuse to answer the question and a considerable percentage refuse to be interviewed at all, it indicates that the interviewing instructions are not adequate or the interviewer training is insufficient. However, *within* the questionnaire or interview some questions will remain unanswered. It is difficult to state an exact figure, but the researcher would do well to restudy carefully any question for which the refusal rate is over 5 per cent. Sometimes the fault lies in a poor *transition*. That is, a taboo subject is brought up without any warning, or a question seems out of context. For example, a questionnaire may seem to be devoted to household budgeting, but within this context the researcher might inter-

ject a question about anti-Semitism. This destroys the pattern of answering and often arouses suspicion. A similar result will sometimes result
from *improper labeling*. Although the title of a study need not convey
an exact picture of its focus, a totally irrelevant or unfitting title may
arouse suspicion once the preliminary questions have been answered. In
this connection a more specialized case may be mentioned. Usually, the
anonymity of the respondent is assured in a cover letter or in the preliminary statement by the interviewer. However, some students have made
the mistake of asking such detailed questions about the respondent that
the latter sees that his anonymity *cannot* be assured. For example, in one
study carried out by a social scientist among faculty members on a college
campus, questions were asked about (1) age, (2) degrees granted, (3) years
in which degrees were granted, and (4) institutions at which the respondent had studied. Thereupon, the researcher began to ask questions concerning the attitudes of the faculty member toward the university administration. A number of respondents became suspicious because from
the preliminary answers anyone could trace the identity of the respondent. Consequently, a number of respondents refused to answer possibly
incriminating questions.

6. SUBSTANTIAL VARIATION IN ANSWERS WHEN THE ORDER OF QUESTIONS HAS
BEEN CHANGED. A frequent check on *reliability* is to rearrange the alternative answer choices to questions so that equivalent samples of respondents
will have, say, a given alternative answer presented first, second, or third.
If, for example, a tabulation of the answers indicates that preferred
"sources of news" vary according to whether newspapers or radio is presented first, we may suspect that the wording of the question is not adequate. This is not always the case, of course, since there is some reason
to believe that first alternatives are chosen more often. If after careful
study it is clear that the question is properly worded but that choice of
order is the only variable, then the researcher will use different schedule
forms, the order being different for each form. Usually no more than two
or three such alternative forms will be necessary. Later, of course, data
from different sequences of questions or sections of the questionnaire may
be tabulated separately to see whether there are other such variations in
the results.

An obvious check of this sort would be that of alternative *meanings* and
wording. Questions which seem to have the same meaning may be inserted at different points in the same schedule form or may be used in
different schedule forms for equivalent samples of respondents. Again,
when the results are greatly at variance, the questions must be carefully re-
studied for subtleties and implications which have escaped the researcher.

This section may be ended by noting that a basic problem of reliability
remains unsolved at the present time. There have been, as noted later,
two major countertrends in the development of interviewing technique:

(1) the standardizing of the interview questions and instructions, so that *less* trained interviewers can do an adequate job; and (2) the development of *highly* trained interviewers who will follow a fairly flexible interview guide, fitting the questions to the respondent's level of knowledge and understanding. Both these developments are important and of value. Yet the first, while being standardized as to form, clearly does not offer the "same question" to each interviewee, since the questions will be interpreted differently by various groups and individuals. Consequently, there is an unknown proportion of unreliability in the results, due to these differences. On the other hand, the skilled interviewer can indeed shape the questions to the individual, instead of requiring him to answer a question which is formally always the same but which is interpreted differently by various respondents. Yet with this flexibility of choice there is a lack of control over the question being asked. However skilled, the interviewer will err at times in his memory of the question asked. No completely accurate record of the interview is available. Consequently, the charge may be made that this type of interviewing is as unreliable as that carried out by less trained interviewers using a standardized form. Some efforts have been made in the direction of making wire or tape recordings of such interviews, in order to have an accurate reproduction of which questions were asked. Thus, variation in form and meaning can be measured. However, these records suggest that the problem is merely recognized and is not even on the way to being solved.

THE PROBLEM OF VALIDITY

The question of validity has been discussed at several points in this chapter. Let us now look at it more closely. Our questions must not only elicit stable or *reliable* answers, but they must also provide the kind of information which the researcher wants. A first question raised here, then, is whether or not respondents answer questions truthfully.[9]

Properly, this discussion should be placed in the chapters on interviewing and some relevant remarks are to be found there. For the basic guarantee of truthtelling, no matter how embarrassing or innocuous the questions, is good interviewing. This is not to say that a good interviewer will always obtain the truth. Most researchers have had some experience with questions which would not be answered truthfully with any but the very finest interviewing. However, a good interviewer will be able to determine to some extent *whether* the answer given is a truthful one, which is another matter. To be able to label a given answer as "doubtful" or "unlikely" is of great worth in research, even when the true answer is never elicited from the respondent.

[9] Herbert Hyman, "Do They Tell the Truth?" *Public Opinion Quarterly,* Vol. VIII (1944–1945), pp. 557–559.

Further, if the interviewer is given greater latitude in probing beneath the answers, the chances of detecting such lapses are much greater. Of course, the self-administered questionnaire does not have this advantage.

More often, the problem of truth is a much more complex one, for it involves that dim sphere in which the respondent is not giving the facts but is not really certain that these are not the facts. All of us reconstruct our personal history to some extent, especially in areas involving our self-conceptions. Only very careful probing can ever separate fact from fiction, and for some respondents even this will not be adequate. This is not cause for despair but a simple recognition of present limitations upon questioning techniques.

A further interesting aspect of validity which must be noted, however, is that of the statement which is technically true but really false. We all have used this evasive technique at times; warned by our parents not to "go swimming in the pond," we have found a more distant and more dangerous swimming hole in the river. The press releases of governmental agencies under public criticism furnish additional examples of this technique. However, the answer to such dissimulation is not only good interviewing but also a good understanding of the kinds of answers which might be given by respondents on the part of the researcher, *so that the additional alternatives will also be asked.* This technique rests upon the greater knowledge which the respondent has of the total situation. If the researcher asks a series of questions without adequate prior research, many of them will miss the mark and the respondent will be able to tell the truth without telling the facts. The danger is particularly great when the research has been sharpened to the point where only a few, specific questions are to be asked. On the other hand, by this time the many alternatives of experience should also have been plotted. Thus, the respondent cannot escape by choosing an alternative missed by the researcher himself. The cooperation of the respondent in the search for the truth can usually be obtained by a good interviewer. However, a good schedule or questionnaire will contain some check questions on crucial issues, variously placed within the document, designed to parallel or confirm each other. Sometimes these will explore other facets of the same behavior. In other cases, the check question will be almost a repetition of the first.

Usually, the cross-check question is a kind of *specification.* That is, a general question is checked by specific references. Thus, a general question may be posed which deals with patterns of neighboring in the locality, and this question may be checked by specific questions about specific neighboring relationships, such as borrowing and lending, "dropping in," etc. As noted later, this technique is a useful device generally for penetrating the cliche answer.

Another type of cross check is the question which can actually be checked by other records. In one study of divorce, all the cases were taken from complete county records, where certain standard data about each couple had been routinely obtained by a trained social worker. Consequently, certain items of information such as number of children, occupation of husband, religion, etc., could be checked, to see whether the respondent had told the truth. A similar case was reported in *The American Soldier,* dealing with the civilian occupations of soldiers and the use by the Army of these skills (Volume 1, Chart VII, page 327; page 325). Here it was found that the soldiers' notions of whether their civilian skills were being used were fairly accurate. The soldiers' comparisons were checked by occupational experts in order to make this test. Afterwards, this laborious matching by the experts was considered unnecessary, for the simpler answers by the soldiers had been shown to be adequate enough.

Another type of cross check of some relevance in a discussion of validity, was used by the Research Branch. This was the use of the "expert panel," to check the responses of the soldiers to questions about objective conditions (Volume 1, page 356). This becomes, of course, a kind of three-way relationship between the reports of the enlisted men, those of the noncommissioned officers, and the objective conditions in a given station (food, housing, recreation, etc.). If questions about such matters could really "get at the facts," then relatively simple questionnaire procedures could substitute for teams of inspectors in geographically distant places. Here, assuming that the noncommissioned officers would have fewer general complaints about the Army and would be in a good position to compare the station with other stations in their experience, the researchers treated this group as "experts" and compared their responses with those of the enlisted men. High correlations suggested that the answers reflected objective differences between conditions at different units. Thus, the questions really got the kind of data needed, and a saving of time and money resulted.

Although it is obvious that not every question may be cross-checked, it is a wise policy to attempt some cross checking so as to gain some notion of the extent to which the questions are actually yielding valid answers.

Questions are often asked in such a way as to invite a stereotyped reply. In the interview, as in daily conversation, the respondent's verbal habits are likely to be in cliché form. That is, questions are ordinarily answered not directly but with formalized answers which really ignore the question. When an acquaintance asks us "How are you?" we do not often tell him how we really are, because we do not believe that this is relevant to his question or that he is interested, anyway. Some such answer as "Fine!" is most commonly employed to avoid further discussion. As more than one wit has remarked, good manners are techniques for keeping possible bores at a distance, and good manners are almost entirely clichés. When a clerical friend inquires about the state of our religious beliefs, we are likely to answer in terms of some religious conformity. When an acquaintance dies, we express and accept sympathy whether or not the appropriate emotion is actually present.

There is, therefore, a general problem of evasion and cliché in all social research. *Good rapport is not a substitute for good questions.* Indeed, the most cliché-ridden interview possible is one in which interviewer and respondent feel so emotionally involved with one another that neither will express an opinion which might hurt the other's feelings. It is here, of course, that the flexibility of the interview guide is most advantageous, for the skilled interviewer may use probe questions which do not allow the respondent to evade the issue behind a verbal formula.

The problem is not the distinction between professed attitudes and actual behavior. This is a false issue, as many have noted before.[10] Verbal behavior *is* one kind of actual behavior and expresses certain dimensions of social reality which are as real as any other kind. The fact that a group expresses an ideal is of great importance for behavior even when there is much nonconformity with the ideal. All of us tell lies, but it would be a false cynicism to state that our professed dislike of lying is mere hypocrisy. Moreover, it would be a shallow view of the complexity of social behavior generally. It is quite true that verbal behavior is not an entirely valid predictor of overt behavior. On the other hand, actual behavior may be equally misleading. Many Southerners in military service showed little overt prejudice, that is, discrimination, against Negroes in their units, without changing any of their attitudes toward Negroes in general or those Negroes in their units in particular. Similarly, for reasons of expediency many liberals in the present South follow patterns of overt discrimination and exhibit verbal patterns of the same kind, while having directly opposed attitudes. There is a cliché of overt behavior as well as a cliché of verbal behavior, and both these may be confused with the clichés of internal attitude and thought.

In short, penetrating a cliché does not involve finding out "what people will really do, not just what they say they will do." Either type of behavior may be a façade. The problem is how to get behind external evasive behavior, of whatever variety, and indeed our research goal may be that of checking certain types of behavior against other types, through questioning *and* observation.

Sometimes a useful aid is found in the *sieve question*. This is a question which sifts out those who should not be answering the question because they do not possess the necessary knowledge or experience. The sieve

[10] Robert K. Merton, "Fact and Factitiousness in Ethnic Opinionaires," *American Sociological Review*, Vol. V (1940), pp. 21ff.; Richard T. LaPiere, "The Social Significance of Measurable Attributes," *American Sociological Review*, Vol. III (1938), pp. 179–181; George A. Lundberg, *Social Research* (New York: Longmans, 1947), 2d ed., pp. 217ff.

question may follow or precede the important question, but only those who have the requisite knowledge will be counted. Thus, one to three questions will determine whether the respondent (1) has heard of the issue, person, problem, etc., and (2) knows any facts about it so that his opinion even roughly refers to the matter. Thereupon, the main opinion question can be asked. Often the respondents who do not know the facts may be tabulated separately to discover which groups in the population do not have the facts.

Similarly, only those with a particular experience may be asked to evaluate the services of a social-work agency, the frightening qualities of different weapons,[11] or the teaching abilities of university professors. Again, by comparing the opinions of those with the experience against those of respondents without the experience it is possible to learn something about the public images of the agency, the weapon, or the professor, as held by members of different groups.

An ancient set of devices for penetrating the cliché is the *assuming* question and the *adverse* question. These have an underlying similarity in spite of differences of form, for they both express to the respondent the idea that the interviewer already knows the facts. The assuming question has been used by investigators of delicate matters such as sex. Thus, Kinsey began with the assumption that any respondent might have participated in any conceivable form of sexual activity. A tax lawyer may begin his interview with the assumption that any client is likely to have broken the law. A student of juvenile delinquency may begin his questions with the assumption that his respondents are likely to have committed almost any crime.

The advantage of this type of beginning is obvious if one is to move behind the façade of conformity and expressions of conformity. The respondent finds the discussion of his behavior much easier because he sees that the interviewer is not going to be shocked. Furthermore, he assumes that the interviewer already knows what has taken place so that attempts at evasion will be useless.

The similarity of this to the adverse question is clear, for the latter becomes almost a more specific case of the assuming question. In its stereotypically humorous form it is expressed as "When did you stop beating your wife?" The common assumption, not always borne out in fact, is that the respondent will deny the charge if it is not true. If the charge is true a basis for frank discussion has been laid. The question is useful when it lies emotionally *between* the point at which the respondent becomes very indignant and the point at which the respondent will admit what is not true simply because of suggestibility. For example, the Research Branch of the Army specified fear situations in which soldiers

11 Stouffer *et al.*, *op. cit.*, Vol. 2, Chart VIII, p. 236; pp. 240–241.

figured, knowing that within the context of combat the expressed assumption that the individual soldier had displayed fear or even cowardice would be met by the facts.[12] The combat soldier, unlike the civilian, was not indignant at the suggestion that he had been afraid, and the experience was vivid enough that suggestibility had little effect on his answers.

These types of questions are akin to *loaded questions*. The student may at times encounter the objection that a given question is loaded, that is, it contains a strong bias. Here, as is the case so often in research, it is the *unknown or accidental biases* which are dangerous. Such questions can be very useful for penetrating a cliché. Thus, a respondent may insist that he has no prejudices against any ethnic groups, but because he is so definite in his identification of them he is suspected of hiding the facts. Often, in this situation, a loaded question expressing definite bias may force such attitudes into the open.

RECALL

Almost all questionnaires and schedules deal in part with the past. Questions about the past range from detailed case histories which delve into the extended family relationships of the respondent, to immediate facts concerning recent voting behavior, purchases, recreation choices, or the preludes to personal crises. The errors, inconsistencies, and biases of our own memories may make us question whether these research tools are adequate. Here we note again that certain factors lead to both low reliability and low validity.

Some attempts to test the consistency of answers have divided questions into those dealing with "objective facts" such as age, years of education, etc., and those dealing with "attitudes" or ideological matters. Most have followed some such pattern as interviewing a group at one time and then attempting to interview the same group at a later date. When the questionnaire has been used, a similar procedure has been followed. Because of the difficult problem of maintaining contacts with the respondents over a period of time, most of these tests have been made with college students. These tests have shown a high correspondence between the answers from the first administration and those from the second. Further, the deviations, that is, the answers which are different, are usually not very great. For example, the age at first moving to the city from a rural area may vary from the first administration to the second, but the variation will usually be no more than a year or so. The answers on "objective" questions, however, seem to exhibit more variation than those on attitudinal questions. In part, of course, this is a function of *precision*. When very exact answers are required, a minor error in memory becomes a perceptible deviation. When, however, the answers are very general, a similar amount of memory

12 *Ibid.*, pp. 236–241.

error will not be registered. To some extent, such variation may be caused by experience with the previous interview or questionnaire. That is, the respondent has been forced to think over the earlier answers and has recognized some errors. However, there is reason to believe that the attitudinal answers are really more stable than those dealing with the more external facts.[13] At all events, if the answers are highly unstable it is not likely that we are really tapping the levels of experience which we wish to understand, and we must correct our questions.

A fundamental point in all question making and one which is of great aid to accurate recall is the necessity of using *units* which are familiar to the respondent. Thus, the skilled worker may be unable to recall how much money he earned in the year 1940, but will be able to recall the weekly wage rate and be able to make a good estimate of the number of weeks of employment. When the unit needed is different from that commonly used by the respondents, the questions must be formulated in commonly used terms. Later calculations can develop the unit data required.

When questions about a distant, specific point in time are to be asked, there is great danger of a quick but unreliable answer. To avoid this or the "Don't know" answer, the respondent must be helped by a *regression in time* toward that point by a series of related questions, each tying one fact with a still more distant fact. Again, this technique can be used by either interview or questionnaire. For example, most of us could not immediately answer the question "What did you do to celebrate Independence Day, July 4, 1939?" Assuming the importance of the information, on the other hand, many of us can remember with some help. As an obvious first step, we might ask ourselves a series of questions to establish *where* we lived at that time, a datum which most people do not forget easily. We would also make a rapid mental calculation to establish how *old* we were at that time to narrow the possible *types* of celebrations. If there have been major changes in the family structure, such as divorce or separation, births or deaths, in this period, we would then adjust for these facts, to determine *who* constituted the possible participants, along with friends, in any such celebration. Finally, some information about school and father's work at the time would narrow the possibilities still further. If the period being investigated was an emotionally important one, it is usually possible by a series of regression questions to stimulate the respondent to recall with considerable exactness.

Why did you—? Perhaps one of the most common types of questions attempts to find out why the respondent made a certain choice. Such

13 John F. Cuber and John B. Gerberich, "A Note on Consistency in Questionnaire Responses," *American Sociological Review*, Vol. XI (1946), pp. 13–15; Robert A. Harper, "The Present Status of Questionnaire-derived Opinion Data," *Social Forces*, Vol. XXV (1946–1947), pp. 294–297.

"decision-making" situations vary from choice of a movie to a resolution to commit suicide. The student will usually find that his first attempt is not satisfactory, because he has failed to include the *dimensions* of the decision and thus does not have comparable data. This is a failure in conceptualization, but it needs to be explained here. If we ask our respondents why they went to a certain motion picture, we may get results like the accompanying tabulation.

Answer	Per Cent
Go to movies all the time	25
Nothing to do that evening	10
Friend told me about it	40
Had been waiting for it	20
Theater conveniently close	10
Critics stated it was excellent	10
Tired of reading	5
Too broke to do anything else	5
Other	30

Note that any individual may have given more than one of these answers. Furthermore, they are really answering different questions. One is telling the *predisposing* factors which led to *any* motion picture. Another is telling us the predisposing factors which led to that *particular* picture. Another is informing us of the *alternatives* among which he was choosing. Another may *describe* the qualities of the picture. Still another is telling us of the *precipitating* event (too tired to read, a friend came along, etc.). Finally, some will be giving the *channels of communication* which informed them of the picture and its quality. Since "why" does have all these dimensions, we will have to transform our question into subquestions, each probing different aspects of the decision. If we wish to probe deeply, we may have to use still further dimensions. It is only thus that we can get answers which allow us to compare each respondent with respect to each dimension. Our original question merely elicited from each respondent the aspect of the decision process which seemed to him to be of more importance or which came to his mind most quickly. The respondent himself may not have a good answer to the general "why" question. We cannot analyze the process of decision in a series of respondents unless we obtain comparable items about the many aspects of any decision. For a complex matter such as the decision to divorce, even these dimensions would not suffice.

Finally, it should be seen that the translation of a "why" question into these aspects of the decision really makes it a "how" question. And, in general, it is true that the answers are likely to be more useful if we ask "How did you happen to . . . ?" If we ask "why?" we are likely to obtain a justification of the decision, rather than a description of it.[14]

14 See Paul F. Lazarsfeld, "The Art of Asking Why," *National Marketing Review,* Vol. I (1935), pp. 26–38, for an early statement of these points.

SUMMARY

In this chapter, we have attempted to show how the social scientist goes about formulating the questions which he will ask his respondents. Although each research is different in many ways, a number of general suggestions have been offered which can be translated into practical advice. The good schedule grows from good hypotheses which have been studied carefully. It is unlikely that an excellent set of questions can be developed without serious library research, much discussion of the problems with colleagues, and considerable experience with the subject matter. The latter may involve various types of personal observation as well as a pilot study. For maximum efficiency, the pretest is suggested, since both the general research design, the interviewing technique, and the schedule itself are thus checked for errors.

Both reliability and validity are sought through the development of well-formulated questions. Investigation of these factors shows that they are interrelated and also have many connections with interviewing problems, sampling, and social theory. Some hints were offered for the detection of poor questions, as well as for their improvement. However, research on these matters is moving forward rapidly. Better ways of handling these problems will be developed. For the present, the student should supplement his knowledge by studies of the questions used in actual research, as well as by working through these suggested steps in the formulation of questions.

Now let us turn to one research instrument which uses these questions, the self-administered questionnaire.

SUGGESTED READINGS

Deming, W. Edward, "On Errors in Surveys," *American Sociological Review*, Vol. X (August, 1944), pp. 359–369.

Jahoda, Marie, Morton Deutsch, and Stuart W. Cook, *Research Methods in Social Relations* (New York: Dryden, 1951), Part II, Chap. 12.

Lazarsfeld, Paul F., "The Art of Asking Why," *National Marketing Review*, Vol. I (1935), pp. 26–38.

Lundberg, G. A., *Social Research* (New York: Longmans, 1942), Chaps. 6 and 7.

Parten, Mildred, *Surveys, Polls, and Samples: Practical Procedures* (New York: Harper, 1950), Chap. 6.

Young, Pauline V., *Scientific Social Surveys and Research* (New York: Prentice-Hall, 1949), Chap. 10.

CHAPTER 12

The Mailed Questionnaire

The preceding chapter dealt with the problem of formulating questions regardless of whether they were to be incorporated in a questionnaire, a schedule, or an interview guide. The questionnaire, it will be recalled, is differentiated from the schedule and interview guide by the fact that it is self-administered. Not all questionnaires are mailed. They may be administered to groups of people who have gathered together for any purpose. In this case, not all the problems which face the mailed questionnaire are present. Since, however, research of the group-questionnaire type differs from interview studies in the same direction, though not as sharply, as does the mailed-questionnaire technique, it seems best to discuss the latter in greatest detail. The student will be able to see for himself at what points the problems of the two are different.

In spite of many abuses, the mailed self-administering questionnaire remains a useful technique in sociological research. So long as this method is employed in appropriate research designs, it can frequently be rewarding. The crucial point in its use is determining whether or not this method of gathering data is the best one possible in the specific situation. The decision to use one method of collecting data over another method is complex and must take many factors into consideration.

THE RELATION OF THE MAILED QUESTIONNAIRE
TO THE RESEARCH PROBLEM

The appropriateness of the mailed questionnaire will depend upon the requirements of the research problem with regard to (1) the type of information required, (2) the type of respondent reached, (3) the accessibility of respondents, and (4) the precision of the hypothesis.

The type of information required. First, very extensive bodies of data cannot often be secured through the use of the questionnaire. It is usually unwise to expect returns from a questionnaire which requires much more than 10 to 25 minutes to complete, and thus its use is restricted to rather narrow areas of data. Further, an extensive, survey type of problem suggests the need for so wide a range of data that personal participation and/or depth interviewing is required. It would, for example, have been impossible to secure the kind of information required by Whyte in his *Street Corner Society* by the use of questionnaires.[1]

Second, the questionnaire is effective only when the respondent is able or willing to express his reactions clearly. A considerable controversy has existed among social researchers as to whether the answers from the anonymous questionnaire are franker, or given with greater openness, because there is less fear when there is no immediate listener. This frankness has been contrasted with the interview situation, since it is claimed that the interviewer may inhibit the answers somewhat.[2]

This, however, seems to ignore the major problem. There can be no question that a good questionnaire can elicit frank answers on almost any subject, even such personal matters as sex and income. It is equally true, on the other hand, for the interview. When good questionnaires are compared with good interviews, it is likely that on the score of simple lying or frankness there is little to choose. The interviewer has the advantage of seeing the evasion, while the person who answers the questionnaire may feel less constraint in telling the truth.

The difference between the two is not in the dimension of frankness, but in that of *depth*. On this matter, there can be little doubt that the good interview can probe far more deeply than the best questionnaire. The reason for this can be seen in both statistical and social-relational terms. With reference to the former, the experienced researcher knows that the most simple question has a great depth of motivation, desire, attitude, and concrete complexity to it. In one project, for example, information was desired about the dating practices of divorced mothers. A simple question for a questionnaire might be, "How often do you date? Almost every night, two to six times a week, once a week, twice monthly, almost never?" However, such a question would not reach the complexity of observable patterns. Some women might have answered, "Almost never," because they were living with their ex-husbands, or with their fiancés, or with boarders. Further, each of the complex patterns breaks down into still further questions to be asked. A simple question to which there are eight possible answers, each of which must be probed by three possible alternatives, demands a series of 24 questions. These not only take up a large section of the space in any questionnaire, but would be very difficult to arrange spatially so that the respondent could thread his or her way through the maze.

At each deeper level of probing, the possible number of answers mul-

---

[1] William F. Whyte, *Street Corner Society* (Chicago: University of Chicago Press, 1943).

[2] Albert Ellis, "Questionnaire versus Interview Methods in the Study of Human Love Relationships," *American Sociological Review*, Vol. XII (1947), pp. 541–553, and Vol. XIII (1948), pp. 61–65.

tiplies enormously, and all these possibilities must be included in the mailed questionnaire.

The more important item for consideration, however, is that the *active work of the interviewer* is required to stimulate the respondent to express these deeper levels of motivation and feeling. It is not that in the interview it is possible to obtain a better rapport with the respondent, although it is likely that the interviewer can get and hold the emotional commitment of the respondent somewhat better. Rapport is not the most important element in this comparison, but it is rather the fact that the respondent is not *able* to give the necessary answers without help.

A social scientist attempted to compare the frankness of answers from the questionnaire and interview by asking comparable questions concerning the love experiences of a group of college girls.[3] Although in general the two techniques gave comparable results, with perhaps a slight advantage in favor of the questionnaire, one or two questions illustrated the present point, that frankness is not the sole issue. One dealt with whether the girl had ever been in love with two boys at once, and the interviews showed a substantially higher number of girls who admitted such attachments. The questions were phrased similarly, but it was discovered that when the interviewer received a "no" answer to this question, the further probe question was asked: "Never?" A number of girls then remembered such an attachment. However, there was no lack of frankness in the first answer. Rather, the probe question forced them to think again, to search their memories in order to be certain. Since the romantic complex in this country is opposed to such double attachments, many persons tend to forget them. This is also true for a number of incidents in the life histories of any individual. Even with the best of willingness to tell the truth, the truth does not come easily to the tongue.

A further point here is the fact that the questionnaire fails when its questions place an emotional burden on the respondent. This is a different dimension from that of being *unable* to answer because of unawareness of the complexity of one's motivation or the details of one's life history. The latter problem is met by the mental alertness of the interviewer, who probes when the answers are vague, meaningless, irrelevant, or contradictory. However, the face-to-face interview offers the *emotional support* of a sympathetic listener, in addition to the purely intellectual help. This factor may be of even greater significance in eliciting the facts than the latter. And, in any event, neither is obtainable when the respondent faces a mailed questionnaire.

The type of respondent reached. Although questionnaires have been used for a wide range of social groups, experience has shown that not all groups respond equally well. At the lowest level of differentiation, it must

[3] *Ibid.*

be clear that it is impossible to obtain a representative sample of the whole population by using this technique. A minimum necessity is the ability to read and write. Further, the amount of reading attention and writing skill required for most questionnaires is much greater than is implied by a minimum definition of "literate." For many who are able to read and write, neither burden is assumed willingly or easily.

The consequence of this aspect of the questionnaire is that it cannot be used for a representative sample of the entire population. This does not detract from its usefulness in specific research situations, when more literate groups are the focus of the study. It is, however, only by recognizing the limitations of any research tool that we can utilize it to the fullest.[4]

Emphasis has been placed on the fact that a substantial segment of the population *cannot* answer a questionnaire. However, the *willingness* of the addressee to answer the questionnaire is a still further problem. The researcher is not there to add his own pleas to those which are printed or typewritten in the letter of introduction.

Both the "cannot" and the "will not" group bias the sample in a *known direction,* but to an *unknown degree.* Since questionnaire studies with a fairly wide population base have reported the percentage answering as from 20 per cent to around 70 per cent, it is clear that this type of sampling bias could be fatal to the validity of the study.

The direction of this bias is toward those who are interested in the subject matter, those who are higher in socioeconomic status, and those who have had more education. Thus, a questionnaire circulated among college professors of English, querying them about the kind of work load they carry, is likely to be answered by a high proportion of the respondents.

In one study, on traveling by train, a substantial proportion of returns was received from the first wave of questionnaires.[5] However, it is now standard procedure, in using the questionnaire, to send a second wave of questionnaires, or a third. Depending on the technique used, these can be sent to everyone on the primary list or only to those who have not answered. In this study, the second wave showed very different characteristics from the first. Looking more closely for the basis of the differences, it was seen that the first wave was mainly composed of those who had actually traveled on the newer types of "super" trains. The group had, therefore, a keener interest in questions about innovations in train travel and were willing to take the trouble of answering the questionnaire. It was only with the second wave, which stimulated those whose interest was less strong, that the peripheral group was tapped, those who had not enjoyed the newer train facilities.

[4] E. Jackson Baur, "Response Bias in a Mail Survey," *Public Opinion Quarterly,* Vol. XI (1947), pp. 594–600.

[5] Cf. Raymond F. Sletto, "Pretesting of Questionnaires," *American Sociological Review,* Vol. V (1940), pp. 193–200; and E. A. Suchman and B. McCandless, "Who Answers Questionnaires?" *Journal of Applied Psychology,* Vol. XXIV (1940), pp. 758–769.

The respondent will ordinarily not answer a questionnaire dealing with a subject with which he is unfamiliar, such as air travel, impending legislation, or experience with a particular branch of the government or an occupation. This lack of knowledge has been classed under the general heading of "lack of interest," for convenience, but it is clear that cases may exist in which these do not coincide at all. In a particular organization, for example, a controversy may have continued in a futile bickering fashion for many months, leaving the members willing to wash their hands of the matter and unwilling to answer a polling questionnaire which seems to bring up the issues once more. Another type of refusal to answer occurs when the questionnaire deals with the use of luxury goods, for in such cases there is a strong bias in the resulting sample, in the direction of those who have used the article in question.

The central point of mentioning these results is to underline the fact that the questionnaire is not an effective research tool for any but a highly select group of respondents. It is not effective because a biased sample is obtained. As noted in the section on sampling, the mere existence of a "bias" is not the primary point, but the fact that the extent of the bias is not measurable. If the exact characteristics of those who do not answer could be known, it would be possible to weight the results accordingly or to restrict the conclusions to the select group who responded.

On the other hand, questionnaires can be fairly effective if such a select group is the object of study. A group of business executives, for example, will answer a Dun and Bradstreet questionnaire with a low rate of refusals. The income-tax blank is a questionnaire and (backed in this case by police power) is fairly successful in eliciting a high rate of response. The *Dictionary of American Scholars* sends a questionnaire to those who are suggested for inclusion, and it is safe to say that the response is very close to 100 per cent.

Accessibility of respondents. Granted that the questionnaire is effective only for a highly select group of respondents, it is a very useful tool for certain situations in which the respondents are geographically widely dispersed. This, of course, actually reduces to a problem of time and money. The savings to be obtained from the use of the questionnaire are not to be formulated by saying that one is always cheaper than the other. To begin with, research on these tools has not proceeded far enough to be able to offer acceptable time and cost breakdowns. Actually, a large part of published research is done by academic or other scholars who, like home craftsmen or weekend farmers, work for the excitement of it. "Costs" include the actual outlay of money, with little allowance for their own time. Especially during a research project, the researcher and his associates are likely to pay little attention to the total number of hours worked. Furthermore, the extra costs on a questionnaire and an interview research are for different things. The questionnaire costs less per questionnaire than the interview costs per interview, but this is true only if immediate costs are considered. A great amount of time may be spent in waiting for successive questionnaire waves to come in. Or, the questionnaire may have to be supplemented by interviews. There may be extra transportation costs for interviewers, and extra costs for added efforts needed to fill in blanks which were left incomplete by the questionnaire respondents. In short, no simple comparison of costs can be made which will hold good in all cases.

However, it is certain that when the group of respondents is widely scattered, the costs will be less if the questionnaire is used. For example, if the researcher wishes to poll the membership of the American Sociological Society, transportation costs for interviewing would be excessive, both in money and time. Similarly, if an attitude study is to be made among the participants at a conference, there is not enough time to make the necessary interviews. However, questionnaires could be distributed to all those attending meetings at a particular hour. A selected group could be interviewed by questionnaire relative to a current controversy, even from a fairly isolated campus as a research base. Further, this could be done by a single researcher, without the large funds otherwise required to hire an interviewing staff, or to pay a national staff, such as the National Opinion Research Center, to carry out the interviewing in various cities.

This is not a blanket statement that the questionnaire is cheaper, only that it can be cheaper under certain circumstances. It must be kept clearly in mind that costs should not be computed on the basis of the *number* of interviews or questionnaires secured, but rather on the basis of the *amount of usable information* secured. For some information, the questionnaire cannot be used at all. For other information, under particular circumstances, the questionnaire is certainly cheaper than the interview and may be as adequate.

The precision of the hypothesis. From the preceding discussion, it is clear that the questionnaire is most useful when a considerable amount of exploratory work has narrowed the questions to be answered. The respondents are not likely to take the trouble to work out careful discriminations of attitude, personal history, and value. The questionnaire itself must do this, for the respondents to choose from. Of course, a great amount of exploratory work must go into any research project, no matter what tools are used. However, the interview remains a considerably more flexible instrument, even at the final stages. What is emphasized here is not the amount of preliminary work, but the sharpness of the hypothesis. The more closely focused the hypothesis, the more effective the question naire. At such a stage, the interview is equally applicable. However, the interview is effective even with a vaguely exploratory hypothesis. Indeed, the *testing of the questionnaire must utilize the interview*. A few questions can be tested by using the questionnaire without interviews. It can be determined, for example, that some of them are not answered or that the answers seem inconsistent. A few respondents will take the trouble to make marginal comments. However, this will not be adequate criticism. The questionnaire will have to be used with a selected sample who are then interviewed further concerning each question. Researchers often do this without selecting members of the respondent group, but the comments of colleagues or students are not sufficient at this stage. The meaning of each question can be adequately tested only by flexible, probing questioning of those who are representative of the final respondent group. This type of test cannot usually be done by the use of the questionnaire alone. As a consequence, it is only when the hypothesis has been rather sharply focused that the questionnaire is most effectively used.

SENDING OUT THE QUESTIONNAIRE

The questionnaire must be thought of as a kind of interview which is surrounded by peculiar obstacles. Consequently, many of the comments to be found in this section are equally applicable to the interview research technique. For example, it is clear that the respondent can judge the study only by what he can see. In interviewing, it is the interviewer himself. In the case of the questionnaire, it is several pieces of paper. These cannot adjust themselves to the situation. They are the same for all respondents. The questionnaire maker, then, must offer as impressive a presentation as possible, if the response is to be adequate. Only the papers are there to make his plea, and he cannot count on any personal charm or social skill when the respondent opens the envelope. He must, then, plan carefully and seek a great deal of professional help, before he sends out his queries. The following are concrete suggestions for building a questionnaire.

The appeal. A cover letter almost always accompanies the questionnaire. This is analogous to the opening "sales talk" of the interviewer, explaining what he is doing, why he is doing it, and for whom. The letter must explain these facts, but must cover as many objections as possible, since an unanswered objection means an ignored questionnaire. The introductory comments of the interviewer need not do so, since in most cases an elaborate explanation is unnecessary. The interviewer has answers ready for the objections, but he need not offer them unless the objections appear. The letter of appeal, however, must leave nothing unexplained.

On the other hand, it must be brief. Most of the recipients are not willing to read a long letter, and lengthiness usually destroys its impact.

Yet within it a number of basic facts must be presented. Some of these follow:

1. THE AUSPICES. Who is sanctioning the study? As in the case of the interview, this information must be given at the outset. If the research bureau is well known as a responsible, scientific group, the response is likely to be good. In some cases, the cover letter may devote a few sentences to explaining the character of the organization sanctioning the study, as well as the one carrying it out. The letterhead should convey the impression of scientific competence, and the address as well as the telephone number should be given to allow an easy check. Nothing should appear to be hidden or suspicious.

2. WHY THE STUDY? The interviewer may include this information in his introductory remarks, but it is often left out unless the respondent asks for an explanation. In the questionnaire cover letter, it is necessary to explain why the sanctioning organization needs the information, or why anyone at all wishes it. This need not be elaborate, but it must be sufficient to explain the need for answers to the questions. Questions dealing with marital relations can usually be explained adequately by referring to the modern "crisis of the family." Studies which explore religious behavior can allude to the secularism of the era. It cannot be assumed that *all* respondents will read the letter carefully, but it must be carefully tested to be certain that every phrase in it conveys the meaning intended. For *someone* will read the phrase, and an unfortunate interpretation will mean a loss of those respondents who found a different meaning in it.

3. WHY SHOULD THE RESPONDENT BOTHER TO ANSWER? Mention of the group authorizing the study, the group carrying it out, and the need for the information merely indicate that someone else is interested in the study. There must be an appeal to the respondent himself, which persuades him that *he* ought to participate. A great number of appeals have been used in the history of the questionnaire. Some have included money or promised it (usually no more than a nominal sum, such as 25 cents). Others have offered special services, such as marketing reports, radio bulletins, or samples of goods. Others have challenged the respondents to "prove what many thought impossible, that thousands of interested people would give information for this cause."

In general, the most effective appeal is an altruistic one. Although these special inducements such as money have increased the proportion of returns slightly, it remains true that no advantage that a research organization is likely to be able to offer will appeal to a large group of respondents. The amount of money that can be offered is trivial, and so are the other advantages, compared to the amount of time and thought requested. Whatever the student may believe concerning the cynicism of

the age or the selfishness of people, extensive research has demonstrated
that an appeal to disinterested motives is strongest. "The information
is needed by thousands of leaders attempting to solve today's problems,"
"You will be contributing to the advancement of science," and "You
will help improve the education of thousands of students who will attend
Xiphosuran College in the future" are all better arguments than attempting to exploit the self-interest of the respondent.

The social scientist will ordinarily test which appeal is most effective
for the group he is investigating, but the final form of his letter must
impel the respondent to action. Mere presentation of the questionnaire is
not enough. The impulse to activity is initially lacking, and the researcher is not even offering the respondent a sympathetic audience, as is
done in the interview. The appeal is the "one-shot" stimulus, and its
failure will result in the failure to gather data at all.

4. THE DIRECTIONS: HOW TO FILL IT OUT. Almost always, the beginning
user of the questionnaire overrates the literacy of the average person. As
anyone knows who has checked questionnaires filled out by civil service
applicants, even those with a great deal of formal education are not always careful in following directions. Therefore, the student must make
certain that a total stranger to the research can follow the directions with
no effort. This aspect of the pretest should utilize individuals *with less
education* than the group for which the directions are ultimately intended, to give a reasonable margin of error. It is not lack of education
or intelligence which is the stumbling block, *but lack of attention and
interest.* There is no primary good reason why motivation should be high.
When high motivation cannot be expected, the demands on time and
attention should be minimal. Directions, then, should be few and simple,
both in the cover letter and in the questionnaire itself.

5. GUARANTEE OF ANONYMITY. One element which is used to back up
the appeal is a guarantee of anonymity. Although many questionnaires do
not ask for information which is embarrassing, respondents will ordinarily
not answer if they have any reason to suspect that information about
them will be made public. This suspicion will be more easily aroused,
of course, if the information itself touches on delicate personal matters.
The letter, then, should include a guarantee that the respondent will
remain anonymous. There should be no request for names and no questions which are so detailed as to make identification easy (such as street
addresses, etc.). The guarantee alone is not sufficient, if the questionnaire
itself seems identifiable.

Such a rule is not to be interpreted too narrowly. When the investigating agency has a long history of making such studies within the same
group, as an annual study of production from specified factories in an
industry, such anonymity may become unnecessary.

TECHNIQUES FOR FACILITATING THE RETURN OF THE QUESTIONNAIRE

As noted previously, the questionnaire is sometimes not mailed, but is administered to groups within the same room. This is the simplest collection situation. Usually, however, the document is mailed to the respondent, with directions to return it by mail. Perhaps the least effective method is having friends or students distribute copies to their own friends, with a request to return them after completion. Not only is the sample biased, but the proportion of loss is extremely high.

The questionnaire maker cannot seriously expect the respondent to exert himself in taking care of this task. Consequently, a stamped, self-addressed envelope should be sent with the questionnaire. There is some evidence that a regular stamp affixed to the envelope is more effective than postage from a mailing machine, or even than the stamped envelopes from the post office. The claim is that respondents do not like to see the stamps wasted. It is equally likely that the regular stamp gives some evidence that the organization is not carrying on a selling campaign. Commercial stamping is often associated with mailed advertisements, and there is a tendency on the part of many individuals to throw such envelopes away almost immediately.

As the student will see from these comments, "techniques for returning" must be thought of as overlapping the "techniques for eliciting response." Facilitating the return of the envelopes yields a greater response. Accurate typography, printed if possible, which is well spaced for easy reading, not only creates a favorable response in the recipient but also helps to eliminate errors in mailing. A slightly larger investment in format and typography will create a very great dividend in number of questionnaires completed and returned. Even the choice of paper is not to be taken lightly. The questionnaire will be handled by the recipient and the researcher, and it will be turned and shuffled many times while it is being coded and tabulated. The paper must, then, be of a good grade and of a convenient size. Many questionnaires, on the other hand, are reproduced on ordinary mimeographed paper, which is likely to smudge or blot when written upon with pencil or ink. As to typography, the researcher should investigate the different methods of reproduction before choosing. A number of new processes are much better than ordinary mimeographing, at only a slightly greater cost. Further, new processes are being developed as time goes on. One simple example of such a process, for the researcher with limited funds, is offset mimeographing, using bold Bodoni type such as is found on modern electric typewriters.

The result is very much like printing and considerably more impressive (and therefore more effective in eliciting responses) than ordinary typewriter type.

CHECKING THE SAMPLE

A major problem in using the questionnaire is the structure of the resulting sample. A low response is almost always indicative of a biased sample. However, a high proportion of questionnaires is not proof that no bias exists in the sample. If the questionnaire elicits a response from only certain groups among the respondents, the sample will be biased. To make certain that the resulting sample is representative, several devices have been used.

One of the most obvious is that of tabulating separately the respondents which result from (1) successive time periods, or (2) successive waves of questionnaires. For most studies, those who answer promptly are different from those who delay their answers. As noted previously, those who answer immediately have a much closer relationship to the subject matter, or wish to offer their opinions about a luxury product, or have a higher level of education. The student, then, may separate the answers received promptly from those received later. When there is very little difference between these two groups, and the percentage of response is high, he will have a fair assurance that the sampling bias is not great.

When successive waves of questionnaires are sent out, in order to obtain a very high level of response, such as 80 to 95 per cent, the same device can be used effectively. By an active follow-up campaign, a good response can be obtained from the group under study. Each new wave will refer to the previous mailing and comment on the importance of the work, appealing once more for an answer.

In order to check the resulting sample more carefully, some researchers have found it useful to assume that there is a final die-hard group who simply care little about the study and cannot be persuaded to bother greatly about it. For the final wave, then, a double postcard is sent, with a few basic questions to be marked with "yes," "no," or similarly brief answers. The double postcard is cheap, and this final group can be compared, for at least a few important characteristics (age, sex, occupation, etc.) with those who answered the questionnaire with little urging. This allows, then, some check on the sample obtained.

A comparable device, to be used with successive questionnaire waves, eliminates some of the cost of duplication. This technique utilizes a small section of the questionnaire, or a separate sheet, on which the respondent can put his name, either with or without cross-tabulation data such as age, sex, etc. This identifying tab is mailed separately by the respondent. The duplicate, stamped envelopes are an added cost, but on receipt of the tab the student can save the cost of sending a copy of the second wave to that respondent. The system preserves the anonymity of the questionnaire, while allowing the researcher to know who has answered the questions.

The further advantage is an obvious one; the unknown character of the sample bias is thereby clarified. The researcher usually knows some thing about his respondents, else he would not be sending his question-naire to the particular persons concerned. Even a few items of informa-tion allow a simple comparison between the answerers and the nonan-swerers. To the extent, then, that any such comparisons can be made, the extent of the bias can be known.

Knowing the direction of the bias, or something about it, may lead to a decision to *weight* the tabulations, under the assumption that those who do not answer have the same characteristics as those who answer very late. A more sophisticated technique was developed by the Bureau of the Census, which involves the use of face-to-face interviews for a certain percentage of those who do not answer the questionnaire.[6] Given the *cost* of such a field interview as compared to the cost of mailing the question-naire, and the *degree of uncertainty* in the sample structure, which is increased as the percentage of response is lower, it is possible to calculate how many interviews ought to be used for any given level of response. It is always assumed, of course, that the *level of precision is not to be changed*. If the answers are not valid and reliable, that is, adequate for the problem, there is little point in doing the study at all. Hansen and Hurwitz have actually calculated hypothetical tables from which the stu-dent can determine how large a proportion of interviews to obtain, given the factors of cost, percentage of response, etc.[7]

Although the beginning student is not likely to be able to use such a technique, it is of great utility in large surveys where a definite level of precision is demanded. The interviews allow a clear picture to be drawn of those who do not answer the questionnaire. In this way, not only is the *direction* of the sampling bias known, but the *degree* and *value* of that bias. Consequently, the resulting tabulations can be weighted with accu-racy. On the other hand, not all the savings of the questionnaire technique are lost unless the level of response is very low.

[6] Morris H. Hansen and William N. Hurwitz, "The Problem of Non-response in Sample Surveys," *Journal of the American Statistical Association*, Vol. XLI (1946), pp. 517–529. This is an adaptation of Neyman's principle of double sampling—J. Neyman, "Contributions to the Theory of Sampling Human Populations," *Journal of the Ameri-can Statistical Association*, Vol. XXV (1938), pp. 101–116—and was used at an early date in sampling lumber production.

[7] Hansen and Hurwitz, *op. cit.*, pp. 521, 523–524.

OPEN-ENDED QUESTIONS

Although the previous remarks have suggested that the most effective questions for the self-administered questionnaire are those which are highly *structured, i.e.,* posing all the possible alternatives for the respondent to choose from, the *unstructured* question may yield further information. Presumably, the work prior to the final formulation of the questionnaire has narrowed the possibilities somewhat, but questions allowing greater freedom to the respondent may still be required. It must be pointed out, however, that such questions are useful with an even smaller proportion of the total population, for such questions require a higher standard of literacy. All the previous remarks on this score are pertinent, with the further emphasis that the open-ended question demands a still greater amount of energy, willingness, and care on the part of the respondent.

As a consequence, unless the sample is extremely carefully chosen and carefully restricted to a rather literate group, the answers to such free questions are likely to be incomplete, couched in clichés, or nonexistent. The problem of coding them is, of course, no different for the questionnaire than for other data-gathering techniques.

If, however, such questions are to be used, the researcher must be rather generous with space on the sheet. A space which is only large enough for a sentence is likely to be filled with no more than a cryptic phrase. It is far better to allow the respondent more space than seems necessary, as a stimulus to a fairly full response.

SUMMARY

The mailed questionnaire has been very useful in social research in the past and is likely to continue to be so in the future. When the student chooses between the mailed questionnaire and the face-to-face interview, he must weight their relative advantages for the purposes and conditions of the project. The questionnaire does not allow complex probe questions which require the respondent to thread his way through many levels of subquestions. Further, the interviewer is not there to give emotional support and other stimuli to increase the respondent's ability and willingness to answer. The questionnaire can be most fruitfully used for highly select respondents with a strong interest in the subject matter, greater education, and higher socioeconomic status. Otherwise, an unknown amount of bias is introduced into the sample. However, when respondents are widely dispersed geographically or will be in one spot only briefly, the questionnaire may be very useful. Whether its cost, for the information needed, is less will depend upon many factors such as degree of response, costs of mailing successive waves, waiting time, etc. Finally, the questionnaire is efficient only when its basic hypothesis is relatively precise. It is not a useful device for gathering preliminary observations concerning social behavior. The present chapter has attempted to analyze the factors which should be weighed in choosing between the interview and the mailed questionnaire and has also described the procedures to be followed in using the questionnaire.

SUGGESTED READINGS

Edgerton, Harold A., Steuart H. Britt, and Ralph D. Norman, "Objective Differences among Various Types of Respondents to a Mailed Questionnaire," *American Sociological Review*, Vol. XII (1947), pp. 435–444.

Parten, Mildred, *Surveys, Polls, and Samples: Practical Procedures* (New York: Harper, 1950), Chap. 11.

Reuss, Carl F., "Differences between Persons Responding and Not Responding to a Mailed Questionnaire," *American Sociological Review*, Vol. VIII, pp. 433–438.

Sletto, Raymond F., "Pretesting of Questionnaires," *American Sociological Review*, Vol. V (April, 1940), pp. 193–200.

CHAPTER 13

The Interview

Just as sampling procedures have developed in complexity and precision far beyond common-sense mental operations, yet are still based on activities common to all men, so is *interviewing* the development of precision, focus, reliability, and validity in another common social act—conversation. When parents attempt to find out what "really happened in school" by questioning children, they are carrying out an interview. Perhaps most readers of this book have been through a "job interview," in which they were asked an embarrassing series of questions designed to find out "What can you do?" Almost everyone has seen a "whodunit" film, in which the master detective carries out a number of interviews with the murder suspects. He "probes" more deeply if he believes the answer does not tell the whole story. He asks a series of questions, designed to cross-check a set of earlier answers. He may ask innocent questions, in order to make the murder suspect relax his guard. The prospective purchaser of real estate becomes an interviewer, also, when he questions the salesman about the property, or returns to the neighborhood later in order to question other residents of the area.

Everyone, then, has been interviewer and interviewee at some time or another, and all have listened to interviews. Some of these have been efficiently performed, while others have failed to elicit the information desired. A few have antagonized the interviewee, while others have become the beginning of a fast friendship. Some have been trivial in nature, and others have been of great significance. It is common to feel, after such interviews, that something different should have been said. Or self-congratulation follows some particularly shrewd question which cleared up an important ambiguity. Once in a while, also, it is recognized that the person who spoke with us "felt a lot better" for having talked about his troubles.

Like other social activities, interviewing has many facets. There are many types of interviews, and their purposes are many. Nevertheless, interviewing can be studied in order to develop skill. Although interviewing is easier for some than for others, everyone can improve his technique by learning to avoid certain types of errors, by developing an alertness to ambiguities and deceptions, and by becoming aware of the purpose of the interview, as well as the interaction between interviewer and respondent.

It is of particular importance that the modern social investigator develop his skill. Increasingly, the social scientist has turned from books to social phenomena in an effort to build the foundations of science. It is true, of course, that speech adds a further complex dimension to research, which the physical scientist does not have to probe. The rock cannot speak. But, as Max Weber once noted, this dimension is also a source of information. If it is not to be ignored, tools for its exploitation must be developed. One can maintain, of course, that every phase of any research is crucial. Errors at any stage may weaken or destroy the validity of the investigation. Yet the interview is, in a sense, the foundation upon which all other elements rest, for it is the data-gathering phase.

Its importance is further seen in the gradual recognition, location, and control of interviewer bias, since the interviewer is really a tool or an instrument. One interviewer may not penetrate the mask of refusal which a potential respondent offers. Another will be given a cordial reception. One interviewer will meet with cliché answers, moderate in tenor and logical in structure, from a certain respondent. Another may find that the same respondent is quite violent in his answers and in his emotion pays little attention to logic. These differences may be extreme cases, but all may be encountered. Important differences between interviewers are generally found, raising the fundamental question of *interviewer reliability:* "To what extent can the answers so obtained be repeated?"

Interviewing has become of greater importance in contemporary research because of the reassessment of the *qualitative interview.* Social scientists of the turn of the century used this type of interview almost exclusively. The interview was likely to be rather unstructured in character and more in the nature of a probing conversation. Guided by a shrewd, careful observer, this could be a powerful instrument for obtaining information. However, it was also an unstandardized instrument. The investigator could not offer definitive proof that his data were as described. The interview was of the character of the anthropological interview, in which no other interviewer was expected to check on the information and the problem of reliability was not often raised.

The development of highly structured schedules was seen as one possible solution to the problem of standardization. Its most complete development, of course, is the polling interview, in which the same questions are asked of every respondent. They were to be asked in the same form, in the same order, with no deviation from respondent to respondent. In this fashion, it was possible to obtain certain items of information for each respondent. This facilitated comparative analysis between individuals or subclasses. However, *depth* was usually sacrificed in order to gain this standardization. As a consequence, there is a movement back to the quali-

tative interview through the use of the *interview guide,* which requires
certain items of information about each respondent but allows the interviewer to rephrase the question in keeping with his understanding of the
situation. This permits the interviewer to express the question in such a
fashion that the respondent can understand it most easily. Further, the
interviewer may probe more deeply when the occasion demands. This
permits a more adequate interpretation of the answers to each question.
In addition, the development of content analysis and qualitative coding
permits some standardization of answers not of the "yes-no" type. Thus,
one of the basic objections to the qualitative interview has been partially
removed.

On the other hand, this method requires an even *higher level of interviewing quality.* The greater the amount of discretion allowed the interviewer, the more necessary is a high level of competence. The application
of more rigid sampling controls takes from the interviewer the choice of
respondent. If, however, his interviewing report contains information
quite different from that obtained by other interviewers, the problem of
"sampling" is reraised—this time, a *sampling of the responses* of the interviewee to these particular questions. If the responses are entirely different
from one interview to another, the adequacy of the data is always in question. Consequently, the development of interviewing skills as well as interviewer controls to a high level is of great importance.

INTERVIEWING AS A SOCIAL PROCESS

Neither reliability nor depth can be achieved, however, unless it is kept
clearly in mind that interviewing is fundamentally a process of social
interaction. Its primary purpose may be research, but this is its purpose
for the investigator. For the respondent, its foundation and meaning may
be different. Even if both have research as an interest, the process of obtaining information is so structured by its character as social interaction
that considerable attention to this aspect is required.

Let us first look at the element in social interaction which is most difficult to define, that of *insight* or intuition. This is an unfortunate term,
since for many it possesses overtones of vagueness, subjectivity, and even
mysticism. Yet no such connotations are intended here. Reference is rather
made to the fact that some of the individuals in a social group seem to
understand the dislikes and likes of the rest better than others do. They
can predict more accurately what the others will say, and respond more
precisely to their intended meaning. They know when one feels offended,
and what lies behind the casual comments of another.

It is commonplace to feel, when on close terms with a friend, that a
casual word, gesture, or look conveys a complete message or story. Yet this
is not usual between mere acquaintances, and this describes the impor-

tance of what may be called *subliminal cues*. That is, everyone betrays his emotions in various ways. As we become accustomed to friends, we learn, consciously or unconsciously, the tiny behavioral accompaniments of these emotions. Those cues which are not recognized consciously, which are below the threshold of perception, are called *subliminal*. A good poker player wins as much by his guesses as to the plans and emotions of his fellow players as by his knowledge of the cards themselves. Indeed, he will play the cards on the basis of these guesses about his opponents. Sometimes guesses are based on a conscious recognition of these cues; other guesses, equally good, which seem to be based on no such recognition, spring from such unconscious observations. If insight refers to such procedures, then it is clear that it can be acquired. To improve his "insight," the student of social relations should attempt consciously to:

1. Develop an alertness to the fact that there *are* many subliminal cues, and that one can learn to "read" them.

2. Attempt to bring these cues to a conscious level, so that comparisons can be made with the hunches of other observers and interviewers.

3. Systematically check the predictions made from these hunches, to see which are correct.

The process of social interaction in the interview is complicated by the fact that the *interviewee* also has insight. This means that the interviewer must not only attempt to be conscious of the real meaning of the answers made by the interviewee; he must also be aware of the fact that his respondent is, in turn, guessing at the motives of the interviewer, responding to the embarrassment of the latter, even to the lack of insight on his part. At times the respondent will give more information because he feels the interviewer "already knows." He responds, then, to the image of himself which he believes the interviewer possesses. This is of real importance when the interviewer must "probe" in order to test or check another answer.

The interviewer must, therefore, become alert to what he is bringing to the interview situation: his appearance, his facial and manual gestures, his intonation, his fears and anxieties, his obtuseness and his cleverness. How do these affect the interviewee? Over some of these characteristics, he may have some control. Others, however, are so much a part of his personality that he can discipline them only slightly. The result will be that every interviewer will meet with some interviewees with whom no rapport will develop, and no adequate interview situation can exist. However, being alert to these characteristics allows him at least to change those elements which are under his control, even if only in the restricted context of the interview situation.

A concrete example lies in one of the most common questions asked by the beginning interviewer: How should he dress? If he is to interview lower class people, for example, should he attempt to dress shabbily? Will he get better answers if he dresses in overalls, or even in poorly cut suits? Further, should he indicate, by using lower class "grammar," that he is a member of that class?

The answers to this series of questions are not entirely certain, but some general rules are apparent. The basic rule derives from the *social role* of the interviewer. Whatever else he may be, he is a researcher in this particular situation, and most of his decisions follow from that role definition. There are research situations in which other considerations enter, but in general this status is a middle-class one. The interviewer will find that "overdressing" is as incongruous with this status as is wearing overalls. Indeed, the latter costume may arouse some disbelief that the interviewer is really a representative of an established research organization. The external characteristics of his functional role include such items as adequate grammar, alertness, confidence and seriousness, and clothing whose aim is neither to attract the opposite sex nor to arouse pity. This is not advice to "steer a middle course." Rather, the interviewer's actions, gestures, speech, and dress should divert attention from himself; in this situation, it is the respondent who is important. Just as extreme dress will arouse attention, so will exaggerated mannerisms or overprecise speech.

These externals are not, be it noted, matters of individual personality and taste, but are the indexes by which the respondent himself will make preliminary judgments. Consequently, they may determine whether the interview will be obtained at all. The social researcher is rapidly becoming a definite status in the society, which means concretely that the student who would pass muster must "act the part." His range of choice in these matters is limited by the public's image of his activities. And, of course, since the interviewer is almost always a representative of some organization, he is limited further by its position in the area. His contribution to the total project will be a negative one if he obtains the interview but manages to arouse antagonism or suspicion toward the organization itself.

This is not to say that for all research situations an apparently middle-class role or behavior will be adequate. Several studies have indicated that a greater range and intensity of attitude are more likely to be expressed when the interviewer is closer to the class and ethnic position of the respondent. This is most especially true, of course, when the opinions to be expressed are somewhat opposed to general public opinion. Thus, to take an extreme case, white interviewers would have a more difficult time in obtaining a true set of attitudes from Negro respondents in Mobile than would Negro interviewers. Similarly, in a town torn by union strife, a very obviously white-collar interviewer might meet with considerable suspicion and might find that many respondents express a suspiciously high proportion of promanagement attitudes.

These facts follow, of course, from the general notion that the respondent, too, has insight and will judge the interviewer by his external characteristics, both gross and subtle. The situation, however, is one to be taken account of in the research design itself, so that the most adequate interviewers are chosen for the particular job. A highly trained interviewer can break through most of these barriers. A poorly trained one will not be adequate even if his class position is superficially in conformity with the group being interviewed. Furthermore, even the average interviewer can learn to become alert to suspicion or reservations on the part of the respondent and to deal with them in an adequate manner.

A common response to a request for an interview is a housewife's, "Oh, I'm much too busy right now. Come back some other time." The interviewer must be able to decide whether the respondent is really too busy or is merely using this claim as a way of avoiding the interview. In some cases, the puzzled or suspicious look on the face of the housewife will tell the interviewer that he should take a few minutes to explain what he is doing and why he is doing it. Even a few casual remarks about the neighborhood, the weather, or his understanding of the housework itself may break through these barriers. In some cases, he may ask a few questions about how to go to his next respondent's house, so as to make known to his interviewee that he is engaged in a quite ordinary activity. It is *not* sufficient merely to ask the respondent if she will set a time for an early appointment. She may be willing to do that, also, in order to avoid the present situation, but there is no guarantee that she will appear. The interviewer, then, must learn to "read" this situation carefully before accepting her claim. She may be obviously leaving the house or may be dressed for housework and annoyed at the interruption. On the other hand, she may really be asking for further reassurance.

Often, when the interviewer has a list of specific respondents whom he must interview personally, his first contact is not with the interviewee but with a member of the family or a friend. In these cases, he must remember that these people must be understood as well, if he is to persuade the respondent to give the interview. A husband or fiancé may be suspicious and refuse permission. A friend of the family may decide that the interviewer is a salesman or a bill collector, and he may give false information or prejudice the respondent so that the latter will not permit the interview. This situation may be very delicate, and particularly so if the subject of the interview is to be explained in detail only to the respondent. The problem must be met before the interviewer goes into the field, so that an adequate answer can be given. However, each situation must be understood as it occurs, so that active cooperation can be obtained from those who may bar the way to the respondent. For example, in one research situation, it was learned that in many lower class areas the statement "I am looking for Mr. Jones" frequently aroused suspicion. Alert to expressions of suspicion such as "What for?" or "Who are you?" or "I don't know the man"—the latter statement made after some hesitation or a long "sizing up" of the interviewer—the decision was made to avoid the question altogether. Instead, the interviewers began their first contact with an expression of smiling, near assurance, "Mr. Jones?" This led more often to a truthful denial of the identity and an offer of information concerning the whereabouts of Mr. Jones. Without this alertness on the part of the interviewer, however, a number of respondents would have been lost because of noncooperation on the part of those who knew the respondents and who had it in their power to misinform the interviewer or refuse access to the ultimate respondent.

ELICITING RESPONSE: RAPPORT

Establishing rapport may seem as elusive an element in interviewing as insight. "Rapport" is indeed a loose term as now used, but its general meaning is clear enough. A state of rapport exists between interviewer and respondent when the latter has accepted the research goals of the interviewer, and actively seeks to help him in obtaining the necessary information. Although the best way to achieve this result may usually be a warm and sympathetic approach, mere friendliness between respondent and interviewer is not sufficient in all cases. If the term "rapport" is to be used exclusively to refer to a state of friendliness between the two, then it must be concluded that rapport is not enough. The goal is to obtain the facts, to the extent that the respondent is capable of presenting them, and in many situations the friendliness must be broken, or suspended, in order to obtain these facts. Although this point will be discussed further in dealing with probe questions, its meaning in the preliminary contact between interviewer and respondent should now be explained.

To begin with, it must be kept clearly in mind that even the inexperienced interviewer will usually meet with an adequate reception. Most students doubt this and approach their first interviews with considerable hesitation and anxiety. Yet it must be remembered that the interviewer is offering a conversation whose focus is the most interesting subject in the world to the respondent: the feelings, attitudes, ideas, and life of the respondent himself. Few can resist this temptation. It has been said that imitation is the sincerest form of flattery, but the most welcome form of flattery is a keen and sympathetic interest in the problems of the person himself. It is still true that Dale Carnegie's *How to Win Friends and Influence People* has much to teach the sociology student who fears that most of his respondents will slam the door in his face. Many people know that the most efficient "line" is simply a good listening ear.

The interviewer must, then, approach the interview with some confidence. Whatever his nervous feelings, he must know that in most cases the respondent will be willing to talk because of the guarantee of a good listener. Confidence, naturally, does not mean brashness. The breezy, cocksure approach is likely to arouse antagonism and refusals more often than even a timid, shy, and awkward approach. The confidence, however, is derived from a calm assurance on the part of the interviewer that the interviewee will find the activity pleasurable. Only experience will teach him the truth of this statement.

The interview is not simply a conversation. It is, rather, a pseudo conversation. In order to be successful, it must have all the warmth and personality exchange of a conversation, with the clarity and guidelines of scientific searching. Consequently, the interviewer cannot merely lose himself in being friendly. He must introduce himself as though beginning a conversation, but from the beginning the additional element of respect, of professional competence, should be maintained. Even the beginning student must make this attempt, else he will find himself merely "maintaining rapport," while failing to penetrate the clichés or contradictions of the respondent. Further, he will find that his own confidence is lessened, if his only goal is to maintain friendliness. He is a professional researcher in this situation, and he must demand and obtain respect for the task he is trying to perform.

The warmth and friendliness—what is usually called "rapport"—can usually be obtained fairly simply. The interviewer greets his respondent with a smile and a simple "Hello" or "How do you do?" It is increasingly the case in modern social research that he is looking for a particular person, rather than any respondent he happens to encounter. Therefore, his next query must establish the identity of his auditor: "Mrs. Jones?" Since the first person to come to the door is not always the desired respondent, there must be a definite procedure for obtaining further information, or locating the respondent. Having learned that the person is the desired respondent, the interviewer will identify himself: "I am Mr. Smith, an interviewer for the Central City Survey. We are making a scientific study of the way people feel about their city, and I'd like to ask you a few questions."

Some respondents will feel ill at ease, at first, because they are afraid that they will have to answer difficult questions. They do not wish to be embarrassed by being unable to answer queries about international relations, impending legislation, and so on. Usually, however, this type of anxiety can be easily allayed by reassuring the person that "This is just a survey, you know. There aren't any right or wrong answers, and this isn't a quiz. We're simply trying to find out how people feel." Or: "There aren't any questions which you can't answer, because they are all about how you feel, the things which have happened to you and to your neighborhood." Such assurances are not always necessary, but they may be very effective when the respondent is hesitant from such a cause.

Some type of conversational statement is often useful in establishing friendly relations with the respondent. A simple statement which conveys the idea that the interviewer is not a superior person, but a professional doing his job, may help to start the interview on a warm basis. A confession that the interviewer took a wrong bus, or that he failed to plan properly for the weather, may be enough. Anxiety on the part of the respondent may be ignored, and the interviewer himself may confess some anxiety: "You know, as much interviewing as I've done, I'm always a little nervous when I begin." When the subject matter is taboo, the interviewer will of course give assurances that the answers will be kept confidential. In addition, however, it may be necessary to make certain the respondent knows that the interviewer himself is not going to be embarrassed by anything which may be said.

Most interviewers find that few respondents require any further identification. However, each interviewer must carry some official card or letter which will satisfy the suspicious interviewee that his mission is a scientific one. Most respondents will invite the interviewer into their homes at this point. Others will wait until further assurances are offered. And, of course, for some studies the interview may be satisfactorily carried out at the door.

A number of fairly standard situations may arise, before the interview is finally granted. The research director, or the student carrying out a term project, must plan for these situations in advance, so that his answers will inspire confidence and ultimately lead to an adequate interview. Most of these can be understood as rapport situations, and they can be most easily seen in concrete terms, as objections offered by the desired respondent. Let us look at some of them:

SITUATION I

RESPONDENT: (*Suspiciously*) Well, I don't know about that. How did you get my name, anyway?

INTERVIEWER: Your name was selected at random, from a list of all the citizens in this city. We wanted to get people from all walks of life, and by chance your name was one of those selected.

Here, the interviewer must be certain whether the answer is satisfactory. If not, he may add a few further comments:

INTERVIEWER: As a matter of fact, the statistical expert who chose your name did not know anything about you personally. He used a mechanical system for selecting names from the entire list, just the way some radio programs pick out names for long-distance quiz questions.

SITUATION II

RESPONDENT: Well, I think I'm too busy now. Why can't you talk to my neighbor, Mrs. Lackland? She likes to talk to people.

INTERVIEWER: I know that I am taking some of your time, Mrs. Jones, but we're trying to get the opinions of all kinds of people, and if we just got the people who like to talk, and left out all the people who are doing things, who *are* a little busy, then we wouldn't have a very good sample, would we? We'd have just one kind of person, and we'd miss the rest. So, you see, we need your own opinions. They're very important for the study.

SITUATION III

RESPONDENT: I'm sorry, but I never give my opinions to people. They're my own business.

INTERVIEWER: I think you're very wise, to follow that general rule. Why, do you know that some people come to the door, acting like interviewers, then try to sell magazine subscriptions, or books, or kitchen utensils?

RESPONDENT: (*Grimly interjecting*) I'd like to see one of them try to sell *me* any books!

INTERVIEWER: It's just because some people want to know more about things before they give their opinions, that all of us on the Central City Survey carry a card to identify us. (*Hands over the card*) That way, you can be sure that this is a *scientific* study, and not just some busybody who wants to find out about your affairs. You see, in a *scientific* study, we don't *even put your name* on our interview records. Furthermore, when the interview goes to the office, only the statistical experts see what you said—and they are interested *only* in the final results, not in the individual comments. It's just like the census interviews, and no outsider can ever learn what your opinions were.

SITUATION IV

RESPONDENT: Well, I suppose so. Won't you come in? We're having a little gabfest, but you go ahead and ask your questions. I'm sure my friends won't mind, and they can help me out, if there's some question I can't answer.

INTERVIEWER: (*After coming inside*) Do you mind if we go in the next room, instead? That way, your friends won't be interrupted, and I can get your own opinions. You see, it's *your* opinions I want, not theirs—and, besides, we're simply trying to find out how you feel about things; we're not trying to test you.

SITUATION V

RESPONDENT: I'm not so sure I want to be interviewed. What kinds of questions have you got there? (*Tries to look at the schedule*)

INTERVIEWER: (*Without trying to hide the questions*) Well, they're really very simple. Suppose I sit down and we'll try a few. Then you can see what kinds of questions they are.

SITUATION VI

RESPONDENT: I think all that stuff is silly. What good does it do, anyway? Why, you people couldn't even predict the 1948 election.

Here the interviewer must decide which of the objections is the real one, and answer that primarily.

INTERVIEWER: With all the new things that are happening to Central City, many people believe that a lot of mistakes could be avoided if we find out what people really think these days. Maybe we can learn how to handle the everyday problems of the city better. You know, a lot of people are too busy to take part in community affairs. But by giving their opinions to a scientific survey like this, they help just the same, and they can have the satisfaction of knowing that someone will actually listen to what they have to say.

Such situations are frequently met, but of course they represent only a sample of the varied circumstances which the interviewer must face. It can be seen, nevertheless, that he is attempting to establish three elements in the interview situation: (1) his own friendliness and interest; (2) the worth of the research itself; and (3) his own competence. Thus, he will sympathize with the personal problems of the respondent, and will adjust to them in every possible way—except in ways which would weaken the interview. The respondent will be less willing to tell the truth if it is embarrassing, when he feels that the interviewer will not see the deception or that the research is of little importance, anyway.

These elements must be continued throughout the interview. Some interviewers are able to maintain a friendly interest but lose the main thread of the interview, since they are willing to listen to anything. Others do not listen carefully and merely go through the motions of sympathetic listening. The consequence may be that the respondent does not attempt to be precise or grows impatient when he has to repeat an earlier statement. Consequently, a number of transitional phrases are often used which let the respondent understand that the material is worth while and is being understood:

"That's a very interesting point. Would you mind repeating it, so that I can write it down exactly as you've stated it?"

"Now, let me be sure I've understood you. You are saying. . . ."

"You were speaking a moment ago about the Camp Fire Girls organization. Would you mind answering a few questions about that?"

CARRYING THE INTERVIEW FORWARD

The process of continuing the interview will vary, depending on the type of interview. Social research has utilized a great number of interviews, which may be classified in numerous ways. Perhaps the simplest variable for classifying interviews is that of *depth,* that is, how deeply the interview attempts to probe. This, in turn, depends of course upon the actual purpose of the research. For some research which attempts to investigate fairly subtle sociopsychological processes, the interview is almost psychiatric or psychoanalytic in character. It will usually be "nondirective" in form, and the interviewer will follow those items which appear so often in the respondent's comments that they seem of great emotional significance. Thus, in the interviewing phase of the Hawthorne research, the interviewers attempted to refrain from any guiding comments or questions at all. Instead, they simply listened, with a judicious "Hmmm," or an interested "Go on," or a similar comment—at times, no more than a gesture of sympathy. In this way, the workers would return again and again to matters which were close to their personal lives. Even when the researchers attempted to ask specific work-unit questions, they found that the workers would bring up apparently extraneous items, indicating that these items were of more personal importance to them than the original questions about the factory itself.

Although the Hawthorne interviews were fairly long, lasting several hours over a period of several interviews, such interview situations may continue for much longer, if the research demands such a depth and range of inquiry into the respondent's life. Indeed, if the research is a cross-discipline study dealing with certain aspects of psychotherapy, a series of interviews may extend over a period of months.

In any event, the types of interviews to be used in social research may vary from extremely lengthy and intensive interviews, which probe into the most intimate aspects of the respondent's life, to the voting poll which merely obtains information about social class, sex, age, and political-party affiliation, along with voting preference. Clearly, then, "carrying the interview forward" must have a very different meaning for such varying types of interviews.

However, all but the briefest of polling interviews do attempt to utilize some questions for which the answers are not easily classified in advance and which must remain "unstructured" or "open-ended." Such questions, as analyzed in the chapter on the questionnaire, give a depth and meaning to the more structured questions. Furthermore, even the most highly structured set of questions is likely to be unsatisfactory to both respondent and researcher if it is not carried forward with some skill.

The process of carrying the interview forward is greatly aided by writing the questions in a fashion which most closely approximates a conversation, while probing those items for which the research is being conducted. It is often useful to insert appropriate transitional phrases as well as introductory comments in the schedule form itself. This is especially the case if the questions are otherwise short and staccato. However, the burden of the interview must ultimately be borne by the interviewer himself. Recognition of this fact has meant that even with the increasing skill in question making, the social research worker in this decade is steadily increasing his use of the skilled interviewer, as against the interviewing crew picked up for a particular study.

Clearly, many of the earlier comments concerning rapport are also appropriate for the task of carrying the interview forward. Some of these may be elaborated further in this immediate context.

Because both respondent and interviewer have been reared through social relationships, in which verbal exchange is almost solely in the form of "conversations," neither can easily adjust to a situation in which the give and take is of an examination character. The respondent is likely to feel that he is being grilled, and the interviewer will feel that the verbal exchange is wooden and mechanical. The student can test this statement very easily by taking his first draft of a questionnaire to a close friend for a test interview. If, in his test interview, he reads the questions quickly, does not pause between questions, cuts off the answers as soon as the needed information is given, attempts to make no transitions between different subject-matter areas of the questions, and ends the interview without further comment when the last question has been answered, he will find that the entire exchange seems forced, unreal, and emotionally unsatisfactory to both.

There are good reasons for placing a strong emphasis on "emotional satisfaction" in a research interview. To begin with, the respondent for one research study does not cease to exist, but tells others about his experience. Social research in a broad sense depends upon the good impression which the interviewer makes on his respondents. This is obviously true when a study is being conducted in a small community, in which news of the interviews will be carried from neighbor to neighbor in a short while. However, the same processes are to be found in any large city. They exist in specific ways, so that one respondent may actually speak of the study to a friend who may later become a respondent in the same study. In more general ways, however, these processes are also important, so that for a later study the good impression made by the interviewer will aid the next researcher.

A further dimension ought to be mentioned. The interview which is developed in an easy, natural fashion, approximating a conversation in its effect on both participants, stimulates the interviewer himself to a better effort. He loses his initial anxiety quickly, and finds time to ask questions which make definite the sometimes vague answers which the respondent may give. He feels more confident and thus—because of the respondent's own insight—makes the respondent feel his competence.

One of the immediate results of attempting to make the interview approximate a conversation is that the silences which occur need no longer be filled quickly by a hurried question, and the respondent does not feel that he has to have a prepared answer. The answer to the silence may sometimes be merely an interested look, or a sympathetic half-smile, or a pursing of the lips to indicate that the comment is being digested. The silence will not be embarrassing, for it can be taken as a matter of course. The interviewer may extend it somewhat by lighting a cigarette, or shifting his questionnaire pad. He may invite the respondent to "think out loud" for a while. Or he may simply wait in a relaxed fashion, as though he is certain that the respondent has a further comment to make. In this manner, what could have been embarrassing becomes an integral part of the give and take of the interview.

In spite of this insistence on the conversational character of the interview, it must not be forgotten that the interview is not merely a conversation. The interviewer's goal is to obtain *information* from the respondent, and he must concentrate upon the respondent. His most efficient method is to treat the latter as a person, giving him a sympathetic hearing. The corollary of this is that the interviewer's attitudes and opinions are not relevant and must not be allowed to intrude into the situation. Again, although it is important for the interviewer to gain the respect of the interviewee, he must not do this by attempting to be "clever," or by arguing with the respondent. Compare, for example, the following two treatments:

I

INTERVIEWER: Would you say that in general you have got along fairly well with your Negro neighbors?
RESPONDENT: Oh, yes! Just fine. They don't bother me, and I don't bother them. Why, I don't suppose we see each other from one week to the next.
INTERVIEWER: I believe you're just kidding yourself. Can't you see that avoiding your neighbors is the same kind of discrimination that is to be found in the South? I don't see any difference at all.

II

INTERVIEWER: Would you say that in general you have got along fairly well with your Negro neighbors?
RESPONDENT: Oh, yes! Just fine. They don't bother me, and I don't bother them. Why, I don't suppose we see each other from one week to the next.
INTERVIEWER: I suppose that once in a while you do meet them face to face on the street. What do you usually do at such times?

The interviewer's attempt, in treatment I, to "educate" his respondent is likely to antagonize the respondent. The result would probably be that the respondent, knowing how the interviewer feels, would change his answers accordingly. In some cases, he simply might not care to cooperate further or might give only polite answers. In treatment II, however, the interviewer is specifying further just what the respondent means by his preceding statement. The interviewer in the first case has pointed out the underlying meaning of the "fairness" of the respondent but has forgotten that the purpose of the interview is to gain information, not to intrude his own opinions.

Similarly, the temptation to be "clever" is very strong in some interviews. Consider the following, for example:

I

INTERVIEWER: You say that you did not begin to date until after the divorce. About how long was it after the divorce before you did begin?

RESPONDENT: Oh, it was a long time, nearly a year. You see, I didn't think anyone would want to have dates with me, after all that mess.

INTERVIEWER: Why, that's very silly. Don't you know that according to a study made by the Metropolitan Life Insurance Company, your chances of remarriage, at your age, are about 94 in 100?

II

INTERVIEWER: You say that you did not begin to date until after the divorce. About how long was it after the divorce before you did begin?

RESPONDENT: Oh, it was a long time, nearly a year. You see, I didn't think anyone would want to have dates with me, after all that mess.

INTERVIEWER: Would you try to think back to that time, and give me some idea of anything that happened that might have made you feel that way?

In the first case, the interviewer has indeed shown that he "knows something," but he has diverted attention to himself and away from the problem he is trying to investigate. Some respondents may feel rebuked by such a remark. Some will not, of course, and may be interested in the fact. However, even to divert the interview to some of the interesting facts about divorce is to miss the point of the interview. It is not to be an exchange of information, but the obtaining of information.

What is the interviewer to do, however, if the respondent really wants information? Suppose the interviewee does answer the question but then asks for the opinion of the interviewer. Should he give his honest opinion, or an opinion which he thinks the interviewee wants? In most cases, the rule remains that he is there to obtain information and to focus on the respondent, not himself. Usually, a few simple phrases will shift the emphasis back to the respondent. Some which have been fairly successful are "I guess I haven't thought enough about it to give a good answer right now," "Well, right now, your opinions are more important than mine," and "If you really want to know what I think, I'll be honest and tell you in a moment, after we've finished the interview." Sometimes the diversion can be accomplished by a head-shaking gesture which suggests "That's a hard one!" while continuing with the interview. In short, the interviewer must avoid the temptation to express his own views, even if given the opportunity.

Nevertheless, the interviewer cannot be efficient if he tries to be only a passive listener. Not only will he fail to impress the respondent with the significance of the research, but he will fail to obtain the information which is the purpose of the interview. He must be a critical and intelligent questioner.

INTERVIEWER: I know it's very hard to remember why you decided to do something a long time ago, but would you try to think back to the time when you first began to think of being a lawyer? How did you happen to change from business administration to law while you were in college?

RESPONDENT: Why, the same reasons then as now. The fact was that I saw in the law an opportunity for service. The lawyer can help his fellow men. All the poor people who come to him need his help, and he has the power to aid them. I've always been one who likes to help his fellow men.

INTERVIEWER: How did you come to believe you could do this better by being a lawyer than being a businessman?

RESPONDENT: Well, all the businessmen I knew were interested only in making money. I was a poor kid in college, and had to work my way through, and I had lots of dealings with businessmen—restaurant owners, hotel men, landlords, clothing store owners, and construction men. They were all hard, grasping men, and I had a hard time of it. I didn't want to be like them.

INTERVIEWER: Did you know any lawyers at the time, who might have played a part in your decision?

RESPONDENT: Oh, yes. I met Mr. Crichton at that time, once when I had gone to the house of a businessman whose store I swept out in the mornings. I went to see him about some money he owed me. He invited me into his house just to tell me he couldn't pay me until Saturday, and I needed the money right then. I guess I was pretty hungry. Why, I can remember his living room still— it was dirty, and it smelled, and the place was ugly. I was sure he was trying to gyp me. Anyway, I had to hitchhike back to where I lived, near the University, and this lawyer, Mr. Crichton, picked me up. I was so mad at Mr. Jones that I couldn't help telling this lawyer about it. Why, right away, he showed how a lawyer can help other people. He agreed to call the man up the following morning, and threaten him with a suit if he didn't pay up. And he did, too. Mr. Crichton was a real gentleman. He invited me to his house for supper, and I was hungry enough to accept. It was a pretty big place, set back from the road, in the middle of a big lawn. Right in the foyer was a great crystal chandelier, and the place was beautiful inside. He was living the way a man ought to live, with servants and fine food. I guess you might say that Mr. Crichton was very important in my decision to study the law.

INTERVIEWER: Then you would say that the personal example of this Mr. Crichton, in helping people in trouble, made you decide to help others too?

Here, the interviewer has not ventured his own opinions. He has listened carefully, and asked the questions in his interview guide. He wishes to avoid a conflict which might antagonize his respondent. Yet his report will be of little value if he does not face the obvious contradiction presented by the lawyer's story. His last question allows the lawyer an easy rationalization, but when the lawyer agrees with these words the interviewer has little opportunity to probe the contradiction. On the other hand, he must understand that the lawyer himself may not be able to face the contradiction.

The rule must again be that his duty is to obtain the facts. He must at least probe once more to see whether the lawyer himself understands his complex motivations. Consequently, the last question must not be asked. Instead, some other formulation must be substituted. One of the following might well be used, depending on the rapport which the interviewer has gained, how far along the interview has progressed, and the interviewer's judgment as to the relative risks involved:

"That must have been a very interesting evening. Could you tell me more about it?"

"Mr. Crichton seems to have been a very successful lawyer, besides helping poor people. Now, I know it's difficult to be sure, but do you think that his way of living—having fine food, a large income, servants, and so on—might have influenced you as much as his being willing to help others?"

"About that time in your life, were you ever invited to the homes of any *businessmen* who made as much money as Mr. Crichton?"

The interviewer must use his ingenuity at such a point, to avoid losing the interview on the one hand, and to gain the crucial information on the other. He must probe more deeply, to avoid the clichés which are used to cover motivations. It is of great importance, in the interview, to unravel sympathetically and intelligently the complex web of paradox which forms much of everyone's life.

Another problem in carrying the interview forward occurs when the question to be asked seems to have been answered previously, as a side comment on an earlier question. The inexperienced interviewer is likely to pass over such a question on these grounds. Yet there is considerable field experience to indicate that the direct question may elicit a slightly different answer, or an entirely different answer, than the earlier comment seemed to suggest. For example, this answer was given to a question about the respondent's parents:

RESPONDENT: My family had a farm in the country, and I lived with them until I was grown. They live in Minnesota, and I haven't seen them in a long time.

A later question centered on the respondent's dating activities following the divorce, and her success in adjusting to the possibility of a new marriage. The interviewer was tempted to ignore the question as to whether the parents of the respondent had helped her to meet eligible men. It was quite clear that they were far away and entirely outside the urban circles in which she moved. Nevertheless, the interview phrased the question in this fashion:

INTERVIEWER: I believe you may have answered this question before, when you mentioned that your parents live in Minnesota, but I'd like to ask the question just the same—Did your parents help you to meet eligible men after the divorce?

RESPONDENT: Oh, yes. As a matter of fact, I met my present fiancé through them. They wrote me a letter about a fellow from our home town who was a chemist here, and they told him about me, and he called me very soon afterwards. And I made a trip home right after the divorce—they saw to it that I met a lot of young men then.

Even under the best of circumstances, the interviewer can bring out only a very thin thread of fact concerning the life of his respondent. What is most obvious to the interviewer, from some casual comment of the respondent, may become entirely opposite in meaning, when a direct question elicits still more facts. The interviewer must not attempt such judgments about answers, but should present each one in turn, for the additional facts may throw great light on, or change basically, the earlier comments and answers. The use of a fairly simple phrase may avoid the awkwardness of asking what seems to have been answered and will often help greatly in understanding the respondent.

THE PROBE QUESTION

Even in a schedule in which most questions demand simple "yes" or "no" answers, there will usually be a number of questions directed toward deeper and more difficult issues of motivation, attitude, and personal history. Furthermore, in the earlier stages of any research, when the questions are being tested, the interviews should not be highly structured in any event, since the range of possibilities will be narrowed too soon. In addition, the interview guide leaves considerable scope to the judgment and skill of the interviewer. In all these situations, then, there will be some questions whose answers will not fall into simple categories. Since these questions may be the most significant ones in the schedule, they must be presented with great care. The interviewer cannot be satisfied with merely writing down the answer. He must be certain (1) that he understands the answer, and (2) that it is actually an answer to the question. Often this will require further questioning, an attempt to "probe" more deeply into the meaning of the response given. Here is a simple case, in which the respondent simply did not answer the question:

INTERVIEWER: Mr. Jones, suppose your son decided to become a lawyer. Would you approve such a decision?
RESPONDENT: Funny you asked me that. I just came from my lawyer's office, and I guess they're all just the worst crooks a man could meet. Why, they're worse than card sharks!

Here a probe question is definitely required. The interviewer cannot assume that, because the respondent has a low opinion of lawyers, he would disapprove his son's decision to become one. Furthermore, he is expressing the anger of an immediate situation and may give a more sober opinion after further conversation. In this situation, if the man's emotion seems fairly strong, the interviewer might well smile and wait in interested silence, encouraging the respondent to talk out his annoyance. Then the question should simply be repeated, and in most situations it does not need to be rephrased at all. The interviewer must recognize that in the interview, as in our private conversations generally, people often fail to answer the question. They respond *in terms of the question*, but the answer will at times simply reflect the enthusiasm or annoyance of the moment. The question has been worked out with much effort, and it should not be lost through failure to see that the words written down are not really an answer.

Another type of probe is required when the interviewee is not able to answer the question. When the respondent simply does not have the information, of course a probe will be of no use, except to be certain that the respondent really does not know. When the purpose of the question is simply to measure the extent of knowledge about a subject, the "don't know" answer represents a definite and useful category. Questions about specific provisions in a new immigration law, or labor legislation, or about local legal and medical services available to low-income groups, would all be examples of this.

However, often the respondent gives a "don't know" answer because he is unable to think of the answer immediately, or is afraid to attempt an answer, or has not understood the question. Of course, as is discussed in the section on making a schedule, a large percentage of "don't know" answers to a given question means that the question itself is not properly phrased. In such cases, it is necessary to discover the communication problem and to rephrase the question in the final draft of the schedule so as to elicit a greater proportion of answers. Nevertheless, the interviewer may meet with a "don't know" answer to almost any question and must learn how to meet this obstacle. Below are a few concrete cases illustrating how some interviewers have solved the problem.

INTERVIEWER: How did you feel when you first heard that the atomic bomb had been dropped on Hiroshima?
RESPONDENT: Why, I don't know. That was so long ago.
INTERVIEWER: Perhaps that *is* a difficult question. Were you living in this house at the time?
RESPONDENT: No, I believe I was living in an apartment on Bleecker Street then. . . . That was in 1946. . . . No, it was in 1945, wasn't it?
INTERVIEWER: What kind of a job did you have then?
RESPONDENT: Well, that was before I married, so I had a job as a stenographer, at Gimbel's. I think I had just been working a few weeks when it happened.
INTERVIEWER: Were you working when you first heard about the bomb?

RESPONDENT: No, I'm pretty sure I wasn't. Oh, no, now I remember. I had a bad cold that day, and stayed at home. I was pretty lonesome, and kept the radio on all day long, just listening to soap operas.

INTERVIEWER: Then you first heard about it over the radio?

RESPONDENT: Yes, that's right. Now, it's all clear to me. When the news announcer first began talking, I thought it was some kind of adventure program, you know, like "Amazing Stories," or "Buck Rogers." Then I began to realize that he was really telling the news. When I did, then I got real scared, and. . . .

In this case, the interviewer adopted an obvious but useful technique in answer to the "don't know" response. He began to reconstruct the early situation by having the respondent recall some of the fairly stable facts which most of us remember fairly easily: where she lived at the time, what kind of job she had, and so on. These set the stage for stimulating her memory to a fairly clear picture of the day on which she heard about the blast. In the case of such an event as the atomic bomb, most people can remember the situation, if reminded of the larger facts which were part of that experience. Naturally, even with such aids, many experiences cannot be recalled. However, it will be noticed that the interviewer did not help the respondent by suggesting what her thoughts might have been. It would have been poor probing if he had asked, "Were you frightened when you first heard of the bomb?" or "What significant ideas went through your mind at that time?" or "Were you proud of the American science which produced the bomb?" No suggestions were given to her about either her ideas or her feelings. Furthermore, the probing questions were not attempts to "force" her to remember.

This technique, of indirectly leading the respondent back to a previous experience, has been utilized not only in research into reactions to crisis, but even in such prosaic matters as the respondent's annual consumption of soap, or the respondent's reaction to a soap opera. The following is a somewhat different case in which the respondent, a civil service worker, seemed afraid to give the answer:

INTERVIEWER: Do you, in general, feel that your boss is fair in giving promotions?

RESPONDENT: Why, I don't know. No, I guess I couldn't give an answer to that.

What does the respondent mean? The interviewer must answer this question before he can proceed. Here are some possible meanings:

1. I am afraid you will tell someone how I feel, and I'll get in trouble.

2. You're asking me to make a judgment about personnel policy in my company, and I don't know all the facts.

3. I've never thought about the matter very much, and I don't know what to say.

In this case, the interviewer could not at first decide between (1) and (2) but felt that his opening explanation and the later development of the interview had made the respondent feel relaxed. Consequently, he decided upon (2).

INTERVIEWER: Of course, you may not know all the facts about your company. You see, we're just trying to find out how you *feel*, your *attitude* about these matters: Do you, in general, feel that your boss is fair in giving promotions?

RESPONDENT: Well, like I said, I don't really know. But I guess I don't much believe some of us get a fair break. There's lots of people in our department, so I'm not sure. But it's always seemed to me that the boss plays favorites a lot.

In this case, the respondent wanted to be correct if he made an intellectual judgment, but his own attitudes were not so impartial. Later questions indicated that he had observed a number of incidents which made him feel that his boss did not promote fairly. He really did "know" the answer to the question, which was a query about his attitude. However, he was unwilling to give an answer as long as he believed that the question concerned the detailed facts of promotion in his department. Assuring him that there were no correct or incorrect answers led to a series of fruitful answers concerning his personal experiences.

In the following case, however, the respondent simply did not understand the question:

INTERVIEWER: Are you in favor of the right of the FBI to tap telephone wires?

RESPONDENT: I don't know. Guess I never thought much about it. Couldn't say at all.

INTERVIEWER: I'd like to get your answer to this question—You know, it's possible to fix a telephone line so that a person can listen to anything that's said over that line. Do you feel that the FBI ought to have the right to do that, so that one of their men can listen in that way?

RESPONDENT: Oh, sure. I think the FBI is a fine organization, and if they think they can catch a crook by listening in, I'm all for it.

Even when difficult words are avoided in the schedule, there will be some respondents who will not immediately understand the question. Sometimes it is necessary only to ask the question over again, in exactly the same fashion. In other cases, when it is clear that this will not or does not help, the interviewer may have to rephrase the question so that it is clear. In the above case, the "don't know" answer was simply a way of avoiding the confession that the question was not understood. Of course, in some studies, the interviewer will be given definite instructions to ask each question without any rephrasing at all. Naturally, then, these instructions will have to be followed, and the answer may have to be recorded as "don't know," if the respondent persists in his inability to answer.

It is clear that the function of a probe question is to get beneath the "easy answer." Sometimes this may take the form of a further "Why?" question, or a phrase such as "That's very interesting. Would you tell me more about that?" As noted above, at times the respondent is not answering the real question or is avoiding it in some fashion, and the interviewer must recognize these answers in order to go beyond them.

A further type of probe, beyond those mentioned, may be called the "antagonistic probe." In general, the good interviewer will not violate the rapport which he has developed, but will attempt to maintain good relations with his respondent. This is usually an excellent interview tool. However, such good relations are not an end in themselves, and if the situation demands antagonism, it must be used. This type of probe may range in emotional tone from a polite reminder of an inconsistency, to the forceful preachment which Kinsey reports he has given to respondents whom he found lying to him.

What must be kept in mind, however, is not that this tool exists, but that it must be used *only deliberately*. It must not be a slip of the tongue, or an accident. It should not be used because the interviewer is annoyed at the respondent, and it should be carried out only with a full understanding of the risk involved. It is usually a last measure to be used only when other techniques fail. In the following case, the interviewer was forced into such a probe in order to be certain of the answer.

INTERVIEWER: Were there any times when you felt you did not play fair with your husband?
RESPONDENT: Never. I always played square with him. I never ran around on him until after the divorce.
INTERVIEWER: Pardon me, but I'd like to be certain I have this correct. You say that you did not date until after the divorce?
RESPONDENT: That's right. I was a good wife, and I thought that would be immoral.
INTERVIEWER: Then I must have written down something earlier that was not correct. Didn't you mention earlier that your main activity, when you were separated, was dating?
RESPONDENT: (*Excitedly*) Well, I never considered that real running around. Dick was like one of the family, a good friend of ours even while we were married. (*In tears*) Anyway, after what he was doing to me, I figured I had the right to do anything I wanted.
INTERVIEWER: Just what was he doing?
RESPONDENT: Well, I said a while ago that we got divorced because we just didn't get along, but that's not right. The truth was, he started to run around with my kid cousin, who was only seventeen at the time, and got her in trouble. Oh, it was a big scandal in the family, and I felt horrible about it. . . .

Here, if the interviewer had simply accepted her statement about feeling that she had treated her husband fairly, he not only would have lost some additional facts but would have missed the point of the divorce crisis in the family. Demanding that the inconsistent facts be faced led to a better understanding of the emotional experiences through which this divorcee had passed. Nor was it necessary to accuse the respondent of hiding facts, although in a few cases such an accusation can be fruitful.

RECORDING THE INTERVIEW

It is the most obvious common sense to state that the interview must be recorded adequately. Yet a careful check of first interviews by beginning students shows that this most obvious rule is not always followed. Considerable experience and repeated corrections are required before the interview is recorded properly. Even for the highly structured questionnaire, in which the interviewer has only to check "yes," "no," or "don't know," or one of a series of answers concerning degree of approval, the beginner will often leave out questions or fail to mark down the answers. In the interesting task of asking questions and trying to understand answers, the interviewer is likely to believe that the answers have been recorded. It is therefore useful to have another person check the interviews even in a relatively small research project so that all the questions are answered for each respondent. For a larger project, of course, checking interviews for completion is a standardized phase in the work flow.

However, just as the interviewer can obtain only a small part of the respondent's total experience, so the interview record presents only a small part of the interviewer's experience in the interview. Increasingly, social research is group research, and increasingly the interviewer is not the person who analyzes the tabulated data. The work of recording the interview, then, becomes still more important. What is quite obvious to the interviewer, observant to the details of his interaction with the respondent, cannot be known to the analyst unless the information is included in the interview protocol. The interviewer may feel, for example, that the respondent is simply hiding the truth, or lying for some reason, but the "yes" and "no" answers do not indicate this important dimension. Failure to include this judgment is a major failure in recording. Again, the respondent may claim that his income is very high, that he prefers certain luxury brands of merchandise, and that he is "getting along very well" in his career—but may live in obvious poverty. If the interviewer fails to record this qualifying fact, his interview protocol will contain a serious error. A similar case occurs when the respondent gives a series of consistent answers but, on taking leave of the interviewer, informs the latter that all the answers are incorrect because of a fear that a neighbor is listening through the wall. It seems elementary that this information must be included in the interview record, but in the bustle and hurry which often characterize a project in the field interviewing stage, such facts may be forgotten or overlooked.

Even in a polling type of interview, consisting of a few carefully chosen questions, to be asked exactly as printed, with no blanks for additional information, the interviewer can sometimes help by including bits of information which help to interpret the answer. However, when the interview is of an intensive, qualitative type, with many unstructured probe questions, the problem of recording becomes crucial. So far as possible, the *exact* words of the respondent should be recorded. They should not be edited for grammar or meaning. Since most interviewers will not have a command of shorthand, it is necessary to develop skill in writing fast and legibly, with some attention to symbols for common short phrases such as "of the," "also," or words common in the particular research study. However, even the best writer will fail to copy all that is said at conversational speed. It will often be useful, at such times, to interrupt by some such comment as "That sounds like a very important point. Would you mind repeating it, so that I can get your words exactly as you say them?" The respondent is usually flattered by this attention, and rapport is not disturbed.

As an additional aid to complete reporting, the interviewer may make it a practice to go directly from the interview to a typewriter or desk, in order to write out the details while the materials are still fresh in his mind. Even under such circumstances, memories can be treacherous, and delay of any proportions may quickly distort or blur the details. The comments which seemed so clear during the interview begin to lose their distinctness, and the "whys and wherefores" offered by the respondent lose their reasonable quality. The comments which are scribbled in haste during an intensive, probing interview will never convey all the richness of material given by the respondent. On the other hand, an alert student without an extraordinary memory can reproduce some 20 to 40 double-spaced typewritten pages of materials from an interview lasting 1½ hours —*if* he goes immediately from the interview to the typewriter with his notes while the experience is still vivid.

CLOSING THE INTERVIEW

The modes of saying "good-by" are many and have many different effects upon the respondent. The question is somewhat complicated by the differing reactions of respondents to the interview itself. In the intensive interview, a common experience for interviewers is to find that the closing is more difficult than the opening. The respondent has found an interested, warm audience and is unwilling to let the interviewer leave. If the interview has touched on fairly deep and troubled matters, the respondent may feel very grateful and exclaim, "This was the first time in months I've had a chance to talk about it." An invitation to stay for dinner, a drink, or coffee and cookies is very common in these circumstances. The interviewer may actually be caught, therefore, by the very web of friendliness he has spun. He has transformed the situation into a conversation between two friends and feels that he would be violating the illusion if he brusquely snatches his papers and mumbles, "Well, I'd better get going."

For the usual polling interview, in which the person's name is not known and in which a few brief questions are asked, a simple "Thank you very much for your trouble," with a friendly smile, will probably be an adequate good-by. However, for the qualitative interview, of longer duration and greater intensity, the interviewer will have to select his occasion for departure more carefully. Since he has presumably obtained the necessary information, there is no particular reason why he may not remain longer, except the obvious one of efficiency. He has spent from 45 minutes to several hours in the questioning process, and he probably has other respondents whom he must see. On the other hand, he should not antagonize the respondent. The good relations which each interviewer develops will, directly and indirectly, help both his own later research and that of others. Besides, he will himself feel embarrassed by social awkwardness at this stage.

Consequently, although his departure should not be abrupt, it can at least be deliberate, open, and continuous. Assembling his papers for a final check, asking a further question to be certain of a previous answer, putting the papers in folder or clipboard, even while continuing the conversation, allows the situation to be defined as one of leave-taking. This restructuring of the situation sets the stage for a final handshake, a thank-you, and a good-by. In some cases, the interviewer may have to reverse the time-honored trick of hosts by asking about some object near the door, such as a lamp, an ornament, or a potted plant. Again, this sets the stage for a good-by. Always, however, the adieu should be accompanied by an expression of thanks in recognition of the respondent's generosity in time and attention.

SUGGESTED READINGS

Hyman, Herbert, "Isolation, Measurement and Control of Interviewer Effect," *Items,* Social Science Research Council, June, 1949.

Jahoda, Marie, Morton Deutsch, and Stuart W. Cook, *Research Methods in Social Relations* (New York: Dryden, 1951), Part II, Chap. 13.

Lazarsfeld, Paul F., "The Controversy over Detailed Interviews—an Offer for Negotiation," *Public Opinion Quarterly,* Vol. VII (1944), pp. 38–60.

National Opinion Research Center, *Interviewing for NORC* (University of Denver, 1946).

Parten, Mildred, *Surveys, Polls, and Samples: Practical Procedures* (New York: Harper, 1950), Chap. 10.

Young, Pauline V., *Scientific Social Surveys and Research* (New York: Prentice-Hall, 1949), Chap. 11.

CHAPTER 14

Probability and Sampling

The purpose of this chapter is to explain the basic principles and techniques employed in sampling. A sample, as the name implies, is a smaller representation of a larger whole. The observation of some phenomena in complete detail would involve such a mass of data that analysis would be slow and tedious. Moreover, to analyze large quantities of material is wasteful when a smaller amount would suffice.

Thus, the use of sampling allows for more adequate scientific work by making the time of the scientific worker count. Instead of spending many hours over the analysis of a mass of material from one point of view, he may use that time to examine a smaller amount of material from many points of view or, in other words, to do a more intensive analysis of fewer cases. Another obvious value of sampling is that it also saves money and thus makes investigations possible which could not otherwise be undertaken.

1. *The generality of sampling procedures*

A vaguely formulated understanding of sampling is part and parcel of what is called common sense and is characteristic of everyday experience. If in casual argument with friends it is asserted that the populace of Red Canyon, Texas, is unfriendly, the reply by defenders of the community will be that the observer met too *few*, and not a truly *representative* cross section, of the population. Whether this be true or not is of no consequence. The important thing is to note the widespread application of sampling theory in an informal and unconscious form.

It might also be pointed out that such everyday uses of sample theory are becoming markedly less informal and unconscious. More and more the informed public, when confronted by the results of a poll or some other conclusion based on sampling procedure, is asking the pertinent questions: *"Who* and what type of persons were interviewed?" *"How many* were interviewed?" No longer are such unqualified statements as "Most of the subjects responded negatively," or "Over half the juvenile delinquents surveyed came from broken homes," taken as serious scientific propositions.

The fact that some increasing sophistication regarding sample design is apparent among the general public might be a function of its increased application in many of the social sciences. Sampling in social sciences as a conscious and careful procedure is relatively new. The U.S. Bureau of the Census first used sampling in a decennial census only in 1940. Although Stephan [1] reports a few examples in the eighteenth century, it seems just to remark with Parten [2] that "the recorded instances of the deliberate use of sampling plans in the fields of social investigation prior to 1900 are relatively few in number." It was in reality not until after 1920 that the field of applied sampling began systematically to develop, and much of the growth was in agricultural rather than social research. At the present, however, sampling is so essential a part of research procedure that every sociologist, though not required to be a sampling expert, must at least be thoroughly familiar with its logic and with some of its basic techniques.

It should be clear by now that sampling is an essential part of all scientific procedure. It is not merely an adjunct of the social sciences. As noted above, it is well developed in biological researches in the field of agriculture. It is also a basic tool in other areas of biology, as well as in physics and chemistry. Science, committed as it is today to the variability of observations in all fields, is forced to sample from a universe of possible observations rather than believing that one observation provides an absolute and immutable truth. Every experiment is indeed only a sample of all possible observations which could be made. The *number* of such observations required as the basis for generalization depends on the number of experimental controls possible and thus may be fewer in the physical than in the social sciences, but all experiments are nevertheless samples from a larger universe of possible experimental situations.

Since an important part of sampling depends upon probability theory, it is first necessary to digress somewhat by discussing the nature and application of probability theory.

There are two ways of looking at probability in so far as scientific method is concerned.[3] According to the first viewpoint, probability refers to the likelihood that a given statement is a true statement. This conception of probability relates to the amount of knowledge lying behind a statement whose "probable truth" is being evaluated. This notion has a special relationship to sampling, but it will be taken up later. It is the second conception of probability which is fundamental to the sampling process.

[1] Frederick F. Stephan, "History of the Uses of Modern Sampling Procedures," *Journal of the American Statistical Association*, Vol. XLIII (1948), pp. 12–40.

[2] Mildred Parten, *Surveys, Polls and Samples: Practical Procedures* (New York: Harper, 1950), p. 106.

[3] See Morris Cohen and Ernst Nagel, *Introduction to Logic and the Scientific Method* (New York: Harcourt, Brace, 1934), Chap. 8, for a discussion of this point.

This second conception of probability is essentially a mathematical one. It holds that probability expresses the frequency of the occurrence of a given event, relative to the frequency of the nonoccurrence of that event, in any series which could produce either occurrence or nonoccurrence. For example, if a coin is tossed into the air it has an equal chance of turning up heads or tails (since it has only two sides). If heads are designated as p and tails as q, then the probability of securing heads may be stated as

$$p = \tfrac{1}{2}.$$

The probability of securing tails is also $\tfrac{1}{2}$. The generalized form of this statement is

$$p = \tfrac{1}{2}N,$$

where $N =$ the possible number of events. Thus the number of heads expected in 10 tosses of a coin would be $\tfrac{1}{2}(10)$, or 5 heads.

The probability of securing more than one of a series of mutually exclusive events is secured by *adding* the probabilities for each. Thus if the chances of throwing a 6 on a die are equal to $\tfrac{1}{6}$ and the chances of throwing a 1 are also $\tfrac{1}{6}$, then the chances of throwing *either* a 1 *or* a 6 are equal to $\tfrac{1}{6} + \tfrac{1}{6}$, or $\tfrac{1}{3}$.

If these two events are considered as one, however, the calculation is different. Thus, in two throws of a die (or one throw of two dice) the probabilities are different if we wish *both* a 1 *and* a 6. What, for example, are the chances of throwing a 7 in a "crap game"? The accompanying table shows the calculation. The probabilities of each of the mutually

Ways of Making 7

Die 1	Probability	Die 2	Probability	Combination Probability
6	$\tfrac{1}{6}$	1	$\tfrac{1}{6}$	$\tfrac{1}{6} \times \tfrac{1}{6} = \tfrac{1}{36}$
1	$\tfrac{1}{6}$	6	$\tfrac{1}{6}$	$\tfrac{1}{6} \times \tfrac{1}{6} = \tfrac{1}{36}$
5	$\tfrac{1}{6}$	2	$\tfrac{1}{6}$	$\tfrac{1}{6} \times \tfrac{1}{6} = \tfrac{1}{36}$
2	$\tfrac{1}{6}$	5	$\tfrac{1}{6}$	$\tfrac{1}{6} \times \tfrac{1}{6} = \tfrac{1}{36}$
4	$\tfrac{1}{6}$	3	$\tfrac{1}{6}$	$\tfrac{1}{6} \times \tfrac{1}{6} = \tfrac{1}{36}$
3	$\tfrac{1}{6}$	4	$\tfrac{1}{6}$	$\tfrac{1}{6} \times \tfrac{1}{6} = \tfrac{1}{36}$

dependent pairs is equal to $\tfrac{1}{36}$. Since all are mutually *exclusive* ways of making 7, the sum of the probability values yields the probability of throwing any 7, which is $\tfrac{6}{36}$, or $\tfrac{1}{6}$.

It should be noticed in these examples that an *assumption of equiprobability* is made between alternative possible events such as throwing heads or throwing not-heads. What is there to justify the assumption that heads are just as likely, no more and no less, to appear as are tails? Or that each side of a die is exactly as likely as any other side to occur? One answer given is "chance." But then chance must be defined. Hagood says,[4] "Chance is generally described as the result of a multiplicity of simultaneously operating independent factors." Another way of putting this is that we know of no reason to expect any one more frequently than the other, and thus we make the assumption of equiprobability.

To see how this concept is transferred to the statistical world, the question of heads and tails can be used for illustration. It is recalled that the

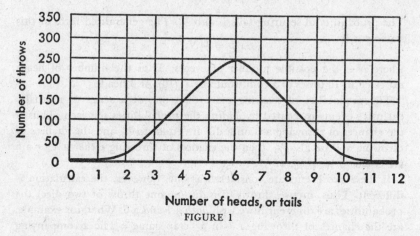

Number of heads, or tails

FIGURE 1

probability of a head on the toss of one coin is $\frac{1}{2}$. Then, what is the probability of *each* of the possible combinations when *two* coins are tossed? Since, as in the case of the dice, these are related results, the probabilities are *multiplied*. Thus the probabilities are

$$2 \text{ heads} = \frac{1}{2} \times \frac{1}{2} = 0.25$$
$$2 \text{ tails} = \frac{1}{2} \times \frac{1}{2} = 0.25$$

$$\left. \begin{array}{l} 1 \text{ head and 1 tail} = \frac{1}{2} \times \frac{1}{2} = 0.25 \\ 1 \text{ tail and 1 head} = \frac{1}{2} \times \frac{1}{2} = 0.25 \end{array} \right\} \begin{array}{l} \text{These being the} \\ \text{same, they are} \\ \text{added} = 0.50 * \end{array}$$

* This disregards the *order,* that is, whether a head or a tail precedes the other.

It can, therefore, be said that, in a *considerable number* of tosses of two coins, the types of results will be in the proportions of 2 heads (0.25) + 1 head and 1 tail (0.50) + 2 tails (0.25) = 1.00 (the full range of possibilities). Now it happens that there is a general mathematical expression for this relationship which can express any number of possibilities rather than the three simple possibilities given in the example. This mathematical expression is known as the expansion of the binomial and takes the general

[4] Margaret Jarman Hagood, *Statistics for Sociologists* (New York: Holt, 1941), p. 406.

form $(p + q)^n$, where n is the number of events. In the case illustrated above, this formula would yield the following:

$$(p + q)^2 = p^2 + 2pq + q^2,$$

in which p^2 refers to 2 heads, pq to 1 head and 1 tail, and q^2 to 2 tails. The *frequencies,* expressed as the coefficients of these terms, are 1 for p^2, 2 for pq, and 1 for q^2. These yield the same proportions as the earlier example, namely, 0.25, 0.50, and 0.25, respectively.

When the binomial is expanded so that n represents a large number of events, the number of combinations increases and the frequencies of each form a perfectly smooth symmetrical curve. This is the familiar "probability curve" or, as it is sometimes called, the "curve

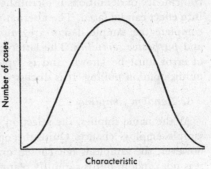

FIGURE 2. Curve of normal distribution.

of normal distribution." This curve, shown in Figure 2, is fundamental in probability statistics. Before discussing the precise application of this conception of probability to sampling in sociology, it will be necessary to discuss some other aspects of sampling.

2. *The requirements of good sampling*

There are only two basic requirements for sampling procedure to fulfill. A sample must be *representative,* and it must be *adequate.* This is a deceptively simple statement because the procedures for achieving representativeness and adequacy may at times be rather complex.

THE REPRESENTATIVENESS OF SAMPLES

By "definition" is meant the careful delimitation of the *universe* to be sampled as well as the definition of the *observations* which are to constitute the sample. Suppose, for example, the universe is defined as all persons who have *ever* been divorced. Suppose also that the observations are defined as interviews with all who admit that they *are* divorced. Since the observations are differently defined than is the universe, we would expect a biased sample. We would, first of all, lose those cases who refuse to admit that a divorce has occurred, and it is likely that these denials would occur differently among different groups. Secondly, we would have a sample with a disproportion of the very recent divorcees, who are younger than the entire group "ever divorced," and those who once divorced and never remarried. The latter group is much *older* than the group "ever divorced." Consequently by failing to make our definitions of universe and observations coincide, we would obtain an unrepresentative sample.

In other words, it should be underlined that careful definition of the universe and the observations, and of the significant relationship between them, is the cornerstone of planning for representativeness. Once this coincidence of definitions is established, the problem of putting the plan into effect can be faced. The alternative techniques which can be used to complete the sample design are *random sampling, stratified sampling,* and *purposive sampling.* The latter type is of little use when the limits of error must be known, and is typically used in market research and public-opinion polling. It is discussed briefly later in this chapter.

1. *Random sampling*

As the name implies, the selection of the units to be included in the sample employs chance. Quite the opposite of what the name implies, however, the sample is not chosen on an accidental basis. In this sense it is not random but is carefully planned. In other words, at this point it is necessary to return to the definition of chance given in the early part of the chapter.

A random sample is one which is so drawn that the researcher, from all pertinent points of view, has no reason to believe a bias will result. In other words, the units of the universe must be so arranged that the selection process gives *equiprobability of selection to every unit in that universe.* This really means that the researcher does not know his universe sufficiently well to duplicate it exactly in his sample. What he is therefore doing is attempting to randomize his ignorance in this area.

Unfortunately, when dealing with social data this is much more difficult than when dealing with such things as patterns of heads and tails, or combinations of figures on dice. People do not exist in such nicely divided patterns. Some are easier to locate than others, and some may refuse to respond. Moreover, there are few lists available which will guarantee a complete definition of the universe. Further, although samples can sometimes be checked against such sources as census data, using the characteristics of age, sex, rental values, location, education, and race, it is frequently the case that the universe we are studying has not been defined in any of these terms. Such indexes, therefore, can often serve as only partial and indirect checks.

A. DEFINITIONS OF UNIVERSES. There are two general technical problems in securing randomness in a sample. One of these is related to the definition of the universe; the other is the mechanical manipulation of that universe in the selection process. Taking up the first of these, it is not enough to define the universe theoretically; it is also necessary to have a *concrete* description of it. Thus, if housing in a community is to be studied, not only must "housing" be defined but the units to be used as physical expressions of "housing" must be carefully outlined. A random sample could then be drawn from all structures in the community which fall within the definition of "housing."

Another type of physical definition of a universe might be a study of all the inmates of a particular penitentiary at a particular time. Such a definition of the universe would make random sampling relatively simple. Most sociological researches, however, do not have such neatly defined universes as houses or prisoners. In some cases, recourse may be had to existing lists of people as possible definitions of universes. This is where the ingenuity and perseverance of the researcher will be taxed to the maximum. Some of the kinds of lists frequently employed are discussed below.

(1) *Changes in marital status.* Although different political subdivisions vary considerably in the accuracy and completeness with which marriages and/or divorces are recorded, some such lists are usually available. They are generally open to inspection and are frequently coded by name, using a system called Soundex, which makes them easily available. With the exercise of due care in regard to their validity and completeness, such data are often of considerable utility to sociologists.

(2) *Juvenile offenses.* This is a complex area in which to work since records are scattered and definitions difficult. Juveniles apprehended will usually appear on the police blotter. Those convicted will appear in juvenile-court records. Both these lists, however, will frequently confuse offenders, suspects, and victims of negligence. Further, the blotter gives a universe of those who were apprehended and charged. The juvenile court provides a record of those apprehended, charged, and convicted. These are two different universes, and, of course, *neither* coincides with the universe of juveniles who actually commit offenses. Great caution is therefore indicated in the use of these lists.

(3) *Distribution of welfare services.* In most medium-sized and large cities the majority of social agencies cooperate in a central record clearinghouse. One problem in working with social-work records is that there is usually an "open" and a "closed" file. The open file will contain only cases currently active. No assumptions about time can be made from this, however, since some of these may have been opened long ago and some of the closed cases may be very recent. Another problem in securing lists in this area, in the absence of adequate clearinghouse records, is the overlapping of various governmental and private agencies.

(4) *Automobile-owners lists.* Such lists are usually available from the appropriate state office. Their accuracy *as far as they go* is probably good. It must be kept in mind, however, that this is a highly select universe. Identification of this list with any other universe is not usually accurate. It was in fact partly its dependence on this source which caused the debacle suffered by the *Literary Digest* in its presidential poll of 1936.

(5) *Telephone directories.* Telephone subscribers may be used for certain purposes but only with great care. These directories have a disproportionate number of higher income families, while omitting many of the lower income groups (without telephones) as well as the very highest (with unlisted telephones). Further, this listing is often out of date, containing many names of people who have moved and not including new arrivals.

(6) *Utility subscriptions.* Where such lists are available they are superior to telephone lists. Here, also, there is a certain amount of exclusion of the lower economic groups. More dangerous than this, however, is the presence of the joint-subscriber problem. In many multiple-family units these services are subscribed to by the management or are shared by two or more families, with only one registration to stand for perhaps several households.

(7) *Voting registrations.* The adequacy of these lists is limited to certain types of the study of political behavior. For any other type of universe they are useless since their adequacy of coverage is unknown, including many who are dead (if a political machine is in control) and not including a large number of the population. Since the characteristics of the omitted population are not known, voters lists as universes are often poorly defined.

(8) *School censuses.* Many states and some school districts conduct special annual censuses of persons of school and preschool age. The type of information in such listings varies, as does the completeness of the enumeration. Particularly in mobile areas, however, a school census, like the telephone directory, may well be out of date by the time of its compilation.

(9) *City directories.* These directories, compiled annually, contain lists of all individuals in the city known to the compilers, and frequently give crude occupational descriptions. Parten argues persuasively for the utility of this listing for sampling purposes.[5] The experience of using such a source for direct-mail advertising purposes, however, is not so encouraging. It is true that city directories are used for commercial purposes, and they are expensive—hence, we assume, carefully done. On the other hand, they do not contain such segments as the transient, rooming-house, hotel-dwelling, or suburban populations. If the researcher is able to fill in these gaps, however, the directory may be of great value. One more problem is the fact that, like other such lists, it quickly is outdated for the more mobile areas of the city. One way in which it is most useful is in its delimitation of a *universe of addresses* which may be a preliminary step in developing an area sampling plan. In this regard city directories are relatively complete, with the exception of rapidly growing sections of the city and of those areas in which there are appreciable conversions from commercial to residential use or *vice versa.*

[5] Mildred Parten, *op. cit.,* esp. pp. 255–261.

B. THE MECHANICS OF DRAWING A RANDOM SAMPLE FROM A KNOWN UNI-VERSE. The essential problem here is a simple one. It involves some method of selecting cases from a listed universe which will depend on chance alone (in the sense that this was earlier defined). One method employed for this (it was used with ostentation to prove impartiality in determining the order of induction notices by Selective Service) is to number every unit on the universe and to record the numbers on identical slips of paper, folded identically and placed in a receptacle. If these are thoroughly mixed and the number required for the sample are drawn, they will appear as a random selection. This method is somewhat laborious, however, and a more mechanical one may be desired. If so, a coin may be flipped or a roulette wheel spun (not by machine) with an appropriate code to relate each chance event (flip of coin or rotation of wheel) to each event in the universe. Thus, for a 50 per cent sample, heads might mean to accept a case for the sample; for a 25 per cent sample, every other head might indicate selection; and so on.

A superior method, however, is the use of a table of random numbers. Like the selection from a jar, this involves numbering serially every item in the universe, so that every number has the same number of digits in it.

Numbers are then read from the table of random numbers, in any way desired—up, down, horizontally, or diagonally—and the corresponding items are selected for the sample. Most commonly used is a table by L. H. C. Tippett.[6] These tables are generally applicable, though some limitations to their use have been described by Yule and Kendall and Babington-Smith.[7]

Another method is to sample a list by fixed intervals or by fixed positions. Thus every nth name on a list or every nth house in a block may be selected for the sample. It must be emphasized that this can be done only where physical position in the list does not affect randomness. For example, the census in 1940 and 1950 wished to sample certain lines (there was one line to each person) in the enumeration with additional questions. Because the use of certain lines for this purpose tended to bias the sample by overweighting certain types of respondents, a number of different schedule patterns, each with the sample cases on different lines, were worked out to offset this selective factor. Another illustration may be taken from the selection of every nth house *within* blocks. If the positional system of selecting at random intervals results in *overselecting*

---

[6] *Tracts for Computers,* Number XV, Karl Pearson, ed. (New York: Cambridge University Press, 1947).

[7] M. G. Kendall and B. Babington-Smith, "Randomness and Random Sampling Numbers," *Journal of the Royal Statistical Society,* Vol. CI (1938), pp. 147–166, and "Second Paper on Random Sampling Numbers," *ibid.,* Vol. CI (1939), pp. 51–61; George V. Yule, "A Test of Tippett's Random Sampling Numbers," *ibid.,* Vol. CI (1938), pp. 167–172.

corner houses, this will introduce a bias, since these houses depart in several important socioeconomic characteristics from those in other locations.

The main considerations in selecting a method of choosing the sample are (1) that it be simple, but above all (2) that it live up to the assumption of equiprobability so that no bias is introduced.

C. SOME DEPARTURES FROM RANDOM SAMPLING.[8] It has already been stated that departures from randomness will cause biases in the resulting sample. Therefore we must make certain that (1) the definitions of the universe and of the observations are precise and coincide with each other; (2) the definition or list of the universe is complete; and (3) the mechanical procedure of drawing the sample is easy to carry out and does not introduce biases of its own. The following examples will illustrate failures to observe such precautions.

(1) *Inadequate definition of universe and observations.* One study set out to discover whether or not there was any religious bias in the "society" coverage of the *New York Times.* The study was set up on the assumption that, if such a bias were present, the newspaper coverage of the actual weddings in the different religious categories would be proportionally smaller for the group against which discrimination was practiced. The *universe* was defined as all weddings occurring in the city of New York for 10 years. The *observations* were defined as all weddings occurring in the month of June—on the assumption that this was the most popular month for weddings—and the *New York Times* coverage of weddings during June for a 10-year period. If there had been no major change in newspaper policy, such a sample would be both adequate and representative from a mathematical point of view.

However, the *definition* of the observations overlooked several important points. If there is any ritual proscription which limits the season of marriage in any religious group, it is likely to affect the proportion of weddings occurring in any month. In the case of couples with a Jewish background, there is such a proscription. For 7 weeks after Passover (Pesach) and for 3 weeks prior to Tishah b'ab (a day of mourning for the destruction of the Temple) weddings are not permitted by either Orthodox or Conservative Jewry, and many Reform groups also accept this prohibition. Although the Hebrew calendar does not fit the Gregorian exactly, it is at least true that when Passover is early in the Gregorian year, the 3 weeks prior to Tishah b'ab cover part of June. When Passover is somewhat later, the 7 weeks succeeding will cover part of June. As a consequence, for most years there will be few Jewish weddings during a large part of this month.

---

[8] Purposive departures are sometimes utilized. There is little to commend such practice in general, although certain types of semipurposive sampling are successfully applied for limited purposes. The outstanding example of this is the use of quota control, particularly in public-opinion polls and marketing surveys. This sampling procedure will be discussed briefly at a later point.

This example of bad sampling was not mechanically, but substantively, in error. Fuller knowledge of the universe would have led to a more adequate sampling. Another point might be made here also, even though the above statement were not true. The use of one month only would not usually provide a good sample in any case, simply on the grounds that a single month could not be considered representative. Knowing nothing about the facts, a random selection of one-twelfth of the total number of days in this 10-year period would have been as simple as taking the 10 June months, and would have answered these objections.

The statistical basis for this difference may be found in elementary works on sampling.

(2) *Inadequate listing of the universe.* Another research was undertaken to furnish certain data which would be of use to a labor union in its pension negotiations with a major corporation. A random sample was drawn by taking every *n*th case from a presumably complete name and address list of union membership. Allowance for difficulty in finding respondents was made by adding to each case drawn either the following or the preceding name, in carefully defined alternative order. If the case drawn was not located, the alternative name was to be used. A defensible sampling plan was necessary, since the corporation would have at its disposal many statistical experts. If the data were to be of any use, the union had to be able to answer any criticisms made by such skilled personnel.

However, because the information was needed quickly, the investigator did not pretest his sample. That is, he did not go into the field with *a sample of the sample,* to see what sort of results the questionnaire would obtain and what type of respondent would be found. A high proportion of the union membership was composed of semiskilled assembly-line workers in a large industrial city. Residential mobility among this group is very high, and an undetermined but large percentage of them do not leave forwarding addresses when they move within the city. It is also possible that the union list of members had never been accurate. Whether this list was adequate, of course, should have been a question to be decided by a pretest, before a substantial amount of money and time had been invested.

The result was that only about one in four of the respondents was at home when the interviewers first called in the evenings. An additional 30 per cent of the respondents could not be located at all without elaborate tracing methods, which were far too expensive at this stage of the research. Yet to accept a high proportion the alternative names on the list would have secured an entirely different type of respondent; the resulting sample would have been heavily biased toward the older, less mobile workers and would have contained a disproportionate number of workers with families, who had bought property. Since a number of questions centered about health and worries about the future, in order to demonstrate the need for pensions, it would be expected that this older group of workers would have more experiences of time lost because of ill health and more worries about their health and financial future, along with a greater number of present physical complaints. These data would strongly support the union position but would be worthless because the sample would be biased. As a consequence, this study was abandoned during the course of the interviewing phase and after several thousand dollars had been spent.

In this case, as is indicated, the original acceptance of the union listing had far-reaching results in destroying the usefulness of the research findings. The case therefore illustrates the importance of carefully investigating the meaning of lists before accepting them as constituting the desired universe.

(3) *Biased sampling in the field-operations phase.* Focusing on the mechanics of procuring a random sample, another point can be made. A study of attitudes toward the use of contraceptives was made in an apartment-house area. The investigators expected to find that most of the women questioned would favor their use, since most studies have demonstrated this point among urban women. However, a proportion even somewhat higher than that among the total urban population was expected in this area, since it contained a high proportion of working women. It was also expected that the reported actual use of contraceptives would be considerably higher than for most other populations. The sample drawn consisted of every fifth apartment, of whatever size, in every apartment house in the delimited area.

However, the investigators found, very early in the collection of data, that their respondents were not giving answers which fitted the hypothesis. Furthermore, on closer checking with the census data for this area, they learned that their respondents had a greater number of children per family than would have been the case for a representative group. They soon learned that their field interviewers were married women with children, and were unable to do much interviewing in the evenings. Since they had done most of their interviewing during the day, especially during the morning, they had captured a sample composed almost entirely of mothers who were staying at home in order to care for their children. Almost no working women were included in the sample. No matter how large the sample, this type of bias would have resulted in a nonrandom sample, of little use for the aims of the inquiry.

This departure from randomness did not result from the mechanics of drawing the sample in the research office. The selection of every fifth apartment would normally constitute a satisfactory procedure. In this case it was a failure of the *field operations* to reproduce the sample which was designed.

2. *Stratified sampling*

While stratified sampling is placed here in distinction to random sampling, this does not mean that it does not employ randomness. Actually it depends upon randomness but combines this with another method calculated to increase representativeness. Because the method does improve representativeness it allows the use of a smaller sample than does simple random sampling, with greater precision and consequent savings in time and money.

A. THE GENERAL CASE. The basic point involved in stratified sampling is the fact that a homogeneous universe requires a smaller sample than does a heterogeneous sample. Thus we need only a small dipper of molasses from a 10,000-gallon vat, in order to determine its contents, if the liquid has been well mixed. However, we would need a much higher proportion if we were sampling from an accidental aggregate of persons. If a series of homogeneous subuniverses can be sampled in such a way that when the samples are combined they constitute a sample of a more heterogeneous universe, then a saving of time and money will result, as well as increased accuracy. The first question involved, then, is the question of how to divide a universe so as to produce significantly homogeneous subuniverses.

The first requirement for the division into homogeneous categories is that the *criteria for division be correlated with the variable being studied.* A second is that the criteria used not provide so many subsamples as to *increase* the size of the required sample over that required by simple random techniques. The following illustration will make these points clearer. Suppose a study of fertility rates in the population of a small town is desired, and further suppose that the investigator knows the characteristics of all the families in the universe, taken as a group. What is the procedure for dividing this universe into useful *strata?* It is in general known, or at least suspected, that fertility is correlated with race, religion, education, socioeconomic status, and age. These would then become logical bases for stratification. On the other hand, we would probably not use height, weight, or membership in a political party, since these are probably little related to fertility levels. From a practical point of view, if all these bases were used, the value of sampling would be lost, for the number of subsamples would become enormous. Consider what would happen if there were two categories of race, four of religion, three of education, three of socioeconomic status, and three of age. Then the number of subsamples would equal $2 \times 4 \times 3 \times 3 \times 3$, or 216. Since a statistically satisfactory number in the smallest cell could not possibly be less than 10 cases, this would require a minimum of 2,160, assuming that the numbers in all cells would be equal. Since we know that the distributions on these criteria are not equal, the actual number would be greatly in excess of this. No one could consider such a number as a *sample* of a small town. This then illustrates the second requirement of the stratification process, that is, that the number of criteria must be practical.

To solve this dilemma it is generally assumed that many such variables occur as *associated factors*. Thus, socioeconomic status may be chosen to stand also for education and perhaps partially for religion. If, further, the community is homogeneous as to race (which is likely in a Northern small town) and if the only significant religious division is thought to be between Roman Catholics and all others (as is also likely), then the number of subsamples could be reduced to 2 (religions) $\times$ 3 (socioeconomic groups) $\times$ 3 (age groups) = 18 subsamples. This is, then, a much more usable sample design than was the first, and it would provide a more representative sample than would the simple random technique.

There still remains the question of how to select the exact cases from within such strata, once they have been set up. This leads back to random sampling methods, since *each* of the subsamples is treated exactly like a universe as in the case of simple random sampling. Any of the randomization techniques previously discussed, therefore, can be applied *within* the strata.

There is another problem in selection, however, which is concerned with *proportionality*. The customary and most frequent procedure is to select from each stratum in proportion to the contribution which that stratum makes to the total universe.[9] Thus in the example given above, if non-Catholic, upper class, older families constituted 7 per cent of the total families in the community, then this stratum should also contribute 7 per cent of the families in the sample.

There are circumstances, however, when *disproportionate* numbers are drawn from a stratum. This is the case when special interest attaches to either the *difference* between two or more particular strata or upon *intensive* analysis of one stratum. We may then use larger numbers for these strata analyses and reduce the results proportionately when we tabulate the whole sample.

B. AREA-PROBABILITY SAMPLES. This is a particular type of stratified sampling which has recently been developed with considerable precision. Its name is somewhat misleading, however, since simple random sampling can be used with areal units as in the case of selecting every nth block, township, county, or even by simply placing an arbitrary grid over the area and numbering the squares as units to be sampled. The area-probability sample, however, is a special type of sampling procedure which is

---

[9] This may frequently be checked by data from the Census or other reliable sources of descriptive data.

based to some extent on the fact that areal *homogeneity* can be used for sampling purposes. Hansen and Hurwitz [10] have described the technique of area-probability sampling as follows:

"The principles introduced in the sample design . . . include: (a) the use of large and heterogeneous primary sampling units, (b) the stratification of these primary sampling units into carefully defined strata, (c) the selection of one primary unit out of each stratum for inclusion in the sample in such a manner that the probability of selection of any unit is proportionate to its 1940 population, (d) the use of an area substratification method which provides that the sample from the selected primary unit be taken so as to represent the entire stratum from which the primary unit is drawn rather than the particular primary unit that happens to be included in the sample, and (e) the subsampling of small areas within the selected primary units and of households within these small areas."

A further statement from this article [11] makes the point that "the technique of sampling within the selected counties is to divide the selected primary sampling units into very small areas such as city blocks or small rural areas, to select a *designated proportion* of these small areas, and to prepare a complete list of all dwelling units in the selected small areas." Although such a sampling plan is fairly expensive to organize, once the data have been secured the plan can be utilized for a series of similar surveys or for other surveys with different purposes, so that the cost per survey is rather small. More important, the precision of information is high per dollar expended. This criterion is, of course, more important than that of cost per interview.

The meaning of a "complete listing of the universe" is clear in the foregoing paragraphs. It is not necessary to make a complete list of all the individuals in the city, state, or nation, or even a complete list of households. Rather, it requires a *complete list of the areas or subareas* in order to select those areas within which still further samples will be drawn. All households, or individuals, are not listed until the final level of drawing the sample is reached. This pattern may be seen in Figure 3.

C. DOUBLE SAMPLING. One useful technique for a number of research situations may, for convenience, be called "double" sampling.[12] This development was first applied by Hansen and Hurwitz, and was based upon theoretical principles presented by Neyman. As originally used, it

[10] Morris H. Hansen and William N. Hurwitz, "Sampling Methods Applied to Census Work," U.S. Department of Commerce, Bureau of the Census, Publication 39505, p. 31. Also, see Morris H. Hansen and William N. Hurwitz, "On the Theory of Sampling from Finite Populations," *Annals of Mathematical Statistics*, Vol. XIV (1943), pp. 333–362, for the statistical principles underlying these techniques.

[11] Hansen and Hurwitz, "Sampling Methods Applied to Census Work."

[12] Morris H. Hansen and William N. Hurwitz, "The Problem of Non-response in Sample Surveys," *Journal of the American Statistical Association*, Vol. XLI (1946), pp. 517–529; J. Neyman, "Contributions to the Theory of Sampling Human Populations," *Journal of the American Statistical Association*, Vol. XXXV (1938), pp. 101–116.

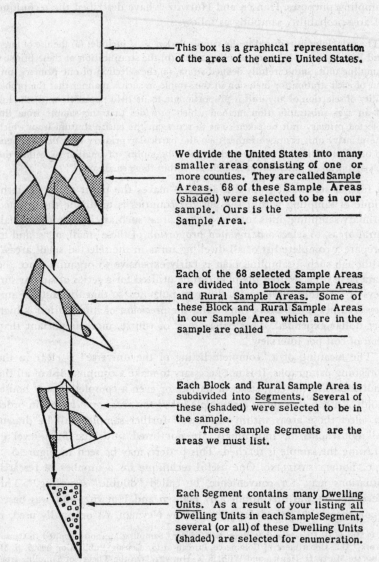

This box is a graphical representation of the area of the entire United States.

We divide the United States into many smaller areas consisting of one or more counties. They are called Sample Areas. 68 of these Sample Areas (shaded) were selected to be in our sample. Ours is the _____ Sample Area.

Each of the 68 selected Sample Areas are divided into Block Sample Areas and Rural Sample Areas. Some of these Block and Rural Sample Areas in our Sample Area which are in the sample are called _____

Each Block and Rural Sample Area is subdivided into Segments. Several of these (shaded) were selected to be in the sample.
These Sample Segments are the areas we must list.

Each Segment contains many Dwelling Units. As a result of your listing all Dwelling Units in each Sample Segment, several (or all) of these Dwelling Units (shaded) are selected for enumeration.

FIGURE 3. Area sampling system of the current population surveys. (*From U.S. Bureau of the Census, How to List, P-1450b.*)

was an attempt to reap the advantages of the mail questionnaire without the biases which are usually involved in that technique. The procedure is to use the mail questionnaire for the entire sample and the field interview for a sample of those *who do not answer the questionnaire.* This technique is discussed in the chapter on the questionnaire. Hansen and Hurwitz have constructed tables and formulas which allow a rapid assessment of the required proportions for questionnaires and field interviews in such cases.

In the 1945 Census of Agriculture a significant application of this technique was used in conjunction with a regular census. Here, however, the entire agricultural population was the sample, and the later sample was an attempt to check by further, concentrated interviewing the results of the census itself.[13] The goal was to determine the accuracy of that census and to point out various problems in the field work that had already taken place. The technique, however, can be generalized to other situations. A check on the field interviewing sample by a selected sample from available records on the same individuals can easily be secured. In some cases it may be necessary to take a sample from our sample, for more intense interviewing. This has been done in a number of cases in political research, as in *The People's Choice,*[14] in studies of daytime radio-serial listening,[15] and in the analysis of a war-bond drive.[16] However, this technique is particularly useful in those surveys in which the mail questionnaire can be profitably carried out, since by its use much of the usual bias of the questionnaire can be avoided.

THE ADEQUACY OF SAMPLES

The preceding pages have dealt with the problem of the representativeness of samples and with some techniques for assuring representativeness. But this, it will be recalled, is only one of the requirements of good sampling. A sample not only needs to be representative, it needs also to be *adequate.* A sample is adequate when it is of sufficient size to *allow confidence in the stability of its characteristics.* This in turn requires a measure of *sampling error.* Just as it was necessary to digress into probability in order to discuss sampling, so it is now necessary to make a similar digression before discussing sampling errors.

[13] W. Edwards Deming and Frederick F. Stephan, "On the Interpretation of Censuses as Samples," *Journal of the American Statistical Association,* Vol. XXXVI (1941), pp. 45–49.

[14] Paul F. Lazarsfeld, Bernard Berelson, and Hazel Gaudet, 1944; reprinted by Columbia University Press, 1948.

[15] Herta Herzog, "What Do We Really Know about Daytime Serial Listening?" *Radio Research, 1942–3,* Paul F. Lazarsfeld and Frank Stanton, eds. (New York: Harper, 1943), pp. 3–23.

[16] Robert K. Merton *et al., Mass Persuasion* (New York: Harper, 1946).

1. *The arithmetic mean and standard deviation*

The arithmetic mean, though only one of several possible averages, is what is commonly called "the average." It is a measure of central tendency which is essential to probability statistics because of some of its properties of manipulation. The definition is

$$\overline{M} = \Sigma X/N,$$

where $\overline{M}$ = the arithmetic mean, Σ = the function "sum of," X = the value of each observation, and N = the number of observations. Thus the mean size of family in a series of six families containing 8, 7, 6, 5, 4, and 3 members, respectively, would be equal to 5.5 members. When data are grouped in class intervals the method of computing the mean is as shown in Table 1.

TABLE 1

Family Size in a Selected Latin-American Sample *

(1) Family Size	(2) Midpoint of Class Interval	(3) Number of Families	(2) × (3)	(4) Deviations from Mean	(5) (4)²	(6) (3) × (5)
1– 2	1.5	6	9.0	−3.9	15.21	91.26
3– 4	3.5	25	87.5	−1.9	3.61	90.25
5– 6	5.5	42	231.0	.1	.01	.42
7– 8	7.5	22	165.0	2.1	4.41	97.02
9–10	9.5	5	47.5	4.1	16.81	74.05
Total		100	540.0			354.00
Mean = 5.4						

* Here we are using the formula $\overline{M} = \Sigma fm/N$, where f = frequency in the class, m = midpoint of that class, and N = total number of cases. We can do so only because the value of every midpoint can be treated as the average for that class. This is permissible, since "number of individuals" is a value marked by discrete individuals and there is no serious problem of distribution within the class. For most grouped data, however, we use the formula $\overline{M} = Mg - \Sigma(fd^1/N)i$, where Mg = the assumed average, d^1 = number of steps of deviation of each midpoint from the midpoint assumed as the working average, and i = the *size* of the class interval. The usual formula for σ should be similarly modified.

The mean, therefore, is $^{540}\!/_{100}$ = 5.4 members per family. Thus, the arithmetic mean is that value in a distribution, the sum of the deviations from which, sign considered, are equal to zero.

The mean is a measure of *central tendency* and as such describes whether a population as a whole is "low" or "high" on a particular value with regard to a particular standard (in this case, number of members in the family). The other descriptive measure which is required for the measurement of error is the *standard deviation*. This is a measure of *dispersion* which describes how closely the individual observations cluster around their mean or how far they depart from it. It is related to the mean in that it is the square root of a figure obtained by squaring the deviations of the cases from the mean and by finding the average amount of deviation squared. It is, then, the square root of the average of the squared deviations from the average. The standard deviation is also related to what was earlier called the probability curve in a way which will presently be shown.

Columns 4, 5, and 6 in Table 1 show the values necessary for the computation of the standard deviation, the symbol for which is σ. Thus each entry in column 4 is equal to the midpoint of the interval *minus* the mean. Each of these is squared in column 5 and this value multiplied by its appropriate frequency from column 3. The sum of these is then used in the formula for the standard deviation which is

$$\sigma = \sqrt{[\Sigma f(x)^2]/N},$$

where $f =$ the frequencies, $x =$ the deviations, and $N =$ the number of cases. In the illustrated case, the values are

$$\sigma = \sqrt{354/540} = \sqrt{0.655556} = 0.81.$$

Because of the fact that the standard deviation is related to the normal curve, it is possible to make a definite statement from these two values. Since it is known that the distribution in the table is fairly close in shape to the probability curve, it can be said that approximately two-thirds (68.26 per cent) of the cases will lie between the value represented by $M \pm 1\sigma$; in this case, 5.4 ± 0.81, or 4.59 and 6.21 persons per family. If two standard deviations (2σ) are taken on each side of the mean, this distance will embrace 95.46 per cent of all cases; in this case these would lie between 3.78 and 7.02 persons per family. Three standard deviations will account for virtually all cases in a normal distribution, embracing as they do 99.73 per cent of the observed values.

With the meaning of these two measures in mind it is possible to see the method of estimating sampling error.

2. *The standard error*

This differs from the standard deviation in that, while the latter is a measure of an *actual distribution*, the standard error measures the dispersion about the mean of a *hypothetical distribution*. The values which make up this hypothetical universe are the means of all possible samples of a universe. Thus the mean of this distribution is a mean of means and can be thought of as the *true* mean of the universe.

The formula for the standard error is as follows:

$$\bar{\sigma}_{\bar{x}} = \sigma/\sqrt{N},$$

where $\bar{\sigma}_{\bar{x}}$ = standard error, σ = standard deviation, and N = the number of observations in the sample. Returning to Table 1 for the data, the values secured are

$$\bar{\sigma}_{\bar{x}} = 0.81/\sqrt{100} = 0.81/10 = 0.081.$$

We do not, however, know the true mean. If we did, we would have no need for a sample. Furthermore, we are not likely to know the true mean. We are here concerned with *stability* of our empirical mean. That is, if we took a similar sample of the same size, how close would its mean be to that of the first sample? We therefore take our empirical mean as the best *estimate* of the true mean. Then, if it were the true mean, and our distribution is normal, we can say that similar samples would have a specifiable probability of varying a determined amount from this assumed mean. We *cannot,* however, say that we know by how much our calculated mean deviates from the true mean, or even the probability of a specified amount of deviation. To know that, we would have to know the true mean.

We are therefore able to say that if our calculated mean is the true mean (and it is our best estimate), means of similar samples have 68.26 chances in 100 of not deviating by more than 0.081 from the empirical mean. In other words, the probability is 2 to 1 that these means would lie between $(5.40 - 0.081)$ and $(5.40 + 0.081)$.* We cannot, of course, state any probabilities for the deviation from the true mean, although this is a common error in interpretation.

Two points should be noted about this method of estimating error. One is that the error is measured in two ways. First, it is expressed as a *probability,* and second, that probability refers to a *band of accuracy* rather than to a point. Thus, in the example above it can be said that the chances are 30 to 1 that, given our assumptions, similar means of samples will not vary more than two standard errors (0.162 persons) away from the sample mean if it is the true mean. This leaves the researcher with two questions to answer: (1) is the probability (30 to 1) high enough to satisfy him, and (2) is the amount of error (0.162 persons) small enough to meet his needs?

The other point to note is that such an analysis, since it depends on the σ of the sample, can only be done after the research is completed. An equally important problem besides evaluating completed research, is planning *in advance* for size of sample.

* Converting standard errors into probabilities is done by reading the per cent of the probability surface reached by any $\bar{\sigma}_{\bar{x}}$ value, doubling it, and expressing this as a proportion. Thus, 34.12 per cent of the cases lie between the mean and one $\bar{\sigma}^{\bar{x}}$. Since the $\bar{\sigma}$ must be considered as either plus or minus, the probabilities are 2×34.12 per cent = 68.26 per cent of occurring against 31.74 per cent (the remainder). Thus the odds are 68.26/31.74, or 2.15 to 1. Tables for reading the proportion of the probability surface are found in any standard statistics text.

For this purpose Parten gives the formula

$$N_s = (\sigma Z/T)^2,$$

where N_s = the required sample size, σ = a preliminary estimate of the standard deviation of the universe, Z = the number of standard error units equal to a desired probability, and T = the permissible tolerance of variation in the sample mean.[17] Using her example, suppose it is desired to estimate reliably the average annual income of families in the $10- to $15-a-month income stratum. Three figures were necessary to solve for sample size. These were T, the permissible range of variation from one sample mean to another (i.e., within what range of precision the mean must fall), which was taken as $100; Z, or the standard error equivalent to the desired probability, which was taken as 99 to 1, yielding a value of 2.57 σ from the normal probability table earlier referred to; and σ, the standard deviation of the universe, which was estimated as $500. These values then gave the following:

$$N_s = 500 \ (2.57/100)^2 = 165.$$

Thus a random sample of 165 cases would yield a mean of which it could be said that the chances were 99 to 1 that it would not deviate more than $100 from other means calculated from a similar sample.

In the final analysis, then, the researcher can plan his sample size with great accuracy, if (1) he knows his universe well enough to estimate accurately its standard deviation, (2) if he can decide upon the range of permissible error, and (3) if he knows what level of probability is necessary for this range of variation.

The statement was made earlier that the sampling error in a stratified sample is less than that in a random sample. Logically this refers to a statement made at the opening of this chapter. There it was said that there are two conceptions of probability—one logical and one mathematical. Thus far only the latter has been considered. The meaning of the former statement is that one use of probability refers to the chances that a given statement, when made, is a *true* statement.

This means that the more that is known about a subject the greater is the likelihood of making a correct statement. When a stratified sample is used properly, it introduces some *additional knowledge* concerning the item to be observed. Consequently the sample size necessary for accurate estimation of the universe decreases. If the methods for measuring the error of a random sample are applied to a stratified sample, they will always be conservative by overstating that error.

---

[17] Parten, *op. cit.*, pp. 316–317. The entire chapter on size of sample (Chap. 9) will help clarify any unclear points and gives particular attention to sample size when percentages rather than means are used. The student should be warned, however, that Parten misinterprets the relation of sample calculation to the "true" mean. For a fuller treatment, see Hagood, *op. cit.*, Chap. 16.

PURPOSIVE OR QUOTA SAMPLING

It is likely that more respondents have been selected by quota sampling than by any other type, since this has been the sampling procedure used in most public-opinion polls. The technique will vary from one researcher to another, but in general the pattern is to leave considerable freedom of choice to the interviewer, with the restriction that certain characteristics (age, sex, socioeconomic status, race, etc.) of the respondents be representative of the area (city, county, state, nation) or the group being polled (readers of a given newspaper, consumers of a certain product, etc.). Thus, if 30 per cent of the adults in a given city have attended at least 1 year of high school, 25 per cent of the adults are earning $2,500 and over, and 55 per cent are married, the interviewers would attempt to obtain a final sample with these characteristics. Usually, of course, there are several classes for each characteristic: *e.g.*, for age, we might wish to have a distribution of our respondents in these classes: 19 years and under, 20 to 29, 30 to 39, and 40 and over. If, toward the end of our interviewing, we find that we have "too many" in the 20- to 29-year-old class, we would stop interviewing individuals in that class and would expend greater energy in locating those in the other "cells."

The process of choosing the individual respondent has sometimes been left entirely to the interviewer. However, this may lead to large biases, since those who are available for street interviews in the center of town are not representative of the whole population. Interviewers often ignored the slums, or areas difficult to reach. Consequently, pollsters have put more restrictions on their interviewing teams and given them more supervision. This may mean taking a group into a particular neighborhood and locating the necessary quota of respondents with the required characteristics. Later, the group will cover a different type of neighborhood. Here again, however, the aim is to secure the proper quota of individuals within each cell.

As the student can see, this is not a satisfactory procedure if high precision is desired. There is little reason to expect that all important characteristics are representative of the population when two or three characteristics are representative. As a matter of fact, there is considerable evidence that this is not the case. Moreover, from the statistical point of view this technique is particularly weak, since there is no way of calculating the limits of permissible error, or the required number for the sample, if strict probability sampling is not used.

Quota sampling has been utilized, on the other hand, because it is cheaper for a given study. Developing a good sampling design for a particular area or city is expensive, even though it may not be costly for the degree of accuracy achieved thereby. In spite of the fact that quota sampling yields rough results, these may be satisfactory for the purpose desired. For example, if public reaction to an advertising campaign, a particular commercial product, or a major public issue is to be the object of study, simple percentage differences may be sufficient. Quota sampling may therefore be successful for practical goals when quick, crude results will satisfy. However, the student should be aware of these weaknesses, or he will otherwise believe that the data from this sampling technique are reliable, merely because a large sample has been used.

These comments also apply when a sample of cities or areas is chosen "purposively," *i.e.*, because they have certain characteristics believed to be "typical." Some precincts, states, or cities are used because election results in them coincide with results from the national results; or because economic patterns show up there before they do in a larger area; or they seem to be "key" regions in other respects. These are tempting procedures, but the logic behind them is the same as that in quota polling samples. Its ultimate weakness is that it does not fit the requirements of probability theory, and the practical consequence is that the sample varies in unknown ways from the universe.

SUGGESTED READINGS

Cohen, Morris R., and Ernst Nagel, *An Introduction to Logic and Scientific Method* (New York: Harcourt, Brace, 1934), Chaps. 8 and 14.

Hagood, Margaret Jarman, *Statistics for Sociologists* (New York: Holt, 1941), Chap. 16.

Jahoda, Marie, Morton Deutsch, and Stuart W. Cook, *Research Methods in Social Relations,* Part II (New York: Dryden, 1951), Chaps. 18 and 20.

Lundberg, G. A., *Social Research* (New York: Longmans, 1942), Chap. 5.

McCormick, Thomas C., *Elementary Social Statistics* (New York: McGraw-Hill, 1941), Chaps. 9 and 12.

Parten, Mildred, *Surveys, Polls, and Samples: Practical Procedures* (New York: Harper, 1950), Chap. 6.

CHAPTER 15

Scaling Techniques: The Basic Problem

PURPOSE

The problem to which scaling techniques are applied is that of ordering a series of items along some sort of continuum. In other words, they are methods of turning a series of *qualitative* facts (referred to as attributes) into a *quantitative* series (referred to as a variable). The complexity of this undertaking, and hence its many pitfalls, can best be seen by considering what is meant by ordering items along a continuum.

If, for example, one wishes to measure the size of a series of families, no problem arises. Families are counted as having a certain number of members. All families which have seven members also have at least six, all those with three also have at least two, and so on. This is obvious and in the nature of the ordinal character of measurement. It is clear that no man can save his second thousand dollars until the first is accumulated. This is because the amount of money in the bank is a quantitative characteristic (a variable), and the comparison between two individuals or groups of individuals can readily be made.

"But," the student may ask, "why bother? What are the advantages of using variables instead of attributes?" The answers involve a number of considerations, but the basic outlines are clear. Sciences vary greatly in their reliance on mathematics. Many original papers in chemistry or biology require no higher mathematics on the part of the reader, while this is not the case for physics. All sciences, however, move in the direction of greater *precision*. This takes many forms, but one fundamental form is *measuring gradations*. Colors cannot be red, blue, yellow, and "in between." They must be *measured* so that every "in-between" color has a place on the color wheel, spectrum, or other scale. Putting it differently, rough categories yield only rough observational data. If a population is divided into "approve—indifferent—disapprove," three perfectly good categories result. However, the more we probe into the problem, the more "in betweens" are found. The classes become too crude. Thus, an increase in the number of ordered classes yields smaller and smaller differences between adjacent classes. This provides more *precise* measurements and at the same time orders the cases according to some principle which becomes more clearly recognizable as our probe continues. Furthermore, attributes are not amenable to mathematical manipulation. Variables, being expressible in a numerical fashion, are more flexible.

In sociology, much of the data consists of qualitative variables which must be so arranged that they represent a quantitative series. If, for example, it is desired to compare two persons, or groups, in regard to social standing, how shall this be done? Accepting, for the moment, that (1) material possessions, (2) amount of community participation, (3) education, (4) family background, and (5) amount of income are all elements entering into general social position, how is it possible to compare those who are low on (3) and high on (2) with those who are high on (3) but low on (2)?

To take another example, suppose a problem requires the comparison of two persons or groups with respect to their attitudes toward a political party. Some may oppose all the party's policies, some may oppose some of the policies and favor others, some may advocate its support only because of opposition to another party, and others may support the candidates of the party but condemn its policies. How is it possible to compare these people or groups on a scale of favorable or unfavorable attitudes toward this particular political policy?

The close reader will immediately see that it is possible to differentiate types *qualitatively* in both cases without necessarily implying that in the one case *higher social standing* could be identified, or that in the other case *greater opposition to the party* could be described. However, the development of a more scientific sociology calls for comparative, quantitative measurement and such qualitative analysis will not always suffice.

The problem of scaling has been encountered in such diverse areas as in the study of attitudes, institutional practices, housing adequacy, social status, neighborhood environment, and occupational prestige, and has been applied in a number of ways. Before presenting an analysis of these techniques, however, it seems useful to make some general remarks about the major problems encountered in this area.

GENERAL PROBLEMS

The following discussion will be confined to those problems which are common to all types of scaling. An exhaustive treatment would require the introduction of specific scales or scaling techniques. Some of these will be dealt with in the following chapter.

1. *Definition of the continuum*

With regard to the examples given above, the question might have been raised as to whether it is reasonable to suppose that there is such a thing as a continuum of social standing or one of favorableness-unfavorableness to a political party. This would obviously be a legitimate question, and it is one which can only be answered by careful logic, conceptual analysis, and empirical test.

Scaling always hypothesizes the existence of a continuum of some kind. Its nature must be inferred from the character of the items selected to make up the scale. *Logically unrelated* items, therefore, cannot be included in the same scale without resulting in a confusion of continua within one scale. Consequently, the first step in scaling procedure, regardless of the technique employed, is a thorough knowledge of the subject. The student must systematically exploit his own observations and those of others through a careful study of the literature and through interviews with "experts" before he can begin scale construction. He must, in short, find out what it is that he wishes to measure quantitatively.

To underline the importance of this step it should be pointed out that every scale is composed of items which are only a *sample* of the possible universe of items. Without the fullest possible knowledge of that universe the researcher can have no confidence in the representativeness of the items which he selects for his tentative list. If, for example, a scale to measure "housing adequacy" is contemplated, two basic steps are necessary: (1) the logical analysis in defense of the hypothesis that such a continuum as housing adequacy exists; and (2) a clear definition of what "housing adequacy" means. Both these steps, of course, imply a thorough knowledge of housing and its problems. It is always necessary to make explicit the rationale for item selection in any construction of scales. This is similar to the problems which were discussed in the chapter on concepts.

Another important point in defining the continuum is to bear in mind the *nature of the population* which is to be scaled. It may well be true that an attitude continuum exists in one group but not in another, or that those items which measure housing adequacy in California have no relevance in New York or Chicago. A scale, therefore, must be treated cautiously and must always be viewed as tentative when applied in a new and dissimilar population. This, of course, is true whether the populations are separated spatially, temporally, or by social distance.

In general, then, scale construction and application require a high degree of consciousness of the logical problems surrounding the twin assumptions of (1) the *existence* of a continuum, and (2) the *representativeness* of that continuum achieved by the particular scale in mind. There are empirical tests which can be applied to check either assumption. The question of *representativeness* is checked by tests of *validity*, which will be discussed below. The *existence* of the continuum can be empirically verified in a number of ways which will be taken up in turn as the various techniques are discussed.

2. *Reliability*

A scale is reliable when it will consistently produce the same results when applied to the same sample. Just as a ruler which shrank or expanded materially when exposed to temperature changes would be useless, so would be a scale which yielded a different result upon each application. Three methods of measuring reliability are in general use.

A. TEST-RETEST. As the name implies, this means that the scale is applied twice to the same population and the results compared. The statistical technique of comparison may employ any of the common measures suit-

EXPERIMENTAL GROUP   CONTROL GROUP

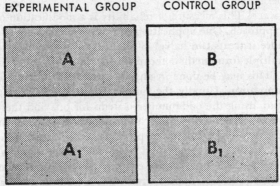

FIGURE 1. A design for controlling test-retest reliability.

able for this purpose. Some form of correlation is generally used, however. A high level of association must be demanded before reliability can be assumed. This method of measuring reliability presents a problem, however, which is rather difficult of solution. The very fact of first application of the scale, if people are the units being measured, may affect their behavior in responding to the second application. This effect can be measured, of course, by randomly dividing the original population into halves and utilizing a control-group procedure. Thus if an attitude scale were to be tested for reliability, the technique illustrated above might be used where only the shaded groups are tested. Thus, if A_1 shifts more from A than B_1 shifts from A, the assumption that the first administration of the scale has affected the second responses would be justified. If this occurred, doubt would be cast upon the reliability coefficient, since the amount of variation which was due to the original stimulus would not be separated from the amount due to the unreliability of the scale. Related to this attempt to avoid the effect of the first scaling is another measure of reliability, discussion of which follows.

B. MULTIPLE FORM. In this method of measuring reliability, two forms of the scale are constructed to begin with, and alternate forms are administered successively to the same sample. It is obvious that this does not completely solve the problem of first scaling effect since, if the two forms are sufficiently correlated to measure the same continuum, then their connection may well be obvious to the subject. Further, answering any series of questions on some segment of behavior may affect the second series of answers.

The level of correspondence between the two forms must here, as in the test-retest procedure, reach a very high level of confidence to ensure satisfactory reliability. In general, the third method of measuring reliability is superior to either of these procedures since it does not involve two scaling experiences.

C. SPLIT-HALF. This measure of reliability is a modification of the multiple-form approach. One application of a scale is sufficient to secure the measure, since it treats two halves of one scale as if they were two forms, as in the multiple-form method above. The scale is divided randomly into two halves. This may be done in any way which is practical and yet assures randomization. Usually the simplest procedure is to separate the scale into two, using the odd-numbered items for one and the even-numbered for the other. This, of course, can be done only when the numbering itself has not involved a systematic principle. It is safer than comparing the first half against the second half since differential informant fatigue or cumulative item effect may lower or raise the true correlation.

Each of the two sets of items is treated as a separate scale and scored accordingly. The two subscales are then correlated and this is taken as a measure of reliability. A further step is to correct the correlation coefficient secured between the two halves by applying the Spearman-Brown prophecy formula $r_n = nr_1/[1 + (n-1)r_1]$. This correction assumes that a scale $2n$ items long will be more reliable than a scale n items long, and since the length of the scale has been halved by dividing it into odds and evens, the full scale will have a higher reliability than would either half. Once again the coefficient should reach a high level before being taken as evidence of adequate reliability.

It should perhaps be noted here that this technique assumes that the scale as a whole hangs together, so that either half may be taken as adequately representative of the whole. This can be true only when two conditions are met:

1. There must be an empirical demonstration that the scale is a unity. This was mentioned in the section of this chapter on the definition of the continuum and will be further discussed under specific scaling techniques.

2. Each half scale must contain sufficient items to be reliable itself. A minimum number for this is probably 8 to 10, so the entire scale should not be shorter than 16 to 20 items.

3. *Validity*

A scale possesses validity when it actually measures what it claims to measure. It can at once be seen that this is very difficult to establish. Since, as was pointed out earlier, a scale measures a continuum which is inferred to exist from the items themselves, there are frequently no independent measures which can be used as a criterion of validity for the scale. Nevertheless every scale, to be useful, must have some indication of validity. The consequence of this is that much work remains to be done with regard to validating scales already in use and with regard to developing techniques of validation. There are four approaches to the validation of scales, which are discussed below.

A. LOGICAL VALIDATION. This is one of the most commonly used methods of validation and certainly one of the most difficult to apply. It refers to either theoretical or "common-sense" analysis which concludes simply that, the items being what they are, the nature of the continuum cannot be other than it is stated to be. Logical validation, or "face validity" as it is sometimes called, is almost always used because it automatically springs from the careful definition of the continuum and the selection of the items. For example, a test of "conservatism" might contain questions about attitudes regarding property, marriage, and the political system. Responses to these questions would be judged in terms of a common-sense definition of conservatism, that is, upholding the *status quo.*

On a question concerning "what should be done about Communism," then, we might agree that the conservatives would suggest further restrictions, while liberals would be somewhat more lenient. We would thus feel justified in including such an item. However, empirical study may indicate that this item is of little use, since some conservatives will be less strict, following a nineteenth-century conception of judicial protection of individual rights. And many liberals, bitter at what they consider a Communist betrayal of reform movements, may suggest that such protections be discarded. Thus it is not wise to rely on logical and common-sense validation alone. Such claims for validity can at best be merely plausible and never definitive. More than logical validity is required to render satisfactory the use of a scale.

B. JURY OPINION. This is an extension of the method of logical validation, except that in this case the confirmation of the logic is secured from a group of persons who would be considered expert in the field within which the scale applies. For example, if a scale to measure the adequacy of housing were constructed, engineers, realtors, janitors, architects, and housewives might constitute a jury to determine the validity of the scale.

Since experts may err and since nothing but logical validity can result from this approach, it would seem that jury validation can be considered only slightly superior to logical validation.

C. "KNOWN GROUPS." This technique is a variant of the jury procedure. In this case the validity is implied from the known attitudes and other *characteristics* of antithetical groups, however, rather than from their specific *expertness*. Thus, if a scale were being devised for the purpose of measuring attitudes toward the church, the questions could be tested by administering it to one group known to attend church, to be active in church activities, and otherwise to give evidence of a favorable attitude toward this institution. These answers would then be compared with those from a group known *not* to attend church and also known to oppose the church in other ways. If the scale failed to discriminate between the two groups it could not be considered to measure this attitude with validity.

This method, while widely employed, always carried with it the danger that there might be *other* differences between the groups in addition to their known behavior with regard to religion, which might account for the differences in the scale scores. For example, the two groups with antithetical behavior patterns might also show differences of age, socioeconomic status, ethnic background, marital status, residential location, and political affiliation. There might also be differences with respect to liberalism, conservatism, attitudes toward various authors and works of art, etc. However, these could not be accepted as *measuring* attitudes toward the church, however correlated with that attitude they might be. We cannot assume that anything is correlated until we have a device for measuring the attitude. Thus there is always the danger that items which discriminate between the prochurch and antichurch *groups* might not be the most significant for discriminating between prochurch and antichurch *attitudes*.

Further, perhaps the known behavior under study might be associated with a differential inclination to agree or disagree on questions in general. As a consequence only very careful use of the known-groups technique should be made. Moreover, such measures of validity are always only plausible and never certain. Nevertheless, a high degree of plausibility may be all that is possible in the study of some problems, and for this reason the known-group technique of validation is frequently useful and should not be discarded for falling somewhat short of perfection.

D. INDEPENDENT CRITERIA. This is the ideal technique, abstractly speaking, but its application is usually very difficult. Ideally, also, it would be called validation by an independent criterion. However, if there is already a single criterion available to measure the continuum in question there is little need to construct a scale. As a result several criteria of validity are generally used so that the scale will serve the function of measuring more simply a continuum that would otherwise be difficult to measure.

For example, if it is desired to produce a scale which will measure social standing, its validity may be measured by checking it against a variety of other factors such as rental value of homes, amount of education, residential location, income, family background, or other similar factors. *On the assumption* that the composite effect of these validating factors will be to measure *true social standing,* the degree to which the scale correlates with these indexes indicates the validity of that scale.

The great difficulty here lies in the fact that the independent criteria may themselves not be good indexes of the continuum which the scale seeks to define. This, of course, is in addition to the point made above that, if these independent criteria are available and reflect the continuum accurately, then there is little reason for the existence of the scale.

However, it should be underlined that where these difficulties are solved, validation by independent criteria is a powerful tool and is perhaps the most effective of all techniques of validation.

In general, it should be understood that the best practice is to employ as many of the four techniques as is possible. In fact, the logical technique should always be employed and made explicit. It will, however, seldom be convincing alone and should be combined with at least one of the other methods.

4. *Weighting of items*

This is essentially a problem in increasing the validity of the scale. Furthermore, it is not a problem in the construction of all types of scales. Nevertheless it is sufficiently different from the problem of validity as such, and it applies to enough types of scales, to warrant separate consideration in this section.

The problem is a simple one to understand, though its solutions are not always equally plain. It will be recalled that the essence of scaling is to combine several qualitative characteristics into a quantitative variable. Thus scales typically present a series of qualities which are either present or absent, and the combination of these provides the scale. The question frequently arises, therefore, whether all the items (attributes) are of equal importance. If this cannot be assumed, then the problem arises as to how this inequality can be allowed for; in other words, how to assign weights to the items.

Three methods are generally employed. Since the purpose of weighting is to secure a scale which will more accurately measure the continuum it purports to measure, it is not surprising to find these closely related to the techniques of validation.

A. KNOWN GROUPS. If a scale without weighting the items has been seen to discriminate between two groups, its accuracy may be improved by applying the same test of validity to *each of the items making up the scale.* Statistical measures which will be discussed later can then be employed to weight each item in terms of its ability to discriminate between the criterion groups. By thus allowing for the validity of each item, the scale as a whole is improved.

B. INDEPENDENT CRITERIA. This technique is essentially the same as that of the known-group method, except that the known groups are replaced by independent criteria. Thus the validity of each item is separately checked against the independent criteria. A statistical measure of the relationship of each to the criteria is then employed as the weight for that item.

C. THE SCALE ITSELF. When a scale is established as reliable and valid, then the total first approximation of the score may be used as a criterion of validity for each item. The procedure in this case is the same as in the two methods above, so that the weighting of *each* item is a function of its relation to the scale as a *whole*.

5. *The nature of the item*

One of the questions closely associated with the validity of scales is that concerning the nature of the items of the scale. There are many who feel that so-called "paper and pencil" tests do not coincide sufficiently well with other behaviors to make them valid instruments. It is felt that such scales structure the situation too arbitrarily to reflect accurately the feelings of the subject. So long as such scales show adequate validity, however, such objections need not be taken seriously. However, in certain cases this objection may be well taken and methods have been developed to deal with this problem. These are all considered as "projective" tests even though they may differ considerably in nature.

The essential nature of the projective item, versus the directive item, is that it avoids as much as possible any structuring of the situation. In this way it is hoped that the response made by the subject will be close to his "real" feelings and will not reflect some biases or prejudices implicit in the structuring itself of the directive items. Projective tests are, at present, most commonly employed by psychologists but are coming into use among sociologists. In the following chapter some examples of attempts to employ unstructured items will be given. At this point it is only necessary to make clear the fact that in some sensitive or controversial areas of study the problem of reducing the directive nature of items is a matter of importance for sociological research. The projective character of "nondirective" interviewing has already been discussed.

6. *The equality of the units*

In the opening paragraphs of this chapter, reference was made to the ordinal character of measurement. Thus the discussion this far has faced only those problems which are related to scaling as a method of *ordering or ranking* units on a continuum. In addition to the problem of *whether* one unit (person or group) is higher on a scale than another, there are also problems of *how much* one unit is higher or lower than another.

The nature of this problem can be clearly seen by returning to the early illustrations of family size or amount of money in the bank. Not only is every family with six members obviously larger than one with only three members, but it can be said to be *twice* as large, or to have three *more* members. Similarly the man who has $2,000 in the bank has more than the man who has only $1,000, but we can make the comparison more precise by noting that he has *twice* as much. This is called the cardinal use of numbers in distinction from the ordinal or ranking principle. It means that the units of measurement can be added, subtracted, multiplied, or divided.

The question as to whether scales as they are applied in sociology can ever be thought of as employing cardinal numbers is often brought up. That is, for example, can one house ranked at the 96th percentile on a housing adequacy scale be thought of as being *twice* as adequate as one ranked at the 48th percentile? This could be true only if the housing scale had two attributes: (1) it would have to have a point of origin at the value zero; and (2) each attribute composing the scale would have to add an equal increment to the scale of adequacy, in the same way that any one dollar added to the bank account is the same as every other one already deposited. No sociological scales in use possess these characteristics. Various ways of dealing with the problem will be presented in the following chapter as indications of the awareness of the problem within the field and as attempts to correct for this shortcoming as much as possible.

It should further be pointed out that it is not necessary for a scale to possess either a zero point or absolutely equal units in order to be useful. These are desirable characteristics, but they are not essential to sound scientific procedure.

STANDARDS FOR SCALING

The foregoing problems, which confront everyone attempting scale analysis, appear formidable indeed. In fact the scale which shows perfect reliability, absolute validity, a zero point, and completely uniform units does not exist.

There are two important facts for the student to bear in mind in regard to the accuracy of scaling: First, that great care must be exercised to achieve as high a degree of reliability and validity as possible, and second, that even when we do not make a scale which can be put in cardinal numbers, the techniques can nevertheless be useful. Such scaling methods as are available range from great crudity to considerable refinement. The research situation will frequently determine the degree of accuracy which can be achieved. Any scale which is reliable and valid, regardless of its crudity of measurement, is better than no scale at all so long as no more refined technique is applicable.

SUGGESTED READINGS

Jahoda, Marie, Morton Deutsch, and Stuart W. Cook, *Research Methods in Social Relations* (New York: Dryden, 1951), Part I, Chap. 4.

Lundberg, G. A., *Social Research* (New York: Longmans, 1942), pp. 211–223.

Murphy, Gardner, and Rensis Likert, *Public Opinion and the Individual* (New York: Harper, 1938), Chaps. 1 and 2.

Rundquist, Edward A., and Raymond Sletto, *Personality in the Depression* (Minneapolis: University of Minnesota Press, 1936), Chap. 1.

Stouffer, Samuel A., *et al.*, *Studies in Social Psychology in World War II*, Vol. 4, Chaps. 1 and 2.

Thurstone, L. L., and E. J. Chave, *The Measurement of Attitudes* (Chicago: University of Chicago Press, 1929), Chap. 1.

CHAPTER 16

Scaling Techniques: Social Distance, Sociometric, and Rating Scales

There are many different ways to classify scaling techniques. For the purposes of this volume most methods can be thought of as falling into one of five major categories with their appropriate subtypes. Thus, they can be thought of as scales measuring social distance, rating scales, ranking scales, scales based upon internal consistency, and latent-structure scales.

SCALING SOCIAL DISTANCE

These are characterized by the continuum with which they deal as much as by their orientation toward a particular technical development. The concept of social distance refers to a continuum described by Robert E. Park [1] as "the grades and degrees of understanding and intimacy which characterize pre-social and social relations generally." Thus described, the continuum ranges from close, warm, and intimate contact on the one hand, through indifference, to active dislike, hostility, and rejection on the other hand.

In applying this technique two problems must be faced. First, it is necessary to define the *remainder* of the continuum, that is, to define the measurement as social distance toward something—a social group, a value, or an individual. The concept of social distance has been applied to all three. The second problem, then, is to measure the social distance which does exist. This technique is quite flexible and can be adapted to a variety of needs.

1. *The Bogardus Social Distance Scales*

These are so named after Emory S. Bogardus, who pioneered in this area. He and his students as well as other sociologists have applied this method to various types of social groups such as ethnic minorities, social classes, and occupational types, as well as to more abstract social values. The two examples which follow will illustrate the procedure.

[1] Robert E. Park, "The Concept of Social Distance," *Journal of Applied Sociology,* Vol. VIII (1902), pp. 339–344.

Table 1 reproduces findings with respect to the degrees of social distance ascribed by 1,725 Americans to a series of ethnic types. There are

TABLE 1

Reactions of 1,725 Americans to Four Different Ethnic Minorities by Percentages *

Regarding ethnic minorities listed	(1) To close kinship by marriage	(2) To my club as personal chums	(3) To my street as neighbors	(4) To employment in my occupation	(5) To citizenship in my country	(6) As visitors only to my country	(7) Would exclude from my country
English	93.7	96.7	97.3	95.4	95.9	1.7	0.0
Swedes	45.3	62.1	75.6	78.0	86.3	5.4	1.0
Poles	11.0	11.6	28.3	44.3	58.3	19.7	4.7
Korean	1.1	6.8	13.0	21.4	23.7	47.1	19.1

* Adapted from Emory S. Bogardus, *Immigration and Race Attitudes* (Boston: Heath, 1928), p. 25.

several points which should be made about this table in the light of the general comments made in the previous chapter about scaling problems.

The first point is, of course, that as it stands the table does not present one scale but rather a series of scales. That is, the series of ethnic groups are ranked on each of seven scales. There is, however, the explicit assumption that these seven attributes are ordered as a continuum of social distance (from acceptability for close kinship by marriage to exclusion from the country). This would indicate the need of a single expression for each ethnic group, which would stand for its position on all seven points. Figure 1, which portrays graphically the frequency of responses for selected groups, shows the difficulty of achieving such a goal. Thus individuals who check either position 6 ("would admit as visitors only to my country") or 7 ("would exclude from my country") are logically prohibited from checking any other item on the scale. This is not the case, however, with responses 1 through 5, where a person might check any combination of the five. This would seem to indicate that points 6 and 7 are so strongly stated that they do not belong on the continuum *as even approximately equal intervals* compared with points 1 through 5. This can be seen by the steepness of the drop of the curves in Figure 1 after response 5. If then, responses 6 and 7 are dropped, is it any simpler to attempt a score for each ethnic type?

Figure 2 shows smoothed curves representing the social distance scores for the same selected groups, ignoring responses 6 and 7. It is clear that an index to describe the position of any group must represent two values for each line. It must first describe the *height* of the line—that is, the point on the scale where it intersects the perpendicular dropped from response

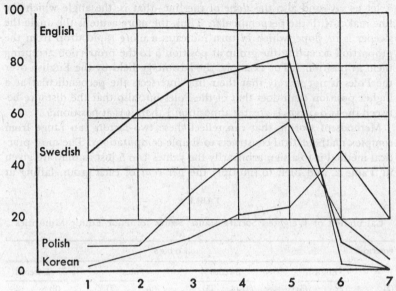

FIGURE 1. Frequency of responses of 1,725 Americans to four different ethnic minorities.

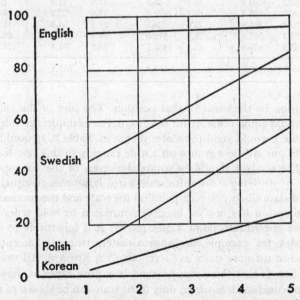

FIGURE 2. Smoothed curves of social-distance scores for four ethnic minorities.

5, let us say—and also the *slope* of the line—that is, the angle which the line makes with the perpendicular. Thus, the more acute is the angle the steeper is its slope, which in turn indicates a more rapid drop from the proportion accepting the group at position 5 to the proportion accepting them at position 1. For example, the advantage held by the English over the Poles is not merely that their line intersects the perpendicular at a higher position than does that of the Poles but also that the distance between the two curves is greater at position 1 than it is at position 5.

Methods of scoring that can reflect these two factors can range from complex mathematical constructs to simple computations. The most practical method is to assign arbitrarily the values 1 to 5 just as they are given in Table 2, and then to multiply the *per cent* of each group falling at

TABLE 2

Calculation of Weighted Social-distance Scores for Four Ethnic Minorities

POSITION	GROUPS							
	English		Swedes		Poles		Koreans	
(1)	(2)	(3)	(4)	(5)	(6)	(7)	(8)	(9)
	Per Cent	(1 × 2)	Per Cent	(1 × 4)	Per Cent	(1 × 6)	Per Cent	(1 × 8)
1	93.7	93.7	45.3	45.3	11.0	11.0	1.1	1.1
2	96.7	193.4	62.1	124.2	11.6	23.2	10.8	21.6
3	97.3	291.9	75.6	226.8	28.3	84.9	11.8	35.4
4	95.4	381.6	78.0	312.0	44.3	177.2	20.1	80.4
5	95.9	479.5	86.3	431.5	58.3	291.5	27.5	137.5
Total		1,440.1		1,139.8		587.8		276.0

each position by the *value* of that position. The sum of the values thus secured would equal the score for the group. For example, the values taken from Table 1 would yield the scores shown in Table 2. It would thus be possible to put all these groups on a scale ranging in this case from 1,440 to 276. The student should be aware, however, of the assumptions involved in quantifying a Bogardus scale. First, it assumes an equal amount of social distance between each point on the scale and the succeeding one. This assumption has not yet been demonstrated to hold true. Further, there is no known zero point. Consequently it is impossible to conclude that Swedes, for example, are approximately twice as "acceptable" as Poles who in turn are twice as "acceptable" as Koreans. All that can be assumed here is that these groups stand in a rank order as shown. Even this can be concluded, however, only if the scale can be shown to meet the requirements set forth in the preceding chapter. Discussion of these points follows.

A. DEFINITION OF THE CONTINUUM. We have already seen how the continuum was verbally defined. The question now is, "What empirical evidence is there to show the existence of a continuum of social distance?" The evidence at hand can be seen by referring once more to Figure 2. Note that all lines slant up from left to right, forming an acute angle with the perpendicular at point 5. This indicates that moving from position 1 to position 5, progressively more people endorse the statements. From this it can be concluded that the scale runs from lesser to greater social distance. Some of the distributions (for example, that for the English) do not show steady increases from left to right and this might cast some doubt upon the existence of the continuum. However, these deviations from regularity are small and statistically nonsignificant. Furthermore, these irregularities appear only among those groups at the *extremes of social distance*. It can be assumed, therefore, that the scale does provide a rough ordering scheme along some sort of continuum between the points 1 through 5. Furthermore, on logical grounds it seems safe to conclude that this can be identified with Park's concept of social distance. This, however, is a question of validity, which will be treated below.

B. RELIABILITY. A scale of this type is not easily tested for reliability by either the multiple-form or the split-half technique. The test-retest approach is the most effective measure of reliability of such a scale.

C. VALIDITY. The logical connection between the scale points and the concept of social distance has already been mentioned. To demonstrate the validity of such a scale further, however, requires careful thinking. The application of the "known-group" method would involve finding groups known to be favorable toward some of the ethnic types and unfavorable toward others. If the responses of these groups fit the requisite pattern, then validity would seem probable.

The use of the method of independent criteria would require showing that the rank order fits some other rank order of social acceptability. Such indicators might be the rank order of desirability as tenants in a large housing project, of ability to secure employment and promotion in industry, of acceptability as members in a union, of actual intermarriage rates, etc. In all cases the cautions concerning inferences of validity discussed in the previous chapters must be observed. Further, the student must keep clearly in mind that the test seeks to measure *attitudes,* not actual "discrimination." Whether the attitudes issue in corresponding action is a separate problem, and the behavior itself may not be determined by attitudes alone.

D. APPLICATION TO VALUES. It was stated earlier that social-distance techniques can be applied to abstract values and individuals as well as to groups. A brief example will show how values can be studied with these techniques. The study of individual social distance will be covered in the next section of this chapter.

If, for example, the relative attractiveness of various types of communities for a given population is a problem, some such scale as that shown in Table 3 might be developed. It is obvious that this scale would present

TABLE 3 *

Mock Table for a Scale to Measure the "Attractiveness" of Different Communities

Place (Region Specified)	(1) I would prefer to live here	(2) I would prefer to spend most of my time here	(3) I would prefer to spend my vacation here	(4) I would prefer to visit here only once in a while	(5) I do not care for this type of community
A large city (1,000,000 or more)					
A city (100,000–999,999)					
A small city (10,000–99,999)					
A small town (2,500–9,999)					
A village (under 2,500)					
In the country					

* Adapted from a manuscript by W. G. Binnewies; cited by Emory S. Bogardus, *The New Social Research* (Los Angeles: Jesse Ray Miller, 1926), p. 215.

certain difficulties, particularly in terms of further describing the types of communities, but it suggests the flexibility of this type of scaling.

E. INVERTING THE SCALE. Another indication of the flexibility of this technique can be seen in the fact that it can be used not only to scale groups or values which are external to the subjects doing the rating, but also to scale the raters themselves with respect to the social distance between them and some specified group or value.

For example, if it is desired to characterize groups or persons as to their willingness to accept, let us say, Poles, then their individual (or group) scores on attitudes toward the Poles can serve as a means of ordering the rates along a continuum of favorableness-unfavorableness toward Poles. In a housing study conducted by the Bureau of Applied Social Research, this technique was used to define groups or subcommunities which had a low level of self-consciousness. By asking questions regarding what kinds of people they "felt most at home with," it was possible to define a small community in terms of the model type of person preferred. Similarly, people could be rated on their "closeness" to farm life by their selection of this one type of community from those listed in Table 3.[2] The general principle in these cases is to consider only one of the rating values as being incorporated in the definition of the continuum, thus producing a variable defined as "social distance toward Poles," "social distance toward farm life," etc.

F. LIMITATIONS AND APPLICATIONS. This scaling technique is not limited so much by inflexibility of application (some examples to the contrary have been given above) as by its crudity as a measure. The chief problems are (1) the assumption of equidistance between the scale points;[3] (2) the assumption that each point is necessarily "beyond" the preceding one; and (3) the fact that it can be tested for reliability only by the rather clumsy test-retest technique. As a consequence the use of this method of scaling will generally be restricted to pilot studies or to researches which for some compelling reason must be completed quickly and do not require a very high level of accuracy.

If this is the case, what are the reasons for having given so much space to discussing this method? The first reason is given above, namely, that under certain circumstances this scaling technique may be satisfactory. The second is that as a pioneer measurement method, a full understanding of the Bogardus scales should be helpful in grasping what sociologists mean by a continuum and in understanding as well as developing newer and more precise scaling techniques.

2. Sociometric measurement

Some 15 years ago, and about 15 years after the appearance of the earliest Bogardus scales, J. L. Moreno and Helen Hall Jennings applied a measure of social distance which differed radically from the Bogardus approach. The chief divergence of this method, usually called sociometry, from the earlier technique lies in the fact that it is concerned with attractions and repulsions between individuals within a small group and with the group structure as defined in these terms. Helen Jennings[4] has described this method as follows:

"Stated briefly, sociometry may be described as a means of presenting simply and graphically the entire structure of relations existing at a given time among members of a given group. The major lines of communication, or the pattern of

---

[2] In fact this was the form originally used. *Ibid.*

[3] Professor Bogardus has worked toward the solution of this problem, chiefly through the use of "juries of experts." See Calvin F. Schmid, "Scaling Techniques" in Pauline Young, *Scientific Social Surveys and Research* (New York: Prentice-Hall, 1949), rev. ed., pp. 335–337.

[4] Helen Hall Jennings, *Sociometry in Group Relations* (Washington, D.C.: American Council on Education, 1948), p. 11.

attraction and rejection in its full scope, are made readily comprehensive at a glance."

This technique has been applied in such widely diversified situations as informal groups, school classes, prisons and other organizations, and industry. Since there is considerable latitude in the application of sociom-

Chosen

Chooser	A	B	C	D	E	F	G	H	I	J	K	L	M	N	O	P
A		3	2				1									
B	2				1	3										
C																
D		3	1			2										
E			3				2									1
F				2			1				3					
G	3								2		1					
H																
I					3		1				2					
J				3		2	1									
K		1					2		3							
L	3								1						2	
M								2	1						3	
N							1		3							2
O				2			1				3					
P							2				3				1	
1st Choice		1	1		1		6		2		1				1	1
2nd Choice	1		1	2		2	3	1	1		1				1	1
3rd Choice	2	2	1	1	1	1			2		3				1	
TOTAL	3	3	3	3	2	3	9	1	5		5				3	2

FIGURE 3. Example of a sociometric matrix showing who chooses whom for membership on a school committee.

etry, it may be well to begin with a consideration of an early statement of its characteristics made by Jennings [5] in 1943:

"The form of the sociometric test as applied up to the present has had three characteristics:

"1. A specific number of choices is allowed, varying according to the size of the groups tested;

"2. A specific criterion for choice is used, varying with the functional activity of the group . . .;

"3. Different levels of preference are designated for each choice."

[5] Helen Hall Jennings, *Leadership and Isolation* (New York: Longmans, 1943), p. 19

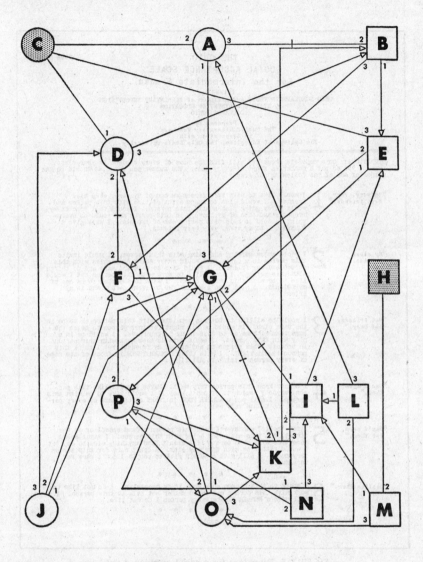

FIGURE 4. Example of a sociogram, presenting data from matrix in Figure 3.

THE OHIO   Form O-3

SOCIAL ACCEPTANCE SCALE

For the Intermediate Grades

Issued by

OHIO SCHOLARSHIP TESTS and DIVISION of ELEMENTARY SUPERVISION
STATE DEPARTMENT OF EDUCATION
COLUMBUS, OHIO

Prepared by
The Euclid Elementary Teachers
in Cooperation with
The College of Education, The Ohio State University

DIRECTIONS: On a separate sheet you will find the name of every student in your class. We want you to put a number in front of every name. The number you put down should be the number of one of the following paragraphs.

"My very, very best friends." **1** I would like to have this person as one of my very, very best friends. I would like to spend a lot of time with this person and would enjoy going places with this person. I would tell some of my troubles and some of my secrets to this person and would do everything I could to help this person out of trouble. I will give a NUMBER ONE to my very, very best friends.

* * * * *

"My other friends." **2** I would enjoy working and being with this person. I would invite this person to a party, and would enjoy going on picnics with this person and our friends. I would like to talk and make and do things with this person. I would like to work with this person and I would like to be with this person often. I want this person to be one of my friends. I will give a NUMBER TWO to every person who is my friend.

* * * * *

"Not friends, but Okay." **3** I would be willing to be on a committee with this person or to be in the same club. It would be all right for this person to be on the same team with me or to live in my neighborhood. I would be in a play with this person. I would just as soon work with this person in school. This person is not one of my friends, but I think this person is all right. I will put a NUMBER THREE in front of the name of every person I think is all right.

* * * * *

"Don't know them." **4** I do not know this person very well. Maybe I would like this person, maybe I wouldn't. I don't know if I would like to be with this person. I will put a NUMBER FOUR in front of the name of every person I don't know very well.

* * * * *

"Don't care for them." **5** I say "hello" whenever I meet this person around school or on the street, but I do not enjoy being with this person. I might spend some time with this person if I didn't have anything else to do, but I would rather be with somebody else. I don't care for this person very much. I will give a NUMBER FIVE to people I don't care for very much.

* * * * *

"Dislike them." **6** I speak to this person only when it is necessary. I do not like to work with this person and would rather not talk to this person. I will give a NUMBER SIX to every person I do not like.

* * * * *

(Over)

FIGURE 5. Directions for a social acceptance test.

DIRECTIONS FOR TEACHERS

1. Provide each student with a sheet of paper on which is listed the name of every student in the class -- OR -- Provide each student with a sheet of lined paper and, as you dictate, have the students write, in an orderly column, the name of every person in the class.

2. Then say: "When you have difficulty in arithmetic I try to help you. I help you with your writing, with your spelling, with reading and many other things. I also want to help you in making friends, in being good companions to other people. But to do this I must know how you feel about every boy and girl in this room and how each boy and girl feels about you. Hence, today we are asking you to tell us how you feel about the other boys and girls in this room. As soon as you have written how you feel about your classmates, all your papers will be shuffled so no one will know who filled out any certain paper.

3. "First, I want you to put the number FOUR in front of your own name. Do that now. Put a FOUR in front of your own name. If you are a girl, write GIRL at the top of your paper. If you are a boy, write BOY at the top of your paper."

4. Pause. Then say: "I am now going to read the first paragraph. Read quietly to yourself as I read aloud. If you don't know the meaning of any word, raise your hand, and I will try to help you to understand the words."

5. Teacher reads PARAGRAPH ONE. After a slight pause she says:

   "If that fits any person in our room, put the number ONE in front of the name. Put the number ONE in front of every name that it fits."

6. Pause for a minute or two while the children are writing. Then read paragraph TWO and say again:

   "If that fits any person in our room, put the number TWO in front of the name. Put the number TWO in front of every name that it fits."

   Pause while students are writing. Then read the next paragraph and continue this way until all paragraphs have been read.

7. Have the students turn their papers FACE DOWN, when they have finished the task. Remind them, several times, that there should be a number in front of every name. Give them time to read the paragraphs over again to themselves. Help them out where they need help in interpreting words or phrases.

8. When the papers have been collected, shuffle them up in front of the class, and emphasize very much the point that you will not know how anybody marked the papers; that nobody can ever find out how they marked their papers.

TABULATING AND USING THE RESULTS:

You have received a CLASS SUMMARY SHEET for this Social Acceptance Scale. On the back of that sheet you will find directions for tabulating and using the results.

FIGURE 5 (Continued)

As an example of this type of sociometric procedure a study referred to earlier has been selected.[6] This is a volume dealing with the technique of studying school classes, and the requirements above are met in terms of this situation. Three choices were allowed each child, and the situation was defined as one in which the criterion for selecting other children in the class was "liking to work with them on a study committee." The levels of choice were designated by asking the children to designate with the number 1 the child they would most like, their second choice with 2, and their third choice with 3.

The major point to note here is the fact of designating the choice situation in such a way as to be meaningful—in this case, by asking the children to name others with whom they would like to do committee work. Obviously there is an infinite number of ways in which the situation can be structured. For example, in an institution it might be: "With whom would you like to eat—share a room—spend your leisure, etc.?" Or in industry: "With whom would you like to work—play—visit, etc.?" The important thing here is (1) that the situation must be a real one to the group being tested, and also (2) that it must fit the sort of sociometric structure which is being studied.

To return to the study of the school children, the next step is the tabulation of the data. A very useful form for this is reproduced in Figure 3. This is known as a sociometric matrix, and it may serve as the basis for analysis.

Another method of analysis, however, employs the sociogram. Figure 4 shows the sociogram resulting from plotting the data shown in Figure 3. The function of this diagram is to make clear the network of acceptances and rejections in a graphic way.

Reference to the bottom four rows of Figure 3 will indicate that the sociogram also offers other possible methods of analysis. Since each child shows a different *frequency* of being chosen, and further a different frequency of the *level* at which he is chosen, there exists the possibility of scaling the individuals as to "acceptability." This in turn implies the possibility of scaling on the basis of *willingness to accept others*. Because of the limitation to only three choices, however, the method described above is not well suited to this approach. An example of a variant of this method suited to such an analysis is found in the Ohio State Social Acceptance Scale, which is reproduced in Figure 5. It will be noted that instead of a series of choices of children, each child is rated on a friendship scale. Thus, if these results are put into a matrix such as that shown in Figure 3, *every cell will have an entry*. The total row at the bottom will then show the relative position of each child in the class in terms of being accepted. In this case there is also the possibility of a total column which would contain the *sum* of the ratings given *by* each child.

6 Jennings, *Sociometry in Group Relations*, p. 11.

These techniques have recently been given increasing application in practical situations, such as administering children's camps, choosing members of flight crews, and the recent Army inauguration of the "'buddy system." They have also been of great utility in introducing new knowledge and techniques in underdeveloped regions, for they aid in ascertaining the channels of power, gossip, and communication within a small village, a rural area, or a larger geographical region.

These and other variants of sociometric techniques offer rather simple methods of ranking individuals on a continuum of "acceptability" or "outgoingness" on the part of group members. Where their use is justified they may be powerful research tools, since they meet the general problems of scaling very well.

A. DEFINITION OF THE CONTINUUM. The existence of a social-distance continuum can be accepted only in so far as it proves valid by other criteria. There seems no trouble in defining the continuum in these scales as social distance, however, *as long as the stimulus, i.e.,* the choosing situation, *is appropriate* to the conclusions drawn.

B. RELIABILITY. This type of scale is suitable only for test-retest reliability measurement. Jennings, however, gives ample evidence that "choice position" is slow to change and that sociometric measurements may therefore be considered reliable.[7]

C. VALIDITY. In the same volume the findings indicate that the independent criterion of case studies and behavior observation provide satisfactory indications of the validity of sociometric tests.[8]

RATING SCALES

This general approach to scaling is very common. The student is almost certain to have had some contact with one mode of rating in the form of grades. When a teacher assigns a grade to a student he is applying a scale of scholarly excellence to that student. If the reader's experience with this scale has been such as to cause him to doubt the reliability and validity of this example of rating scales he may wish to dispense with this technique altogether. That would be somewhat hasty, however, until the problems and applications of rating scales have been more fully discussed.

The design of the rating technique must always take into account the existence of three elements: the judges who will do the rating, the phenomena to be rated, and the continuum along which they will be rated. If the design does not adequately define all three, as well as assure that (1) the judges, (2) the subjects, and (3) the continuum are logically re-

[7] Jennings, *Leadership and Isolation*, pp. 27–31.
[8] *Ibid.*

lated, then only unreliable and invalid results can be expected. All three components must be very carefully selected.

1. *The judges*

In general, pooled judgments increase the accuracy of any rating scale. The rating situation and the subsequent use of the scale will determine the number of judges to be employed. Any number may be used, of course, from one to a very large population. Under some circumstances one judge is all that is possible. This is true, for example, of the teacher-student-grade situation. Since pooled judgments are more accurate, however, it would be expected that a student's grade average—representing the pooled judgment of many teachers in many different subjects—would be a more accurate reflection of his general ability than would any one grade in any one course.

A great many studies are to be found in sociological and psychological literature, using various numbers of judges. Perhaps the most common form of multiple judges is the use of a college class. Mapheus Smith, for example, used 345 college students to secure prestige ratings of occupations.[9] The final position of the occupation was reckoned as the mean value of all the ratings.

The use of such judges, while increasing the reliability of the ratings, has a serious weakness. The *number* of judges is very satisfactory, but the *selective* characteristics which define college students make it dangerous to apply their ratings in a broader context. That is, the judges are not representative of the population nor are they experts. The result is to limit sharply the use of scales based upon such narrowly selected judgments.

One way of avoiding this problem is to use several judges but to select them on the basis of expertness in relation to the continuum under examination. The difficulty here is that of finding such experts and demonstrating their expertness. Further, in many continua, such as "prestige of occupations," expertness has no meaning. Each person is an expert in regard to his own ratings. Another way of avoiding the problem of selectivity of judges is to use as judges a sample of the population in which the scale will subsequently be applied.

Such a procedure was followed by North and Hatt in studying the same problem approached by Smith above, that is, the prestige of occupations.[10] In this case a cross section of the American population was

[9] Mapheus Smith, "Empirical Scale of Prestige Status of Occupations," *American Sociological Review*, Vol. VIII, No. 2 (April, 1943), pp. 185–192.

[10] C. C. North and Paul K. Hatt, "Jobs and Occupations: A Popular Evaluation," in Logan Wilson and William Kolb, *Sociological Analysis* (New York: Harcourt, Brace, 1949).

interviewed by the National Opinion Research Center. The problem of ignorance is often raised by this type of judging, and it is best solved by the use of experts. In this particular case, however, relatively few occupations were unknown to the population, so that the scale did not suffer materially.

2. *The continuum and the subjects*

The rating scale itself is always composed of two parts—an *instruction* which names the subject and defines the continuum, and a *scale* which defines the scale points to be employed in rating. There are two general methods of doing the latter—the use of verbal descriptions and the graphic technique.

A. THE GRAPHIC TECHNIQUE. This perhaps will be most familiar as the type of item found on many evaluation blanks. For example, this item appears on a teacher rating scale:

You are asked to rate your instructor in terms of a number of characteristics. Will you place a check mark (∨) at the place on each line which you think best describes his usual manner of teaching?

1. In regard to enthusiasm for his subject, does he appear to be:

Intensely interested in his subject matter?	Definitely interested but not intensely so?	Mildly interested?	Rather more disinterested than interested?	Definitely bored by the material?

Within the general limits of the use of rating scales, the graphic method can be used with effectiveness. In using it, however, Guilford suggests that the following principles be adhered to carefully: [11]

"1. Each trait should occupy a page by itself. This rule is rarely observed. When numbers of individuals are to be rated, it is far better that all of them be rated in one trait before going on to the next.

"2. The line should be at least 5 in. long but not much longer, so that it can be easily grasped as a whole.

"3. The line should have no breaks or divisions. A broken line may suggest a discontinuous variable.

"4. The 'good' and 'poor' ends should be alternated in random order so as to avoid a constant motor tendency to check at one side of the page.

"5. Introduce each trait with a question to which the rating gives an answer, that is, 'How has he responded when praised?'

"6. Use three or five descriptive adjectives—two extremes and one or three intermediates.

[11] J. P. Guilford, *Psychometric Methods* (New York: McGraw-Hill, 1936), pp. 271–272.

"7. The descriptive phrases should be in small type with considerable white space between them.

"8. Only universally understood descriptive terms should be used, avoiding slang and other colloquial expressions.

"9. Decide beforehand upon the probable extremes of ability (or of the trait) to be found in the group or groups in which the scale is to be used.

"10. The end phrases should not be so extreme in meaning as to be avoided by the raters.

"11. Have the extreme phrases set flush with the ends of the lines.

"12. The average or neutral phrase should be the center of the line.

"13. Descriptive phrases need not be evenly spaced. The meaning of the intermediate ones should be nearer the middle one than the extremes.

"14. In the scoring use a stencil which divides each line into several sections to which numerical values are assigned.

"15. The divisions of the scoring stencil need not be equal; they may be made to conform to the distribution of ratings.

"16. Do not require any finer distinction in rating than are used in scoring. If anything, the scoring units may be smaller than the rating units."

B. THE DESCRIPTIVE TECHNIQUE. There are two general approaches to this mode of defining the continuum and locating the points. One is best illustrated by Smith's occupational scale already referred to. His instructions asked the judges to rate

"each occupation on a scale of 100 points, the lower limit of this scale being conceived as reserved for the occupation having the lowest prestige in the United States according to the rater's personal estimation, and the highest as being reserved for the occupation having the highest prestige, regardless of whether the extreme limits were included in the occupations of the study. The rater was also directed to give the same rating to more than one of the occupations, if they appeared to be exactly equal. All ratings were made in terms of whole numbers.

"The title and definition of each occupation employed in the study was placed on a separate slip of paper to facilitate comparison and ranking. It was suggested to the evaluator that a preliminary arrangement of the occupations be made quickly into several groups, each representing a general degree of occupational prestige, such as very high, high, slightly above average, average, slightly below average, low and very low."

It will be noted in this case that only the end points are given and these are specified as 0 and 100. All other positions are assumed to lie at unit points between these. Such an approach is, of course, similar to a graphic scale with 100 graduations but with only two described. Generally speaking, this technique is not likely to be generally applicable. It throws great weight upon the judges by not specifying intermediate reference points and also assumes a facility in the use of percentages. A few of the occupations in Smith's study are given in the accompanying table.

Means and Their Standard Errors for Prestige Status Ratings
of 100 Representative American Occupations

Rank Order	Description	Mean	Standard Error
1	U.S. Supreme Court Justice	99.02	0.120
2	U.S. ambassador to foreign country	97.56	0.145
3	U.S. cabinet secretary	97.08	0.161
4	U.S. senator	96.21	0.145
5	Governor of state	95.25	0.170
6	College president or chancellor, 3,000 + students	92.30	0.229
7	Banker, large city	89.41	0.360
8	Mayor of city of over 500,000 population	88.76	0.423
9	Medical doctor, city of over 500,000 population	88.19	0.368
10	State prosecuting attorney	85.36	0.588

A somewhat different approach to the descriptive technique was employed in the rating scale of occupational prestige devised by North and
Hatt as described in Chapter 11. It will be recalled that in this case the
judges were a representative sample of the United States rather than college students. Therefore, no assumption of familiarity with the abstraction of a 100 per cent range could be made, and a simpler method was
required. An adaptation of the method used in the Ohio Social Acceptance Scale was employed as follows:

"The rating process was introduced by the interviewers as follows:

" 'Now I am going to ask you how you would judge a number of occupations.
For example, a *railroad brakeman*—which statement on this card (HAND RESPOND-
ENT [rating] CARD) *best gives your own* personal opinion of the *general standing*
of a *railroad brakeman?* (PAUSE) What number on that card would you pick out
for him?' (RECORD ANSWER.)

" 'Try not to judge a job according to your own opinion of some one person
you know who has such a job. Now, how would you judge a . . .?' (PROCEED
THROUGH LIST OF OCCUPATIONS.)

"The rating card handed the respondent is reproduced below:

" 'For each job mentioned, please pick out the statement that best gives *your
own personal opinion* of the *general standing* that such a job has.

1. *Excellent* standing.
2. *Good* standing.
3. *Average* standing.
4. *Somewhat below average* standing.
5. *Poor* standing.
X. I don't know where to place that one.' "

It is clear that such a technique has at least two weaknesses. It assumes
an equal distance between each of the descriptions and it limits the fine-
ness of choice. Both the graphic scale and the 100 per cent method of

Smith avoid this problem. It seems clear, then, that the entire study design will usually determine the method to be employed in those cases where a rating technique is called for. In general, it does not appear that results will be too dissimilar if each of the methods is carefully applied.

3. Reliability

Reliability here is a function of the number of judges and of the number of discriminations required. In general, not less than eight to ten judges should be used and not more than seven discriminations required. Reliability is best measured here by the test-retest method, although the multiple-forms technique can also sometimes be applied. An indication of the latter can be seen in the NORC study in which two occupations were repeated by different names. In this case the paired occupations of "automobile repairman" and "garage mechanic" received almost identical responses, as did "school teacher" and "instructor in the public schools."

4. Validity

The problem of validity has no special aspects and it may be tested in any of the usual ways.

5. Limitations and applications

The major limitations of this technique lie in its dependence upon judges, instead of independent criteria. However, in this particular case this is not a problem, since "prestige" is usually defined in terms of being rated high or low by the population, and on the other hand it possesses the advantage of being a very flexible and simple procedure.

SUGGESTED READINGS

Bogardus, Emory S., "Social Distance and Its Practical Implications," *Sociology and Social Research*, Vol. XVII (1933), pp. 265–271.

Guilford, J. P., *Psychometric Methods* (New York: McGraw-Hill, 1936), Chap. 9.

Jahoda, Marie, Morton Deutsch, and Stuart W. Cook, *Research Methods in Social Relations* (New York: Dryden, 1951), Part II, Chap. 17.

Lundberg, G. A., *Social Research* (New York: Longmans, 1942), Chap. 10.

Schmid, Calvin F., "Basic Statistical Concepts and Techniques" in Pauline V. Young, *Scientific Social Surveys and Research* (New York: Prentice-Hall, 1949), pp. 377–382.

CHAPTER 17

Scaling Techniques: Ranking, Internal Consistency, and Scalogram Scales

RANKING SCALES

The ranking technique is quite similar to the rating technique in its employment of judges, but rather than requiring the judgments to be made on an absolute scale, it requires them to be made by comparing the series of stimuli itself.

1. *Paired comparisons*

The simplest case of this would be to present two stimuli, define a continuum, and ask the judges which is larger (greater, hotter, better, etc.). When the number of stimuli is greater than two, however, other problems develop and other possibilities appear. A simple example may be taken from a field study of Puerto Rico. A representative sample of Puerto Rican adults was told by an interviewer, "I am going to read several occupations in pairs. When I pause after each pair will you tell me which of the pair is the more desirable employment for a woman?" The occupations were as follows: office worker, nurse, clerk in a store, domestic servant, farm laborer.

The 10 pairs of occupations were arranged so that each occupation appeared first in a pair as often as it appeared second. No occupation was repeated in any two succeeding questions. This procedure raised the question as to the consistency (*i.e.*, reliability) with which people responded. Table 1 shows what is meant by consistent and inconsistent responses.

The consistent pattern shows no contradictions while the inconsistent one shows that while occupation 5 was preferred to occupation 2, 2 was preferred to both 3 and 4, which in turn were preferred to 5.

If items are well chosen, that is, if the continuum is clearly defined, there will be relatively few such inconsistent responses. In this particular instance, a test sample of 150 cases revealed less than 9 per cent of inconsistencies.

The simplest way of scoring a ballot such as that reproduced in Table

TABLE 1

Response Patterns to a Paired Comparison of the Desirability
of Selected Occupations for Women, Puerto Rico, 1947

	CONSISTENT PATTERN Occupation Preferred *						INCONSISTENT PATTERN Occupation Preferred *				
	1	2	3	4	5		1	2	3	4	5
1	–					1	–				
2	x	–				2	x	–			x
3	x	x	–			3	x	x	–		
4	x	x	x	–		4	x	x	x	–	
5	x	x	x	x	–	5	x		x	x	–

* x indicates occupation listed in the heading was preferred over occupation listed
in stub of table.

1 is merely to add the number of preferences and consider this a score for
each occupation. Thus, in the consistent pattern, occupation 1 has a
score of 4, occupation 2 has a score of 3, and so on. The average score of a
number of such rankings would then constitute a scale value for that
occupation. This is crude and possibly somewhat misleading, since it assumes an equal interval between an item chosen twice and one chosen
three times. If the consistency of votes is high, however, this need not
be a serious problem.

A more complex and precise scale value can be secured from a paired-
comparison matrix by a method described by Guilford.[1] Should the student find this technique suitable to a research problem and also require
the highest accuracy, he would do well to consult this reference.

How well the continuum is defined by the scale may be seen from the
consistency of response. The problems of reliability and validity are the
same as those which attach to rating scales which use judges. One difficulty is the involved calculations required for the refined scale values
when the number of judges and choices is large.

2. The method of equal-appearing intervals

This is often referred to as the Thurstone technique of attitude measurement, reflecting the fact that L. L. Thurstone developed this particular
adaptation of the psychophysical method. To explain briefly what is
meant by the term "equal-appearing" intervals it is necessary to take an
example from experimental psychology. If a large number of objects of
the same size and appearance but of differing weights are given to a series
of judges it is possible to arrange them in order, from lightest to heaviest.

[1] J. P. Guilford, *Psychometric Methods* (New York: McGraw-Hill, 1936), Chap. 7.

Moreover, if the number of these objects is large and the total range of weight small, there will be a very slight difference between any two which are next to each other on the weight scale. Thus, if this number is increased to the point where the difference between any two neighboring weights is "just discernible," the differences between any neighboring pair can be thought of as representing the same "distance" on the scale; in other words, as constituting a scale unit. It will be remembered, of course, that the analogy may not be complete, since in sensory experiments such as those measuring the perception of weight differences, the "just discernible differences" are definitely not equal as between the lower and upper ends of the scale. As the classical experiments by Fechner indicated, a much greater increment in our stimulus is required at the upper end of the scale before we perceive a difference. Whether any such relationship creates a problem (or is even relevant) for social research has not been determined.[2]

If such a technique could be applied successfully with primary sensory stimuli there is no reason why it should not be applied to other types of stimuli. The discerning student will see immediately that this transfer or extension of the technique into attitude measurement poses two problems. One is the familiar difficulty of defining the continuum. This has already been discussed sufficiently to require no further elaboration here. The other problem is that of finding the "just discernible" differences.

It will be recalled that in the case of weights a large number of stimuli are required to establish the scale units. The same, of course, is true in the case of the attitude continuum. Thurstone and Chave, for example, began with 130 statements about the church in the construction of one attitude scale. These statements were constructed with six major criteria in mind: [3]

"1. As far as possible, the opinions should reflect the present attitude of the subject rather than his attitudes in the past. By wording the opinions in the present tense one avoids the situation in which a subject might indorse two conflicting opinions, one referring to his past attitude and one to his present attitude. The scale-value of the subject should naturally describe his present attitude.

"2. It has been found that double-barreled statements tend to be ambiguous. The material should be edited so that each opinion expresses as far as possible only one thought or idea. The subject is confused in reading a double statement in which he might want to indorse one idea but not the other. Example: 'I believe in the ideals of the church but I am tired of denominationalism.' Perhaps this statement would serve better if it were divided into two opinions.

"3. One should avoid statements which are evidently applicable to a very restricted range of indorsers. Example: 'I go to church because I enjoy good music.

---

[2] For a simple discussion of this problem, see Edwin G. Boring, *A History of Experimental Psychology* (New York: Appleton-Century-Crofts, 1929), Chap. 13.

[3] L. L. Thurstone and E. J. Chave, *The Measurement of Attitude* (Chicago: University of Chicago Press, 1929), pp. 57–58.

I am in the choir and get musical training and chorus-singing.' The first sentence can be indorsed by a fairly wide group of indorsers, but the second statement can be indorsed only by those who happen to be members of a church choir. It is probably not worth while to include opinions which are so restricted by factual qualifications in an attitude scale. What we want to measure is attitude and in doing so we should avoid so marked an influence on the range of possible in- dorsers. The foregoing statement would probably be much improved for our purposes if only the first sentence were retained for scaling.

"4. Each opinion selected for the attitude scale should preferably be such that it is not possible for subjects from both ends of the scale to indorse it. Such opinions will be canceled by the objective criteria, but when this defect is con- spicuous the statement might as well be discarded at the start. On the other hand, there will probably always be a certain number of opinions in a list which have this defect and which are not recognized when read by the investigator. Later, when they are discarded by the objective criteria it is usually easy to see why it is that these statements are eliminated. In other words, it is easier to have the objective basis for discarding a statement and then to see why it should have been discarded by inspection than to spot these defective statements in the read- ing of the original whole list of statements.

"5. As far as possible the statements should be free from related and confusing concepts. In the present material we have a number of statements which mention 'true religion' and 'the religion of Jesus.' These statements are likely to be diffi- cult to interpret because, in addition to the assertions about the church, these statements involve also additional though related concepts which might as well be avoided wherever possible. Example: 'I think the church allows denomina- tional differences to appear larger than true religion.' A statement of this type can just as well be written directly with reference to the alleged over-emphasis of denominational differences by the churches without involving the uncertainties of interpretation of the phrase, 'true religion.'

"6. Other things being equal, slang may be avoided except where it serves the purpose of describing an attitude more briefly than it could otherwise be stated. For example, to say that most sermons are 'all bunk' may be justified if it should be considered a natural way of expressing an attitude which is to be represented on the scale."

When a number of statements as great as this have been carefully con- structed in accordance with the above criteria, however, the problem has only begun. The next step, if the actual method of just discernible dif- ferences were employed, would be to have judges compare every state- ment with every other statement to see which was the more or less favorable statement toward the church. This, of course, would actually be an application of the method of paired comparisons discussed above. As was noted there, such a series of judgments would require an impossible amount of labor from the judges. In this case, for example, with 130 items, each judge would be required to make 8,385 judgments. Additional labor would then fall to the student who would have to analyze this number of judgments from *each* of the judges.

The palpable impossibility of such a procedure led Thurstone to modify the technique of just discernible differences and thus to develop his technique of equal-appearing intervals. The basic reasoning is as follows. If an attitude continuum is thought of as ranging from the strongest possible appreciation of a value to the strongest possible depreciation of that value, then it can be also thought of as being theoretically divisible into any number of equal intervals. If, therefore, these equal-appearing intervals are given beforehand to judges, they can be asked to assign items (statements of attitudes) to the appropriate positions along that attitude continuum. Then it is possible to secure equal-appearing intervals on the attitude scale represented by those items assigned to them, since each item is placed in a group corresponding to its appropriate position equidistant from the group immediately below and above itself. Thus, in the case referred to above, Thurstone and Chave gave the following instructions to 300 subjects: [4]

"DIRECTIONS FOR SORTING SLIPS

"1. The 130 slips contain statements regarding the value of the church. These have been made by various persons, students, and others.

"2. As a first step in the making of a scale that may be used in a test of opinions relating to the church and religion we want a number of persons to sort these 130 slips into eleven piles.

"3. You are given eleven slips with letters on them, A, B, C, D, E, F, G, H, I, J, K. Please arrange these before you in regular order. On slip A put those statements which you believe express the highest *appreciation* of the value of the church. On slip F put those expressing a neutral position. On slip K put those slips which express the strongest *depreciation* of the church. On the rest of the slips arrange statements in accordance with the degree of appreciation or depreciation expressed in them.

"4. This means that when you are through sorting you will have eleven piles arranged in order of value-estimate from A, the highest, to K, the lowest.

"5. Do not try to get the same number in each pile. They are not evenly distributed.

"6. The numbers on the slips are code numbers and have nothing to do with the arrangement in piles.

"7. You will find it easier to sort them if you look over a number of the slips, chosen at random, before you begin to sort."

It can be seen from the above instructions that the technique of equal-appearing intervals now appears to be more of a rating scale than a ranking scale procedure. It is treated as a ranking scale here (1) because it is logically derived from paired comparisons and the method of just discernible differences, and (2) because the ends of the continuum are defined by the most extreme statement submitted to the judges. In a sense, then, each item is ranked in relation to every other item rather than in terms of a more abstract scale.

After the judges' ballots are in, the next step is to secure a scale value for each item. This is done by assigning it the median position given to it by the group of judges. Because of its further utility the graphic method of assigning scores is illustrated in Figures 1 and 2. Both of these curves are ogive or cumulative curves of proportions of the judges assigning the various values from one to eleven. Thus in Figure 1, which represents the statement, "I believe the church is absolutely needed to overcome the tendency to individualism and selfishness. It practices the golden rule fairly well," it can be seen that almost 100 per cent thought this statement fell in the first five, or "favorable to the church" side of the scale. The median can be graphically determined by finding the value on the abscissa corresponding to 0.50 on the ordinate. In this case that value is 1.8, which becomes the scale value of the item in question.

Figure 2 represents a somewhat different pattern for statement 9, showing that about 75 per cent of the judges felt it belonged on the unfavorable side of the scale in regard to the church. The item represented here reads, "I don't believe church-going will do anyone any harm." The scale value of this item can be seen to be 5.3, or just slightly above the noncommittal position.

So far so good. At this stage of scale construction there exists a series of items with their scale values which, if they were well chosen, will cover the full range of positions from one to eleven. It is now necessary to select from these the items which will constitute the final scale. This requires the application of two criteria. The selection should be made in such a way as to (1) include no ambiguous items, and (2) represent the full scale range.

The first process, therefore, should be the measurement of ambiguity for the items. Returning to Figure 1, one line can be seen on each side of the arrow. Just as the arrow represents the median position, or scale value of the item, these lines represent the quartile values. Thus, for the curve on the left of the figure it can be seen that $Q_1 = 1.3$ and $Q_2 = 2.6$. The distance between these, which Thurstone calls the Q value, is a measure of disagreement on the placement of the item. In this case the Q value $= 1.3$. The smaller is this value the more satisfactory is the item, since it is a measure of deviation; the greater the amount of deviation, the less secure we can be that the median itself is a useful figure.

Using the Q values as a measure of ambiguity, items are so selected as to secure the best possible representation of the full continuum by items possessing the lowest possible Q values. From 12 to 18 well-selected items will provide a usable scale.

The administration of such a scale is a simple matter. The items are presented in random order so that simple instructions will suffice. The

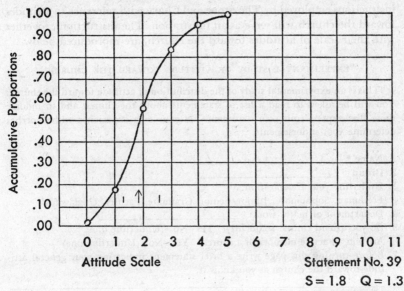

FIGURE 1. Judgments on the item: "I believe the church is absolutely needed to overcome the tendency to individualism and selfishness. It practices the golden rule fairly well."

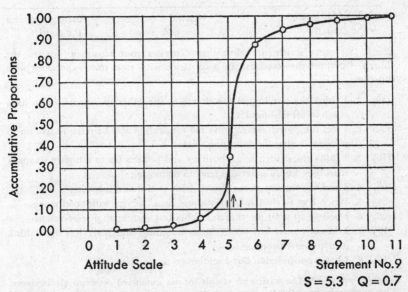

FIGURE 2. Judgments on the item: "I don't believe churchgoing will do anyone any harm."

instructions employed by Thurstone and Chave with reference to attitudes toward the church will serve as an illustration. The instructions, together with their scale of attitudes toward the church, are reproduced below.[5]

"EXPERIMENTAL STUDY OF ATTITUDE TOWARD THE CHURCH

"This is an experimental study of the distribution of attitude toward the church. You will be asked to read a list of statements about the church and to indorse those that express your own sentiment. Let your own experience with churches determine your indorsements.

1. Name * _____
2. Group _____
3. Underline your classification:
   Freshman, Sophomore, Junior, Senior, Graduate, Faculty, Unclassified.
4. Department of major work: _____
5. Do you attend church frequently? Yes No (Underline one)
6. Are you an active member of a church? Yes No (Underline one)
7. Before turning this page write a brief statement indicating your general attitude toward the church as you know it.

_____

_____

8. Write an X somewhere on the line below to indicate where you think you belong.

_____

Strongly favorable   Neutral   Strongly against
to the church   the church

Check (√) every statement below that expresses your sentiment toward the church. Interpret the statement in accordance with your own experience with churches.

(40) 1. I think the teaching of the church is altogether too superficial to have much social significance.

(50) 2. I feel the church services give me inspiration and help me to live up to my best during the following week.

(110) 3. I think the church keeps business and politics up to a higher standard than they would otherwise tend to maintain.

(103) 4. I find the services of the church both restful and inspiring.

(54) 5. When I go to church I enjoy a fine ritual service with good music.

(28) 6. I believe in what the church teaches but with mental reservations.

(77) 7. I do not receive any benefit from attending church services but I think it helps some people.

(13) 8. I believe in religion but I seldom go to church.

[5] Ibid., pp. 60–63. The statements of this list are numbered consecutively as shown. The number in parentheses before each statement refers to the original list of 130 statements.
* You need not sign your name, if you prefer to give your opinions anonymously.

(69) 9. I am careless about religion and church relationships but I would not like to see my attitude become general.

(96) 10. I regard the church as a static, crystallized institution and as such it is unwholesome and detrimental to society and the individual.

(93) 11. I believe church membership is almost essential to living life at its best.

(21) 12. I do not understand the dogmas or creeds of the church but I find that the church helps me to be more honest and creditable.

(7) 13. The paternal and benevolent attitude of the church is quite distasteful to me.

(19) 14. I feel that church attendance is a fair index of the nation's morality.

(34) 15. Sometimes I feel that the church and religion are necessary and sometimes I doubt it.

(114) 16. I believe the church is fundamentally sound but some of its adherents have given it a bad name.

(65) 17. I think the church is a parasite on society.

(64) 18. I feel the need for religion but do not find what I want in any one church.

(38) 19. I think too much money is being spent on the church for the benefit that is being derived.

(11) 20. I believe in the church and its teachings because I have been accustomed to them since I was a child.

(87) 21. I think the church is hundreds of years behind the times and cannot make a dent on modern life.

(89) 22. I believe the church has grown up with the primary purpose of perpetuating the spirit and teachings of Jesus and deserves loyal support.

(113) 23. I feel the church perpetuates the values which man puts highest in his philosophy of life.

(51) 24. I feel I can worship God better out of doors than in the church and I get more inspiration there.

(128) 25. My experience is that the church is hopelessly out of date.

(33) 26. I feel the church is petty, always quarreling over matters that have no interest or importance.

(95) 27. I do not believe in any brand of religion or in any particular church but I have never given the subject serious thought.

(125) 28. I respect any church-member's beliefs but I think it is all "bunk."

(74) 29. I enjoy my church because there is a spirit of friendliness there.

(41) 30. I think the country would be better off if the churches were closed and the ministers set to some useful work.

(101) 31. I believe the church is the greatest institution in America today.

(27) 32. I believe in sincerity and goodness without any church ceremonies.

(74) 33. I believe the church is the greatest influence for good government and right living.

(72) 34. I think the organized church is an enemy of science and truth.

(56) 35. I believe the church is losing ground as education advances.

(24) 36. The churches may be doing good and useful work but they do not interest me.

(119) 37. I think the church is a hindrance to religion for it still depends upon magic, superstition, and myth.

(107) 38. The church is needed to develop religion, which has always been concerned with man's deepest feelings and greatest values.

(36) 39. I believe the churches are too much divided by factions and denominations to be a strong force for righteousness.

(48) 40. The church represents shallowness, hypocrisy, and prejudice.

(127) 41. I think the church seeks to impose a lot of worn-out dogmas and medieval superstitions.

(14) 42. I think the church allows denominational differences to appear larger than true religion.

(90) 43. I like the ceremonies of my church but do not miss them much when I stay away.

(100) 44. I believe the church is a powerful agency for promoting both individual and social righteousness.

(73) 45. I like to go to church for I get something worth while to think about and it keeps my mind filled with right thoughts."

The method of scoring such a scale is equally simple. An individual's score is equal to the average of the scale values attached to the items he endorses. This average may be either the median or the mean, though the latter is more generally employed.

There is considerable evidence that so long as they are constructed with satisfactory care, scales with good reliability and validity can be constructed with this technique. The chief problem here is the accuracy exercised in selecting items and defining the continuum, and the number of items and judges originally employed. The larger is the number of these, the greater is the chance of developing a useful tool. This will also point out two problems associated with the technique. The first of these is the fact that the scale values depend upon judges. Thus, not only is an inadequate number of judges dangerous, but the use of careless, uninformed, or biased judges will endanger the utility of the scale. The second problem is the amount of labor involved in tabulating and analyzing a large number of responses from a large number of judges. Once this is done, however, the Thurstone technique provides an instrument whose simplicity in administering and scoring is admirable.

INTERNAL CONSISTENCY SCALES

1. *Thurstone scales*

Thurstone was, of course, not unaware of the difficulties which confronted his method and, in fact, made the point that the scale values were dependent on the number and character of the judges chosen. Consequently he suggested another line of procedure: [6]

"Ideally, the scale should perhaps be constructed by means of the voting only. It may be possible to formulate the problem so that the scale-values of the state-

[6] *Ibid.*, p. 56.

ments may be extracted from the records of actual voting. If that should be possible, then the present procedure of establishing the scale-values by sorting will be superseded."

Not only did Thurstone suggest the general proposition that ideally the scale should be constructed from the responses of those to whom it was administered, but he also devised a technique which was later improved and which became the method of internal consistency. This was called by Thurstone, "an objective criterion of irrelevance." [7] In the case of the Thurstone scales this consisted in relating all items on a scale with all other items, to determine the frequency with which each item was endorsed at the same time that every other item was also endorsed by the same person. Thus, if an item were relevant it would be endorsed together with other items only when they possessed nearly equivalent scale values. If it were irrelevant then it might be endorsed together with all other items in the scale in a random fashion. Such items were deleted from the scale on the grounds that they did not belong on the continuum defined by the other items, but rather reflected some other attitude.

These two contributions of Thurstone's, then, the criticism of the use of judges and the objective measure of irrelevance, set the stage for a simple, more precise mode of attitude scaling. Credit for working along these lines must be given to many, but perhaps the most thorough and complete presentations of the method of internal consistency were those of Murphy and Likert [8] and Rundquist and Sletto.[9]

Bearing in mind that the first fundamental difference between the techniques is that the subjects being studied replace the group of judges, it is obvious that in this method *all subjects* must be asked to respond to *all items*. Thus, in the Thurstone method the subjects are asked to endorse only those items with which they agree, while in this method a response representing disagreement must be added. Further, since it is not feasible to expect all subjects to be able to make a definite decision on all items, this implies adding a response to stand for the doubtful response. The minimum categories, then, for this procedure are "agree," "doubtful," and "disagree." In practice, however, it is found that the introduction of a *measure of intensity* is helpful and the conventional responses are "strongly agree," "agree," "uncertain," "disagree" and "strongly disagree." For example, an item from the Thurstone and Chave scale on attitudes toward the church, quoted earlier, is

"I believe the church is absolutely needed to overcome the tendency to individualism and selfishness. It practices the golden rule fairly well."

[7] *Ibid.*, pp. 45–56.

[8] Gardner Murphy and Rensis Likert, *Public Opinion and the Individual* (New York: Harper, 1938).

[9] Edward A. Rundquist and Raymond Sletto, *Personality in the Depression* (Minneapolis: University of Minnesota Press, 1936).

In a Thurstone scale this item would simply stand as above and the subject would check it only if he agreed with it. In the method of internal consistency, however, the subject would be asked to place a check mark opposite the response which most closely expressed his feeling toward such a statement, as in Table 2.

TABLE 2

	Strongly Agree (1)	Agree (2)	Uncertain (3)	Disagree (4)	Strongly Disagree (5)
The church is absolutely needed to overcome the tendency to individualism and selfishness.					

The student will see at once from this that each item has become a scale in itself and that the total scale is actually a battery of scales. Another conclusion may be drawn from this fact. If each item is a scale and a total score on several such items is taken as the attitude measurement, it is no longer necessary to begin with as large a number of items as is true in the Thurstone method. This, then, constitutes an advantage for the method of internal consistency.

A. ITEM SELECTION. This is the part of scale construction which gives its unique character to the method of internal consistency. Items from the preliminary form of the scale are selected on the basis of how they will relate to the score on the scale as a whole. At this point it might be well to set forth the preliminary steps leading up to this procedure.

Possible items should be selected from all available sources—newspapers, magazines, books, motion pictures, and the student's own knowledge of the problem. These should then be put in the form of items exactly as in the case of the Thurstone technique. This means, of course, that the criteria for item selection given above on pages 263–264 should be applied rigorously. Informal help from competent judges should always be sought at this point in the effort to secure good items. While the number of items required for this type of scale is small, perhaps as few as 15, it is necessary to begin with many more, usually at least 30.

Having reached this point, the student is ready to apply the criterion of internal consistency in the process of item selection. Since, however, this consists in correlating each item with the average score on all items it is necessary to digress at this point for the purpose of discussing scoring techniques, after which the process of item selection will be dealt with further.

B. SCORING THE SCALE. The simplest method of scoring a scale of this type is quite obvious. It is to assign arbitrarily the values 1 to 5 to the responses as the columns in Table 2 are numbered. In this case the value of 5 would indicate the strongest feeling against the church and the value of 1 the strongest feeling for the church. It must be noted here that if the item were stated so that agreement with it indicated opposition to the church, the value of 1 would be given to the most favorable response to the church, which in this case would be the "strongly disagree" response. Thus 1's will sometimes be assigned to "strongly agree" and sometimes to "strongly disagree," depending on the form of the statement. There is, of course, no difference whether the high score is given to the favorable or the unfavorable end of the continuum so long as its use is consistent with favorableness or unfavorableness toward the church. An objective check of correct assignment is available, as will be shown later.

While this yields a simple scoring technique, it makes at least two assumptions which remain to be demonstrated. These assumptions relate to the problems of (1) weighting items and (2) weighting each response within an item. Thus, in the simple method, an arbitrary weight of 1 is given to the most favorable position on all items regardless of how they are stated. The difficulties of this assumption can easily be illustrated. In an attitude scale on anti-Semitism there might appear such diverse items as, "The United States would be better off if all Jews were placed in concentration camps," and "I prefer not to have social contacts with Jews." Clearly the person who strongly agreed with the first statement must be considered as more anti-Semitic than the person who strongly agreed with the second but not the first. Should not these two responses be given different weights rather than arbitrarily classed as the same?

Before answering this question the other assumption should be examined. Thus not only does arbitrary weighting assume an equality between similar responses to all items but it also assumes that the distance between "strongly agree" and "agree" equals one unit and therefore is the same distance as that between "agree" and "uncertain," which is also one unit. Is it possible to assume that this is true without distorting the outcome?

There are two approaches to answering this question—the logical and the empirical. Taking up the empirical approach first, it can be seen that weighting both items and responses can be done by utilizing the standard deviation of the distributions on the items. Thus, it is likely that very few people would strongly agree with the placing of Jews in concentration camps, whereas a somewhat larger number might strongly agree with the milder statement. The consequence of this, of course, is that, expressed in standard deviations, the person who strongly agrees with the first statement will be *more of a deviant* from the average response than will be the person who strongly agrees with the second. Consequently he would secure a higher anti-Semitic score than the second.[10] The important ques-

10 For the student who wishes to study this sigma-scoring technique further, excellent discussions are available in Murphy and Likert, *op. cit.*, pp. 39–44, and in Rundquist and Sletto, *op. cit.*, Chap. 3. It might further be noted that the latter reference

tion to be answered is "Does this rather laborious method 'pay off' in the sense that it modifies the scores secured by the arbitrary method of any significant degree?" Using the converted sigma technique described in the preceding footnote, Murphy and Likert report a negative answer to this question. They report correlation coefficients between the arbitrary and converted sigma scores in nine instances ranging from .987 to .995.[11] Rundquist and Sletto report similar results, so that these cases give strong empirical support to the use of the simple methods.[12]

The fact that these empirical checks indicate the utility of the simple method of scoring leads back to the second approach to the relation of the two, that is, to the logical nature of the relation between the two scoring methods. It will be recalled that in a previous chapter the point was made that equality of units was not a necessary quality of a useful scale. So long as the scale orders people in a sensible way it is valuable. Thus, in the case of the two anti-Semites mentioned earlier, one would have a score composed of his agreement to two items whereas the other would have agreed to only one. Consequently the two would be properly ordered with a higher score for the subject who agreed with the stronger statement. The possibility of inconsistent responses, however, indicates the need for a scale containing *many* rather than *few* items and the additional need for having a *wide range of intensity* of statements, both favorable and unfavorable, in any attitude scale.

From the foregoing it can be seen that in the case of well-constructed scales the simpler scoring technique, though not as safe as the sigma-scoring method, will serve quite adequately to produce a useful instrument.

C. ITEM SELECTION (CONTINUED). Having made the point that the arbitrary method of weighting responses is an adequate scoring technique, it is now possible to return to the application of the criterion of internal consistency to item selection. When the scale has been administered to the first sample of subjects (at least 100; an even larger number is desirable) each item should be scored on the 1-to-5 scale. These scores should be totaled and divided by the number of items in the scale. The resulting average item score for each individual should be entered on the top of his sheet. This average item score can then be correlated with each of the

---

discusses two sigma-scoring methods. One of these uses sigma values computed directly from the distribution on each item and the other assumes a normal distribution and converts the percentage falling at each response position into a sigma value for a normal distribution. This is a highly technical point, however, and will not interest every student. Perhaps it is sufficient to say that Rundquist and Sletto report empirical findings showing correlation between the two methods of weighting on six scales ranging from .953 to .978 (p. 98). Obviously, in these cases at least, it would make no important difference which weighting technique were employed.

[11] Murphy and Likert, *op. cit.*, p. 44.

[12] Rundquist and Sletto, *op. cit.*, p. 98. Still further evidence of this nature is reported in Paul K. Hatt, *Social Attitudes and Anti-Semitism*, M.A. thesis, unpublished, University of Washington, 1940.

actual item scores. The simplest technique for this is the tetrachloric co-efficient of correlation from the computing diagrams, which may be found in standard statistics textbooks.

The items may then be ranged in order from high to low in accordance with the value of the coefficient of correlation. Those with low coefficients should be discarded and the selection made from the remainder.

Note, however, that the size of the measure of internal consistency alone is not the only criterion to be employed in selection, since this is ultimately only a measure of reliability. The final scale of 15 to 18 items should also (1) contain approximately as many favorable as unfavorable items, and (2) contain a wide range in each type of "weak" and "strong" statements.[13]

D. ITEM ANALYSIS—AN ALTERNATIVE TO THE METHOD OF INTERNAL CON-SISTENCY. Another method of selecting items which will yield an internally consistent scale is that of item analysis. The problem in both, of course, is to find items which will consistently separate those people who are "high" from those who are "low" on the attitude continuum. Item analysis merely uses a technique different from that of correlation. In this alternative method each item is subjected to a measurement of its ability to separate the "highs" from the "lows." This is called the *discriminative power of the item*.

In calculating the *DP* (discriminative power) the investigator sums the arbitrarily scored items for each person and places the sheets or scores in an array (from the lowest to the highest scores). He then selects out those who fall above Q_1 and those who fall below Q_3, *i.e.*, the ranges above the

TABLE 3 *

Group	Number	Item No. 22 Score					Weighted Total (Score × number checking that score)	Weighted Mean (Weighted total ÷ number cases)	DP (High Weighted Mean − Low Weighted Mean)
		1	2	3	4	5			
High	9	0	1	2	3	3	35	3.89	
									2.00
Low	9	1	8	0	0	0	17	1.89	

* Adapted from Murphy and Likert, *Public Opinion and the Individual* (New York: Harper, 1938), p. 289, Table 68.

upper quartile and below the lower quartile are compared. A computing sheet such as that in Table 3 is then constructed for each item.

[13] An additional note here should be made to the effect that positively worded items are more difficult to construct than negatively worded ones. To ensure a balance between the two in the final scale the student will do well to overweight the preliminary list of items with positively phrased items, which favor the value or group toward which an attitude is being measured.

The *DP*'s are then arrayed precisely as were the *r*'s (coefficients of correlation) in the use of the method of internal consistency and applied as one of the criteria of item selection. The example given in Table 3 shows an exceedingly high *DP* because in this case the upper and lower deciles (10 per cent of the cases) were used, rather than the upper and lower quartiles. It is safer to employ the quartiles, however, and as many items as possible should reach a *DP* of 1.00, and few, if any, should drop below 0.50.

E. FURTHER POINTS ON DISCRIMINATIVE POWER AND INTERNAL CONSISTENCY. The use of these techniques also yields an objective check on the correctness of the arbitrary scoring of the items. If the correlation between the score on any one item and the average item score has a negative sign it is clear that the item has had its values assigned wrongly and they should be reversed. The same is true, of course, if the *DP* bears a negative sign, for this would indicate that "lows" on the test as a whole were "highs" on this item, and also the converse of this.

A further point to be made here is that after item selection has been made, either the internal consistency or the *DP* should again be computed on the basis of the shortened scale. This will ensure the use of only consistent or discriminating items in the final scale.

F. RELIABILITY AND VALIDITY. Any of the tests of validity discussed in the previous chapter are applicable to these scales. Also, any of the measures of reliability may be employed. However this type of scale is particularly adapted to the split-half reliability test.[14]

2. *Other scale forms to which the criterion of internal consistency may be applied*

Some writers have objected to the use of the type of item scales described above. They have felt that either such statements are too obvious, thus leading to evasive answers, or that such statements have a "bad" effect simply by being read. The example given earlier of an item stating that Jews in the United States should be placed in concentration camps might be a case in point. Thus, some might feel that no one would ever agree with so extreme a statement even if he privately thought this a fine idea. Others might feel that the result of printing such a statement would be to increase anti-Semitism on the part of those who were exposed to it. There may be some validity in both of these objections, and at any rate they have resulted in attempts to develop more subtle stimuli as scale items in attitude scales dealing with socially explosive issues.

The following instances of such attempts, however, may utilize all the procedures of scale construction by internal consistency. It is the form alone of the stimulus which is altered.

[14] See Murphy and Likert, *op. cit.*, pp. 47–52, and Rundquist and Sletto, *op. cit.*, Chap. 5.

A. THE "CAFETERIA" QUESTION. This is so called because it offers a variety of answers to the subject. The usual reason for employing it is to avoid the narrowness of the "forced" responses demanded by the agree-disagree continuum. Some examples can be taken from a scale, devised by Murphy and Likert,[15] for attitudes toward Negroes.

"In a community in which the Negroes outnumber the whites, under what circumstances is the lynching of a Negro justifiable?

(a) Never.
(b) In very exceptional cases where a specially brutal crime against a white person calls for swift punishment.
(c) As punishment for any brutal crime against a white person.
(d) As punishment for any gross offense (felony or extreme insolence) committed against a white person.
(e) As punishment for any act of insolence against a white person.

"How far in our educational system (aside from trade education) should the most intelligent Negroes be allowed to go?

(a) Grade school.
(b) Junior high school.
(c) High school.
(d) College.
(e) Graduate and professional schools.

"In a community where the Negroes outnumber the whites, a Negro who is insolent to a white man should be:

(a) Excused or ignored.
(b) Reprimanded.
(c) Fined and jailed.
(d) Not only fined and jailed, but also given corporal punishment (whipping, etc.).
(e) Lynched."

It can easily be seen that the optional responses provided in these items range from a lesser to a greater antagonism toward the Negro. It is not always simple, however, to be certain that this is so. As a result the difficulty of securing a large enough number of such items to meet the demands of good scaling practice is very great. In general, it is better to employ the simpler approach and include each of the "cafeteria" answers in a separate direct statement. Thus, in the first example above, the item might be stated "It is never justifiable to lynch a Negro no matter what the conditions" and then ask for agreement or disagreement. However, for certain special purposes the "cafeteria" question may have to be used, usually in cases which do not demand the higher precision of carefully

[15] Murphy and Likert, *op. cit.*, pp. 17–18.

defined scales. When this is the case the greatest care must be taken to assure that the answers offered the subject actually do constitute a graded series of intensity along the selected attitude continuum, rather than merely being equal alternatives.

B. THE "STORY INTERVIEW." The reader will see that the "cafeteria" question, while still directive in that it provides the answers, attempts to be somewhat "freer" than the statement scales with their uniform agree-disagree responses. Another scaling method goes still further in the direction of projective techniques. In this case the items are stories, and as can be seen from the following quotation, no answer was provided the respondents. The interviewer, however, was provided a scale into which he fitted the reply given by the subject. The instructions below make clear the method by which the scale may be made self-administering: *

"Although the main body of our investigation took the form of verbal interviews with single persons, a method was worked out for use in groups. Following a modification of this, it will be possible for the reader to interview and score himself and his friends.

"The stories as given below correspond exactly to the interview. After reading each one, fix upon the answer closest to your own feelings in the matter, and make a note of the corresponding number. Follow the special instructions for the eight numbers.

"The interviewers in Akron were instructed not to give the scores 1 or 3 on any of the stories, unless a real qualification was expressed. Hence, do not score yourself 1 or 3 merely because you have trouble making the decision, or merely because you do not feel strongly about it, but rather if you have a real qualification which can be put in words.

"There may be a tendency on the part of certain readers to put themselves in the position of the group whose actions are being judged, and make their decisions accordingly. Of course in such cases the interview fails to achieve its purpose. Instead, the attempt must be made to judge each action in the light of what the reader feels to be right, and what wrong, from his own point of view, if he has any."

Some examples of the stories follow:

"Anthracite coal mining in Eastern Pennsylvania was a 'sick industry' even before the depression. In the 1930's still more mines shut down, the companies deciding to keep their coal in the ground until prices for it should go up. There was great unemployment and distress among the miners. In these years the unemployed miners began going into the idle mines and taking out the coal. They did this without the interference of the local police, so that no violence resulted. They have both burned the coal themselves, and sold it.

QUESTION:
What do you think of this sort of action on the part of the unemployed miners?

* Alfred W. Jones, *Life, Liberty, and Property* (New York: Lippincott, 1941), pp. 357–360.

ANSWERS:

0. I approve.
1. I think it may have been all right if they were really in distress, but I'm doubtful about it.
2. I can't decide.
3. I suppose it is wrong, but I must qualify my feeling. For example, I think it wrong for them to sell the coal, but not if they merely burn it to keep warm.
4. I disapprove, and cannot let my sympathies interfere."

"In early 1938 negotiations took place between the Utility Workers' Organizing Committee, and the Consumer's Power Co., of Michigan. The union wanted a renewal of its contract with the company which was about to expire, and a year's guarantee against wage cuts. The company refused this and negotiations broke down at the same time as the contract expired. A strike followed, in which the workers took possession of the company's power plants, in the Saginaw Valley area, and expelled the company's superintendents and foremen. During the several days that this stay-in strike lasted, the property of the company was not damaged in any way. Nor was it a sitdown strike, since the workers continued to operate the power plant, so that the interests of the consumers did not suffer. Although the company officials were strongly opposed to this strike action, they settled with the union after a time and it is safe to say that the union won better terms by this action than they would have won in any other way.

QUESTION:
What do you think of the action of the workers in this case?

ANSWERS:

0. I approve.
1. I approve, but with qualifications.
2. I cannot decide.
3. I disapprove in general, but I find points in favor of this action.
4. I disapprove."

"The B. F. Goodrich Company in early 1938 asked the workers in its plant in Akron, Ohio, to accept a wage cut and a longer working week. The company maintained that if the workers refused, some departments would have to be moved away from Akron, involving the removal of some four or five thousand jobs. They held that only in this way could they compete with the other rubber companies which already had a smaller proportion of their operation in Akron, where a strong union exists and maintains high wages. Assume that the Goodrich Company can stay in business and continue to pay the old wages. They will not make much money, if any, and they will not be able to pay much dividends, if any, but they will at least not be driven into bankruptcy. Assume also that if they move out of Akron they will be able to hire workers cheaper, make more money and pay more dividends, at least at first.

QUESTION:
The company has the next move. What would you think of its action if the company should move these jobs away from Akron?

ANSWERS:

0. I would disapprove.
1. I would disapprove, but with qualifications.
2. I cannot decide.
3. I would approve, but with qualifications.
4. I would approve."

The purpose of these stories is to explain the story stimulus very fully in order to avoid difficulties of decision which sometimes attach to single and simple statements. In the effort to avoid the effect of stereotypes, however, such a story method runs the risk of introducing additional stereotypes and also increases the possible ambiguity of the items. Furthermore, it shares with the "cafeteria" method the difficulty of securing enough items to apply rigidly the criterion of internal consistency. In general, unless special conditions demand it, this technique is not yet sufficiently developed to warrant wide application.

C. THE "OVERHEAR" TECHNIQUE.[16] This is another attempt to overcome the difficulties of the direct-statement approach to attitude measurement. It is not presented to the student as a perfected technique, for the results revealed difficulties not yet resolved. However, it possesses value as indicating still another method of presenting items in a semiprojective way.

"This experiment was designed to yield tentative information concerning the possibility of constructing an attitude scale composed entirely of items which are neither for nor against a given issue, but neutral in character; a scale which does not require one to express agreement or disagreement with items, but merely to judge how favorable or unfavorable they are toward the issue in question. Subjects were asked after reading each item to imagine they had just *overheard* someone make the statement and then to judge the attitude of the person making the statement. This method is a departure from usual attitude measurement procedures in which the items are definitely favorable or unfavorable and the individual is asked to agree or disagree. While this scale is not projective to the same degree as the projective techniques used in personality diagnosis, the basic mechanism relied upon is similar.

"Specifically, then, it hypothesizes that if a judgment of neutral statements relating to an issue or institution is forced, an individual with a favorable attitude toward the issue or institution will, in the absence of other standards of judgment, judge the item to be favorable; while one with an unfavorable attitude will judge it to be unfavorable.

"For the experiment it was decided to attempt the measurement of attitudes toward the Republican party among a group of college students during the period immediately prior to the 1948 presidential election. Fifty-two items about the Republican party were prepared. Insofar as possible, they were designed so that they were neither pro-Republican nor anti-Republican, but neutral in character. Examples of the kind of statements used are:

---

[16] Taken from an unpublished manuscript by Franklin P. Kilpatrick and Paul K. Hatt. The experiment was performed on 100 Princeton freshmen in 1948.

"1. 'Since the Republicans got control of Congress, its record has been extraordinary.'

"2. 'Dewey is a small man.'

"3. 'More people ought to study the Republican party platform.'

"4. 'If only the *little* people knew more about the Republican leadership.'

"5. 'Dewey has a lot of powerful men behind him.'

"At the end of the form were two questions, one asking which presidential candidate the person preferred, and the other how strongly he felt about the matter. These forms were then submitted to one hundred elementary sociology students. Instructions were to read each item, imagine that one had just overheard someone make the remark, and then judge how the person making the remark felt about the Republican party. Judgments were recorded on a six-point forcing (no neutral point) scale: SP (strongly pro-), P (pro-), MP (mildly pro-), MA (mildly anti-), A (anti-), SA (strongly anti-). One hundred correctly filled out forms were returned to the experimenters.

"The first step in the analysis was to establish the scale values of each of the items. Successive integers from one through six were assigned to the judgment series starting with SP and running through SA. Using this numerical scale, the median of the one hundred judgments of an item was found and designated as the *scale value* of the item. After scale values had been determined for all twenty-seven items, a scoring system based on deviations from scale values was devised. An individual's total score was thus the algebraic sum of his deviations from the scale values of all items. In order to avoid the complication of negative numbers, the value of ten was assigned to the midpoint of the judgment interval in which the scale value fell. Then the judgment positions on either side were assigned values in terms of their positive or negative deviations from the corrected scale value. Under this system an item having an original scale value of 4.4 would be assigned judgment position values as follows: 4.4 falls in the MA interval, so MA becomes 10.4; the series becomes SP = 13.4, P = 12.4, MP = 11.4, MA = 10.4, A = 9.4, and SA = 8.4. An individual's total score is the sum of the values of his judgment positions on all the items, and is a numerical representation of the overall extent and direction of his disagreements with medians of the judgments of the other judges. Perhaps the rationale of this scoring system should be repeated at this point. It is assumed that, in general, there is little objective basis for judging any item as either pro- or anti-Republican, and that what little objective information there is will be corrected for by finding the scale value. Assuming our theory to be correct, the direction and extent of departure of an individual's judgment from scale value should represent the attitude he is projecting, both in kind and in degree.

"After total scores on all the items for all individuals were obtained, an item analysis was performed. The twenty-seven papers with the highest scores were placed in one group and the twenty-seven with the lowest scores in another, and then each item tested (mean difference) for the degree to which it discriminated between these two groups."

While it was possible to secure a scale of about 15 items which showed satisfactory discriminative power, the relation of the score to the expressed preference for Dewey or Truman was not adequate to meet validity requirements.

This required further item analysis which showed that four items gave high discriminative values between Dewey and Truman supporters —but in the "wrong" direction. Nine items, on the other hand, showed excellent discriminative power between the two groups and in the "correct" direction. An examination of the four "failures" was revealing with regard to item constructions for a test of this type. All of them were rather personal remarks which could be thought of as "cracks." In these cases the projection of pro-Republicans tended to be defensive. An example of this type of item was the one given earlier, "Dewey is a small man." Items which dealt with broader issues, however, such as "More people ought to study the Republican party platform," were not only internally consistent but showed good validity value.

As has been stated, this technique is not well developed but offers possibilities for future development. The findings of this single experiment show its feasibility, though they warn against the inclusion of any-thing which could be considered a "smart crack." They further underline the need for the use of items which deal ambiguously with broad and general issues rather than specific ones.

D. THE INDIRECT PICTURE STIMULUS.[17] Still another application of the semiprojective technique is suggested by Seeman.[18] In his study Seeman was not concerned with the actual construction of a scale but rather with demonstrating a rationale which would allow for scale development. The question posed was, "Will the presence in the picture of a Negro in connection with the judgment of a moral issue produce a different response than if the picture involved a white person?" He answers this question affirmatively in an experiment performed on a sample of Ohio State University students.

The technique involves the same principle as the "story technique" described above, with the difference lying in the fact that the questions ask for an answer to the story but assume that the responses will relate not only to the story itself but also to the picture which illustrates the story. The stories which were used in this study were taken from the Cuber-Pell "Moral Evaluations Questionnaire." [19] The carefully selected

17 While the use of pictures and visual stimuli other than words has proceeded far in clinical psychology, their application in sociology is thus far limited. Considering this and the high level of training required for the use of these projective techniques, such tests as the Rorschach, TAT, and the Rosenzweig P-F tests are not considered to fall within the scope of this volume.

18 Melvin Seeman, "Moral Judgment: A Study in Racial Frames of Reference," American Sociological Review, Vol. XII, No. 4 (August, 1947), pp. 404–411.

19 J. F. Cuber and B. Pell, "A Method of Studying Moral Judgments Relating to the Family," American Journal of Sociology, Vol. XLVII, No. I (January, 1941), pp. 12–23.

pictures were divided into two groups, Negro and white, so that each respondent answered with reference to one race, either Negro or white. An example follows:

"DIRECTIONS:—In each of the following cases you will be given a set of facts about someone, either a real person known to the writer or a character of fiction. After you have read the 'case,' answer the question or questions relating to it. Do not go on to later cases until you have answered or decided to omit the current one.

"1. Glenna has been married almost a decade. There are two children. Her husband's work takes him away from home often during the evening. Glenna does not object to this but is annoyed by neighborhood gossip regarding a friend of hers and her husband's who often comes to spend the evening with her while her husband is away. This man has been a good friend of hers and of her husband. 'In fact,' she says, 'my husband often asks me why I don't invite Dale to come over oftener. Dale seems just like one of the family. He's alone much of the time himself and seems to appreciate coming over. He writes a great deal and likes to read to me what he has written—says I can give him a great deal of much-needed criticism, understanding, and encouragement to go on. That is about all we ever do.'

a) Is this wrong for Glenna?   Yes_____No_____Uncertain_____

b) Is this wrong for Dale?   Yes_____No_____Uncertain_____

Any remarks?"

The limitations of this method are great. First, it is difficult to use the pictorial method for any large number of groups or values toward which attitudes may be measured. Further, in common with the simple story technique the construction of enough items to provide a reliable and valid scale is a formidable task. Nevertheless, in certain types of situations an adaptation of this method may prove valuable to the researcher, and in any event it illustrates another of the attempts being made to improve on the direct-statement type of scale.

3. Internal consistency applied to other than attitude scales

While the preceding sections have dealt with the application of this technique to the measurement of attitudes, it should not be supposed that this is its only application. As a means of item selection or item weighting the criterion of internal consistency has been applied in numerous other areas.

A. PREDICTION STUDIES. The simplest form which these take is the selection of criterion groups and the determination of differences between them. These differences may then be combined into a scale to predict the behavior of other groups. For example, suppose it is desired to secure a scale which will predict the likelihood of children becoming delinquent.[20] The first step might be to select a group of children who actually were delinquent (this being carefully defined). This group should then be *carefully matched* on such characteristics as age, sex, socioeconomic status, neighborhood of residence, school experience, etc. The two groups should then be studied carefully. All the information which can be hypothesized as related to delinquency should be gathered. Each of these characteristics can then be separately tested as to whether or not it differentiates between the delinquents and the nondelinquents. Any of the tests of significance may be employed for this purpose.

When the items which do not differentiate the two criterion groups are dropped, the remainder, if they are sufficient and if they yield an accurate predictability, may be taken as constituting a prediction scale of juvenile delinquency.

This general method of prediction scaling has been applied to a wide variety of problems, including success on parole,[21] success on probation,[22] happiness in marriage,[23] and occupational adjustment.[24]

The actual techniques of prediction-scale construction raise the same problems as those of attitude scaling, but in addition pose other complex problems dealing with weighting of items. Since these are complex problems, the student who wishes to pursue this further is urged to consult the works cited above and also the Social Science Research Council monograph on the subject,[25] which contains excellent advanced bibliographies.

B. SCALING VALUES. The method of internal consistency is also applied to the scaling of a variety of social values. Thus Chapin has scaled the phenomena of urban social status and community participation;[26] Sewell,

[20] H. Ashley Weeks and Margaret G. Smith, "Juvenile Delinquency and Broken Homes in Spokane, Washington," *Social Forces*, Vol. 18 (1939), pp. 48–55.

[21] Elio David Monachesi, *Prediction Factors in Probation* (Hanover, N.H.: Sociological Press, 1932).

[22] George B. Vold, *Prediction Methods and Parole* (Hanover, N. H.: Sociological Press, 1931).

[23] Lewis W. Terman, *Psychological Factors in Marital Happiness* (New York: McGraw-Hill, 1938); E. W. Burgess and Leonard S. Cottrell, *Predicting Success or Failure in Marriage* (New York: Prentice-Hall, 1939).

[24] E. L. Thorndike *et al.*, *Prediction of Vocational Success* (New York: Commonwealth Fund, 1934).

[25] Paul Horst *et al.*, *The Prediction of Personal Adjustment* (New York: Social Science Research Council, 1944).

[26] F. Stuart Chapin, "A Quantitative Scale for Rating the Home and Social Environment of Middle Class Families in an Urban Environment: A First Approximation to the Measurement of Socio-economic Status," *Journal of Educational Psychology*, Vol. XIX (1928), pp. 99–111. See also F. Stuart Chapin, *Experimental Designs in Sociological Research* (New York: Harper, 1947), pp. 191–194; Louis Guttman, "A Revision of Chapin's Social Status Scale," *American Sociological Review*, Vol. VII (1942), pp. 362–369; and George A. Lundberg, "The Measurement of Socio-economic Status," *American Sociological Review*, Vol. V (1940), pp. 29–39.

rural social status; [27] Shea, the adequacy of home environment; [28] and the American Public Health Association, the quality of housing.[29] The American Public Health Association has also constructed an *Appraisal Form for Local Health Work,* which combines various categories of community health indexes into a scale.

It should be clear that the method of internal consistency is a very flexible and useful method of scale construction. Before the student applies it, however, it is suggested that he consult carefully the works referred to in this chapter as well as some other fuller explanation of the methods.[30]

SCALOGRAM ANALYSIS

One of the basic criticisms leveled at the method of internal consistency is that a scale constructed by this method contains not one but several dimensions. Thus, such a scale can give only a crude measure, for the definition of what it actually measures is always open to question.

To illustrate what is meant by the problem of unidimensionality versus multidimensionality, an example may be borrowed from the physical world. Suppose a series of volumes are to be ranked on a scale of cubic inch capacity. A series running from very small to very large can easily be arranged. However, the question still remains, "How much then is known about each of the items in the series?" Obviously, only its volume; the shape and the size of each component cannot even be guessed at. Thus the scale might include a small cone, a medium-sized sphere, and a large cube. Now, it may be sufficient to rank the items by volume if that is all that is desired. If, however, more knowledge is required, then volume is inadequate and the items must be scaled in other ways, none of which includes a combination of other dimensions. They could not be scaled by shape, since this is nonmetrical, but they could be scaled by height, breadth, or depth. These, then, are unidimensional scales. It must be pointed out again that volume may be satisfactory if that is all that is desired. The danger with social data is that other dimensions which

[27] William H. Sewell, *The Construction and Standardization of a Scale for the Measurement of the Socio-economic Status of Oklahoma Farm Families* (Stillwater, Oklahoma: Oklahoma Agricultural and Mechanical College. Agricultural Experiment Station. Technical Bulletin No. 9, 1940).

[28] Alice Leahy Shea, *The Measurement of Urban Home Environment* (Minneapolis: University of Minnesota Press, 1936).

[29] *An Appraisal Method for Measuring the Quality of Housing,* especially Vol. 1, "Nature and Uses of the Method."

[30] Particularly, Raymond Sletto, *Construction of Personality Scales by the Criterion of Internal Consistency,* Ph.D. thesis, University of Minnesota, 1936 (Minneapolis: Sociological Press, 1937). Quinn McNemar, "Opinion-Attitude Methodology," *Psychological Bulletin,* Vol. XLIII (1946), pp. 289–374. For critical views on this technique see Louis Guttman, in Paul Horst *et al., op. cit.,* Parts III and IV; and Louis Guttman, in Samuel A. Stouffer *et al., The American Soldier* (Princeton, N.J.: Princeton University Press, 1951), Vol. 4, "Measurement and Prediction," Chap. 6, esp. pp. 181–185.

are not wanted actually become involved and obscure a dimension which we wish to study.

The concern with the imprecision of multidimensional scales constructed by the earlier methods led to the search for a solution to the problem.[31] One such solution was factor analysis. This technique provides principal components for any set of intercorrelated data. Thus, if the items of a scale constructed by the method of internal consistency are subjected to factor analysis, the number of dimensions contained in the original list can be determined, as can the items making up each of the dimensions, or principal components. Since, however, as was stated earlier in this chapter, scaling is the process of ordering *qualitative* characteristics and since the coefficients of correlation underlying factor analysis apply to only *quantitative* variables, there was criticism of this mode of approach.[32] One alternative suggested was to abandon the factorial technique and in so doing to abandon the concept of a *latent-attitude continuum*, substituting the idea of a *scalable unidimensional universe* dealing only with the *manifest* function. However, the notion of a latent-attitude structure which under certain conditions can be derived from manifest data has been developed into a potentially important analytic tool by Lazarsfeld. The tool is used for dichotomous answers, but has close logical connections with a Thurstone scale and with Guttman's scalogram pattern.[33] The Guttman scalogram technique has developed from the idea, noted above, of a scalable unidimensional universe.[34]

The term "scalogram" derives from the response patterns which are yielded by this method when it applies to a set of data. Stouffer refers to Guttman's work with scale analysis as follows: [35] "He [Guttman] considered an area scalable if responses to a set of items in that area arranged themselves in certain specified ways. In particular it must be possible to order the items such that, ideally, *persons who answer a given question favorably all have higher ranks than persons who answer the same question unfavorably.* From a respondent's rank or scale score we know exactly which items he indorsed. Thus we can say that the response to any item provides a definition of the respondent's attitude." This quality of being able to reproduce the responses to *each* item, knowing only the *total* score, is called *reproducibility,* which is one of the tests

[31] It should be noted that multidimensionality is not necessarily a fault in an attitude scale. In the given example above it is clear that if the solids were to be scaled *as containers,* volume alone might be a sufficient (and perhaps the necessary) scale, even though the vessels have other dimensions. Thus in measuring social attitudes it may be sufficient or necessary to scale a composite attitude. For example, if one wishes to measure, let us say, anti-Semitism, an over-all measure may be required without reference to the subuniverses which make it up. Even so, however, there can be no doubt that the charting of its components would increase the precision of knowledge about the universe of anti-Semitism, and help provide a better over-all measure.

[32] See Stouffer *et al., op. cit.,* Chap. 1, esp. pp. 6–7.

[33] *Ibid.,* Vol. 4, Chaps. 10 and 11, by Paul F. Lazarsfeld.

[34] *Ibid.,* esp. Chaps. 2–11, by Louis Guttman and E. A. Suchman.

[35] *Ibid.,* Chap. 1, p. 5.

as to whether or not a set of items constitutes a scale in Guttman's sense. This statement provides a good statement of the general meaning of scalogram analysis, but an illustration is included here for additional clarification.[36] The example is also taken from *The American Soldier.*[37]

1. Are you over six feet tall?	____ Yes	____ No
2. Are you between 5 feet 6″ and 6 feet tall?	____ Yes	____ No
3. Are you between 5 feet and 5 feet 6″ tall?	____ Yes	____ No
4. Are you under 5 feet tall?	____ Yes	____ No

This illustration, by the nature of the questions, must, except for respondent error, provide a perfectly scalable universe. The pattern resulting in Table 4 is called a "scale pattern" because it shows obvious reproducibility.

TABLE 4

Scalogram of Height Responses

Rank Order of Respondents	Says "Yes" to Item				Says "No" to Item			
	1	2	3	4	1	2	3	4
1	X					X	X	X
2		X			X		X	X
3			X		X	X		X
4				X	X	X	X	

Four specific techniques for the establishment of a scale in this sense have been described.[38] All these give substantially the same results, since

[36] The statement in the quotation to the effect that "the response to *any* [italics added] item provides a *definition* of the respondent's attitude," seems a little ambiguous. It seems more accurate to the writers to say that the respondent's response to that item which is least frequently endorsed by the entire sample provides a definition. Clearly the "weakest" item, that is, one which is generally agreed to, cannot define the attitude of the respondent who endorses not only this but all other items in the scale.

[37] P. 11.

[38] The scalogram board technique in Samuel Stouffer *et al., Studies in Social Psychology in World War II,* Vol. 4, "Measurement and Prediction," Chap. 4; the least-squares method in Louis Guttman, "The Quantification of a Class of Attributes: A Theory and Method of Scale Construction" in Horst *et al., op. cit.,* pp. 319–348; the tabulation technique in Ward H. Goodenough, "A Technique for Scale Analysis," *Educational and Psychological Measurement,* Vol. IV, No. 3 (1944), pp. 179–190; and the so-called Cornell technique in Louis Guttman, "The Cornell Technique for Scale and Intensity Analysis," *Educational and Psychological Measurement,* Vol. VII, No. 2 (1947), pp. 247–280. See also Chaps. 1, 3, 4 and 7 in Stouffer *et al.,* "Measurement and Prediction," *Studies in Social Psychology in World War II;* Louis Guttman and Edward A. Suchman, "Intensity and Zero Point for Attitude Analysis," *American Sociological Review,* Vol. XII (1947), pp. 57–67; Allen L. Edwards, "On Guttman's Scale Analysis," *Educational and Psychological Measurement,* Vol. VIII (1948); Allen L. Edwards and Franklin P. Kilpatrick, "A Technique for the Construction of Attitude Scales," *Journal of Applied Psychology,* Vol. XXXII (1948), pp. 374–384; Leon Festinger, "The Treatment of Qualitative Data by Scale Analysis," *Psychological Bulletin,* Vol. XLIV (1947), pp. 149–161; and Louis A. Guttman, "On Festinger's Evaluation of Scale Analysis," *Psychological Bulletin,* Vol. XLIV (1947), pp. 451–465.

they are all based on the same theory. Because of its relative simplicity and general utility, the Cornell technique has been selected for discussion here.

The example given by Guttman in discussing the Cornell technique is that of a series of seven questions concerning the book *A Nation of Nations*, by Louis Adamic, asked of the members of a Cornell University class who had used it as a textbook. These questions were:

1. *A Nation of Nations* does a good job of analyzing the ethnic groups in this country.

    _____ Strongly agree 4   _____ Agree 3   _____ Undecided 2

    _____ Disagree 1   _____ Strongly disagree 0

2. On the whole, *A Nation of Nations* is not as good as most college textbooks.

    _____ Strongly agree 0   _____ Agree 1   _____ Undecided 2

    _____ Disagree 3   _____ Strongly disagree 4

3. Adamic organizes and presents his material very well.

    _____ Strongly agree 4   _____ Agree 3   _____ Undecided 2

    _____ Disagree 1   _____ Strongly disagree 0

4. As a sociological treatise, Adamic's book does not rate very high.

    _____ Strongly agree 0   _____ Agree 1   _____ Undecided 2

    _____ Disagree 3   _____ Strongly disagree 4

5. Adamic does not discuss any one group in sufficient detail so that a student can obtain a real insight into problems of ethnic group relations in this country.

    _____ Strongly agree 0   _____ Agree 1   _____ Undecided 2

    _____ Disagree 3   _____ Strongly disagree 4

6. By providing a panorama of various groups, *A Nation of Nations* lets the student get a good perspective on ethnic group relations in this country.

    _____ Strongly agree 4   _____ Agree 3   _____ Undecided 2

    _____ Disagree 1   _____ Strongly disagree 0

7. *A Nation of Nations* is good enough to be kept as a textbook for this course.

    _____ Strongly agree 4   _____ Agree 3   _____ Undecided 2

    _____ Disagree 1   _____ Strongly disagree 0

There are 11 steps involved in applying the technique of scale analysis to the results shown in Table 5 on pages 290–291.[39]

[39] Taken from Louis H. Guttman, "The Cornell Technique for Scale and Intensity Analysis," *Educational and Psychological Measurement*, Vol. VII (1947), pp. 248–279.

1. The *preliminary weights* are arbitrarily, but not finally, assigned as 4, 3, 2, 1, 0, with 4 standing for the response most favorable to the book.

2. Each student is assigned a *total score* on the basis of the values in (1) above. Scores have a possible range for the seven questions of 0 to 28.

3. The next step is the *ordering of the respondents*. The questionnaires are placed in order from 28 to 4, that is, from lowest to highest, as in Table 5.

4. Each student has seven x's in his row, since he answered all seven questions, and the total frequency of responses is entered as in the bottom row of Table 5. The table, therefore, is a *complete* record of the responses to the questionnaire.[40]

5. Now we come to the test for *scalability*. If the universe is a scale and if the order in which we have placed the people is the scale rank order, then the pattern of X's in table 5 must be of a particularly simple kind. Let us consider the first question in the table. If response 4 is higher than response 3, and if 3 is higher than 2, and if 2 is higher than 1 (response 0 happens to have no frequency in this case), then the nine people in category 4 should be the top nine people. Actually, six of them are the top six and the other three scatter farther down the column. Similarly, the twenty-seven people in category 3 should be below the first nine people and should go down to the thirty-sixth person ($36 = 9 + 27$). Again, this is not perfectly true for our data. A similar examination for the other items shows that there is a substantial error of reproducibility in their present form. The approximate number of errors need not be counted at this stage, since it is evidently more than 15 percent of all the 350 responses ($350 = 7 \times 50$, the number of questions times the number of people) in table 5.

6. It has seldom been found that an item with four or five categories will be sufficiently reproducible if the categories are regarded as distinct. One reason for this is the verbal habits of people. Some people may say "Strongly Agree" where others may say "Agree," whereas they have essentially the same position on the basic continuum but differ on an extraneous factor of verbal habits. By *combining categories,* minor extraneous variables of this kind can be minimized. By examining the overlapping of the X's within the columns of each question, it can be determined how best to combine the categories so as to minimize the error of reproducibility for the combinations. In question 2, for example, categories 4 and 3 seem to intertwine, so they are combined. Similarly, in the same question, categories 1 and 0 seem to intertwine, so they are combined. In question 4, on the other hand, we combine categories 3, 2, and 1, leaving categories 4 and 0 separate. The way to combine categories is determined for each question separately. The combinations decided upon for this example on the basis of table 5 are given in table 6 on page 292.

If it is desired to keep many scale types, then as little combination as possible should be done. However, if not many scale types are desired, the categories may be combined as far as one wishes even though this may not raise reproducibility.

[40] Points 1, 2, 3, and 4 paraphrase the explanation given by Guttman (*ibid.*); points 5 through 11 are quoted directly, with italics added.

TABLE 5

A Nation of Nations

First Trial: Content

(Data for the Cornell Techniques of Scale and Intensity Analysis)

SCORE	1					2					3					4					5					6					7				
	4	3	2	1	0	4	3	2	1	0	4	3	2	1	0	4	3	2	1	0	4	3	2	1	0	4	3	2	1	0	4	3	2	1	0
28																																			
25																																			
25																																			
24																																			
23																																			
23																																			
22																																			
21																																			
21																																			
21																																			
21																																			
20																																			
20																																			
20																																			
19																																			
19																																			
18																																			
18																																			
18																																			

		Frequency
4	5 11	11 19
1	7 12	9 21
7	5 21	3 14
10	16 14	7 3
0	8 7	10 25
5	0 13	8 24
0	2 12	9 27

17 17 16 16 16 16 15 15 15 14 14 13 13 12 12 11 11 10 9 8 7 7 7 6 5 5 4

TABLE 6

Combinations of Categories

Question	Combination
1	(4) (3) (2,1,0)
2	(4,3) (2,1,0)
3	(4,3,2) (1,0)
4	(4) (3,2,1) (0)
5	(4,3,2) (1,0)
6	(4,3) (2,1,0)
7	(4) (3) (2,1,0)

There is no harm in combining categories that could otherwise remain distinct with respect to scale error; all that is lost by such a combination is one scale type. On the other hand, categories may *require* combination in order to reduce error; they should be combined in the manner indicated by table 6 and not arbitrarily.

7. A second trial rank order for the people cannot be established on the basis of the combined categories. This is done by *reassigning weights*. Since the first question now has three categories (that is, three combinations), these are assigned the weights 0, 1, and 2. Question 2 now has two categories. These could be assigned the weights 0 and 1. In the present example the weights 0 and 2 are used instead, since keeping the range of weights relatively constant from item to item often helps to establish a better ranking for the people when there is error of reproducibility present.[41]

8. Each person is now given a *new score* which represents his *second trial rank order*. This is done by re-scoring his questionnaire according to the new weights. This re-scoring is easily done from table 5. Using a strip of paper which is as wide as the table, the new weights for the old categories can be written directly on the edge of the strip. Placing the strip across the row for a person, the weights are added according to where the X's lie. For our example, the strip would have for its first five columns the weights 2, 1, 0, 0, 0, weight 2 being placed in the column which was the old category 4, the weight 1 in the column which was the old category 3, and the 0's being in the old columns 2, 1, and 0 which are now combined. For question 2, the strip would have for the five columns the weights 2, 2, 0, 0, 0. Similarly, the new weights for the other questions can be written down to be used over the old columns of table 5. The person who was formerly first on table 5, with a score of 28, now has a score of $2 + 2 + 2 + 2 + 2 + 2 + 2 = 14$. The second person in table 5 also gets a score of 14. The third person in table 5 now gets a score of $2 + 2 + 2 + 1 + 2 + 2 + 2 = 13$; and so on for each person.

9. The people are now shifted into the *rank order of their new scores*, and table 7 is prepared from the combined data just as table 5 was prepared from the original data. Question 1 now has three columns, question 2 has two columns, etc. The data of table 5 are modified to fit table 7 according to the combinations indicated in table 6. The columns of table 7 now refer to the combined categories, and the scores of table 7 are the second trial scores just obtained in the preceding step.

[41] In a perfect scale, *any* set of weights, provided they have the proper rank order for the categories, will yield a perfect rank ordering for the people.

TABLE 7

A Nation of Nations

Second Trial: Content

SCORE	1 (2)	1 (1)	1 (0)	2 (2)	2 (0)	3 (2)	3 (0)	4 (2)	4 (1)	4 (0)	5 (2)	5 (0)	6 (2)	6 (0)	7 (2)	7 (1)	7 (0)
14	x			x		x		x			x		x		x		
14	x			x		x		x			x		x		x		
13	x			x		x			x		x		x		x		
13	x			x		x			x		x		x		x		
13	x			x		x			x		x		x		x		
13	x			x		x			x		x		x		x		
12	x			x		x			x		x		x		x		
12	x			x		x			x		x		x			x	
11		x		x		x			x		x		x			x	
11		x		x		x			x		x		x			x	
11		x		x		x			x		x		x			x	
11			x	x		x			x		x		x		x		
11		x		x		x			x		x		x			x	
11		x		x		x			x		x		x			x	
11		x		x		x			x		x		x			x	
11		x		x		x			x		x		x			x	
11		x		x		x			x		x		x			x	
10		x		x		x			x			x	x		x		
10		x		x		x			x		x		x			x	
10		x		x		x			x		x		x		x		
9	x				x	x			x		x		x		x		
9		x		x		x			x		x		x			x	
9		x		x		x			x		x		x			x	
9		x		x		x			x			x	x			x	
9		x		x		x			x			x	x			x	
9		x			x	x			x			x	x			x	
8		x		x		x			x			x	x				x
7		x		x		x			x			x	x			x	
7		x			x	x			x			x	x			x	
7			x		x	x			x			x	x			x	
6			x	x			x		x			x		x		x	
6		x		x		x			x			x		x			x
6		x		x		x			x			x		x			x
6		x		x		x			x			x		x			x
6			x		x	x			x			x		x			x
5			x		x	x			x			x		x			x
4		x			x	x			x			x		x			x
4		x		x			x		x			x		x			x
4			x		x	x				x		x		x			x
3		x			x	x				x		x		x			x
3			x	x			x			x		x		x			x
3		x			x	x		x				x		x			x
2			x		x	x				x		x		x			x
2			x		x	x				x		x		x			x
2			x		x	x				x		x		x			x
2			x		x	x				x		x		x			x
1		x			x		x			x		x		x			x
1			x		x		x			x		x		x			x
1			x		x		x			x		x		x			x
0			x		x		x			x		x		x			x
Frequency	9	27	14	32	18	43	7	3	37	10	22	28	30	20	11	19	20

10. The error of reproducibility in table 7 seems much smaller than in table 5, and we shall now count up the actual errors. This is done by establishing *cutting points* in the rank order of the people which separate them according to the categories in which they would fall if the scale were perfect. For question 1, which has three categories, we need two cutting points. The first seems to fall

between the last person with score 12 and the first person with score 11. All people above this cutting point should be in category 2, and all people below should not be in category 2. Since there is one person in category 2 below this point, we have one error for category 2. A second cutting point is needed to separate category 1 from category 0; since these two categories overlap some-what, its exact location is not essential since moving it slightly up or down will not change the amount of error. It should be placed so as to minimize the error, but this may be done in several adjacent ways. One way is to place the cutting point between the second and third persons with score 4. Below this point we find three errors in category 1, and above this, we find five errors in category 0. The total number of errors in question 1 is $1 + 3 + 5 = 9$. Since there are 50 responses to question 1, this means 18 percent error. This error could be reduced, of course, by combining the last two columns and leaving question 1 as a dichotomy. Then there would be only the one error in the first column. Such a further dichotomization need not be done if there is relatively little error in the other questions so that the error over all questions is not much more than 10 per cent.

Question 2 has two categories in the second trial, and the cutting point which will minimize the error is between the last two scores 6, which makes two errors in the first column and four errors in the second column of question 2. Similarly, question 3 has a cutting point between the last score 2 and the first score 1, leaving three errors in its second column. Question 4 gets two cutting points, questions 5 and 6 one cutting point, and the whole of table 7 is 40, which is 11 percent of all the responses. We can, therefore, conclude in view of the fact that much of the error occurs in question 1 and could be eliminated by combining two categories in that question, that this area is scalable. From a person's rank order, we can reproduce his response to each question *in terms of combined categories* with 89 percent accuracy (or better, if we combine the last two columns of question 1).

11. The percent reproducibility alone is not sufficient to lead to the conclusion that the universe of content is scalable. The *frequency of responses to each separate item* must also be taken into account for a very simple reason. Reproducibility can be artificially high simply because one category in each item has a very high frequency. It can be proved that the reproducibility of an item can never be less than the largest frequency of its categories, regardless of whether the area is scalable or not. For example, question 3 in table 7 has quite an extreme kind of distribution. Forty-three students are in one category, and seven in the other. Under no circumstances, then, could there be more than seven errors made on this item, regardless of whether or not a scale pattern existed. Or again, question 4 in table 7 has thirty-seven cases in its modal category and thirteen cases in the other two categories. Under no circumstances, then, could item 4 have more than thirteen errors. Clearly, the more evenly the frequencies are distributed over the categories of a given item, the harder it is for reproducibility to be spuriously high. Questions 5 and 6 in table 7 each have high reproducibility, each having five errors; these are not artificially high because question 5 has only twenty-eight cases in its more frequent category and question 6 has thirty cases for its modal frequency. The maximum possible error for question 5 is twenty-two, and for question 6 it is twenty. The scale pattern represents quite a substantial reduction from this maximum error. An empirical

rule for judging the spuriousness of scale reproducibility has been adopted to be the following: no category should have more error in it than non-error. Thus, the category with weight 2 in question 1 (table 7) has eight non-errors and one error; category with weight 1 in this same question has twenty-four non-errors and three errors; category 0 has nine non-errors and five errors. Thus question 1 fits this rule. Question 3 comes perilously near to not fitting the rule. While the first column of question 3 (in table 7) has no error the second column has three errors compared to four non-errors. Similarly, the first column of question 4 has one error compared to two non-errors. It is because evenly distributed questions like 5 and 6 have little error and because the errors in the other questions, like those in 3 and 4, are not too widely displaced from where they ought to be, that we consider this area to be scalable.

In constructing a sample of items to be used in a test for scalability, at least some of the items should be constructed, if at all possible, to obtain a uniform distribution of frequencies. Such items afford a good test of scalability. However, items with non-uniform frequencies are also needed in order to get differentiated scale types, so both kinds of items must be used. The more categories that are retained in an item, the sharper is the test for scalability, because error —if it really should be there—has a better possibility to appear when there are more categories.

LATENT-STRUCTURE ANALYSIS

As noted above, this approach to scaling, like "scale analysis" constitutes a solution to the problem raised by the fact that a scale constructed by the criterion of internal consistency may contain more than one variable. In contrast to the Guttman technique it does not depart from factor analysis but rather develops a method for factoring qualitative data, and in addition is very useful in problems of scaling.

This is a most promising technique, but it is so new that few examples of its application have appeared. Another problem posed by latent-structure analysis, as in the case of factor analysis, is the fact that its computations are both arduous and complex. This, of course, is no reason for not employing the method where results seem to warrant it, but it cannot be presented in the limited space of this chapter. The interested student therefore is directed to Volume 4 of *Studies in Social Psychology in World War II*, Chapters 1, 10, and 11, for a presentation of the technique and its application.

SUGGESTED READINGS

McNemar, Quinn, "Opinion-Attitude Methodology," *Psychological Bulletin*, Vol. XLII (1946), pp. 289–374.

Sargent, Helen, "Projective Methods: Their Origins, Theory and Application in Personality Research," *Psychological Bulletin*, Vol. XLII (1945), pp. 257–282.

Stouffer, Samuel A., *et al.*, *Studies in Social Psychology in World War II*, Vol. 4, Chaps. 3–11.

Thurstone, L. L., and E. J. Chave, *The Measurement of Attitudes* (Chicago: University of Chicago Press, 1929), Chaps. 2, 3, and 4.

CHAPTER 18

Research in Population

The study of population growth is a subject of interest to others as well as to sociologists. The biological sciences in addition to economics and political science have provided many studies of population. There are actuaries and demographers who are population experts per se. As a result, at least in part, of the increasing recognition of the fact that births, marriages, migration, and deaths—all of which are major demographic factors—are greatly affected by sociocultural factors broader than the economic or political, demographic research is interesting an increasing number of sociologists. The methods of population research are very complex and few sociologists will become expert demographers; all sociologists, however, require at least a basic understanding of demographic techniques.

Since demography is essentially a study of additions to and subtractions from a population, the basic formula as Davis puts it is simple.[1] It follows that

$$P_2 = P_1 + (B - D) + (IM - OM),$$

where P_2 = a population at any given time, P_1 = that population at some previous time, B = the sum of births in that population, D = the sum of deaths in that population, IM = the sum of additions to the population through in-migration, and OM = the population's total loss through out-migration.

Ignoring for the time being the matter of migration, the remaining factors of fertility (births) and mortality (deaths) are the essential factors in demographic analysis. Since raw numbers are seldom adequate to answer the researcher's questions, these must usually be turned into rates in order to give some idea of the speed with which a population is increasing or decreasing and to make possible the comparison between two or more populations.

[1] The formula and a discussion of it can be found in Kingsley Davis, *Human Society* (New York: Macmillan, 1949), pp. 551–553.

SIMPLE RATES

Like other rates, a population rate is a frequency of the occurrence of an event per standard unit of a base population, within a given time. Birth and death rates are usually expressed as the frequency of these events per thousand of the base population, per year.

1. *Crude rates*

The most common measures of fertility and mortality are the crude birth and the crude death rates, respectively. These are defined as equal to

$$\frac{\text{Number of births (or deaths) per year} \times 1,000}{\text{Total population}}$$

It is this figure which is usually called "the" birth or death rate. In order to secure a measure of population increase or decrease (ignoring migration) it is only necessary to combine these rates. Thus the crude birth rate minus the crude death rate yields the *crude rate of natural increase*. If a population shows a crude birth rate of 23 per 1,000 and a crude death rate of 11 per 1,000 then it can be said that the rate of natural increase is 12 per 1,000.

2. *Specific rates*

While the above rates give some idea of the rapidity with which the population is adding to itself by births and losing by deaths, it does not tell us whether these are *really* high or low in the light of *potentials* for births and deaths. If such an estimate is desired the crude rates must be refined. This is done by adjusting for a more accurate base.

This is because the crude rate, computed on the basis of the total population, includes components which may be differently represented in two or more populations and also be correlated with fertility. The problem, therefore, is to hold constant the most important of these interfering factors so that the fertility measure may be "purer" and hence more accurate. Thus in computing refined birth rates it should be kept in mind that only women bear children. Therefore, men should be dropped from the denominator of the crude calculation. Furthermore, not all females can be expected to bear children, since some are too young and some too old for this. The conventional adjustment for this is to include the period between ages 15 and 44. The specific birth rate, then, is equal to [2]

$$\frac{\text{Number of children born per year} \times 1,000}{\text{Number of women ages 15 to 44 in the population}}$$

[2] Specific rates may, of course, be refined by any other factor of significance to a particular research, *e.g.*, race, nationality, marital status, or rural-urban residence.

Comparisons between two populations using this figure may yield very different results from those obtained by using the crude rates, if sex ratios and age composition of the two populations differ widely.

The same general principle, of course, also applies to the refining of mortality rates. In this case, however, age is the principal refinement, though sex is often included since the mortality rates of the sexes differ. Thus mortality between populations can best be compared, age group by age group, for the two sexes considered separately. There is no conventional procedure for the computation of a specific mortality rate as in the case of the specific birth rate. The problem of over-all comparison is usually solved by the use of a standardized rate, as explained below.

3. *Standardized rates*

A rate may be said to be standardized when it is related to some age, or age and sex, distribution which is accepted as a standard. That is, a number of factors are held constant, thus making it possible to compare other factors between groups, with the spurious factors eliminated. In many demographic analyses the population used is one representing the age distribution of England and Wales in 1911, so that we recalculate the age distribution of any group by reapportioning in such terms. This is a purely conventional "standard million," however, and the researcher may adopt any appropriate method of standardization. The procedure for comparing mortality in two counties within a state might involve the use of the state population as a standardization, or the comparison of two states might employ the population of the entire United States. Another common method is to use the life-table population [3] for this purpose as is illustrated in Table 1.

It can be seen in Table 1 that, whereas Mississippi appears to have an advantage over Texas when the crude mortality rate is employed, Texas has a slight advantage over Mississippi when the age-specific mortalities are considered. More than this, the calculation makes it clear that Mississippi does have an advantage at all the younger age groups, while Texas shows lower mortality rates at the older ages.

Such a procedure provides much more complete knowledge of mortality than the crude rate yields. For still greater accuracy it would be well to compute these separately for the sexes, especially if there is considerable disparity between the sex ratios of the two populations.

Clearly, if this procedure can be applied to mortality it can also be applied to fertility analysis. It is not necessary to do so, however, since births do not occur throughout the entire life history and the specific

---

[3] A life-table population is a hypothetical age distribution which will be discussed in detail later in the chapter.

TABLE 1

A Comparison of White Mortality, Texas and Mississippi, 1940, Using the 1939–1941 Life-Table Population* of the United States as a Standard

AGE INTERVALS	LIFE-TABLE POPULATION	AGE-SPECIFIC MORTALITY RATES		EXPECTED DEATHS	
		Miss.†	Texas	Miss.	Texas
Under 1	192,735	53.0	77.7	10,215	14,976
1–4	760,628	3.8	5.0	2,890	3,803
5–14	1,885,084	1.0	1.2	1,885	2,262
15–24	1,861,969	1.8	2.7	3,352	5,027
25–29	917,319	2.5	3.4	2,293	3,119
35–44	1,764,760	4.0	5.5	7,059	9,706
45–54	1,653,312	8.4	10.4	13,889	17,194
55–64	1,432,567	18.8	20.6	26,932	29,511
65–74	1,042,210	45.1	42.8	47,004	44,607
75–84	494,457	114.0	100.7	56,368	49,792
85 and over	99,075	354.7	230.3	35,142	22,817
Total	12,104,116	8.8	9.8	207,029	202,814

* Louis I. Dublin, Alfred J. Lotka, Mortimer Spiegelman, *Length of Life* (New York: Ronald, 1949), pp. 12–15.

† John C. Belcher and Morton B. King, Jr., *Mississippi's People* (University of Missis-sippi, Bureau of Public Administration, 1950), p. 28.

birth rates discussed above provide fairly accurate adjustments, as well as because more accurate fertility measures, to be discussed later, are avail-able.

POPULATION COMPOSITION

The importance of age and sex composition of a population in dis-torting mortality and fertility rates has already been touched upon. The systematic treatment of *composition,* however, is a sufficiently basic aspect of population research to require its consideration as a separate topic.

The population pyramid is a simple graphic method for portraying age, sex, or other population characteristics. As can be seen from Figure 1 below, it is essentially a pair of bar charts placed back to back with each half representing one of the sexes. The bars are arranged in order by age groups, and the length of the bar indicates the percentage of the total population constituted by that category.

There are two elaborations of the population pyramid which are commonly employed. One of these, shown in Figure 2, is to add another variable, in this case rural-urban residence. The bars can logically be split into as many categories as are desired, but the complexity involved in using more than two will usually defeat the purpose of the pyramid, which is to convey a meaning simply and graphically.

The other use of the pyramid which is fairly common is the comparison of two populations. This may be either the same population at different periods as shown in Figure 3, or two totally different populations.

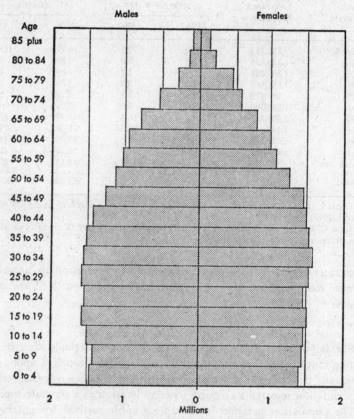

FIGURE 1. Typical population pyramid.

The population pyramid allows a quick view of the basic variables in population composition, age, and sex. If, for example, the pyramid shows a deep indentation at the lower ages, it is clear that at any given time in the future that same cohort will be unable to replace the cohort just older than itself. If there is a large bulge in the 0- to 5-year group (as has been the case in the postwar period) it can be seen that schools and other facilities will have to be expanded to take care of the added numbers. Further, the balance of the sexes at various age groups is made clear by the population pyramid.

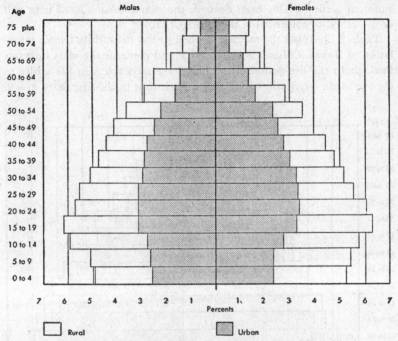

FIGURE 2. Population pyramid for rural and urban populations.

THE LIFE TABLE

The life table is a method of treating the age-specific mortality rates, *i.e., mortality rates for definite age categories,* of a population in such a way as to show what the mortality experience of a cohort would be throughout its collective lifetime (if age-specific mortalities remained unchanged). A *cohort* is simply a group of people, real or hypothetical, who enter life at the same time. In the case of the life table the cohort is hypothetical and the construction of the table merely consists in reducing that cohort by age-specific mortalities until the last surviving individual member disappears. The life table is essentially a straightforward process of cumulative subtraction. There are, however, some complicating factors. For this reason, and because the life table is of such central importance in demographic research, its construction will be analyzed in some detail.

The most accurate life-table construction requires the use of mortality rates for each age of life. Since, however, most information available to the student is given in 5-year intervals except for the first 5 years of life, and since methods of constructing these abridged life tables with sufficient accuracy have been devised, the example considered here will be a method of constructing the abridged table.[4]

Table 2 illustrates the method applied to the 1940 white female population of Texas. *Column 1* is headed *x* and contains the class intervals throughout the life period. The symbol *x* always refers in life tables to the age at the *beginning* of a class interval; thus in the first entry $x = 0$,

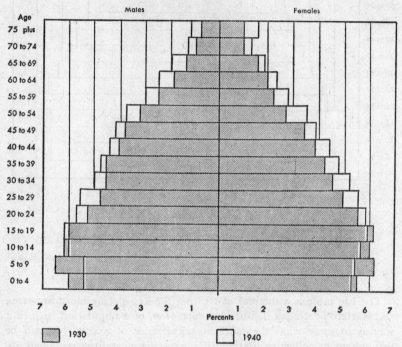

FIGURE 3. Comparison of age and sex structures of a population at different time periods.

in the second $x = 1$, etc. The first interval is 1 year, that is, 0 to 1 or from birth to age 1. The second is 4 years, from age 1 to age 5. The remainder should be 5-year intervals and must continue as long as is required by the life table; 100 years is usually sufficient. The student will encounter a difficulty here in that most population sources with which he will work do not give 5-year intervals after age 75.

[4] The values for the probability of dying are taken from the Reed-Merrell tables. The computation of L_x is taken from Louis I. Dublin, Alfred J. Lotka, and Mortimer Spiegelman, *Length of Life* (New York: Ronald, 1949) and from Margaret Jarman Hagood, *Statistics for Sociologists* (New York: Holt, 1941). See Lowell J. Reed and Margaret Merrell, "A Short Method for Constructing an Abridged Life Table," *American Journal of Hygiene*, Vol. 30 (September, 1939), pp. 33–62; Hagood, *op. cit.*, pp. 881–883.

TABLE 2

Construction of an Abridged Life Table for White Females, Texas, 1940

(1) x Age Interval	(2) n Size of Interval	(3) P Population	(4) D Number of Deaths in 1940	(5) $_nm_x$ Mortality Rate (4 ÷ 3)	(6) $_nq_x$ Probability of Dying (Reed-Merrell Tables)	(7) l_x Number Entering Each Interval	(8) $_nd_x$ Number Dying in Each Interval (7 × 6)	(9) $_nL_x$ Number of Years Lived in Each Interval (8 ÷ 5)	(10) T_x Number of Years Lived in Interval and all Succeeding Intervals	(11) $\overset{o}{e}_x$ Life Expectancy at Age x (10 ÷ 7)
0-1	1	47,291	3,187	.0674	.059923	100,000	5,992	95,662 *	6,431,240	64.31
1-4	4	194,634	964	.0050	.019217	94,008	1,807	371,209 †	6,335,578	67.39
5-9	5	246,291	261	.0011	.005486	92,201	506	460,185 ‡	5,964,369	64.69
10-14	5	261,588	251	.0010	.004989	91,695	457	457,000	5,504,184	60.03
15-19	5	267,816	540	.0020	.009954	91,238	908	454,000	5,047,184	55.32
20-24	5	240,589	616	.0026	.012920	90,330	1,167	448,846	4,593,184	50.85
25-29	5	235,799	643	.0027	.013414	89,163	1,196	442,963	4,144,338	46.48
30-34	5	213,718	672	.0031	.015389	87,967	1,354	436,774	3,701,375	42.08
35-39	5	189,797	721	.0038	.018833	86,613	1,631	429,211	3,264,601	37.69
40-44	5	159,209	742	.0047	.023245	84,982	1,975	420,213	2,835,390	33.36
45-49	5	139,379	834	.0060	.029590	83,007	2,456	409,333	2,415,177	29.10
50-54	5	115,208	984	.0085	.041676	80,551	3,357	394,941	2,005,844	24.90
55-59	5	92,084	1,176	.0128	.062147	77,194	4,797	374,766	1,610,903	20.87
60-64	5	73,720	1,352	.0183	.087742	72,397	6,352	347,104	1,236,137	17.07
65-69	5	58,069	1,783	.0307	.143105	66,045	9,451	307,850	889,033	13.46
70-74	5	34,535	1,880	.0544	.240395	56,594	13,605	250,092	581,183	10.27
75-79 §	5	19,348	1,716	.0887	.373242	42,989	16,045	180,891	331,091	7.70
80-84 §	5	11,243	1,686	.1500	.538143	26,944	14,500	96,667	150,200	5.57
85-89 §	5	4,880	1,021	.2092	.666978	12,444	8,300	39,679	53,533	4.30
90-94 §	5	1,432	398	.2779	.769321	4,144	3,188	11,472	13,854	3.34
95-99 §	5	260	95	.3654	.859214	956	821	2,247	2,382	2.49
100 and over §	00	30	30	1.0000	1.000000	135	135	135	135	....

* $_1L_0 = 0.276\,l_0 + 0.724\,l_1$ (see text).

† $_4d_1 = 0.034\,l_0 + 1.184\,l_1 + 2.782\,l_5$ (see text).

‡ $_5d_5 = -0.003\,l_0 + 2.242\,l_5 + 2.761\,l_{10}$.

§ These values are secured by distributing the number of those 75 years of age and older in the same proportions as they are found in the life table population for U.S. white females 1939–1941 (see text).

The solution of this problem is to find a life table of a population whose composition is similar and distribute the group 75 and over in the same proportion as they are found in that population. Deaths are usually given by 5-year age groups up to age 100, but where necessary they may also be proportioned as they occur in the table taken for a standard. This anticipates columns 3 and 4 somewhat, but the next two paragraphs explain their meaning in more detail.

There is no great error involved in this arbitrary procedure. In the first place, enumerations and deaths are themselves not accurate at these advanced ages; and second, the number of total life years which these ages contribute to the life table is minimal.

Column 2 is headed n and contains the *size, i.e.,* the number of years, for each class interval. This column is not always included in life tables, but in the present case it will aid in clarifying a later step.

Column 3 is headed P and contains the observed population within the specified age ranges. The population listed in the census as of unknown age is distributed as if it were of the same age as the known population.

Column 4 is headed D and contains the number of registered deaths in the population within each of the age classifications. Deaths for which age is not reported are distributed throughout the series as if the individuals had died at all ages in the same proportions as those whose age at death is known.[5]

Column 5 is headed $_nm_x$ and represents the mortality rate for each class interval beginning at age x and including n years. Thus, the mortality rate for the first interval is the rate of death for 1 year beginning at age 0. There are two differences between the entries in this column and mortality rates as they were described earlier in this chapter. First, these are for varying periods, 1 year in one case, 4 years in another, and 5 years in the remainder; and second, these rates are not multiplied by the constant one thousand. Their computation is simply the entry in column 4 divided by the corresponding entry in column 3.

Column 6 is headed $_nq_x$ and refers to the probability of dying in an interval of n years beginning at age x. This column is a modification of column 5 secured by reading the appropriate number from the Reed-Merrell tables. There are three such tables, the first of which is read by locating the value of the observed $_1m_0$ (mortality during 1 year beginning at age 0) in the left-hand column and reading the value in the second

---

[5] Greater accuracy in the life table can be secured if columns 3 and 4 can be computed for 3 successive years centering around the desired life-table years. In this case these years would be 1939, 1940, and 1941. The reason for this is that 3-year rates are more stable than single-year rates. Because data for the three periods will not usually be available to students, the 1-year rates are illustrated here. Further and more detailed discussion of various rate corrections can be found in Hagood, *op. cit.,* p. 874, pp. 820–823, pp. 835–836, and pp. 852–853.

column. This is the entry $_1q_0$, or the probability of dying in the first year of life. Similarly the second table provides $_4q_1$, while the third and all subsequent values are designated as $_5q_x$. The third column in these tables, headed Δ, is merely the difference between each value and the succeeding one, thus providing help in the interpolation of values.

The reason that $_nq_x$, the probability of dying, is not the same as $_nm_x$, the mortality rate, is as follows: The mortality rate has as a base an *observed population* within which *all* living persons of a particular age group are counted. The life-table population, however, it will be recalled, is a *cohort* analysis. Thus the deaths between, let us say, age 5 and age 9, will reduce the life-table base at each year. To apply the mortality rate to the entire number entering the age group, therefore, would understate the actual number of deaths in the cohort and thus reduce the probability of dying.[6] The Reed-Merrell tables provide the corrections of $_nm_x$ necessary for accurate $_nq_x$ values.

Column 7 is headed l_x and shows the number surviving to the beginning of each age interval. This column, as will be seen, is computed together with *column 8*, which is headed $_nd_x$ and which contains the number of individuals dying in each age interval.

It will be noted that the first entry in column 7 is 100,000. This is the hypothetical cohort which enters the life table. The corresponding entry in column 8 is the product of the entry in column 7 and the appropriate $_nq_x$ from column 6. The second entry in column 7, then, is the preceding entry minus the number of deaths. This number of survivors is again multiplied by its corresponding value from column 6 to compute the number dying in this interval. This process is then repeated throughout the life table until no survivors remain.

Column 9 is headed $_nL_x$ and contains a computation of the total number of years the cohort lives *in each age period*. With the exception of the first two intervals, this can be computed quite simply. It is assumed that the mortality rate in the life-table population is the same as that in the observed population. Now, since the number of life years lived in each age period can be thought of as constituting a population of that size (if this is not clear it should become clear later), then the age-specific death rate of the life-table population is equal to $_nd_x/_nL_x$. This means that if

$$_nm_x = {_nd_x}/{_nL_x},$$

then

$$_nL_x = {_nd_x}/{_nm_x},$$

so that the entries in column 9 are secured by dividing the values in column 5 into the corresponding values[7] in column 8.

---

[6] This is true for all ages except 0 to 1, where because of the skewed character of the age distribution of deaths, $_nm_x$ overstates $_nq_x$.

[7] Dublin, Lotka, and Spiegelman, *op. cit.*, pp. 312–313.

The first three intervals must be computed differently, however, because the deaths in these periods cannot be assumed to be distributed evenly throughout the age period. The formulas for these calculations are given in the footnote to Table 2 and are taken from Hagood.[8]

Column 10 is headed T_x and its entries show the number of life years lived by those attaining age x and in all subsequent years. These values are secured by cumulating the entries in column 9 beginning with the last one. The first entry, therefore, represents the total life years which will be experienced by the entire cohort.

Column 11 is headed $_eo_x$ and contains the number of years of life expectancy remaining to the average individual at any age x. This value is easily computed by dividing the value of T_x in column 10 by the number of individuals who enter age x in column 7, since these are the individuals who share the total expectancy value given in column 10.

The life table in general provides a conservative estimate of life expectancy, since underenumeration exaggerates mortality and since the assumption that mortality will remain constant is not warranted. Actually mortality in most age categories decreases during the lifetime of a cohort; at least this has been true for the past several generations.[9]

APPLICATIONS OF THE LIFE TABLE

1. *Gross and net reproductive rates*

The calculation of these rates provides measures of the *generational* rate of replacement, as distinct from the *annual* replacement rates discussed earlier. The *gross reproductive rate* provides an estimate of the number of female births which will be experienced by a full generation of females in a population, without any consideration of mortality, *i.e.*, a reproductive potential if all effects of mortality are removed. The first three columns of Table 3 provide the necessary information for its calculation.

Column 1 is simply a figure taken from a census enumeration; in this case, it is the same number used for the computation of the life table on page 303.

Column 2 is the number of female births occurring in each age interval of the mothers. As in the case of mortality rates in the life table, a 3-year average rate will provide more stability than a 1-year rate and where possible should be used.

Column 3 is a female fertility rate computed by dividing the column 1 entries into the corresponding column 2 entries, times 1,000.

[8] Hagood, *op. cit.*, p. 877.

[9] For an illustration of this see Dublin, Lotka, and Spiegelman, *op. cit.*, pp. 174–182, esp. p. 177.

TABLE 3

White Gross and Net Reproductive Rates, Texas, 1940

Age of Mothers	(1) Number of Women in Observed Population	(2) Number of Female Births in 1940	(3) Annual Female Births per Thousand Mothers	(4) Pivotal Age	(5) Proportion of Daughters Surviving to Pivotal Age *	(6) Surviving Daughters (5 × 3) †
10–14	261,588	56	.214	12.5	.914665	.196
15–19	267,816	8,048	30.050	17.5	.907840	27.280
20–24	240,589	17,349	72.111	22.5	.897465	64.717
25–29	235,799	14,203	60.234	27.5	.885650	53.346
30–34	213,718	8,646	40.455	32.5	.872900	35.313
35–39	189,797	4,454	23.467	37.5	.857975	20.134
40–44	159,209	1,218	7.650	42.5	.839945	6.426
45–49	139,379	104	.746	47.5	.817790	.610
50–54	115,208	3	.026	52.5	.788725	.021
Total			234.953			208.043

* Values secured by linear interpolation from the life table.
† Assuming no change in fertility and mortality.

Gross reproductive rate = (5 × 234.953)/1,000 = 1.174765
Net reproductive rate　 = (5 × 208.043)/1,000 = 1.040215

The sum of column 3 values, when multiplied by 5 (since each of its entries stands for a 5-year period), will yield the number of female births per 1,000 mothers which will be experienced by this particular generation. Dividing this value by 1,000, then, gives a value of female births per mother. This is the form the gross reproduction rate usually takes.

It is clear, from looking at the life table, that the gross reproductive rate overstates the actual population growth, since some of the cohort will die and mortality is ignored in this computation. The *net reproductive rate* is a modification of the gross rate allowing for the effect of mortality on the cohort. Hence *column 4* in Table 3 shows the central, or pivotal, age of each interval. *Column 5* represents the fraction of the daughters who will survive to the pivotal age of the mothers. This figure is a linear interpolation from the life table. Since the cohort will be exposed to the birth rate in column 3 for each of these years, a multiplication of the entries in column 3 by those in column 5 will yield, in *column 6*, the expected frequency of surviving female births for each age group of mothers. Their sum is the total number of female births expected for a cohort of 100,000 women born *if mortality and fertility remain unchanged*. Like the gross reproductive rate, the net reproductive rate is usually expressed *per woman*, which in this case requires the division of the sum of column 6 by 1,000, since the original cohort, the survivors of which are represented in column 5, were originally that number, and its multiplication by 5, the number of years in each interval.

Two weaknesses of the net reproductive rate are (1) that it assumes constancy of mortality and fertility rates over a generation, an assumption seldom warranted, and (2) that it provides only a generational replacement measure. Without knowledge of the *length* of generation, therefore, it is not possible to know actually how fast a population is growing or shrinking. This problem is taken care of by a still more refined rate which will be referred to later as the "true" or "intrinsic" rate of natural increase.[10]

2. *Stable and stationary population*

A. THE STABLE POPULATION. It can be shown that if age-specific fertility and mortality rates remain constant within a population, then that population will *ultimately* assume a stable age distribution which will not alter.[11] Since the form of this stable age distribution can be computed, the rate of natural increase characteristic of this age composition and the constant fertility and mortality schedules can be calculated. Therefore, it seems proper to say that such a rate, which is an annual rather than a generational rate, represents the tendency which is *intrinsic* in any observed set of mortality and fertility schedules.[12] Even in this rate, however, it should be noted that the assumption of continuing mortality and fertility levels does not allow the use of the rate in *predicting* actual future population size, for these may change at any time and in most cases are constantly changing.

B. THE STATIONARY POPULATION. This is the concept of a population in which the birth and death rates are exactly equal so that the population is neither increasing nor decreasing. With a known age-specific mortality schedule, therefore, the life table provides a picture of the age distribution of such a population. This is so because in a stationary population just enough people must enter the population to balance the number of deaths. Thus, the entries in column $_nL_x$ of the life table can be thought of as a number of separate individuals alive at that age instead of life years lived by a cohort. The entire column $_nL_x$ is therefore proportional to the age distribution of the stationary population. One characteristic of the stationary population is that the reciprocal of $_e o_0$, or the life expec-

---

[10] Other factors which interfere with the accuracy of fertility measures are relative sterility, marital status, and previous parity, as pointed out by P. K. Whelpton, "Reproduction Rates Adjusted for Age, Parity, Fecundity and Marriage," *Journal of the American Statistical Association*, Vol. XLI (December, 1946), pp. 501–516.

[11] Dublin, Lotka, and Spiegelman, *op. cit.*, p. 237*ff.*

[12] There are alternative modes of calculating this rate. Should the student wish to examine them they can be found in Dublin, Lotka, and Spiegelman, *op. cit.*, pp. 239–243, and in D. V. Glass, *Population Policies and Movements* (New York: Oxford University Press, 1940), pp. 405*ff.*

tancy at birth, will yield both the crude birth and crude death rates for the stationary or life-table population.

Two applications of this way of looking at the life table, that is, seeing it as a stationary population, have already been made. The first was in the construction of the life table itself while computing the values of $_nL_x$. It will be recalled that this was computed as

$$_nL_x = {_nd_x}/{_nm_x}$$

This follows from the other formula,

$$_nm_x = {_nd_x}/{_nL_x},$$

which states that mortality in any age period is equal to deaths in that period divided by people living in that period. Thus, $_nL_x$ is used to represent the number of people of a given age, rather than life years lived.

The other application of the life-table population was in the computation of the net reproductive rate. In this case the entry in column 5 of Table 3 contained a figure based on the life-table values of $_nL_x$, which were multiplied by age-specific fertility rates. Thus, the entries in column 5 were in reality thought of as being that number of women in a given age group which was determined by the life-table population.

A third application of the life-table population is its use as a standard population for the standardizing of fertility and mortality rates. In the example of this given earlier it was suggested that in the comparison of two counties on either mortality or fertility the application of the rates to the age distribution of the state as a whole would facilitate the comparison of the two populations. The general rule here is that the population chosen as a standard should not be too dissimilar in age distribution from the populations being compared.

A somewhat more accurate standardization, therefore, could be secured by computing the life-table population for the two counties together, or for the state as a whole, and using the resulting $_nL_x$ column as a basis for standardizing the rates.[13]

3. Estimating net reproductive rates

It is possible to estimate net reproductive rates when age-specific fertility schedules are not available. The basis of this estimate is the *fertility ratio*, sometimes referred to as the "effective fertility" of a population. This index is computed as the ratio of children to the number of women of childbearing age in an observed population. The customary definition of these terms is children under 5 years of age as a proportion of women ages 15 to 44, although other definitions may be used if desired.

---

[13] If a standardized population for both sexes is required, two life tables are needed, since these are computed separately for the two sexes. The method for constructing such a joint standardized population can be found in Hagood, *op. cit.*, pp. 883–888.

It follows that if this ratio is larger than the equivalent ratio in the stationary population that the fertility of the observed population is above that required for mere replacement at the same mortality schedule. The ratio between these two gives a measure of replacement and constitutes a rough estimate of the net reproductive rate. This is called the *replacement index* and is computed by the formula

$$\text{Replacement index} = \frac{\text{observed fertility ratio}}{\text{life table fertility ratio}}$$

MIGRATION

The problem of securing an accurate measure of internal migration [14] is very complex and one which is not yet systematized in the way that the measures of fertility and mortality are. It will usually, therefore, tax the ingenuity of the researcher who undertakes its study. This is due to two major causes. One of these is the problem of defining migration. How far must one move to become a migrant? Is a move within a city a migration? Or if not, is a move within a county sufficient? Or should a minimum distance be established which must be traversed before a move becomes a migration? Such questions obviously cannot be answered in any final sense but the definition must rather be related to the problem the researcher seeks to solve.

1. *Direct methods*

Data which bear directly on internal migration are found in two forms in the United States census. One of these is the tabulation of state of residence by state of birth, which appears in every census from 1920. Carter Goodrich and his associates have made use of these figures by computing a "birth-residence index of population movement." [15] This index is secured by subtracting the number of persons born in a state, but living outside of it, from the number of persons living in a state but born outside of it. If the result is positive the state has gained through migration; if negative it has, of course, suffered a loss.

The limited use of this census tabulation can be seen at once. An individual who moved in infancy is classed as a migrant, whereas another who was born in one state but who spent his life in another state, only to return to his "home" state, is not a migrant. Second, since the data are not tabulated by age and length of residence, little light on the type and time of migration can be secured. Third, the data tell nothing about the intervening history of the migrants. Finally, the unit of state provides a wide

[14] Immigration and emigration are not treated here, as their significance is relatively slight for the current American scene and because the basic problems of their analysis are the same as for internal migration.

[15] Carter Goodrich *et al.*, *Migration and Economic Opportunity* (Philadelphia: University of Pennsylvania Press, 1936), pp. 676–687.

and varying definition of migration. To move 500 miles in Texas may not be migration, whereas it is certain to be so considered in most states.

Beginning with 1940 in the Sixteenth Census of the United States, an additional tabulation of place of residence 5 years earlier by present place of residence is available. The unit of residence here is the county or quasi county (a device to include large cities which are parts of other counties).[16] The difficulties in the use of this measure are essentially the same as those of state-to-state migration.

2. Indirect methods

The most accurate method of measuring population loss or gain between censuses is to combine census enumeration and vital-statistics data. Thus, if the population of a state is known in 1930 and 1940, the procedure involves taking the earlier figure as a base.[17] This base figure is then subtracted from by the number of deaths and added to by the number of births known to have occurred during the decade. The difference between this figure and the 1940 enumeration then represents the gain or loss through migration.[18]

A refinement of this method is the use of survival rates for each age group so that each group can be properly followed through its mortality experience in the decade. The survival rates are computed from life tables constructed for each of the years defining the decade. To these are added the appropriate births modified by their survival rates. The advantage of this procedure is that it not only provides the amount of migration (in or out) but also yields the age structure of the migrants.

It can easily be seen by the student from the foregoing that the study of migration poses complex and difficult problems. For the student who wishes to pursue the matter further, it is suggested that he consult the references in this section and also Dorothy Swayne Thomas, *Research Memorandum on Migration Differentials,* and Rupert B. Vance, *Research Memorandum on Population Redistribution in the United States* (New York: Social Science Research Council, 1938, Bulletins 43 and 42).

POPULATION PROJECTIONS

A population projection is the attempt to outline the size or composition of a population at some future data. These are based upon separate

---

[16] T. Lynn Smith criticizes the accuracy of these returns in his *Population Analysis* (New York: McGraw-Hill, 1948), Chap. 18, on the grounds that too few rural-to-urban migrants are reported to conform to otherwise known facts. While his criticism may be valid, it is not known to what extent *intracounty* migration which is not recorded may account for this difference.

[17] Because of mortality differences it is usually better to do this separately by sex and race.

[18] A more detailed account of this procedure can be found in Hagood, *op. cit.,* pp 807–809.

projections of the factors which determine population size. Thus fertility trends as reflecting trends in family size, age at marriage, age of mother at birth of children, and marriage rate must be combined with projections of mortality and migration trends.

If, however, it is desired to project the proportion of the population which will be 65 years of age and over in 1975, this is a simpler problem, since all such persons are already living and their mortality can be predicted quite accurately on the basis of the fact that mortality is changing relatively slowly among the upper age groups.

The more complex problem of predicting total size and/or composition of a population at a future date such that fertility is involved is too technical a matter to go into in this volume. The student, if he wishes, may find detailed discussion of the problem in Frank W. Notestein *et al., The Future Population of Europe and the Soviet Union* (Geneva: League of Nations, 1944) and in Warren S. Thompson and P. K. Whelpton, *Population Forecasts of the United States, 1940–1970*. It should be noted in this connection that population projections are frequently erroneous because of the great difficulty in projecting economic, social, and psychological factors which are reflected in changing marriage patterns and changing fertility behavior. On this point, recent discussions by Notestein and Dorn will be helpful.[19]

SUGGESTED READINGS

Hagood, Margaret Jarman, "Selected Techniques for Population Data," in *Statistics for Sociologists* (New York: Holt, 1941), Part V.

Jaffe, A. J., *Handbook of Statistical Methods for Demographers,* preliminary ed. (Washington, D.C.: Government Printing Office, 1951).

—— and C. D. Stewart, *Manpower Resources and Utilization: Principles of Working Force Analysis* (New York: Wiley, 1951).

Methods of Using Census Statistics, United Nations Population Studies No. 7, 1949.

Notestein, Frank W., *et al., The Future Population of Europe and the Soviet Union* (Geneva, League of Nations, 1944), Chap. 1.

Population Census Methods, United Nations Population Studies No. 4, 1949.

[19] Harold F. Dorn, "Pitfalls in Population Forecasts and Projections," and Frank W. Notestein, "The Population of the World in the Year 2000," both in the *Journal of the American Statistical Association,* Vol. XLV (1950), pp. 311–345.

CHAPTER 19

Some Problems in Qualitative and Case Analysis

A main thread of thought running through this volume is that sociology rests upon the same foundations as do all other sciences. Its assumptions regarding the empirical world are the same, and the precautions which the sociologist must observe in carrying out research must also be observed by scientists in other fields. We are, then, at the beginning of an era in which the conscious application of scientific methods to sociological problems should be marked by great advances.

This promise is also based upon a fundamental assumption of sociology, constantly borne out by daily observation, that there is an orderliness within social phenomena. Just as the psychiatrist finds a system or structure within the seemingly most incoherent expressions of a schizophrene, so can the sociologist find predictability and order within the most anomic or disorganized strata and social groups. The intimate spontaneity of friendship groups exhibits this orderliness no less than the impersonal memoranda within a bureaucracy. Indeed, if the behavior of other members of society were not predictable, it would not be possible to communicate, interact, or maintain any of the common enterprises in which we take part.

It follows, then, that modern research must reject as a false dichotomy the separation between "qualitative" and "quantitative" studies, or between the "statistical" and the "nonstatistical" approach. The application of mathematics to sociology does not ensure rigor of proof, any more than the use of "insight" guarantees the significance of the research.

The fundamental questions to ask about all research techniques are those dealing with the precision, reliability, and relevance of the data and their analysis: (1) how precise are the observations? (2) can other scientists repeat the observations? and (3) do the data actually satisfy the demands of the problem, that is, do they actually demonstrate the conclusion? If the observations are crude, casting them in a statistical form will not help the research. If other scientists cannot repeat them, mathematical manipulation is futile. If the data do not satisfy a rigorous logic of proof, the conclusion remains doubtful.

Furthermore, no matter how precise measurement may be, *that which* is measured remains a *quality*. Quantification simply achieves greater precision and reliability in *measuring the qualities which are considered important*—intensity of anti-Semitic attitudes, degree of social cohesion, conformity with moral rules, etc. The process of achieving precision leads to the clarification of ideas and helps to recast substantive knowledge, but in a fundamental sense the research may nevertheless be called qualitative.

Similarly, the most "qualitative" of social research attempts rough *measurement*. The historian speaks of "a growing antimonarchical feeling during the reign of Louis XVI." The anthropologist contrasts the intensity of emotion aroused by, say, the murder of a kinsman as against the murder of a tribal enemy. The economist may single out those who find the security of income far more important than the promise of great rewards when they are considering the choice of an occupation. The sociologist comments that the individual who is well integrated within a strongly cohesive group is better able to withstand emotional shocks than other individuals. In each of these statements, there are implied *measurements* of important qualities. We may or may not be satisfied with the *degree* of precision in these notions, but they are essentially attempts to measure the effect of different variables. It is equally clear that, when data *are sufficiently precise*, statistical techniques can simplify the task of understanding them. Such techniques are aids in research, just as good methods of recording data can be, and they should be used whenever the problem permits it.

Thus, the increasing use of statistics is not the distinguishing feature of modern social research. Rather, it is the increasing precision and reliability of research techniques, and higher standards of proof, which have made the use of statistics more fruitful. In turn, the increasing *fruitfulness* of statistical manipulation has stimulated further developments in both sampling and statistical theory; while the *needs* of modern statistics have stimulated still greater precision and reliability in the collection of data.

These developments have occurred on many fronts, such as the better identification of the important social variables, increased precision of the questions used in schedules, and a better grasp of interviewing techniques, among others.

However, most of this growth may be classified as techniques for stimulating responses, or obtaining observations, *which are easier to categorize*. More precise questions allow the answers to be analyzed more easily. The mastery of interviewing permits deeper probing in the search for more precise answers from respondents. What, then, of those sources of data which have *not* been structured previously by such techniques? Most of our daily observation and experience, the newspapers and magazines we read, the radio programs to which we listen, as well as historical records and the recorded protocols of psychiatric and other depth interviews, are all essentially "unstructured" but may be important sources of data for certain sociological problems. If such data are eliminated from consideration, the range of information available is narrowed and much of the richness of social experience may be lost. On the other hand, if they are utilized as they occur, little order appears in them, and few fellow scientists might agree to any one interpretation of them.

Techniques are therefore being developed which permit us to order and analyze such data. Since most of these procedures are really ways of *classifying data which were not originally created for research purposes,* the term *qualitative coding* is usually applied to them. When qualitative coding is applied to the content of various communication media such as magazines, newspapers, radio programs, or similar materials, it is called *content analysis.* Since the most effective application of the *case history* or *case study* to social research depends in large part upon qualitative coding, that special problem is included in the following discussion.

Succeeding sections will, then, deal with these subjects: (1) simple coding operations, (2) qualitative coding, (3) content analysis as one application of qualitative coding, and (4) the case study.

SIMPLE CODING OPERATIONS

The student may feel that there is little point to a discussion of coding operations, since they are usually bracketed with large-scale surveys. Although it is true that such surveys almost always code the materials gathered, the student may find it profitable to consider whether a small project might also benefit from coding the data. If the class attempts a joint project, or breaks into several project groups, coding may be the most effective means of handling the data. A brief explanation of this tool will allow the student to make a decision concerning the use of coding.

When to code. Coding is an operation by which data are organized into classes, and a number or symbol is given to each item, according to the class in which it falls. Thus, counting the symbols gives us the total number of items in any given class. The basic operation, of course, is that of *classification.* Assigning the number or symbol to a given datum then becomes a mechanical procedure. *How* to classify must, naturally, depend upon the questions which have been asked and the concepts which are used in the particular research. These problems are discussed in the earlier chapters of this volume, and examples are given in this chapter. Let us now ask the practical question, "When is it profitable to code?"

The answer depends mainly on three variables: (1) the number of *respondents* or *sources* of data in our study; (2) the number of *questions* asked; and (3) the number and complexity of *statistical operations* planned for the study. If the number of cases is large, any kind of tabulation becomes difficult unless the data are coded. The individual sheets for each case become separated after a few shufflings, or they become torn and worn.

Small errors in counting the answers require handling all the sheets once more. By the use of coding procedures, however, retabulations may be avoided or minimized. If the number of questions is large, the same set of considerations holds.

Most important, however, there is no easy way to carry out complex cross tabulations without some form of coding. Any statistical operation requires the manipulation of numbers, which in turn must represent the data from the schedule. It is possible either to make many piles of sheets for each comparison or analysis, or to give numbers to the answers and summarize these separately on other sheets or cards. In the latter case, the operations are much simpler. The more complex the operations planned, the more useful is some form of coding.

At what stage to code. Coding can be carried out at any phase in the study, from the interview itself to the period just prior to the tabulations. In the section on formulating the questionnaire, mention was made of *precoded questions.* These were questions which had already been field-tested for meaning and range of possible answers, and which were physically set up on the schedule so that checking the answer automatically coded the data. An example would be the following:

Are you a veteran of World War II? (Circle answer)　　$\dfrac{1}{\text{YES}}$　$\dfrac{2}{\text{NO}}$

Answers which are set up in this fashion can be tabulated very easily by hand, or they may be punched directly onto cards for machine tabulation. In this case the interviewer is actually *coding* as he goes along, although no separate operation is required.

Similarly, the interviewer may be asked to do the coding as soon as he hears the answer. This can be done in a fairly cautious fashion, as an almost automatic operation:

How did your husband feel about this? 1. Strongly approved; 2. Mildly approved; 3. Indifferent; 4. Mildly disapproved; 5. Strongly disapproved.　 2

When the respondent answers, the interviewer has only to mark the proper number in the coding margin.

Suppose, however, that the goal is to classify respondents in terms of *annual income,* while many of them are laborers who typically think of their earnings in terms of daily wages. It would be possible to ask them for their total annual earnings directly. This, however, might cause them to make important errors in arithmetic. Second, the interviewer might carry out the operation mentally, coding the total earnings in its proper class after calculating daily earnings times the total estimated number of days or weeks worked. Although this is a simple procedure, experience shows that even the best interviewers may make errors. Most important, however, there is no way of discovering the error, since the only figure recorded will be the code number. Consequently, a third procedure is indicated: (1) recording the daily wage; (2) recording the estimated number of days or weeks worked; and (3) carrying out the necessary calculations and coding in the office, from these original figures. Although errors can be made, at least they can be checked.

The decision as to the *time* of coding must, then, be a matter of choosing the phase at which the least number of errors, and the greatest amount of control, will be achieved.

Paper aids to coding. When only simple tabulations are required, there is little advantage to *transcribing* the coding. A heavy colored pencil can be used to mark the code symbols opposite the answers, and the answers can be hand tabulated. If the number of cases is small, some type of *summary sheet* may be used. This may be attached to each schedule, for later independent use, or it may be designed on a larger scale to take care of *all* the cases. If a *special* sheet is used for *each* schedule, it should be very heavy so as to withstand considerable handling, and designed for ease of tabulation. Such sheets have the advantage that several persons can work on this stage of the operation at one time.

The *larger summary sheets,* containing data from *all* the cases, are sometimes useful for quick overviews of the data, especially when the number of cases is small. The accompanying illustration shows a simple sheet of

Respondent	Age Group					Religion	Weekly Wage
	20 to 29	30 to 39	40 to 49	50 to 59	60 & over	1 2 3 4	1 2 3 4 5 6 7 8 9
1. Jones, Carpenter							
2. Smith, Plumber							
3. Roe, Plasterer							
etc.							

FIGURE 1. Example of a summary sheet for simplifying analysis of the study data.

this kind. The code symbols can be used instead of full headings, as a solution for the space problem. It is possible to design such sheets from accounting paper, affording an easy method for the cross tabulation of a small number of cases.

However, when the numbers of cases go much beyond 150, the student may find some form of *punch card* of advantage. Unless IBM machines are easily available, the use of Hollerith cards is not a good solution for students. A great amount of time may be wasted in obtaining access to the machines, or in planning carefully the exact operations to be carried out, so that adequate written instructions to the operators can be given. The net result may be a loss in efficiency.

On the other hand, even for student group projects there may be a net advantage in using the McBee Keysort punch card. For both this card and the Hollerith card, it is necessary to use *numbers,* for the coding techniques are the same. The McBee card is relatively inexpensive and is procurable in several styles, depending on the number of items being coded. It is basically a card with a row of holes punched around its edge. In most studies, a single card will carry the data for one respondent or group. However, more than one card may be used, if an identifying punch or written symbol is used for both cards to prevent any confusion.

Each hole around the edge of the card is numbered. The technique, then, is to *open up* the hole corresponding to the code number. Thus,

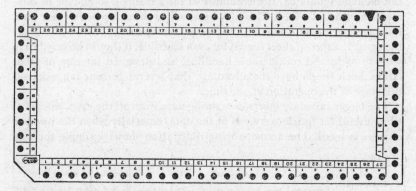

FIGURE 2. Sample of the McBee card, showing method of opening holes.

with a simple three-choice code, "Approve" (1), "Indifferent" (2), and "Disapprove" (3), and a response of "Approve," which is No. 1 in the code, the hole corresponding to No. 1, on the right-hand upper edge of the card, is opened as in the accompanying illustration. When this set of answers for all respondents has been thus coded and punched, it is possible to separate those in any desired category by inserting a needle through the holes. When the needle is lifted, all the cases corresponding to that punch will *drop out* (because that section of the card has been opened). The remaining cards, with intact holes, will remain on the needle. Having coded and punched *all* the answers in a similar fashion, it is possible to select all the males who are over twenty years of age, and who are married, by three insertions of the sorting needle. Since this method is used only on *small* samples, the actual counting is a minor task. What is important is that all the data have been classified and recorded permanently on the cards, for any kinds of complex operations which may later be decided upon.

Since the number of questions may rapidly exhaust the number of holes, it is possible to use *combinations* of the numbers in the two rows. This requires *double* punching and thus a double insertion, but more data can be placed on the single card. Thus, for the first section in the upper right-hand corner, we could obtain eight classes, as shown in the table. Further

Coded as Hole Number

Top Edge of Card

Income Level			
$ 10.00 to	$ 24.99	(punch)	1
25.00 to	39.99		2
40.00 to	54.99	(2 plus 1)	3
55.00 to	69.99		4
70.00 to	84.99	(4 plus 1)	5
85.00 to	99.99	(4 plus 2)	6
100.00 to	114.99		7
115.00 to	129.99	(7 plus 1)	8

instructions may be obtained from the McBee Company for still other operations made possible by the Keysort system.[1]

For large surveys, however, the need for greater ease and speed of sorting and tabulation requires the use of IBM and similar equipment. First

FIGURE 3. Sample of a punched Hollerith card used in IBM counting, sorting, and tabulating machinery.

developed for the needs of the United States census, such mechanical aids have come to be applied to many complex statistical problems in both business and research. The punch card used, which is called a Hollerith card, is reproduced here. Each one of its 80 columns contains 10 numerical choices, so that for any given item (such as "wages") it is possible to have 10 coding classes. There are two additional punches, called "fields," which can be used for further classes. However, these "fields" are more often used to direct the various machines to carry out statistical operations. That is, fairly complex statistical manipulations can be wired into the

[1] McBee Keysort Company, Detroit, Mich.

machine by changing the circuits on a removable wiring board. The "field punches," then, control some of these operations.

The advantages of such an aid are obvious: greater amount of information on each card, greater ease and speed in carrying out simple sorting and tabulation, and the possibility of performing complex statistical computations within the machines themselves. However, for most student projects and for most projects with low funds and small numbers of cases, these advantages do not outweigh the low cost and ease of independent operations represented by the Keysort system.

Checking the coding operations. Even when the student himself is carrying out the coding of his schedules, careful instructions should be written and should be followed without deviation. Further, such directions should be tested by having fellow students code a sample of the schedules according to the instructions. If the coding carried out by others deviates from his own, the instructions may be ambiguous, or they may fail to take into account some of the problems presented by the data. This precaution may uncover some difficulties in *classification* which the researcher has not clarified adequately.

Since it is possible to make errors no matter how simple the problems of classifying and coding, a definite sampling of the coding should be made, and every nth schedule should be recorded to see whether there are many errors. This is called "spot checking," and it is a further precaution against errors in the mechanics of coding.

QUALITATIVE CODING

One of the more important forward steps in recent social research is the investigation of qualitative coding as an *explicit* problem. The term "qualitative coding" is given to all the techniques for classifying reliably those social data on which very little order has been previously imposed by the researcher. Such a definition highlights the fact that coding is basically a matter of *classifying*. When the data have already been classified with respect to our theoretical needs, as was assumed in the previous section, our problems are mainly mechanical. However, when the data have not been structured in neat categories by carefully designed questions, the problems are more complex.

As has been noted several times, not only all social research but also all social interaction requires this kind of classification. We are constantly ordering the manifold social experiences in which we participate. When we investigate a past historical epoch, we must begin to organize data which were not recorded for our purposes. If we attempt to study the social patterns of a small community, or of a work unit, or of a primitive society, we must learn how to classify the relevant data.

Similarly, when schedules are tested, intensive interviews which are essentially unstructured are often used, and these answers are classified before a more structured set of questions is formulated. By this kind of approach, it becomes possible to use important sources of data beyond those already patterned by narrow sets of questions. Historical records, case records of various clinics or agencies, diaries and letters, propaganda and advertising, or nondirective interviews may thus become grist for the researcher's mill.

Most research based on such records has, however, been open to the criticism that the reader did not "see" the order created by the researcher. The conclusions were based on perhaps adequate data, but the reader did not agree that the data had been interpreted correctly. Yet each researcher must eventually meet the criticisms of his peers, and unless he sets forth a set of instructions for classifying the same data, no one is bound to accept the results. "Intuition" is useful in the search for creative ideas, but the *demonstration* of their truth cannot be founded upon any expectation that the intuition of others will come to the same conclusions. It is therefore necessary to develop an *explicit* set of instructions for handling data, thus forging a link between apparently unordered observations and adequately demonstrated generalizations.

Research experience in this area has not, however, been adequately organized and published as yet. It will therefore be useful to outline here some of the main steps which are ordinarily followed in qualitative coding, along with some of the problems which may arise.

1. CLARIFY WHAT IT IS THAT IS DESIRED FROM THE MATERIALS. Let us suppose that pilot interviews concerning residential mobility have used the question, "Would you mind telling me, in detail, just how you came to decide on moving from your last address?" If the interviews were careful, there should be several remarks from each respondent. Presumably, these answers represent many different *types* of decisions, or housing situations, or families, or even modes of participation in the community. That is, since the question is only partly structured, the answers may be ordered in many ways. How should they be classified?

The answer must be found in the purposes of the question. If the question was considered ambiguous by the respondents, the answers may be studied only to see whether it was understood accurately. However, if the question has been developed beyond this stage, from among the many ways of classifying the answers, the one which best suits the aims of the total research is chosen. If we are mainly interested in *who* makes such decisions, we will note which persons are mentioned. We may instead seek cues to the *process* of reaching the decision and look for statements about its phases. If we are seeking *motives*, comments which attempt to justify the move will be sought. If we are seeking *predispositions*, we will attempt to classify the answers according to the descriptions of the previous housing accommodations, or according to the housing values expressed.

2. STUDY THE COMPLETED SCHEDULES CAREFULLY. This is an obvious second step. It is sometimes a disillusioning process, since the answers may seem less rewarding on the schedules than they seemed while the interview was under way. However, it is these records on which the demonstration of the facts must be based. If there was more in the interview situation than appears on the schedule, it is wise to attempt to develop better ways of recording such data before proceeding with the research.

3. WORK OUT THE CLASSES AND THE INDICATORS OF THE CLASSES. After closely studying the data, it is likely that a rough idea of the classes will be developed. In some cases, of course, these classes have been in mind from the beginning. In others, the possible groupings will only gradually take shape.

However, it is at this point that a first approximation of the *indicators* to be used in coding should be made. Since the respondent has chosen his own words, they will not fall into neatly prearranged classes. Slang words may appear. Both simple and complex rationalizations may be recorded. It is necessary to work out both the *classes* and the cues, comments, or phrases which are accepted as *equivalent* indicators for those classes. For example, housing respondents may be grouped into (1) those who are anxious to move; (2) those who are looking for a definite type of housing; and (3) those who are confronted by a housing "opportunity." This, of course, is only one type of classification, which may be used to interpret other comments on the process of decision. However, the respondents may not have used such phrases. The solution exists, then, in developing *coding instructions* (for the researcher himself as well as for others) which list the *indicators* for each class. For example, one respondent may not use the term "anxious" but may state, "What a dump that was! But we had to find some place to live, so we put up with it for a year." Or, "My cousin picked it out while we were in Idaho. We were certainly sick when we saw it, but what could we do?" Both these comments indicate the respondents had a strong predisposition to move and were dissatisfied with their housing from the beginning.

On the other hand, a clear indicator for the "opportunity" group might be any comment which suggested general satisfaction with the housing, until a "bargain" was discovered accidentally. This type of comment would be the clearest case, and further details could be used to delimit the class in the case of respondents who were not very satisfied but who state that they would not have moved if the new housing had not been found unexpectedly.

The goal, therefore, is to work out a set of instructions which will enable others to classify these comments into the types which are relevant for the research. Since, ordinarily, exactly the same wording cannot be expected, the practice is to look for equivalent *meaning*. To do this, the phrases and cues which will unequivocally indicate the proper class are listed and checked by seeing whether several different coders using them will secure the same results.

In some cases, the indicators are known from the beginning. For example, one might be interested in discovering the extent to which nursery-age children use various ethnic stereotypes in their play language. The records might consist of observations made through a one-way visual screen, supplemented by wire recordings. In this case the coding problem would be simple, for the phrases used in ethnic stereotypes are fairly well known.

A somewhat more difficult problem occurs when a *continuum of intensity* is the object of the coding operation, such as the classification of answers from those expressing a strong degree of disapproval, to those expressing strong approval, of a particular object. As noted in the sections on scaling, this problem is sometimes met by the use of judges, who classify independently a series of responses along a continuum of approval and disapproval.

Even when judges are employed for a preliminary group of responses, the problem of which *indicators* are adequate for classification must still be faced, for we are dealing here with *unstructured* data. How many degrees can be used will depend on the detail to be found in the responses. "Strong disapproval" or "strong approval" may be fairly easy to classify. The less intense responses will sometimes be indicated by favorable or unfavorable comments which are accompanied by various qualifications: "They're all right, but some of them . . ."; or "I don't have much to do with them, but I never have any trouble. . . ."

4. FIT THE CLASSES TO THE DATA. Having worked out a preliminary set of indicators, the gradual process of fitting classes to the data must be begun. A first use of this procedure is to discover whether or not the instructions are clear. By working out the preliminary indicators and applying them, it is often possible to add new details to the instructions, as well as to understand more clearly the nature of the classes.

At this stage it is particularly important to pay attention to the *deviant cases*. No matter how carefully the first set of instructions have been worked out, some responses will occur which do not fit. The indicators may not apply, or they may seem fuzzy and vague. These cases should be studied in detail, for they may require a new set of indicators, or a new set of classes.

Further, it is likely that a small group of "unknown" or "unclassifiable" respondents will remain throughout the coding process. If this group is large, the instructions, classes, or data are poor. On the other hand, if this class is minute, it will not affect the conclusions to any important degree.

5. CODE ALL THE ANSWERS. Having gradually fitted the instructions to the classes needed, an attempt to code all the answers should then be made. Here, again, it is necessary to test the coding of one person or group against that of another. It is only by such fitting and testing that it is possible to check whether or not merely impressionistic judgments have served as the basis of interpretation.

Special problems. Before showing how qualitative coding is applied to communication content, such as newspapers, radio programs, speeches, etc., some common problems which occur often will be discussed.

A common result of the attempt to code is the discovery that one has failed to clarify the *concept itself* by which the comments are to be ordered. For example, a question about "belief in democracy" may elicit comments which are difficult to organize, precisely because the concept itself has not been properly defined. In some cases, the problem can be solved by a series of questions or by wording them more precisely. In other cases, it may be necessary to think through the problem once more. For example, if an attempt to order the comments in terms of "shop morale" confuses job satisfaction, acceptance of group standards in the shop, belief in job mobility, or other possible meanings of this term, only confusion in coding can result. In such a case, the focus of the research must be more clearly defined.

The failure to elicit the data desired is another type of problem which is sometimes met. Usually, this will be caused by faulty wording of the original question. Thus, one might use a direct question, such as "What made you commit this crime?" when the aim is to obtain information on the *process of deciding* to undertake a *particular* criminal act. Many respondents, however, will answer in terms of familial backgrounds, slum neighborhoods, gang behavior, etc. Then, of course, it is necessary to formulate the question differently.

Coding may result in an equally disheartening discovery—that most of the answers prove to be of one type. Thus, the earlier question about residential mobility, "Why did you decide to buy a house?" may elicit a set of answers which may all be classifiable as cost factors. Other questions indicate clearly, however, that cost cannot be the main factor. Respondents do not know much about comparative costs, and most of their comments suggest that familial discussions did not deal with costs to any great extent. We then see that "cost" is a kind of rationalization for other motivations, in terms which are acceptable in conversations with friends and outsiders. The answers to the formal question may have been so nearly identical merely because the basic question was not really being answered.

Such "one-class" tabulations often result when the question is answered by a cliché: "I decided to become an engineer because I've always been interested in it." "We were married because we were in love." "I never punish my children because they must be allowed to express their personalities." Reformulation of the question, or the use of probe questions, may be required. In any event, the coding process clearly points to a set of answers which seem to require further analysis before being accepted as satisfactory.

On the other hand, the attempt to find order in essentially unstructured data may lead to *further* insights, useful in understanding the tabulations already made. For example, in one unpublished study there were questions which dealt with ethnic opinions and friendship patterns. These answers were adequately coded in terms of attitudes toward various ethnic groups and also in terms of friendship patterns. However, this process suggested that the comments contained further data. When the respondents spoke of their friendships with members of other ethnic groups, they made "individual exemptions"; *i.e., their* friends were *different*. Their Irish friends were not pugnacious or of a low culture, or their Jewish friends were not commercial-minded (or radical). Consequently, a further coding operation was carried out, in terms of the individual exemptions used. Later cross tabulations demonstrated the fruitfulness of this operation, since a relationship existed between the degree of ethnic prejudice and the types of individual exemptions made.

Attempting to make procedures explicit is merely following one requirement of scientific work—that operations must be repeatable by others. If interview protocols are seen as "observations," it is clearly necessary that these observations actually be classifiable by others as they are by the researcher. When these observations are neatly structured, the problem of classification has been solved. However, many records such as case records in psychological clinics or social-work agencies, or observations of children, or protocols of free answers to open-ended questions, may be closer to the "real" attitudes of our sample. Qualitative coding is one set of techniques for locating and specifying the order which exists in such materials, and to which our theoretical questions point.

CONTENT ANALYSIS

We shall not at this point attempt to introduce the *substantive* field of communication analysis, which has had its main development within the past generation. All that we wish to do is point out that the data from all fields of communication may also be treated as sociological data. Whether we wish to understand the T'ang Dynasty in China or the Protestant Revolution, the propaganda of revolution or of reaction, the radio programs of the lower class housewife or of the highbrow, the available materials must be somehow coded. Whether these materials support or weaken a hypothesis in communication theory can only be determined by the usual criteria of good research design. All that is attempted here is to show how such materials can be exploited *as observations*, so that their underlying order, if any, is clearly demonstrated.

A simple case from the field of communication follows, in which such coding is indispensable for content analysis. While measuring the kinds of stimuli to which the newspaper public was exposed during a given period, a researcher may come to the conclusion that a particular newspaper was in sympathy with the Nazis at that time. A number of people may object to this statement, pointing out that the owner is a respectable man in the community, that he is "a 100 per cent American," that he does not belong to any political party, and so on.

If the researcher has been following a merely intuitive analysis, he would have to argue the point interminably. If he cites an example, they may cite a counter-example or an explanation. He may be charged with bias, with not understanding the situation, and so on. Many of our daily arguments with friends are similarly inconclusive.

However, a good sampling plan for the newspaper issues analyzed, an adequate logical structure uniting the data and the conclusions, and a systematic technique for coding the content of the newspaper make it possible to provide genuine evidence, such as Table 1 contains. With

TABLE 1

Number of Statements in *The True American* Consistent with or Opposed to Nazi Propaganda (March 3, 1943 to December 31, 1943) *

	Consistent	Opposed
The U.S. is internally corrupt	301	34
The foreign policies of the U.S. are un-Christian	41	0
The President of the U.S. is objectionable	150	17
Great Britain is internally corrupt	34	0
The foreign policies of Great Britain are un-Christian	80	2
Nazi Germany is just and virtuous	56	2
Japan's foreign policies are morally justifiable	22	6
Japan is powerful	30	2
The U.S. is weak	345	41
Nazi Germany is strong	41	2
The U.S. and the world are menaced by:		
a. Communists	55	0
b. Jews	99	0
c. Meddlers in the affairs of other countries	45	0

* See Harold D. Lasswell, Nathan Leites, *et al.*, *Language of Politics* (New York: Stewart, 1949), Chap. 9, "Detection: Propaganda Detection and the Courts," pp. 173–233, esp. the table on p. 187. Table above is adapted from Lasswell's presentation.

this table might go a comparison with other publications, such as the second tabulation here.

TABLE 2

Percentages of Articles and Editorials Consistent with Nazi Themes *

Magazine	Percentage
Time Magazine	0.11
True American	55.67
Liberty	1.12
Saturday Evening Post	0.54

* See similar tables in Harold D. Lasswell, Nathan Leites, *et al.*, *Language of Politics* (New York: Stewart, 1949), pp. 198–199. This table is an example of Lasswell's "consistency test"; the former, of his "parallel test."

Without going into the logic of the research design, which was developed during the war and used for actual court proof, we can see that such pinpoint use of data is at the polar extreme from an intuitive approach. It will be noted that the researchers have actually counted the presence or absence of Nazi themes within a publication. Whether the focus is on editorials alone, or on the entire publication, these examples show a translation from the qualitative complexity of the total content, to the quantitative simplicity of counting Nazi themes. Since these themes are already available, the coding problem would not be difficult. For high reliability, coding instructions would simply list the major themes to be observed, and coding the publication over a selected period would yield an accurate count, which could be verified by other researchers. Of course, not all the material from this publication is utilized. Many other analyses could be made, with relevance to other problems, and "theme" analysis is only one possible unit of investigation.

Let us now select another example, dealing with the status of various ethnic groups in the United States, as depicted in popular fiction. A great number of interesting critical essays could be written on the subject, depending on the writer's literary knowledge. These might be suggestive and stimulating, but most of them are open to the criticism that the reader "knows of exceptions," or he "does not see" how the writer arrived at such conclusions. By developing an adequate sampling plan and a set of clear coding operations, it is possible to demonstrate a number of facts about popular fiction which do not depend on the researcher's personality or insight alone but which can be tested by any trained social scientist.

One study of this sort focused on the treatment of ethnic groups in popular short stories.[2] The method of classifying the data was fairly

[2] Bernard Berelson and Patricia Salter, "Majority and Minority Americans: An Analysis of Magazine Fiction," *Public Opinion Quarterly*, Vol. X (1946), pp. 168–190.

simple. Each story has a number of characters, and each of these characters is described more or less fully. The student can extract this list of characters with their descriptions from each story.

Any such set of characters can then be analyzed, in order to discover whether there is any identification of class, race, ethnic origin, religion, occupation, the goals which they seek, and so on. The process of developing explicit coding operations, as noted previously, depends on the purpose of the analysis and on the difficulty of securing adequate indicators for the desired classes. For the case in question, let us take a few examples of hypothetical characters as met in popular fiction. A simple decision might be reached on the following individual, who is presented with the description used in the story about him:

Character	How Identified	Treatment in the Story
John Adams	White (story illustration)	Hero of the story
	Descendant of New England family	Idealist (is trying to force realtors to accept a city plan which will beautify the community, but reduce their income)
	Lawyer	
	High income (has custom-built convertible, seashore summer cottage)	
	Episcopal (has conversation with minister regarding early church experience)	

Similarly, the following character seems adequately identified to allow some judgment concerning his treatment in the story:

Character	How Identified	Treatment in the Story
Johnny Turridu	White	Minor role. He is defeated by hero
	Came to this country from Italy at the age of three (father speaks broken English)	Makes money from numbers rackets
	High income (spends vacations at expensive resorts, owns buildings)	Rejects his old priest
	Catholic	Cynical materialist (expresses interest only in his success; bribes city officials)

Any such sketches would, of course, be only the first steps toward more precise directions for identifying the ethnic backgrounds and the roles which the characters play. There would be fewer data for minor characters, and instructions must be flexible enough to allow identification by using any one of the many indicators which might be used. For example: (1) the ethnic membership might be specifically noted; (2) obvious ethnic names might be used; (3) some supposedly ethnic phrases may occur; (4) membership in ethnic organizations may be cited; or (5) the home neighborhood may be described closely enough to allow identification. A similar set of possibilities exists for "treatment in the story," although this is somewhat more difficult, involving as it does a set of cues to locate and specify to what extent there is "discrimination" against the ethnic group member. So long, however, as the category, "unknown" is not a large one, the basic conclusions will not be affected.

Note, further, that for many minority groups there may be no representatives at all. This is not surprising, since popular fiction must rely upon commonly recognized ethnic images. Consequently, in this case the researchers used these categories: "The Americans," "The Anglo-Saxon and Nordic minorities and foreigners," and "The Others" (Jews, Italians, Negroes, etc.). The treatment of these groups in the fiction sample was then tabulated as shown in the accompanying table. "The

TABLE 3

A Content Analysis of Ethnic Groups in Current American Literature

	The Americans, Per Cent	The Anglo-Saxons and Nordics, Per Cent	The Others, Per Cent
Major characters	52	38	30
Approved characters	80	78	62
Highest socioeconomic status	39	24	16
Top occupations	59	29	20
"Heart" goals (*i.e.*, idealist, love, family, as against money, power, etc.)	69	61	49

rule seems to be that the character receives better treatment the closer he is to the norm of *The American, i.e.,* white, Protestant, English-speaking, Anglo-Saxon" (page 186).

Thus, by working out fairly simple rules for identification and treatment, it was possible to determine that within popular short stories there is a demonstrable "discrimination" against the various minority groups, especially those which are at present disadvantaged in the society. By using fairly large categories, the problem of decision was reduced considerably.

The data contained in the short stories were not originally presented or organized for the purposes of research, but by formulating instructions for locating and identifying the characters and the themes which are used to describe them, the coders could *reliably* classify the data as presented. The further analysis of the meaning of these data will always depend on the goals of the research, but the data are no longer guesses or hunches: they are empirically verifiable by other observers if the same operations are followed.

It is also clear that there are many *units* of the communication content which can be used for sampling and analysis, from small units such as words or symbols, to journal issues or volumes. Similarly, there are many ways of organizing the materials: by symbol count, by item analysis, by thematic analysis, in terms of the *structure* of the ideas and facts presented, or even (in propaganda materials) in terms of the campaign. Clearly, it is equally possible, in the case of content addressed to an audience, to analyze these spoken or written materials in terms of the *response.* However, for such further treatments of content analysis as a substantive field, the student should read the literature cited at the end of this chapter.

THE CASE STUDY

The case-study approach may be introduced at this point, since traditionally it has been thought of as a kind of qualitative analysis. More important for our purposes, however, is the fact that it is through the developments of qualitative techniques, such as qualitative coding, that the case study can be most efficiently used in social research.

References in the sociological literature to "the case-study method" are decreasing. In part, this would seem to be one result of the false distinction between "the statistical approach," and "the nonstatistical approach," as a consequence of which the case study is sometimes identified with the use of less reliable research techniques. It is often thought of as a kind of intuitive approach, derived from much participant observation and using all sorts of personal documents such as diaries, letters, autobiographies, etc., without adequate sampling design or checks on bias or distortions resulting from personal views of social reality.

However, such an identification fails to distinguish the case-study *approach,* a method of looking at social reality, from the specific research *techniques* which accompanied it in the research of a generation ago. It is true that much of case-study research at that time failed to follow good sampling design and often came to conclusions with no explicit description of the operations which led to those conclusions. However, this was true for most social research, and in any event there is no intrinsic connection between the case study and unsophisticated research techniques.

Similarly, the case-study approach has been praised as a set of useful research techniques, such as the use of personal documents, probing many facets of the respondent's life, adjusting the wording of questions to fit the peculiar experience of the respondent, sharing experiences with the individuals being studied, collecting life histories, gathering data over the lifetime of the individual, etc. Such praise is equally unwarranted, since these techniques may be used in almost any type of social research. The use of qualitative coding permits the use of personal documents in a systematic way. The interview guide is one form of the questionnaire which allows flexible and alternative wordings of questions, when that is needed. Participant observation, while it has not been systematically studied in recent years, is used when possible in the early stages of formulating the research problem. Life histories may also be used in the preliminary stages of research, or as the basic body of data, and may be employed in conjunction with the techniques of qualitative coding for many types of social research. In short, modern social research has attempted gradually to systematize and make precise the various special "qualitative" techniques which were once thought to be the exclusive characteristics of the case-study approach.

The case study, then, is not a specific technique. It is a way of organizing social data so as to preserve the *unitary character of the social object being studied.* Expressed somewhat differently, it is an approach which views any social unit as a whole. Almost always, this means of approach includes the *development* of that unit, which may be a person, a family or other social group, a set of relationships or processes (such as family crises, adjustment to disease, friendship formation, ethnic invasion of a neighborhood, etc.), or even an entire culture.

Before pointing out some of the difficulties and advantages of this approach, let us clarify it somewhat by contrasting this holistic view with that of much modern research. A simple case taken from public opinion polling yields an extreme comparison. Suppose the respondents are asked a series of questions about their attitudes toward war. For further analysis, a series of cross-tabulation questions, such as age, sex, economic ranking, urban-rural residence, and veteran status, may also be asked. The answers to each question are classified, in order to cross-tabulate by strata. Thus the answers to the question on economic ranking are put into the classes A, B, C, and D. Perhaps three to five age groupings and two sex groupings (male and female) may also be used. Having thus classified and coded the data, all these can be transferred to the punch cards.

However, from this point onward the individual unit, the *person,* disappears from the analysis, which instead merely compares *traits.* Thus, for example, cross tabulations may reveal whether the old object to war more vigorously than do the young, or whether women disapprove of war more vigorously than do men, or perhaps how the various economic rankings compare in their attitudes toward war.

The answer to each of these questions is obtained by sorting out all the cards into the first group of traits (old as against young), then tabulating under each group the responses to questions about war. For example, the cards could be sorted into those with a punch meaning "65 and over," one which means "under 20," and another group which includes all the rest (or any other age classification desired). Then, for each

such group obtained in this fashion, the responses to the questions concerning war are tabulated.

Note, however, that it is only the *traits* which are immediately involved in the cross tabulation. All other characteristics on each card are
ignored. What is being emphasized here is not the *narrowness of the
questions,* for even the most elaborate research represents a relatively
thin slice of any respondent's life. Rather, it is important to see that
most of our analyses are cross-tabulating the distribution of one *trait*
with the distribution of another. This is equally the case for elaborate
cross tabulations, as it is for correlations. The individual representing
the "wholeness" of those traits does not figure in these analyses.

Such a characterization is, of course, essentially negative and seems
almost a polemic cliché. In order, then, to specify the case-study approach
as an alternative mode of handling respondents, groups, or social relationships, let us attempt to show wherein the differences lie. In a more
practical form, how *can* the wholeness of cases be preserved? We shall
attempt to outline the answer briefly under four rather complex rubrics:
(1) breadth of data; (2) levels of data; (3) formation of indexes and types;
and (4) interaction in a time dimension.

A few preliminary remarks are in order, however. First, the *wholeness*
of any object, whether physical, biological, or social, is an intellectual
construct. Concretely, there are no limits which define any process or
object. Every variable ultimately links with any other. As theoretical
biology has pointed out, from some points of view even the living animal
is a construct, and the point at which the animal stops and "the environment" begins is arbitrarily defined. Similarly, "the individual," or "the
formation of a gang" must be such a construct, defined in terms that
are most fruitful for the research problem.

From this point we see, further, that not only is it difficult to set the
limits of any social object, but it is difficult to state at what point it is
profitable to stop gathering data about the object so delimited. As has
been noted before, an infinite number of observations may be made
about even the dullest or most unimportant person. Consequently, neither
the case study nor any other approach can be characterized as the analysis
of the individual in all his uniqueness. The point at which data are
adequate must be determined by the research problem itself. There is
no inherent or intrinsic limit. One implication of this must be added:
when we speak of the "social object as a whole" we cannot mean the
"social object as a unique unit." It is precisely the unique elements in
any phenomenon which are eliminated by scientific abstraction. To the
extent that characteristics are really unique, it is impossible to account
for them in terms of scientific generalizations. Consequently, the case-
study method cannot be thought of as capturing the unique, but as at-

tempting to keep together, as a unit, those characteristics which are rele-vant to the scientific problem being investigated.

Breadth of data. Clearly, one of the ways by which the unit is studied as a totality is the collection of a broad array of data about it. This is true whether the subject is a set of social relationships, a person, or a group. The "person" who is recorded on a polling schedule is not only dis-solved by becoming a set of traits individually tabulated; he almost fails to exist from the beginning, by virtue of the narrow range of the data concerning him. Although mere quantity of data is not sufficient, since the collection must be guided by the research problem, there is a greater opportunity to grasp the pattern of the individual's life if a substantial body of data concerning many facets of that life is available.

Levels of data. The case-study method is further distinguished by the use of data from other abstract levels than the purely sociological. Al-though many sociologists do incorporate economic, political, psycho-dynamic, and even biological data into their analyses, social research has in the main been moving in the direction of a clearer definition of the sociological, together with better techniques for abstracting it from the complex of other relationships. In the case-study method, such data from other levels are deliberately incorporated into the records. Although it may be pointed out that such data should be viewed in terms of their sociological meaning, so that a biological defect, for example, is seen as it affects social relationships, it is clear that recourse to other levels does give added dimensions to the individual being studied. When we see the individual in his total network of relationships, it is more difficult to lose sight of him as a unit.

Formation of indices and types. However, the most important tech-nique in preserving the wholeness of the social unit is the development of typologies and indexes, so that the various traits are actually used in characterizing the unit. Note that this technique is not confined to the case-study method and is used in any qualitative analysis. Furthermore, elaborate cross tabulations attempt the same goal. Thus, cross tabula-tions in terms of sex, age, and socioeconomic ranking serve to character-ize those who are (for example) male, *and* aged 20 to 29, *and* poor.

The same operations may be performed in a case study, and the problem may be somewhat simplified by qualitative coding beforehand. Because of the breadth and added dimensions of the data, moreover, the choice of *which* type or class the case falls into will be simplified. In addition, by the time the types begin to emerge clearly, enough of the process of interaction between various facets of the individual's life will be known so that this choice may be made with greater certainty. Finally, cases will be concerned with developing "natural types," that is, types which are already discerned in the culture (such as "lovers' quarrels," "life of the party," "village philosopher," or the religious revival meeting), and the case-study approach can ordinarily single out such types at an early stage.

Interaction in a time dimension. To the breadth and additional levels of the data gathered in the case-study method must be added the emphasis upon *process and time.* Any cross tabulation is essentially a static analysis, although the relative numbers of cases found in various subcells may be used to *test* hypotheses of interaction. For example, according to some theories we would expect to find a causal relationship between class position and continuation in school. It is possible, then, to cross-tabulate these characteristics (possibly holding IQ constant) and thus check the hypothesis.

Nevertheless, we do not observe "process" in such tabulations. We are limited to the traits on the punch card, which have not recorded any of their relationships to one another. In the case study, the attempt to hold these characteristics together in both the data-gathering and the data-analysis phases emphasizes the *changes* in time, as well as the *processes* by which those changes took place. The period of time may be short or long. An individual's life from childhood until the time of a study, or the formation and reformation of cliques in Congress over a very short period of months may be studied equally well. In either case, however, the concern is with recording the relevant characteristics *as they appear* in interaction, not merely recording them at two separate instants in time for a before-and-after comparison. The emphasis on the interaction process makes the maintenance of the unitary character of the social object somewhat simpler.

Problems of the case-study technique. Most of the difficulties in the use of this method can be reduced to one, although a more complex classification is possible. Interestingly enough, the basic danger in its use is the *response of the researcher.* The researcher comes to feel a false sense of certainty about his own conclusions. The danger, then, does not lie in any technical weakness of this approach to social processes or individuals as wholes.

The student may feel that this is a constant danger in all research. Yet it should be remembered that in most research there are constant reminders that a very narrow range of experience is represented by the data. However long our interviews, gaps are all too obvious, and there is no way to fill them. However, each *case* which is developed as a unit takes on complete dimensions in the mind of the researcher. He comes to feel certain that he could answer many more questions about his case than can be answered from his file records. The case has a definite form and pattern, and as the researcher probes more deeply into the process or person being studied, he finds there are few surprises left. It is quite comparable to our feeling of certainty about our close friends, or the neighborhood in which we have lived for years, or our families. There is, in short, an emotional feeling of certainty which is much stronger than in the case of other types of research. This is particularly true as compared with much survey work, in which the analyst has only the completed schedules before him and knows he cannot capture the varied experiences of the many interviewers who carried out those interviews.

Yet the student can test the accuracy of this knowledge very easily, by submitting to questioning about his close friends or his own family, the "cases" he knows best. Most of us find that our feelings of certainty deceive us. We know far fewer data about these cases than we believe. Important facts are forgotten. Other facts are distorted, or surprising facets of these lives are unknown to us. For example, children usually believe that they "understand" their parents, but are often oblivious to the many deep conflicts between them. Brothers and sisters are often unaware of important experiences happening to each other outside the family circle. What most of us feel is a kind of at-homeness with these close acquaintances, so that we fill in or ignore those facts or dimensions of the person which are really unknown to us.

This danger, then, is one which the observer *himself* creates. The *consequences* of this feeling of certainty are many, but most of them can be grouped under one main heading: *a temptation to ignore basic principles of research design.* Since the researcher feels so very certain about the area of experience he is investigating, he feels no need to check the over-all design of proof. For example, after the student has collected, say, 200 cases of juvenile delinquency from social-work records, supplemented by interviewing and other sources, it is difficult for him to feel that he does not have an adequate sample. The range of delinquency experience in his cases is so wide, the types of people so varied, the depth of detail so vivid, that the researcher ordinarily has a strong conviction that his selection is "representative." He was not, usually, following any known pattern of sampling, so that he feels certain there is no bias. It must be repeated at this point that we are not separating one type of researcher from any other type. *Any* investigator who absorbs the facts from a large number of cases will begin to feel that he really has a satisfactory sample, no matter how much knowledge he has about sampling design.

The result is, naturally, a strong temptation to extrapolate unwarrantedly. Perhaps an equally important consequence of this feeling is the failure to make explicit just what are the generalizations underlying the analysis of the cases. One boy's refusal to give up his pilfering may be explained by his desire for economic gain. Yet, in a similar case, and without explaining the *bases* for the different explanation, another boy's refusal to give up thievery may be explained by his desire to humble his parents, a psychodynamic explanation. Although both explanations may be correct, we are likely to forget that any such analysis requires a *system* of explanation. It is not scientific to apply various explanations which by common sense or intuition seem to fit particular cases, on a purely *ad hoc* basis. Some set of generalizations is being used, and it is necessary to make explicit just why one or the other may or may not be applied. However, when the investigator feels so much "at home" with each case, he may be tempted to "feel" the right explanation—even though a second reader of our cases might come to an entirely different explanation. This is what is known as *ad hoc* theorizing. The previous reference suggests a further danger resulting from this feeling of certainty: *the failure to test the reliability* of the data recorded, the classifications used, or the analysis of the data. As the researcher is likely to point out, no one else knows the data nearly so well as he, so that no one else could check his work adequately. Furthermore, case gathering is a time-consuming activity, and it is difficult to find others who are willing to study the cases with such completeness.

Avoiding these problems. Nevertheless, these difficulties can be avoided by the student who is willing to follow good research planning. Being warned of the dangers which result from such a feeling of certainty, he will develop a research design which takes account of these dangers. He cannot avoid the feeling of certainty, but he can use an adequate sampling pattern. Knowing that his sampling is good, he has a rational basis for making estimates about the universe from which it was drawn. Instead of relying on intuition for his conclusions, he will make certain that whenever he analyzes a given factor, there are actual data for all case records concerning that factor. Further, he will develop his theoretical framework from the beginning of the research, so that he avoids speculations made on the spot to fit the peculiarities of each case.

Furthermore, he will attempt, as far as possible, to utilize the technique of qualitative coding for individual factors and traits which are amenable to such classifications. If he is to use categories like "selfish," or "adjusted," or "anomic," he will develop a set of instructions for deciding whether a given case falls into the category. If other investigators cannot use such instructions, they are likely to contain many implicit judgments, intuitions, common-sense guesses, and the like. The good student will recognize that a description of research operations must be so written that other scientists can repeat them. If not, either the description or the operations are unclear. The student *must* make this test, if he is not to remain open to the charge from others that they "simply can't see" what he sees. It is usually good procedure to carry out this stage of analysis with the aid of a number of collaborators or assistants who can act as judges of the reliability of even simple classifications.

One may almost claim that it is at this point—that of developing categories, of defining and delimiting types of behavior already recorded— that the case study requires the closest criticism. For it is at this stage that the systematization of much of the mass of data begins, that is, condensation, excision, reinterpretation, etc. The final report cannot simply repeat the recorded observations. The steps in this transformation, then, must be carefully marked, if the researcher expects to have his conclusions accepted.

It is worth recording that this problem is not peculiar to sociology. When the historian begins to reduce the mass of individual observations from original sources, he faces the problem of showing his operations to fellow historians, so that they can follow them exactly, should they wish to do so. Much of the objection of social scientists to the published analyses of psychiatrists and psychoanalysts is simply that, whatever the details of the case, there is no clearly outlined set of operations by which the next scientist can use the same data to come to the same conclusions. The economist who studies the marketing process among tobacco farmers may find similarly that each case is so very different that colleagues are suspicious of conclusions until the operations of the analysis are made clear. As noted above, the best way of clarifying these steps is to develop definite coding instructions for most of the important qualitative items, with definite tests for coding reliability.

Costs in time and money. It is clear that this approach is a costly one in time and money. Each case becomes a research in itself, and the collection of even 100 adequately documented cases may easily consume 2 years of the student's time. Since the data are not usually standardized, the system of keeping records and of developing techniques for standardizing the observations must be rather elaborate. Over such a lengthy period, the loss of potential cases from the sample drawn may be very great, and the resultant costs of tracing cases similarly great.

These costs need not deter the researcher from this technique. They simply remind him of a cardinal fact, that *all* research is expensive, and there must be an early judgment as to *which* kind of study will be most adequate for the kinds of facts needed. For some types of analysis, the use of case studies will be fruitful. For others, a simple polling study or mailed questionnaire may be adequate. When detailed *processes* of social interaction are being analyzed, some preliminary recourse to case study is needed, even if there is not complete reliance upon this method. One type of simple, less expensive, substitute is a panel sample, which is re-interviewed over a period of months.

Advantages of case study. Nevertheless, as was noted previously, most good research has some recourse to case analysis, even if it does not appear in the final publication of results. Its fruitfulness is indicated by the preceding discussion of its characteristics. Before a final questionnaire is developed, it is likely that the careful researcher will attempt the analysis of many cases which center on his major problem. He cannot rely on the reports from a few trial interviews. He will want to go over the field of interaction with a number of respondents, in great detail, to find out just how their life pattern is being affected by the item being studied. For example, if the aim is to develop a good schedule for the analysis of stratification, simply trying out a number of schedule drafts will usually not be adequate. The student must attempt to develop a body of much more intensive, detailed, and subtle observations about many individuals, learning about their responses to the phenomena of class barriers, mobility, class perspectives, etc. In addition, it is here that the added data allow the study of the deviant cases, that is, those which seem to negate the theory. Such analysis may lead to considerable clarification of the theory itself. Such observations may or may not be formalized into definite case histories. Such a practice is recommended, since at this exploratory stage the student is likely to see *selectively*, that is, see those items which seem outstanding to him, while neglecting perhaps equally important data. Only by *recording* them for analysis and then analyzing them, prior to the next stage of formulating the final version of questionnaire or schedule, can he make certain that all the pertinent data are being incorporated into the research instrument.

Of course, the researcher may be interested in certain social processes, such as the courtship process, clique formation, postdivorce adjustment, or boys' gangs, and in such a case the unit selected need not be the life history of the individual person. It will instead be the *process* selected for study. Here again the preliminary study of the processes is greatly facilitated by case documents, incorporating the pertinent data which will guide later stages of the research.

Whether the student approaches his data through the framework of the case study at *later* stages of the investigation will depend on many factors. As was noted above, the time and money at his disposal may lead to a decision to study only a limited number of factors. In this case, he may well utilize a questionnaire or some form of single interview as his main technique. If he wishes to study a much wider range of data, he may be willing to limit the number of cases. He will ordinarily not be able to generalize safely from a small number of cases, but it is often true that the depth of insight afforded by case study will yield fruitful hypotheses for a later, full-scale study.

The most important theoretical advantage of the case study has not been fully exploited as yet. As noted earlier, most research has become "trait" research, that is, cross tabulations between *traits* of individuals. Even when these individuals are being studied in groups, very few individuals or groups as units are being analyzed.[3] Even though many of the apparently group traits can be approached through combining indi-

[3] For a recent discussion, see Patricia L. Kendall and Paul F. Lazarsfeld, "Problems of Survey Analysis," *Continuities in Social Research*, Robert K. Merton and Paul F. Lazarsfeld, eds. (Glencoe, Ill.: Free Press, 1950), pp. 187–196.

vidual data, they may also be approached through an organizing framework emphasizing the characteristics of the group, or process, or social structure as a whole. The case study, attempting to organize data around the unit of growth, or group structure, or individual life pattern, does force the researcher to think in these terms rather than fall back on trait analysis alone.

Emphasis should also be placed on the *wider range of personal experience* which the use of the case study gives to the student. This advantage has been implicit in the previous discussion, but it deserves special comment at this point. Precisely because of the narrowness of most survey work, the researcher actually derives most of his wider range of experience in such investigations at the stage of *analysis,* when the meaning of the questions is probed more deeply. This latter stage is most fruitful, however, if there has been a *prior* period of absorbing the varied experience of others. The case study is particularly useful because of its attempt to find the meaning of the recorded data within the life of the individual, and only later in terms of *classes* of individuals. Often, too, these experiences yield new insights because of their very differences from the ordinary experiences of the researcher; he may never have been divorced, been a safecracker, a pickpocket, a member of a boys' gang, a member of an ethnic group becoming Americanized, etc. In a sense, then, he is able thereby to live many quite different lives by sharing these experiences. Such materials are not only useful within the confines of his particular research, but may become raw materials for further reflection and research. Since the researcher, whether academic, industrial, or governmental, is under pressure to lead his life entirely within his own middle-class group, attention to these further dimensions of social life prevents his sociological thinking from becoming increasingly narrow.

It is seen, then, that although it is not possible to identify the case-study "method" as a particular *technique* for eliciting data, it is a *mode of organizing data* in terms of some chosen unit, such as the individual life history, the history of a group, or some delimited social process. In order to obtain such holistic data, one may use all the techniques which any other mode of organization uses: intensive interviews, questionnaires, self-histories, documents, case reports by others, letters, etc. Maintenance of the unitary character of the case is aided by the breadth and added levels of data gathered, the use of indexes and typologies, and the emphasis on interaction in a time dimension. There is, then, some attempt to make of each case a research in itself. This is a time-consuming process, and the collection of a large number of cases may be unnecessary, if the research goals are limited. The absorption in the detailed material of social relationships and interaction gives the researcher a wider range and a greater depth of experience, which may be of great use in interpreting the data and in further research. However, by such close contact with the individuals or groups studied, it is likely that the observer will have a strong effect on the data themselves. At least, it may be claimed that this danger is perhaps greater in this approach. The absorption in the data also creates such a feeling of certainty about his knowledge, on the part of the researcher, that he is often tempted to be less cautious in following the basic rules of research design. Nevertheless, for preliminary research in any field, most investigators will use some form of the case study; and for the purpose of *group or process analysis,* as against the analysis of individual traits alone, it is a highly fruitful approach, as yet insufficiently exploited by those who are currently doing research into research techniques.

SUGGESTED READINGS

Berelson, Bernard, and Patricia J. Salter, "Majority and Minority Americans: An Analysis of Magazine Fiction," *Public Opinion Quarterly,* Vol. X (Summer, 1946), pp. 168–190.

Jahoda, Marie, Morton Deutsch, and Stuart W. Cook, *Research Methods in Social Relations* (New York: Dryden, 1951), Part I, pp. 252–276, 295–304.

Lazarsfeld, Paul F., and W. S. Robinson, "The Quantification of Case Studies," *Journal of Applied Psychology,* Vol. XXIV (1940), pp. 817–825.

Lundberg, G. A., *Social Research* (New York: Longmans, 1942), Chap. 11.

Parten, Mildred, *Surveys, Polls, and Samples: Practical Procedures* (New York: Harper, 1950), Chap. 14.

Young, Pauline V., *Scientific Social Surveys and Research* (New York: Prentice-Hall, 1949), Chap. 12.

CHAPTER 20

The Analysis of Data

Thus far the emphasis has been on the necessity of carefully *planning* the collection of data so that significant questions can be answered and on the problems of *collecting* data so that the answers will be reliable and valid. It is quite obvious, however, that performing these two steps alone will not provide an answer to the original hypothesis. Rather, they will provide a means for answering it. This chapter aims at clarifying some of the ways in which such data can be so ordered as to provide the desired answers.

Under ideal conditions of precision and simplicity this presents very few problems since the statement of the hypothesis and the elaboration of the experimental design will automatically provide for the analysis of the data. Consider, for example, a hypothesis stated as follows: If lights are selected as visual stimuli in such a way that each is subliminal (not perceivable) to each eye taken separately, then if they are applied simultaneously (but still separately) they will be perceived by the subject. Such a hypothesis is so stated that either there will be perception or there will not. An analysis of the data would constitute no problem at all. If, on the other hand, the responses were such as to show not an absolute presence or absence but rather proportions or degrees of presence, the problem of analysis would become more complex. If, in addition, the proportions of those perceiving the light appears to be different among different types of subjects, *e.g.,* men and women, or older and younger persons, the problem becomes rapidly still more complex.

In other words, the problems raised by the analysis of data are directly related to the complexity of the hypothesis or hypotheses. Suppose, for example, a study is carried on to test the hypothesis that family size is directly related to size of the home in which the family resides, with the results shown in the table which follows. Such findings would force a rejection of the hypothesis *as stated* and should lead to its reformulation in more specific, and hence more complex, terms. Thus, it might be restated as follows: The size of the home is positively correlated with family size, *when the opportunities for choice are equal.* This, of course,

FAMILY SIZE	PERCENTAGE OF FAMILIES RESIDING IN:		
	Small Houses	Medium Houses	Large Houses
Large families	25.0	55.0	20.0
Medium families	30.0	60.0	10.0
Small families	30.0	55.0	15.0

requires a clear definition of what factors influence freedom of choice. Clearly, financial ability to buy or rent at various levels is such a factor, since size of home is correlated with its costliness. A retabulation, therefore, such as the following one might then appear. This type of find-

ECONOMIC LEVEL OF FAMILY	PERCENTAGE OF LARGE FAMILIES RESIDING IN:		
	Small Houses	Medium Houses	Large Houses
High	5.0	35.0	60.0
Medium	35.0	65.0	10.0
Low	40.0	55.0	5.0

ing would tend roughly to support the hypothesis as restated. If similar tabulations were carried out for "medium" and "small" families, and coincided with the above findings, then the hypothesis would be affirmed even more strongly.

However, economic ability is not the only factor which interferes with the choice of a home. In some areas being a member of a "non-Caucasian" race will inhibit choice through restrictive covenants. Therefore, it might be necessary to retabulate the above in terms of race. Thus such an analysis would lead to two racial divisions (white and nonwhite) within three economic levels (high, medium, and low) for three sizes of family (large, medium, and small). This would yield $2 \times 3 \times 3$, or 18 such tables. As will be seen later, it is not always necessary to perform the task in so cumbersome a fashion, but the logical problem must nonetheless be dealt with.

If all the relevant factors are known in advance, then there is no serious problem in analysis, for as pointed out in the earlier chapters, the experimental design would have gathered the data in only the crucial instances. There are two aspects of scientific research, however, which make the occurrence of so ideal a situation relatively infrequent. The first of these is the appearance of an anomalous empirical regularity or the absence of an expected regularity. Such instances require analysis not anticipated by the original design. Similar to this is the use of data, gathered for one purpose, for quite another problem. Both these represent what is called *secondary analyses*. From a very "pure" experimental point of view, such analyses are considered to yield answers which are "plausible" but not capable of being stated in the customary "probability" terms of science.

For example, in the case of the housing study referred to above, if race and economic status had been considered in the original design, the sample employed would have been so constructed as to contain an *adequate* and *representative* selection from all the various subtypes. That is, a satisfactory sample of each family size within each racial group within each economic level would have been secured. If this were *not* done because the later analysis was the result of an afterthought, it becomes difficult to assess the value of the old sample for the new purpose.

However, secondary analysis is not only common but necessary, and it is certainly of great value, even if it produces no more than plausible statements to serve as hypotheses for subsequent verification in more stringent terms.[1]

In a sense, then, problems of data analysis involve all the questions raised in the chapter on research design, for secondary analyses do involve the designing and redesigning of substitutes for the controlled experiment. This indicates that there are two types of questions about analysis which may be raised. One of them relates to the techniques of *representing the data*, and the other to the methods of *logically ordering* them so that questions can be raised and answered.

The first of these general problems cannot be treated exhaustively in a book such as this and are, in any case, part of the usual content of statistics courses. A few basic comments concerning the methods of repre senting the data will be made, but the major object of attention will be the logical processes involved in secondary analysis.

STATISTICAL REPRESENTATION

The frequency distribution. The simplest form of representing research findings is the frequency distribution or tabulation. All that is meant by this is the presentation in one column of different qualities of an attribute, or different values of a variable, together with entries in another column showing the frequency of the occurrence of each of the classes. The only problems connected with the preparation of a useful frequency distribution, or simple table as it may also be called, is to use common sense with respect to three things.

---

[1] A detailed discussion of this point can be found in *Continuities in Social Research*, Robert K. Merton and Paul F. Lazarsfeld, eds. (Glencoe, Ill.: Free Press, 1950), *passim*, esp. pp. 133–143 and pp. 197–211.

First, the units entered in the left-hand column describing the qualities or values must be mutually exclusive, as well as inclusive of the vast majority of observations which will be made. Overlapping values or attributes can only lead to confusion. For example, in a study of Puerto Rico one of the authors found that besides Catholic, Protestant, and "no religion" categories, there were some who professed Spiritualism. This would have made no problem except for the fact that it appeared possible to combine Spiritualism with either Protestantism or Catholicism. Therefore, instead of just adding a category, Spiritualist, it was necessary to add also Catholic *and* Spiritualist as well as Protestant *and* Spiritualist.

Second, the tabulation, to be of the most utility, must have *internal* logic and order. It seems quite obvious that, if one were tabulating such a variable as the height of men or the size of cities, he would tabulate in order either from the tallest or largest to the shortest or smallest, or vice versa. However, when tabulating qualities, where the order may not be so obvious, the need for a logical treatment is equally great. For example, one survey asked women for their reasons for buying a certain face cream.[2] One tabulation of the results is shown in the accompanying table.

Reasons for Buying Face Cream *

Reasons	Percentage of Respondents
Recommendation	28.0
Beneficial to skin	21.0
Heard it advertised over the radio	18.0
Saw it on the counter	15.0
Reasonably priced	10.0
Scent appealed	8.0
Because of special skin conditions	7.0
Total	107.0

* This is not strictly speaking a frequency, but a percentage distribution. This problem will be taken up later.

First of all, since the total reaches 107 per cent, it is clear that this table violates the first requirement, namely, that the categories be mutually exclusive. Ignoring this fact, however, it is clear that there is no sensible order to the types of reasons given. How is it possible to improve the utility of the tabulation for analytical purposes? Since there is no continuum such as that for height or size, the procedure is to search for logical groupings of the responses. It is possible to discover three such larger categories, and the use of the table increases greatly if it is modified in this way.

[2] Adapted from Hans Zeisel, *Say It with Figures* (New York: Harper, 1947), 2d ed., pp. 7–8.

Reasons for Buying Face Cream

Reasons		Percentage of Respondents
Pertaining to respondent:		28.0
Beneficial to skin	21.0	
Special skin condition	7.0	
Pertaining to product:		18.0
Reasonably priced	10.0	
Scent appealed	8.0	
Pertaining to way heard of product:		61.0
Recommendation	28.0	
Heard radio advertising	18.0	
Saw it on counter	15.0	

Not all tabulations will have a logical structure, but in most cases it is possible to find a logical order to use as an analytical principle, even in simple tabulation.

Third, when the left-hand column of a tabulation is a quantitative variable such as size of city or monthly rental value, the class intervals must be carefully and reasonably chosen. Schmid suggests three criteria for this: [3]

"1. Ordinarily there should not be less than 8 or 10 and not more than 18 or 20 class-intervals, depending on the nature of the data and on the number of cases being studied. In order to obtain a clear understanding of the original data the individual items are frequently arranged in either ascending or descending order of magnitude. Such a classification is known as an *array.* After noting the highest and lowest values as well as the characteristic features of the data, the number of intervals can be determined more easily.

"2. Every effort should be made to have intervals of uniform size. The intervals should not be so small as to lose the advantages of summarization or so large as to conceal the more important characteristics of the distribution. Moreover, if the class-intervals are too small, vacant or blank intervals might occur. If comparisons are to be made between similar data, it is advisable to select class-intervals of the same size for all the distributions. Whenever possible the class-intervals should represent common and convenient numerical divisions such as 5 or 10, rather than odd divisions such as 3 or 7.

"3. After the size of the class-intervals has been determined, it is important that they be clearly designated in the frequency table. Each interval must have definite lower and upper limits, and must be expressed in such a way as to obviate any possibility of misinterpretation or confusion."

These seem like simple principles, and indeed they are. In practice, however, they are somewhat difficult, and many analyses of data have become difficult to perform or understand because of ignoring them.

[3] Calvin F. Schmid, "Basic Statistical Concepts and Techniques," in Pauline V. Young, *Scientific Social Surveys and Research* (New York: Prentice-Hall, 1949), pp. 291–292.

Summarizing the frequency distribution. There are two general ways of stating a frequency distribution in simple ways. These are used singly and together, depending upon the problem at hand. One of them is to compute a value which represents the *central tendency* of the distributions. Such measures are called averages and include among others the common average, technically known as the *mean;* the *median,* a value such that half the entries in a frequency table fall below and half above it; and the *mode,* or the value represented by the greatest frequency.

The other general type of summary of a frequency distribution includes measures of *dispersion* such as the *standard deviation* and the *coefficient of variation.* These measures are used to compare the relative wideness of spread in any two or more frequency distributions. Their characteristics, applications, and methods of computation can be found in any elementary textbook on statistics and will not be considered here. They are mentioned merely as being widely used ways of summarizing frequency distributions.

Comparing frequencies. A common and simple method of comparing frequencies is the use of the *ratio.* A ratio is merely an indicated or actual quotient which relates the size of one number to another.[4] Their chief utility is to act as a relative measure and thus permit the comparison of otherwise unequal numbers. For example, if we wish to know the relation of the female to the male death rates at various ages, a series of ratios, as shown in the accompanying table, will help. This adds to the knowledge,

Deaths per Thousand Native White Population by Age and Sex in Cities of 100,000 or more, Ohio, 1930 *

Age	Male	Female	Ratio of Male to Female
0–4	17.2	13.6	1.26
5–9	2.4	1.7	1.41
10–14	1.5	1.2	1.25
15–19	2.4	1.9	1.26
45–54	12.3	10.0	1.23
55–64	25.8	19.9	1.30
65–74	59.1	45.9	1.29
75 and over	135.6	114.5	1.18

* Adapted from Warren S. Thompson, *Population Problems* (New York: McGraw-Hill, 1942), p. 228.

shown by the second and third columns, that male death rates are generally higher than female, by showing that this female advantage is constant through life, except for being somewhat larger than usual at ages 5 to 9, and somewhat smaller at ages 75 and over. The figures in column

4 See Margaret Jarman Hagood, *Statistics for Sociologists* (New York: Holt, 1941), pp. 113–115.

four are actual quotients; they could have been expressed as 172 to 136, 24 to 17, 15 to 12, etc., but it is the actual quotients which are most useful since they reduce the right-hand figure to 1 in every case, thus allowing the comparison to be made easily.

A related method of comparing values is the *proportion*. This measure is a fraction such that the numerator is one of two observed frequencies and the denominator the sum of observed frequencies. Thus the previous table could have been expressed as the proportions of all deaths at various ages which were male deaths. Thus the ratios 1.26, 1.41, 1.25, etc., expressed as proportions would read 0.558, 0.585, 0.555, etc. When proportions are expressed in multiples of 100, they are *percentages*. Thus in the above example, 55.8 per cent of all deaths in large Ohio cities in 1930 between ages 0 and 4 were experienced by males, etc. Whether ratios, proportions, or percentages are used in the analysis of data is purely a matter of preference and of the way in which the researcher wishes to communicate his findings.[5]

The purpose of using percentages (and ratios and proportions as well) is to simplify the problem of comparison. It is important, therefore, to see exactly what their use implies so that they will not be misused. First, they can serve to put *qualitative* characteristics into numerical form. Thus it is possible to compare two college classes on the basis of sex by saying that one class is 60 per cent male and the other only 40 per cent. This is a perfectly good comparison, but care must be taken not to translate this statement by saying that one is more *masculine* than the other and thus implying that masculinity is a quantitative characteristic. Such errors in logic are common and easily fallen into, but the consequences may be disastrous.

Second, percentages reduce two frequency distributions to a common base, as was illustrated above, thus making comparisons much simpler. It must be noted, however, that this obscures *absolute* comparisons, and sometimes it is these rather than the relative comparisons which are important. Zeisel gives an example of this problem [6] as shown in the accompanying table. Here the absolute and the relative figures produce ap-

Comparative Growth of Cities M and N, 1941–1946

City	1941	1946	Increase	Percentage Increase
M	1,000,000	1,200,000	200,000	20.0
N	500,000	650,000	150,000	30.0

[5] See *ibid.*, pp. 115–123.
[6] Zeisel, *op. cit.*, p. 77.

parently opposite results. The problem, then, is which is "correct." Did city *M* grow more or less rapidly than city *N?* It is clear that this is a problem in logic. Thus it could be reasoned that, if the growth were "normal," we would expect the larger city to attract more people than the smaller and hence would say the percentages are the "significant" figure. If, on the other hand, the growth of cities depended not upon previous size but other factors such as the addition of new industries, then we might say that the larger city grew faster in the ratio of 200,000 to 150,000, or one and one-third times as fast.

In other words, while percentages are a great aid to communication through simplification, they are also susceptible to misuse by obscuring significant facts. This underlines the importance of never presenting a table of percentages without also showing the actual numbers which they represent. This not only guards against the kind of misinterpretation of the kind described above, but also assures the reader that there is an adequate base for the calculation of a percentage. For example, the statement that three of a total of only four people interviewed favored the Democratic party becomes very misleading in the form "three out of every four" or "75 per cent" of those interviewed favored the Democratic platform.

Bases for computing percentages. When a simple frequency distribution is turned into percentages it is usually for the purpose of making clear the comparisons between the several class intervals. In this case there is seldom a problem as to what the base of the percentages should be. One case, however, in which a difficulty may arise, is where the tabulation includes residual categories, or more than one dimension. An example will show this more clearly. If a sample polled in relation to a bond issue gave the results shown in the accompanying table, there would be a problem of interpretation. Thus if the base for percentaging were taken as the

Responses to Question, "Do You Favor the School Bond
Issue Which Will Be Voted On in November?"

Responses	Number
Yes	97
No	78
Undecided	44
Refuse to Answer	31
Total	250

total sample, those favoring would be reported as 39 per cent; if the base were all *those replying,* the result would be 44 per cent; and if it were taken as *those who would answer and who had made up their minds,* it would be 56 per cent. It is very important, therefore, that the base of a percentage be fully and carefully described to avoid confusion.

The more common problem arises when a cross tabulation is used, for in this case, even though the categories are complete, it is still necessary to make a choice as to whether the percentages should be computed horizontally or vertically. Zeisel gives a general rule which can usually be followed, by stating [7] that *"the percentages should be computed in the direction of the causal factor."* This does not mean that one of the factors *must be* the actual cause of the other, but merely that in the mind of the analyst one of them is thought of as influencing the other. The illustration given by Zeisel makes this clear. First of all, percentages may be calcu-

Deaths from Cancer in the United States by Race

RACE	CAUSE OF DEATH		
	Cancer	All Others	Total
White	139,627	1,055,804	1,195,431
Negro	9,182	169,391	178,573
Total	148,809	1,225,195	1,374,004

lated to either the vertical or the horizontal totals. Thus the figures given in the first of the accompanying tables could be expressed in percentages calculated vertically, so as to appear as shown in the second table. Such

Race	Cancer	All Others	Total
White	93.8	86.2	87.0
Negro	6.2	13.8	13.0
Total	100.0	100.0	100.0

a presentation shows the racial composition of two groups, those dying of cancer and those dying of some other cause. This is a clumsy way of presenting the analysis, since we are not likely to think the cause of death will affect materially the relative number of whites and Negroes. Rather it is more probable that the hypothesis was that for various reasons death accompanied by a diagnosis of cancer is more common for one group than another. Therefore the percentages should be computed horizontally, as shown in the third table. Such an arrangement points directly to the de-

Race	Cancer	All Others	Total
White	11.7	88.3	100.0
Negro	5.1	94.9	100.0
Total	10.7	89.3	100.0

[7] *Ibid.*, p. 88.

sired Negro-white comparison, rather than requiring still further analysis as did the other mode of calculating the percentages.

It will frequently be the case that this "causal principle" will not be applicable as clearly as in the above case. For example, suppose the number of years of school completed were being cross-tabulated with "economic worth" for a series of adults; would higher education be considered as the "cause" of higher economic standing, or vice versa? Clearly it could be viewed either way. The general principle, then, is to compute in the direction of the factor which the analyst wishes to emphasize.

That the analyst's concept of causality or desire for emphasis is not always the sole determiner of the direction in which percentages should be computed, however, is shown by another principle stated by Zeisel.[8] This principle is that percentages should be run *only in the direction in which a sample is representative*. The illustration of this rule deals with the collection of political preferences from a representative sample of 8,000 persons in each of two states, with the results shown in the accompanying table. If these results are analyzed from the point of view that

STATE	FAVOR PARTY		Total
	XX	YY	
A	2,500	5,500	8,000
B	3,500	4,500	8,000

differences between the states are "causal" for differences in party allegiance, then the table would be percentaged horizontally, as shown in the second table. Such results would be "sensible" in showing that party YY

STATE	PERCENTAGE FAVORING PARTY		Total
	XX	YY	
A	31.0	69.0	100.0
B	44.0	56.0	100.0

was in a favorable position in both states, but especially so in state A.

If the original question were reversed, however, and it were hypothesized that the differences in the *parties* rather than the differences in the *states* was the "cause" of the distribution, the percentages would have been calculated vertically, as shown in the third table. If this table were an

8 *Ibid.*, p. 101.

STATE	PERCENTAGE FAVORING PARTY	
	XX	YY
A	42.0	55.0
B	58.0	45.0
Total	100.0	100.0

accurate analysis it would seem to say that 42 per cent of the votes of party XX would come from state A. If it is recalled, however, that the samples were representative of each state and *not* of the two parties, it is clear that these percentages are meaningless. Since we do not know the relative contribution of the two states to the total vote, no such percentages can be meaningful. Therefore where cross tabulations are representative in only one direction, percentages can be computed only in that same direction.

Presenting complex tables. Several examples have been given in which two-dimensional tables or simple cross tabulations have appeared. Often such tables are not adequate for the problem at hand where more than two dimensions must be simultaneously presented. The example of the size of houses given at the beginning of the chapter is a case in point. There it was pointed out that a complete presentation would involve at least six tables placed side by side. It is clear that such a presentation would be exceedingly confusing and thus poses the problem of simplifying the presentation. Suppose we had only three variables to deal with: size of family, size of house, and economic status. Suppose further that we are provided with the data shown in the accompanying table.

The Relation of Size of House to Size of Family, by Economic Status

INCOME	LARGE FAMILIES			MEDIUM FAMILIES			SMALL FAMILIES		
	Small House	Medium House	Large House	Small House	Medium House	Large House	Small House	Medium House	Large House
High	5	35	60	5	70	25	10	60	30
Medium	25	65	20	10	65	25	40	55	5
Low	35	55	10	35	55	10	75	25	0

One way of reducing the table is to remove one variable. Now any dichotomous percentage can be expressed by one figure only, since the second is then determined. If we say 65 per cent of a group are men it is not necessary to state also that 35 per cent are women. Thus if it is possible to turn any of the trichotomous variables into dichotomous ones, the table can be greatly simplified. So suppose the analyst's interest is in

showing the problem of crowding, and he therefore rewords the table title
and reenters the data as shown in the second table.

Percentage of Families of Various Sizes, by Income Groups,
Residing in Small Houses

INCOME	FAMILY SIZE		
	Small	Medium	Large
High	10.0	10.0	5.0
Medium	40.0	10.0	25.0
Low	75.0	30.0	40.0

It would be possible to conclude from these data that income, more
than family size, determined the proportion of small houses occupied.

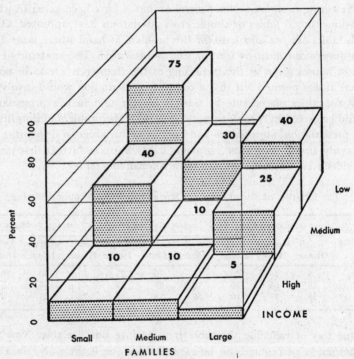

FIGURE 1. Graphic presentation of a trichotomous cross tabulation (income and size
of families) for families living in small houses.

Figure 1 graphically illustrates what such a tabulation actually does to
the data by showing the three-dimensional character of the cross tabulations. However, turning a trichotomy into a dichotomy is difficult and

sometimes obscures the real point. Another method of summarizing the distribution, it will be recalled, is the use of an average. This table, if the values of "small," "medium," and "large" houses are known, can be simplified by the use of an average such as the mean, as shown in the third table.

Average Number of Rooms in Houses for Families of Various Sizes, by Income Groups

INCOME	FAMILY SIZE		
	Small	Medium	Large
High	4.7	4.6	5.7
Medium	3.2	4.5	4.4
Low	2.1	3.4	3.4

Again, the table becomes quite readable. The logic involved should be clear. In both cases the cell entries have been changed from frequencies or percentages, representing every category of the frequency distribution, into *single values,* each *standing for* the entire distribution.

General problems of presenting frequency distributions. This section has been concerned primarily with showing some of the ways of summarizing, simplifying, and presenting frequency distributions. Some of the more common problems have been spelled out and others indicated as belonging to the realm of statistics. With these in mind, the next section turns to some of the logical problems underlying simple analyses by cross tabulation.

LOGICAL ORDERING OF DATA

The cross tabulation of two or more attributes or variables is merely a formal and economical method of arranging the data so that the logical methods of proof may be applied. Thus, the methods of agreement, differences, or concomitant variation (correlation) may all be used in drawing conclusions from a cross tabulation. This should further underline the point made earlier in this chapter, that what can be gained through cross tabulation depends entirely on the logical design of the study and the insightfulness of the investigator. There are no "tricks" of cross tabulation which can guarantee that an analysis will provide the most significant and meaningful results possible.

It is possible, however, to discuss some of the modes of thought which lead to fruitful cross tabulation. First of all, the use of cross tabulation is, in effect, an approximation of the controlled experiment. This means that the analyst is really thinking in terms of cause and effect. That is, he has in mind one or more variables, variation in which can be used to *explain* variation in another variable. These "causal" dimensions are termed *independent variables* and the values to be explained are called *dependent variables*. It is because the analyst is really thinking in causal terms that there is a need for elaborating survey results through cross tabulation. If all that the analyst desires is an empirical statement of concomitant variation, simple cross tabulations will suffice. The need, however, to know the "meaning" of a relationship leads to asking many other questions which can be answered only by introducing other variables into the analysis.

Kendall and Lazarsfeld have given a classification of three types of elaboration which they call *interpretation, explanation,* and *specification.*[9]

Interpretation. This is the process of stratifying a previous cross tabulation by another variable (called a *test variable*) under circumstances such that the test variable has occurred (1) subsequent in time to the independent variable, but (2) prior to the dependent variable. One other requirement is that the test factor be correlated with both independent and dependent variables. Such a procedure allows the further interpretation of an original relationship in terms of a third factor, in this case called an *intervening* variable.

This may be diagrammed as follows:

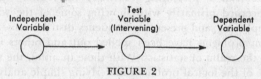

Independent Variable → Test Variable (Intervening) → Dependent Variable

FIGURE 2

For example, when the men students at a private university were cross-tabulated by whether they attended public or private secondary schools and by their university academic records, those attending public schools showed a superior record. On the face of it, such a finding would suggest an explanation of the dependent variable (grades) in terms of the excellence of preparation in the independent variable (public versus private secondary schools). Anyone conversant with the admissions policy of private universities might suspect, however, that events could have occurred between secondary training and acceptance at the university which might give the finding an entirely different meaning.

Thus an intervening variable in terms of excellence of academic work in secondary school could logically be introduced. If there were circumstances in the application procedure which meant that public school graduates had to meet higher academic standards than private school graduates, the original correlation between the type of secondary school and subsequent grades would disappear. In this case, the test factor, high school

[9] Patricia L. Kendall and Paul F. Lazarsfeld, "Problems of Survey Analysis," *Continuities in Social Research,* Robert K. Merton and Paul F. Lazarsfeld, eds. (Glencoe, Ill.: Free Press, 1950). The entire paper is relevant here, but especially pp. 148–158.

record, would serve to interpret the original finding since when men of the *same high school achievement level* are compared, the relation of type of school to undergraduate success would disappear.

Explanation. This is essentially the same kind of reasoning as interpretation in that it seeks to reduce an originally observed correlation through the use of a test factor. In this case, however, the test factor is an *antecedent variable* rather than an intervening variable. In other words, an observed relationship is explained in terms of a third factor which occurred earlier than the independent variable and which is related both to it and the dependent variable.

This may be diagrammed as follows:

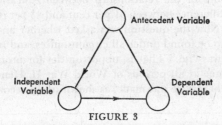

FIGURE 3

For example, a study of birth rates in Puerto Rico produced a cross tabulation which showed a negative correlation between economic status and the birth rate. Both the variables in this case were measures of adult life experience, and since "causal" reasoning was involved, the question was asked as to whether or not there was some variable characterizing the earlier portion of the life history which might "explain" this correlation.

Consequently education was used as an antecedent test variable, with the result that the correlation between economic status and birth rates all but disappeared when cross-tabulated separately for comparable educational levels. In this case, then, the use of a test factor "explained away" an original observation and substituted another for it. We should describe the relationship between economic status and birth rates in Puerto Rico as a *spurious* correlation. This raises the question, "How can we be certain that the relationship between education and birth rates is actually a causal one and not merely another spurious correlation?" The only answer to this is to say that if the application of all known relevant test factors fails to reduce this correlation materially, the assumption of causality can usually be made.

Specification. Whereas in explanation and interpretation the question asked is whether or not the use of a test variable will cause the sharp reduction or disappearance of an observed relationship, the goal of specification is quite different. In this case the "causal" sequence is modified by specifying varying conditions under which the original correlation will exist in greater or lesser intensity. The example given by Kendall and

Lazarsfeld uses the findings from *The American Soldier* [10] shown in the accompanying table.

Educational Level

Rank	High School Graduate or Better	Less than High School Graduate
Non-com.	61.0	43.0
Pvt., Pfc.	39.0	57.0
Total cases	3,222	3,152

A crude measure of the relationship between education and rank is taken to be the difference between 61 per cent and 43 per cent. This value, called f, is 0.18. Now the question was asked whether an f value of 0.18 would be likely to be found under all circumstances, and it seemed logical that the answer was "no." That is, opportunities for promotion may not have been the same at all periods of World War II. Hence a cross tabulation by length of service was made, as shown in the second table.

Rank	Have Served for Less than Two Years		Have Served for Two Years or More	
	High School Graduate or Better	Less than High School Graduate	High School Graduate or Better	Less than High School Graduate
Non-com.	23.0	17.0	74.0	53.0
Pvt., Pfc.	77.0	83.0	26.0	47.0
Total cases	842	823	2,380	2,329
	$f = 0.06$		$f = 0.21$	

Since the f's are quite different for the two length-of-service categories, the analyst can now state that the relation between education and rank is greater for those who entered the Army early than for those who entered it later.

Specification, then, is the process of describing the conditions under which a particular relationship may exist or not exist, or may exist to a greater or lesser degree. Like explanation and interpretation, therefore, it makes any "causal" analyses more acceptable and meaningful.

General aspects of elaboration. There seem to be two major problems with respect to this aspect of analysis. The applications of test factors in

10 *Ibid.*, pp. 163–164.

the three preceding paragraphs doubtless seem simple enough. The two practical problems, however, are (1) whether or not to elaborate, and (2) what test variables to apply.

With respect to the first problem it can be pointed out that unexpected consequences may impel the analyst to elaborate. If the findings conform to anticipation, there is little stimulus for further analysis. This is a somewhat dangerous situation, for it may result in the acceptance of spurious or uninterpreted relationships. As Kendall and Lazarsfeld put it:

"Our first concern is whether or not the relationship is a spurious one; consequently our initial efforts of elaboration are usually of the explanatory type. Once we have gained some assurance that the original relationship is not a spurious one, we try to interpret the result or to specify it.[11] We ask ourselves what variables might provide the links between the 'cause' and the 'effect,' or what conditions might show the original relationship to be even more pronounced than we originally saw it to be. The elaboration of a particular result can go on almost indefinitely. We are limited only by our lack of ingenuity in thinking of factors by which to elaborate the result, by the absence of data to check the relevance of factors which we have thought of, or by the difficulties of dealing with few cases as the process of elaboration is extended."

Elaboration, therefore, is a process which is limited only by the analyst, on the one hand: his ability, his patience, and his purposes; and, on the other hand, by the nature of his data.

Unfortunately, it is not possible to give concise directions for selecting the factors to be used as test variables. It should be recalled that the selection of every test variable actually constitutes the formation of a hypothesis which can be tested by the data at hand. Therefore all the materials in the chapters on hypotheses and experimental design will apply here.

In other words, the ingenuity of the analyst coupled with his knowledge of the field in which he is working will be the major source of test variables. Two methods of inducing such hypotheses, however, may be mentioned. First, it would be possible in some studies to cross-tabulate routinely every factor with every other factor. In practice this is usually clumsy and the number can be cut down substantially by reference to existing theory. In any case, wide ranges of cross tabulations will often suggest the selection of test variables. Second, the study of deviant cases will also often indicate the kind of interpretation, explanation, or specification which will improve the analysis.

In the most general sense it must be said that the whole process of analysis is not so much a matter of manipulative techniques as it is of the

[11] We must stress that the failure of one antecedent test factor to disqualify the causal connection between two variables is in no way a definitive demonstration of that causal relationship.

rigorous application of the basic principles of scientific method. The research worker who is fully acquainted with the problems of *designing* research will have fewer troubles in *analyzing* his data.

SUGGESTED READINGS

Jahoda, Marie, Morton Deutsch, and Stuart W. Cook, *Research Methods in Social Relations* (New York: Dryden, 1951), Part I, pp. 276–295.

Kendall, Patricia, *Psychological Factors Affecting Stability of Response,* Ph.D. thesis, Columbia University, 1951.

Lazarsfeld, Paul F., "The Statistical Analysis of Reasons as a Research Operation," *Sociometry,* Vol. 5 (1942), pp. 29–47.

Parten, Mildred, *Surveys, Polls, and Samples: Practical Procedures* (New York: Harper, 1950), Chap. 15.

Schmid, Calvin F., "Basic Statistical Concepts and Techniques," in Pauline V. Young, *Scientific Social Surveys and Research* (New York: Prentice-Hall, 1949), Chap. 13.

Zeisel, Hans, *Say It with Figures* (New York: Harper, 1947), 2d ed.

CHAPTER 21

Preparing the Report

Although the research process itself is often fascinating, sooner or later it will be necessary to complete the study report. Other time commitments of the scientist or beginning student demand that the investigation be ended. Further analysis of the data seems unrewarding. Further, at times the materials which have been developed may appear so interesting that the researcher wishes to share them with other people. Finally, all those who have contributed to the study in the form of money, advice and help, or time will want to "see how it all came out." The preparation of the report is, then, the final stage of the research, and its purpose is "to convey to interested persons the whole result of the study, in sufficient detail and so arranged as to enable each reader to comprehend the data and to determine for himself the validity of the conclusions." [1]

It seems clear that a report could be simple to write, since it is merely an exposition of the question asked, the techniques used to answer it, and the answers which were finally developed. Actually, it is rarely so. Instead, the entire research grows in many directions. Some parts of the research design must be changed, while others will be dropped. Many more facts seem to be needed than was originally supposed and many questions turn out not to have any simple answers. Neither positive nor negative, many of our answers must be placed in the "doubtful" category.

Nevertheless, even a research project which has errors in it may be useful for other investigators, since it will warn them of dangers which might be avoided by additional thought. Moreover, it is likely that the research of which the student has despaired because of its patent errors will nevertheless have some worth-while data in it. The present chapter, then, offers several suggestions and reminders which may aid the student somewhat in preparing his research report.

Nature of the problem. As with so many practical problems of living, the principles of report writing are easier to draw up than to follow. As a consequence, drawing them up may serve little purpose here. If the student is a careful reader, he will already have found many errors in the

[1] American Marketing Society, *Technique of Marketing Research* (New York: McGraw-Hill, 1937), p. 299.

359

sociological works he has studied. Many sentences are unclear, and some-times there is no apparent development of any main line of thought. Crucial data are omitted, and at times the tables of data do not demon-strate the conclusions offered. Although the student may feel that such errors can always be avoided by "following the rules," he will find that his own attempts at report writing are worse in these regards.

Naturally, carelessness and accident play a role in this situation. How-ever, there are other factors which should be noted, in order that the student may more easily develop a good presentation. Perhaps primary among these factors is the lack of a commonly accepted conceptual system in the field. This is partly a linguistic matter. Obviously, to the extent that concepts differ in meaning, communication will be difficult. How-ever, mere linguistic confusion is not the crux of the problem. Rather, the lack of a clear system of abstraction means that we cannot indicate quickly and easily just how much knowledge is to be assumed and how much is to be presented.

The student can make the comparison easily by looking at a standard journal in the physical sciences, and a standard sociological journal. In the former, the scientist can assume a great amount of technical knowl-edge on the part of the reader, and a few references to the specific research problem identify it clearly. The problem can be identified easily because it occupies a definite place in the existing theoretical and conceptual structure. The sociologist, on the other hand, must write many pages attempting to identify his problem and the level of abstraction at which he is attacking it, as well as to sketch many of the facts which are necessary to orient the casual reader.

Note, however, that to the extent that the problem itself is not clearly identified, the writer must either risk confusion or write in tedious detail everything about the study which might be of interest to other social scientists with somewhat different definitions of the general problem.

The lack of a systematically abstract theoretical structure is merely an index of the youth of the science. This also means, however, that both laymen and social scientists are expected to be able to read the report. Most sociologists, then, are very sensitive to the criticism that they have used difficult words or that their data are tedious. As the science grows, of course, this sensitivity will decrease, since it will be taken for granted that the sociologist has a technical vocabulary. A scientific report is likely to be written for scientists, and to deal with matters which he understands well enough to require no more than a few words of explanation. At the present time, however, most monographs in sociology are also written for the intelligent layman, and considerable effort is expended toward drama-tizing case histories, omitting footnotes or placing them where they are difficult to consult (so as not to frighten off the potential buyer), or em-phasizing the moral aspects of the study rather than its factual aspects.

There are, then, pressures toward popularizing sociological reports. No argument is required for the need of making scientific data known to the public. It is necessary, on the other hand, to avoid confusing the two audiences. Further, and more important for the present discussion, this fact means that the sociologist is tempted to write with an eye more toward style than clarity, drama than facts, and persuasiveness than incisiveness.

One further result is that since the writer of the report cannot easily indicate the level of abstractions he is using, the report seems empty or lifeless without including anecdotal and other material that is irrelevant to the theoretical problem being attacked, or to the problem of proof.

What is obvious, then, is that the writing of a report can be difficult, and that there are added difficulties in the case of a sociological report. Let us now attempt to look at some of the individual problems in turn.

Who is the audience? This problem has already been suggested, and it is necessary to comment only that the process of communication requires some definition of hearer and speaker. The social scientist, like the *avant-garde* literary man, is likely to think that when he has understood his substantive problem, the audience must come to him on his own terms. If the scientist has made a superlative contribution, this may indeed occur. However, failure to recognize the audience may mean that the scientist has no listeners for a long period after publication, or must engage in useless polemics occasioned by the failure to communicate.

Of course, a basic distinction must be whether it is important to have the audience know *how* the study was done. It is this item, and not the difficulty of language, which distinguishes the scientific from the lay audience.

The scientist is most interested in facts which have been established by good techniques. However, even when this is not the case, the report may be useful if the techniques themselves can be seen clearly. Their usefulness or their weaknesses can then be judged. Similarly, it is possible to judge the worth of the facts.

Within the field itself, it must be clear that the report must contain considerably more details regarding techniques or the general theoretical approach being used, when they *deviate* considerably from current practice. In this case, the fellow scientist may be a layman to some extent. Here again, the problem is not vocabulary in the usual sense, but a lack of knowledge about how the reporting scientist came to his conclusions. In short, the report must tell others how to repeat the investigation, since it is only by fairly exact repetition that facts can be adequately established.

Of course, in this book we have assumed that primary interest is in the scientific audience. However, the materials which sociology investigates have wide appeal, and as a consequence the researcher may at times have a popular audience. In addition, considerable commercial research, such as marketing studies, analyses of social patterns in factories, investigations of the effect of radio or television programs, etc., will also have an essentially lay audience. Finally, much research is "action research," *i.e.*, it is part of a program aimed at changing existing conditions, whether slum conditions, race tensions and prejudice, or the effectiveness of an organization. Here, too, the audience is lay, but there are special problems in writing reports for such a group.[2] In action research, the report is usually made to a small group, some of whom are specialists in their respective fields, while they are laymen with regard to the particular study. On the other hand, since they are to implement or reject the recommendations of the report, special attention must be given to persuading the group.

The research report is not usually presented to the popular lay audience, since this task is taken over by journalists. Few social scientists are able to communicate to such a public, partly because in the process much of his achievement is simplified, dramatized, and even presented as banal, and the scientist himself shrinks from the task.

However, the increasing use of research by lay audiences means that the social scientist must begin to settle some of the professional and ethical problems which are thereby raised. If the scientist fails to give his colleagues a clear and adequate description of his research operations, or if he fails to test his conclusions, his work will be open to attack. If others fail to come to his conclusions, the reason for this situation will be discovered. There is, then, a self-corrective process in reporting to one's colleagues. However, the lay audience is not similarly protected. For example, the fact that all science operates in terms of probabilities is not well understood, and as a consequence the problems of sampling are only beginning to be recognized. It follows, then, that anyone can appoint himself as a "survey expert." While in most cases the result may be no more than spurious advertising claims, in other areas the results may be more far reaching.

It is precisely because so much of sociology is close to common experience that the popular audience is a problem. Although the physicist may be annoyed at the newspaper publication of errors regarding nuclear reactions, such errors do not usually change social action. On the other hand, the popularization of reports on bilingualism as a supposed factor in mental retardation, on juvenile delinquency among ethnic or racial groups, or the supposed "overbreeding of the unfit" may lead to definite changes in social and even legal action. The qualifications on any research are omitted, the problems of sampling are usually ignored, the statistical tests of significance of differences are dropped, and the original study becomes propaganda.

[2] For various cases of this kind, see Marie Jahoda, Morton Deutsch, and Stuart W. Cook, *Research Methods in Social Relations* (New York: Dryden, 1951), Vol. 2, esp. Chap. 10.

The implications which are involved can only be noted here, as a set of problems to be solved. The writer of the report certainly has the obligation to include the operations which led to the conclusions. He would also seem to incur the obligation, if he allows his study to be popularized, of following the study through publication, so that he may correct erroneous interpretations of his results. It is very likely that the journalist is unwilling to put as great a strain upon public understanding as might be possible, and he may actually exaggerate the difficulty of explaining at least some of the simple but useful qualifications on the research conclusions. In any event, the scientist has not discharged his duty when he has drawn up the scientific report, if he has also agreed to its being published in a popular form. He owes a duty to science as a profession, to his colleagues, and to society, to prevent if possible the distortion of his work.

The basic outline. After the student has made his tabulations and systematized his observations, he will have a fairly clear idea as to the accuracy of his original hypotheses. The application of tests of significance will tell him to what extent he may rely upon his conclusions. Although he will by that time have a *mental* outline of his report, it is useful to draw up a *formal* outline of the entire paper before he begins to write.

Usually, the work can be done more efficiently if a sentence outline rather than a topical outline is prepared. That is, instead of merely *noting the topics* and subtopics to be touched upon, it should be possible actually to *write out the statements* which are to be expanded in the report itself. This requires more thought, since it is then necessary to know what one is going to say and not merely the various topics one is going to touch.

A brief excerpt from a sentence outline might be the following:

I. The term "applied research" implies a false dichotomy
  A. Research has many dimensions, but they are along other continua than "applied-theoretical":
    1. Are the implications of it great or small for the field, or other fields?
    2. How abstract?
    3. How manipulable are the controls used?
      a. In *ex post facto* research we manipulate symbols
      b. When we seek to implement values in action, we may be unable to manipulate many variables
    4. There is careless and careful research
  B. Therefore, if the study is really research, its scientific value does not stem from its being "applied"

Obviously, it is more difficult to write such an outline than a topical outline, since we are thus required to have a clear idea of our major statements. It is equally obvious, however, that such a report almost "writes itself" if it is based upon such an outline. Since it is much easier to change the outline than to change the rough draft of the paper, it is actually more efficient to write a sentence outline before attempting the more detailed draft.

After the first attempt at an outline has been made, the student should then study it carefully. Since the report represents a considerable amount of work whether the study is poor or excellent, an effort should be made to see that whatever it actually contains is presented well. One aid toward this end is a series of reminders such as the following:

1. Have you made your hypothesis explicit? Often the problem has many ramifications, each of them interesting, and it is difficult to discipline oneself enough to subordinate the minor to the major propositions. Yet the reader will not have had your experience, and he will find the presentation puzzling unless it is clear just what the report attempts to prove.

2. Have you given the observational and reading background which led to the hypothesis? No matter what the origin of the hypothesis, its justification must be intellectual. This discussion will inform the reader just why the hypothesis seems reasonable in the first place. This means, further, that the reader should be shown the connection between this hypothesis and existing theory on the subject. Since the major purpose is likely to be a proof of one hypothesis as against another, for the purpose of developing a better theoretical system, this explanation will help the reader place the study in its proper context. Giving the intellectual background of the project will aid in its being understood as a whole.

3. Have the problems and hypotheses been stated in scientific terms? As noted elsewhere in this chapter, this does not mean that the writer should use complex and esoteric language. Rather, the writer should not attempt to develop his own terminology, peculiar to himself, but should utilize existing terms if they are clear enough. Further, this means that the writer should clearly label his own values and ideals, and keep such statements at least intellectually separated from the description of phenomena. Polemics are, of course, much easier to write than straightforward analyses, just as obscure or literary language is easier to write. Nevertheless, the concepts and the descriptions should represent an attempt to demonstrate, not merely persuade. Of course, if the existing terminology is believed to be confused or useless, the paper may try to clarify existing usage.

4. Has the plan of the research been presented in detail, so that its logic is apparent? Scientific writing allows the reader to know what actually took place and not what the researcher hoped would take place. There are disasters and disappointments in research, and particularly in sociology the paper plan may deviate from the actuality. However, it is not merely honesty that dictates a full report. It is a measure of self-protection. Sooner or later, the study may be repeated by someone, and the resulting data will show that the earlier study was not reported correctly. Thus, it

is necessary to present both the plan as originally drawn up, with its underlying logic of proof, and the plan as it was realized during the course
of the work. If the development of indexes or scales was attempted, the
technique for developing them should be indicated. If various data sources
were used, the way in which they were integrated must be outlined. Obviously, not every operation need be reported, but enough must be given
so that a competent reader can judge the merit of the resulting conclusions. In showing how the plan of the research was carried out, the simplest
mode of exposition is to describe it chronologically, from the development
of the schedule to the analyses of the observations and tabulations, but it
may also be presented under such headings as "schedule," "field interviewing," etc.

5. Have the various subpropositions been derived from and tied to the
observations and tabulations which are in the report? The report is actually a summary of the total research. There are always more data than
can be presented. Some of these only suggest the correctness of a given
proposition. Others are relevant to it, but do not yield proof at all. Other
data actually prove the proposition, but have many other implications as
well. The writer should, then, be certain that the data he has selected are
the best for the purpose. Although this is an obvious point, the researcher
sometimes "sees" in the report many data which he possesses but has
actually failed to include. Consequently, after the outline or draft is in
rough form, it is useful to check once more to be certain that the necessary data have actually been used for the propositions stated.

6. Does the summary really summarize, and point to further research?
Perhaps the best way to ensure that the summary actually contains the
essence of the report is to write it directly from the outline. In writing a
summary, there is often a temptation to claim more than was performed.
This occurs because the researcher always finds many "suggestive" data,
and sees far more uniformities than the project itself could demonstrate.
However, it is wiser to frame such suggestions as ideas for future research.
If the research actually represents a link in the cumulative growth of
science, then the study does point to the future. The summary carries
knowledge on the particular point through the contribution made by this
research, and the next hypotheses to be tested can then be stated.

The use of scientific language. One of the most common complaints
made against sociological reports is that they are difficult to read. For
example, Samuel T. Williamson complains of the social scientists whose
work he has had to edit, and comments further: [8]

"I am not picking on my little group of social scientists . . . ; they are so used
to taking in each other's literary wash that it has become a habit for them to

[8] Samuel T. Williamson, "How to Write Like a Social Scientist," *Saturday Review of
Literature,* Vol. XXX (1947), p. 21.

clothe their thoughts in the same smothering garments. Nor are they worse than most of their colleagues. . . ."

A good example of the kind of writing he objects to is the following sentence, taken from an important work of a major sociologist:

"These concepts can hold only for ranges of variation of circumstances not too large to invalidate the assumption that for practical purposes the particular constant relations between the values of analytical elements which these type concepts in the concrete case represent, will not be so unreal as to exceed an acceptable margin of error."

Very likely, it is possible to find unclear writing in the works of most sociologists. It seems probable, although the data are not at present available, that there is more unclear writing in sociology than in the natural sciences.

Such charges are often denied by an insistence that the social sciences, and sociology in particular, are sometimes difficult to understand because the scientist must use a technical language. He must develop a set of concepts with scientific definitions. In the earlier chapter on the use of concepts, we have pointed out that there is no reason why the lay reader should find such concepts easy to understand. To the extent that they represent the shared experience of scientists, and this experience is different from ordinary experience, the layman would of course find scientific language obscure, unreal, or complex. However, there is some justice to the claim that the failure of the social scientist to communicate easily is not due to his use of abstract and technical terms, but to his failure to master *nontechnical* language.

Sociology has grown from a literary and philosophical tradition, and those who are now writing have usually studied that tradition, at least as graduate students. Since actual research has only recently become a usual experience in graduate training, the first papers of most social scientists have been concerned with conceptual and theoretical analysis. Patterns of language are thus learned which are difficult to destroy. These patterns may often continue, therefore, even when the subject matter no longer demands such linguistic virtuosity.

Clarity of language, in any event, is hard won. The student is rare who presents his research materials in a straightforward way. This is not the place to teach the student how to write clearly, and indeed there are teachers of English who despair of the possibility. All that can be stated here is that one consequence of obscure writing is that the report is not understood or is not well received. And perhaps the best safeguard is simply to write genuine rough drafts which are to be shown to others. It will usually be discovered that the fine literary style, so consciously sought, is felt by others to be coy. The pounding epigrams will very likely seem to be forced, mechanical, or similar to advertising copy. The subtle points of conceptual analysis will appear to be deliberate obscurantism. What this means, often, is that the reader of a scientific report usually resents the intrusion of the writer's personality. If there is genuine originality, the study itself will show this. On the other hand, no amount of verbal play will substitute for it, and the best time to discover obscurity is before the final draft has been written.

Mechanical aids to clear presentation. Although the best guarantee of a good report is a well-organized study, there are common aids to clarity which deserve mention. These are well known, but the reasons for their use should also be noted.

1. FOOTNOTES. The student is likely to look upon footnotes with some annoyance, and upon rules for footnote style with even more. However, the latter source of annoyance can be easily dispelled by following some standard manual of style, of which the *Manual of Style* published by the University of Chicago is a good example. As to the general antipathy to footnotes which simply quote or cite books, it is frequently misplaced. It is true that they can be manufactured easily and that they may distract the reader from the significant to the irrelevant. However, they have remained part of the scientific and scholarly tradition for good reason.

Footnotes serve the primary function of giving credit to those who have preceded the writer in attacking a given problem. Every scientific advance is made on the basis of previous work, and in a real sense footnotes are the deference we pay to our intellectual forebears.

In addition, however, they serve the further function of informing the reader just how we are attacking the problem, and just what kind of problem it is. That is, we cite previous, related works, and thereby indicate the larger context of our problem. We not only warn the reader that the problem has many ramifications, but we also tell him where to learn more about it.

Most important, however, is the use of the footnote to distinguish our own contribution from that of previous researchers. When the writer of a monograph fails to give footnote citations for the ideas or facts expressed, he thereby serves notice to his readers that everything in the monograph is new and original—or nothing is. Since such complete originality is highly unlikely, the reader is forced to look for the sources himself. After he has found many of them, he may grow skeptical of the rest of the monograph. Thus it happens that the practice of giving footnote credit actually protects the writer from attack. On the other hand, by thus distinguishing the contribution by others, the genuine contribution of the report is likewise seen more clearly. The writer will show that the work of previous workers carries the problem up to a certain point, at which his own study began. His addition to knowledge is then difficult to question.

2. SUBHEADINGS. Another mechanical aid to clarity is the use of many subheadings in order to call the attention of the reader to the materials being presented and to their organization. Its basic service to the writer is that he is better able to see his own errors. It is difficult to find the points of organization in a paper of 50 to 100 pages if there are few or no headings in it. Since few people can remember the total pattern, all that the reader notes is whether paragraphs relate to one another.

With detailed subheadings, however, even the casual reader can see the organization, and a friendly critic can help the writer repair the damage before it is too late. Furthermore, the reader is not led to expect more than the report will give, if these headings are fairly specific. The student is likely to give a broad title to his first research paper, and indeed this is difficult to avoid, since an accurate descriptive title will be long and repelling (*e.g.*, "Some Aspects of Television Viewing among Certain Nonrandomly Selected Families in Neighborhood *X* at Period *Y* . . ."). However, by breaking the presentation into smaller units with limited headings, the limitations of the paper can be seen. Frequent reference to the fact of the basic organization in the paper will alert the reader to grasp it. The use of clear headings will force the writer himself to stay within the organization. Finally, rewriting is considerably easier when this rule is followed, since it is possible to delete sections or to recombine and expand others, without destroying the basic plan of the report.

3. MAPS, CHARTS, GRAPHS, ETC. These are basic aids in translating complex statistical tabulations into a form which can be easily grasped. Of course, they may also serve to prove the conclusions being reached. For example, the map is sometimes used in ecological analysis to show the position of natural barriers, the flow of commerce or traffic, etc. The graph is one of the most common devices for proving a trend.

However, we should keep clearly in mind that even in most ecological analysis our final proof is likely to be in the statistical analysis of our tabulated data. Graphs which show a trend can be most accurately described by mathematical equations. Bar, "pie," or picture charts only crudely represent the data which they represent. On the other hand, such aids not only present the data in a readable form but also help the reader to understand the more complex tabulations which are given. For example, the common bar chart is often used to compare two groups with respect to some characteristic. This clear comparison may then be used in the report to call attention to the cross-tabulation cells in which those groups fall—and to point to *other* comparisons in the same cross tabulation. This is especially useful when a series of bar charts is not thought to be necessary. These common aids to clarity of presentation are well known to the student and need no further discussion. When the final report is being planned, however, it may be useful to look at a statistics textbook or a manual on graphic presentation for suggestions as to the range of such aids available, and as to the details of technique.[4]

Presentation of technical details. If the student will peruse several technical journals in various scientific fields, he will discover that most of the articles seem to give few details of the experiment. This will be as true of sociology as it is of chemistry. Nevertheless, a report cannot omit such details without good reason. In most reports, a few brief phrases will suffice to describe the techniques, for those used are well known. The scientist need only refer to the procedure used, with perhaps a citation to an earlier, detailed exposition of the technique.

In sociology, such references are likely to be more adequate for sampling and statistical procedures than for observation and interviewing. Of course, as the former techniques become standard in the field, there is less need to cite any original description of them. At the present time, however, it is necessary to explain the sampling technique, for some writers are not careful to use the term "random" in a technical sense. Sometimes, it may mean only that the investigator is not aware of any bias. Often, unfortunately, it means that the researcher has "checked" his resulting sample by such categories as age, sex, etc., and has found that it is "representative" of the total population (not always the universe which it is supposed to represent). As a consequence, additional explanation may be necessary, so that the reader can see clearly that the researcher understands the technical meaning of "random," and actually used a design for a random sample.

On the other hand, with reference to observation and interviewing, neither the techniques themselves nor knowledge about the techniques are sufficiently standardized. As a consequence, a report of research which utilized participant observation would give as much information as possible concerning the entrance into the group, which group members knew that the investigator was an outsider, how records were made, etc. Nevertheless, we would still not have enough information about the impact of the investigator upon the group. Until the technique is better standardized, this will remain the case. With reference to interviewing, we do have somewhat more information, and a discussion of the technique would indicate the amount of training the interviewers received, and the type of training; the age, sex, and other relevant characteristics of interviewers; the type of interview; special devices used; etc.

Of course, not all the information may be presented in any one report. Preliminary data may be published, when they are of particular interest. What is important, as a general rule, is that the details be given if a technical problem is to be discussed at all. A partial report may delete,

4 See Herbert Arkin and Raymond R. Colton, *Graphs, How to Make and Use Them* (New York: Harper, 1940), rev. ed.; or American Society of Mechanical Engineers, *Engineering and Scientific Graphs for Publications* (New York: 1943).

as being of little interest to the audience, the difficulties encountered in the interviewing stage. However, in that case, it is better practice to avoid much discussion of interviewing at all. Instead, reference should be made to later reports which will contain the details, or to a complete appendix which will deal with all the research operations.

What is typical? A minor problem in the presentation of a report occurs when the writer wishes to illustrate either a summary observation or a statistic. This may be a problem of synthesis or of abstraction. The researcher may wish to synthesize a case history, an interview, or a description of an individual family from his records. After tabulating all his data, he knows what a "typical" case is. On the other hand, he may have few or no cases which are like this "typical" case in all respects. Furthermore, he may fear that data from a real case would be identifiable. As a consequence, he may attempt to bring together the data from several cases. Most textbooks in the field of social disorganization contain numerous interviews or case histories of this kind.

In other cases, some item is to be abstracted from a larger interview or history in order to illustrate a more general proposition or even to show that the general statement is a cautious one. For example, Whyte comments that almost everyone in Cornerville played the numbers. He illustrates this statement by a preceding statement from Doc that he had too little money even to play the numbers: "When a Cornerville fellow doesn't have the money to put on a number, then you know he's really batted out. Put that in your book." [5]

Such individual excerpts, as well as longer, synthesized interviews, give an apparent reality to the less exciting tabulations or general statements. They seem to furnish a kind of peephole into these people's lives. Furthermore, they persuade us. If they are pertinent, well-phrased comments, they have a ring of authenticity which statistical data rarely have. Finally, when most of the data in a study have been obtained from participant or quasi-participant observation and informal interviewing (as in *Street Corner Society*), such synthesized interviews or abstracted excerpts may constitute the main body of "proof" which the researcher can offer in the published study.

In view of these obvious advantages, there can be no criticism against the judicious use of such illustrations. However, the persuasiveness of the illustrations or the drama of the case must not confuse the writer into believing that they are adequate proof of the conclusions presented. The writer can make an easy test of this confusion: clip pieces of paper over all the "live" material, and read the report through once again. If the data continue to prove the conclusions, then these live materials

[5] William F. Whyte, *Street Corner Society* (Chicago: University of Chicago Press, 1943), p. 115.

contribute no more than they are supposed to contribute, *i.e.*, illustrative materials.

The fundamental queries, then, are (1) whether the materials merely illustrate, and (2) in what sense they can be thought of as typical. When we read over our interviews, we are tempted to select those with the most quotable phrases, or the most dramatic incidents. If we synthesize a typical interview or case history, it is likely to illustrate our latent literary wishes rather than the data. It is necessary, as a consequence, to compare with great caution our tabulations and our illustrations.

Scope of the study. The limitations of the study should be explained to the reader. An explicit statement of this kind not only gives an important datum to the reader but also protects the researcher from obvious criticism and from his own indiscretion. As the investigator masters his research data in any project, he begins to see clearly many relationships which cannot be proved by the data at hand. Although his data refer to one class group, he believes that he knows how other strata act. He has data on the behavior of divorcees, but he is certain that cases of desertion are similar. He has studied rural neighboring patterns in Louisiana, but he "knows" that they are the same in central Pennsylvania. If, however, he states that his data actually refer only to the more limited set of cases, he serves notice on himself as well as others that such extrapolations are unwarranted.

A description of the sampling design is particularly important in a statement of the limitations on the study, because good sampling practice is not always followed at the present time. Often, the data will be useful or worth reporting, even when the sampling practice was not entirely satisfactory, but the reader must be allowed to know the facts.

"Scope" includes more than a mere designation of the population being studied, however. It must also include the level of generality of the study. Although many studies represent a "contribution to the theory of functionalism," the reader should be informed at an early point in the report that the contribution is actually a study of the percentage of apartment-house superintendents who receive Christmas gifts from the tenants. If the reporter seriously believes his study makes a contribution of high generality, then the line of reasoning being followed must be clearly presented. As a rule, the research does have implications beyond the immediate data, since it was designed with that notion, but these implications must be stated.

Finally, the study may end with some suggestions for future research, or a statement of further problems which were uncovered by the investigation. It is worth commenting that this is not merely a ritual gesture. It is also a way of stating how far the data have actually carried the problems being investigated, thus once more indicating the limitations of the investigation.

The use of statistics. "Scope of the study" is particularly relevant to a discussion of the use of statistics, since the student is likely to fall into a very obvious trap when he attempts to use his own data in statistical analyses. In the usual statistics textbooks, he will have learned some of the elementary statistical operations, such as the arithmetic mean, the standard deviation, and simple correlations. However, the mechanical application of such operations may obscure the fact that the data themselves are not reliable. If the student carries out his own research project, it is likely that it will not be satisfactory in important respects. This is not cause for dejection, since the beginner must expect some failures. However, when he outlines on paper the research procedure followed, he may become aware that a correlation would be meaningless, since the sample itself has unknown biases and is not normally distributed. Similarly, tabulations of poorly phrased questions may have little significance.

The student may decide to carry out various statistical operations in this case, but he must understand that these do not change the underlying design of the study. No amount of refinement will remedy such weaknesses. We must remember in this connection, consequently, that in writing the report such qualifications of the apparent meaning of the statistical computations must be openly stated.

However, the research report should also present the *statistical* limitations on the analyses. These limitations are discussed in elementary statistics, but it is good to cite a few examples here. As an illustration, it is common to use the arithmetic mean to express the average for any group. However, the student should remember that a few extreme cases will bias sharply such an average, and in the resulting analysis it may be useful to note this fact, while presenting the mode or median for comparison.

Similarly, if percentages are used it is important to present the bases on which the percentages have been calculated. Not only does this allow the reader to check the writer's computations, but it is thereby also easier for the reader to keep in mind the scope of the comparisons being made and to make at least a rough guess as to the statistical reliability of the sample used.

The use of samples means that we can never be sure that our data represent our universe exactly. It is for this reason that the measurement of standard error is suggested as an elementary but useful computation. Similarly, when differences between groups are shown, it is important to test the statistical significance of these differences. The operations are relatively simple, but they serve to protect the writer against improper claims. And, in both these expressed limitations, it must be kept in mind that we are speaking of probabilities. We cannot know how close our data are to the universe parameters. If we did, then we would know the data for the universe. It is an error, then, to say that our mean has 95 chances in 100 of being 3.5 units from the universe measure, unless we are merely using such a phrase for the sake of verbal simplicity.

Our measure merely gives us some judgment about the stability of our answers over repeated investigations of the same kind.

Another limitation ought to be mentioned, since it is frequently overlooked by the student who has mastered these elementary computations. Although a difference is "statistically significant," it may nevertheless be of little importance for the research. When a measurement of a racial attitude, for example, shows that two groups differ by only one or two percentage points, it is likely that for any purposes of prediction the difference is insignificant, no matter how statistically significant the answer is. Such measures deal with the reliability, or the stability, of answers, and tell us nothing about their theoretical importance.

The problem of statistical limitations becomes more complex when the report is meant for relatively wide circulation. As Doob has commented, with respect to the pollsters,[6]

"At the same time, polling organizations are in a dilemma. If they present results cautiously and accurately, their releases may be dull and lacking in news value. If their releases are dramatic and newsworthy, on the other hand, they may sacrifice caution and accuracy."

As he notes later, most of the polling releases of 1948 failed to note the limitations which the use of a sample imposes upon any tabulations. As was noted earlier in this chapter, until popular audiences have come to understand better the problems of sampling, this problem will not be solved. Many of the governmental releases, such as Sample Surveys, do attempt to present such limits of error, but in general these are technical releases and used by a technical audience.

In any event, the writer of the report must show by his statistical operations the probabilities yielded by his sample.

This is particularly important in the analysis of cross tabulations. If we begin distributing a sample of 400 into several levels of categories, they are quickly exhausted. As the student will discover by an examination of Kinsey's tables, it is difficult to fill all these cells even with a sample of over 5,000.[7] In a simple tabulation, this point is not important, since we are only interested in the relationship of *one* cell to the *entire* distribution. However, when we begin to compare the differences between one subcell and another in a complex cross tabulation, the absolute number in each cell is important. Since the temptation is often to accept differences between such cells as being significant, it is useful to check

[6] Leonard W. Doob, "The Public Presentation of Polling Results" in Frederick Mosteller *et al.*, *The Pre-election Polls of 1948*, Social Science Research Council Bulletin No. 60, 1949, p. 30.

[7] A. C. Kinsey, W. B. Pomeroy, and C. E. Martin, *Sexual Behavior in the Human Male* (Philadelphia: Saunders, 1948).

this temptation by a simple statistical computation. An ordinary test of significance of differences will usually show that these cells are not worth comparing.

What the student should keep clearly in mind is that no great statistical sophistication is required to avoid most of the improper uses of statistical tabulations. However, considerable self-control may be needed in order to force oneself to test the "obvious" facts of a tabulation against the simple computations needed. It is only then that the reader can know how far he can trust the conclusions which are being presented.

Perhaps a final point is in order here, especially relevant when the research is to be used for action purposes, whether slum clearance or a new selling campaign. Since all research conclusions are based upon probabilities, the question may arise, just how accurate should the data be? With what margins of error should the statistics be accepted? The answer must be found in the type of analysis called *quality control,* which is a standard body of techniques for calculating the margins of tolerance for rejecting or accepting an individual product as it comes from the factory. This matter is discussed in analyses of research design or statistics under the heading of the *null hypothesis.*

The general principle must be sought in the *consequences* which follow from rejection or acceptance of the conclusions.[8] For example, if a parole-prediction index is developed and applied, obviously it will reject some individuals who are really good risks, and it will permit some to be paroled who are not good risks. Similarly, a marketing study which compares the buying habits of different groups may err by showing them to be different when they are really the same, or the same when they are really different. In short, the fact that we work with probabilities means that we can err in either direction.

We see, however, that errors in different directions may have quite different consequences. *How* we weigh such consequences may depend upon how intense our values are concerning any problem, but it is clear that we must at least be aware of these differences. To use a simple manufacturing case, if the manager allows some matches to be sold which will not light, the consequence will usually be that a smoker is frustrated or annoyed. On the other hand, the druggist who used such rough margins of rejection and acceptance might cause many customers to die. Correspondingly, a marketing study with rough standards of accuracy might be satisfactory to all concerned, simply because the consequences of being wrong are not great for a rather wide band of accuracy (*i.e.,* large margins of error) in either direction. On the other hand, the manufacturer of a new product might feel that it is extremely important not to make more

---

[8] Russell L. Ackoff and Leon Pritzker, "The Methodology of Survey Research," *International Journal of Opinion and Attitude Research,* Vol. V (1951), pp. 324ff.

than small errors in the proportion of individuals who *dislike* something about it. Similarly, a test which predicts future marital adjustment of a couple might well have a rather wide band of accuracy if the researcher feels that in the light of current courtship practices these scores will not affect anyone's decision very much. This does not mean, of course, that for purposes of continuing research the investigator need be satisfied; merely that for action purposes we must look at the consequences of error.

On the other hand, if the results of research are to be used in the settling of a legal precedent, as has actually occurred, most would agree that the margins of permitted error must be narrower.[9] Whether the student accepts this situation as "more important" than the prediction of marital adjustment is irrelevant here. All that is asserted is that the limits of error must be determined by the consequences of the action to be based upon the research. The "action" may be the rejection or acceptance of a hypothesis, and in this case there must be a prior judgment as to the accuracy needed. The calculations are not complex, and there are standard "quality-control" charts which indicate how many errors in which direction will occur, with a given level of accuracy and under the usual assumptions of normal probability. Since the researcher who is helping to plan action is making predictions about the future, it is useful for him to have a clear understanding of these possibilities when he recommends one program over another.

SUMMARY

The preparation of a scientific report is different in one fundamental respect from an argumentative essay or a literary effort: the self-conscious presentation of negative and positive evidence, along with the techniques by which that evidence was obtained. Linguistic and intellectual clarity is necessary, of course, for communication at all, and this set of problems must be worked out in relationship to the audience which is being reached. Since, however, the scientific report is expected to become part of the cumulative body of verifiable knowledge, it must be presented so that its data can be repeated, its logic followed, and its significance ascertained. As noted earlier in this volume, there is an inescapable public character to research, and the investigator who is unwilling to face both the strength and the weakness of his work will soon have them brought to his attention by others. It is this which puts such harsh demands upon the social scientist, but thereby is created the only possible basis for developing, accepting, and utilizing the conclusions of this young, exciting science.

[9] Cf. Tracy S. Kendler, "Contributions of the Psychologist to Constitutional Law," *American Psychologist*, Vol. V (1950), pp. 505–510.

SUGGESTED READINGS

American Marketing Society, *Technique of Marketing Research* (New York: McGraw-Hill, 1937), Chap. 17.

Doob, Leonard, "The Public Presentation of Polling Results," in Frederick Mosteller *et al., The Pre-election Polls of 1948,* Social Science Research Council Bulletin No. 60, 1949, Chap. 4.

Jahoda, Marie, Morton Deutsch, and Stuart W. Cook, *Research Methods in Social Relations* (New York: Dryden, 1951), Chap. 10.

Wolfle, Dael, Rensis Likert, Donald G. Marquis, and Robert R. Sears, "Standards for Appraising Psychological Research," *American Psychologist,* Vol. IV (1949), pp. 321–328.

INDEX

A

Absolute comparisons, 347–348
Abstraction, 332–333, 370
  level of, 371
  in report writing, 360
Accessibility of questionnaire respondent,
  174–175
Ackoff, Russell L., 374
Action research, 362, 374
Ad hoc theorizing, 335–336
Adamic, Louis, 288
Adequacy of sample, 225–231
Age composition, 299–301
Age-specific mortality rates, 301
Agreement, method of, 74, 78
  negative canon of, 75–76, 78
Ambiguity, 266, 321
Analysis of data, 341–357
  elaboration of, 356–358
  explanation, 354, 355
  interpretation, 354
  secondary, 343
  specification, 354–356
Anderson, Nels, 121, 131
Anomalous fact, 342
Anonymity, 178, 181, 192, 193, 370
Antagonism, 205–206
Antecedent variable, 354–355
Anxiety of interviewer, 196
Applied science, 29–39
  and common sense, 33–34
  pressures away from, 30–31
  pressures toward, 27–30
  related to pure science, 34–39
Area probability, 222–225
Area sampling, 222–223
Arithmetic mean, 226–231, 346, 353, 372
Arkin, Herbert, 369
Array, 346
Association of factors in sampling, 222
Attitude continuum, 262–265, 275, 278
Attitude measurement, 262–275, 277–278,
  280–283, 325

B

Attitudes, 243–249
  and facts, 203–204
  of interviewer, 196–198
Attributes, 232–233
Audience for report, 361
Auspices, of research, 188
  of study, 177
Authenticity, 370
Automobile owners, 215–216
Average, 226–231
Avoiding refusals, 189–194

B

Babchuck, Nicholas, 123
Babington-Smith, B., 217
Bales, R. Freed, 128
Banks, Seymour, 154
Barnes, Harry Elmer, 6
Baur, E. Jackson, 173
Becker, Howard, 6
Berelson, Bernard, 225, 327, 340
Bergmann, Gustav, 55
Bias of sample, 180–181, 218–221
Bibliography, 103, 109
Binnewies, W. G., 248
Binomial expansion, 212–213
Birth rate, 297–298
Birth-residence index, 310–311
Bogardus, Emory S., 243, 244, 248, 249,
  260
Bogardus scale, 243–249
Boring, Edwin G., 263
Bowman, Claude C., 28
Boyd, A. M., 116
Breadth, of data, 332–333
  of experience, 339–340
Britt, Steuart H., 183
Brown, Everett S., 117
Burgess, Ernest W., 39, 61, 284
Burke, Cletus J., 154
Bush, Vannevar, 22

J

Jaffe, Abram, 312
Jahoda, Marie, 102, 125, 147, 169, 208, 231, 242, 260, 295, 340, 358, 362, 376
Jennings, Helen Hall, 249, 250, 254, 260
Jones, A. W., 278–280
Judges, in coding, 323
sampling of, 256
in scaling, 255–260, 264–266, 270, 271
Jury in scaling, 237–238
Just discernible differences, 262–265
Juvenile offenses, 215

K

Kendall, M. G., 217
Kendall, Patricia L., 89, 135, 338, 354, 355, 357, 358
Kendler, Tracy S., 375
Keysort card, 318–319
Kilpatrick, Franklin P., 280, 287
Kinsey, A. C., 373
Kiser, Clyde V., 100, 101
Kitt, Alice, 50, 135, 156
Klineberg, Otto, 72
Kluckhohn, Florence, 123, 130
Known groups, 238–240, 247, 283–284
Kolb, William L., 40, 256
Komarovsky, Mirra, 158
Komidar, Joseph S., 103
Kornhauser, Arthur, 155

L

Langer, Suzanne K., 55
Language, 375
scientific, 362–367
LaPiere, Richard T., 164
Lasswell, Harold D., 326, 327
Latent-attitude continuum, 286
Latent-structure analysis, 294
Lay audience, 360, 361, 363
Lazarsfeld, Paul F., 49, 61, 65, 89, 135, 158, 168, 169, 208, 225, 286, 338, 340, 343, 354, 356–358
Leites, Nathan, 326, 327
Length of interview, 195
Levels, of abstraction, 360–361, 371
of data, 332–333
of theory, 335
Levy-Bruhl, Lucien, 71
Library, 103–118
Library of Congress system, 107
Life expectancy, 302–310
table of, 301–310
Likert, Rensis, 242, 271, 273, 274, 276, 277, 295, 363, 376
Limitations of study, 371–374

Limits of error, 374–375
Listings, 223
errors in, 219–220
obsolescence of, 216
Literacy, 178, 182
Locating of respondent, 189–191, 219–220
Logic in tabulation, 344–345
Logical validation, 237
Lotka, Alfred J., 302, 305, 306, 308
Lundberg, George A., 6, 17, 28, 39, 164, 169, 231, 242, 260, 284, 340
Lynd, Robert S., 22, 28

M

McBee Keysort card, 318–319
McCandless, B., 173
McCormick, Thomas C., 231
MacIver, Robert M., 3, 28
McNemar, Quinn, 285, 295
Mailed questionnaire, 170–183, 223–225
and bias, 173
and cost, 175
directions for, 178
facilitating return of, 179–180
open-ended items, 182
rapport, 176–178
sampling, 172–174, 180–181
Malthus, Thomas, 66
Manifest function, 286
Maps, 368–369
Margin of error, 374–375
Marital status, changes in, 213–215
Marquis, Donald G., 363, 376
Martin, C. E., 373
Marx, Karl, 70
Marx, Melvin H., 17, 55, 73
Mass observation, 121
Masters, Ruth D., 117
Mauss, Marcel, 71
Mayo, Elton, 82, 83
Mean, arithmetic, 226–231, 346, 353, 372
Measurement, 232–233, 235, 313, 314
of intensity, 271
Mechanical aids to presentation, 367–368
Median, 346
Meier, Norman C., 154
Melinat, C. H., 116
Memory, 202–203, 206–207, 335
Merrell, Margaret, 302
Merton, Robert K., 6, 13, 17, 46, 49, 50, 65, 72, 89, 123, 125, 131, 135, 147, 156, 164, 225, 338, 343, 354
Method, of agreement, 74, 78
of difference, 76–77
Migration, 310
calculation of, 310–311
Mill, John Stuart, 74, 86, 91
Miller, H. A., 61